AN ECONOMIC ANALYSIS OF CRIME

AN ECONOMIC ANALYSIS OF CRIME

SELECTED READINGS

Edited by

LAWRENCE J. KAPLAN
John Jay College of Criminal Justice of the
City University of New York

and

DENNIS KESSLER
Brooklyn College of the
City University of New York

CHARLES C THOMAS · PUBLISHER
Springfield · Illinois · U.S.A.

Published and Distributed Throughout the World by
CHARLES C THOMAS • PUBLISHER
Bannerstone House
301-327 East Lawrence Avenue, Springfield, Illinois, U.S.A.

© 1976, by CHARLES C THOMAS • PUBLISHER
ISBN 0-398-03407-9 (cloth)
ISBN 0-398-03408-7 (paper)
Library of Congress Catalog Card Number: 75-2013

With THOMAS BOOKS *careful attention is given to all details of
manufacturing and design. It is the Publisher's desire to present books
that are satisfactory as to their physical qualities and artistic possibilities
and appropriate for their particular use.* THOMAS BOOKS *will be true
to those laws of quality that assure a good name and good will.*

Printed in the United States of America
W-11

Library of Congress Cataloging in Publication Data

Kaplan, Lawrence Jay, 1915-   comp.
    An economic analysis of crime.

    Includes bibliographies and index.
    1.   Organized crime—United States—Addresses,
essays, lectures.   2.   Crime and criminals—Economic
aspects—United States—Addresses, essays, lectures.
I.   Kessler, Dennis, joint comp.   II.   Title.
HV6791.K36   364-1'06'073   75-2013
ISBN 0-398-03407-9
ISBN 0-398-03408-7 pbk.

CONTRIBUTORS

RALPH BLUMENTHAL: An ardent Manhattan moviegoer and reporter for the *New York Times*.

DONALD R. CRESSEY: Professor of Sociology at the University of California at Santa Barbara.

MICHAEL DORMAN: A journalist and author of five books.

ROY A. FEIGENBAUM: A Counselor in the Methadone Treatment Program of St. John's Episcopal Hospital, New York City.

CARL R. FOGELBERG: A Washington Attorney who served as Project Director of the Washington Lawyers Committee for Civil Rights Under Law.

CHARLES GRUTZNER: A veteran newspaperman and expert on organized crime who writes for the *New York Times*.

PETE HAMILL: A columnist for the *New York Post*.

LAWRENCE J. KAPLAN: Professor of Economics, John Jay College of Criminal Justice, The City University of New York.

DENNIS KESSLER: An Instructor of Sociology at Brooklyn College of The City University of New York.

RUFUS KING: A Washington attorney and one of the nation's leading experts on gambling laws and enforcement.

LEO C. LOUGHREY: Professor of Law and Police Science at John Jay College of Criminal Justice, The City University of New York.

JAMES M. MAHER: A superior officer in the New York City Police Department.

SALVATORE MATTEIS: A superior officer in the New York City Police Department.

JOHN McDONALD: Former editor of *Fortune Magazine.*

RICHARD B. MILLER: A contributing editor of the *Bankers Magazine.*

ROGER LEROY MILLER: An Assistant Professor of Economics at the University of Washington.

MICHAEL J. MURPHY: Formerly Police Commissioner of the City of New York and is currently head of the Police Foundation in Washington, D.C.

DOUGLAS C. NORTH: Professor and Chairman of Economics at the University of Washington.

MATTHEW W. RAFFA: A graduate student in criminal justice and doing research on organized crime.

RALPH SALERNO: An organized crime consultant, "The Johnny Appleseed against organized crime," who, until recently served in the Central Intelligence Bureau of the New York City Police Department.

THOMAS C. SCHELLING: A Professor of Economics and a faculty member of the Center for International Affairs at Harvard University.

RICHARD F. SULLIVAN: Economic Consultant to the Solicitor General of Canada and Visiting Professor of Law, McGill University Law School, Montreal, Canada.

JOHN S. TOMPKINS: A journalist with extensive experience writing for the *New York Times,* the *Wall Street Journal,* and *Business Week.*

LESLIE WALLER: A journalist and author.

PAUL A. WEINSTEIN: An Associate Professor of Economics at the University of Maryland.

PREFACE

Amid the welter of controversy surrounding the macro-sociological concept of crime, scant attention has been paid to the economics of crime. While existing literature abounds with theoretical explanations, the monetary aspects have often been overlooked. Discussions in this volume center primarily on organized crime; its sources of income; and its impact on the American consumer.

It has been estimated that the annual cost of crime in the United States is in excess of $50 billion. This includes the annual return to organized crime derived from illegal gambling, loan-sharking, narcotics and other illegal activities; crimes against people, including homicide and assault; crimes against property, including burglary, larceny, auto theft, embezzlement, forgery, and property destroyed by arson and vandalism; other crimes, such as driving under the influence of liquor and tax fraud; public law enforcement, which includes the cost of police, courts, and corrections; and, finally, private business costs, including the cost of theft insurance, burglar alarms, night watchmen, and other expenses for guarding against crime. Surprising as it may seem, the total of $50 billion is modest. It excludes illegal tax evasion, bribery and graft, and compensation to victims, a new form of payment which has been enacted into law by California, Massachusetts, New York, Maryland, and Hawaii.

A $50 billion annual cost of crime absorbed by about sixty-five million households in the U.S. comes to about $800 per household per year, or on a weekly basis about $16 per household per week. These costs come out of the pockets of the nation's consumers in the form of higher taxes and higher prices.

The articles in this book of readings attempt to show how the vast network controlled by organized crime affects every single individual. The editors have drawn from the most recent literature and have presented a body of material which is reliable, comprehensive, informative and authoritative. It is not fiction, but fact. It is a body of knowledge which should be brought to light and disseminated before action and legislation can be considered to protect the American consumer who has too long been victimized.

INTRODUCTION

Every American is affected by the cost of crime, which imposes a heavy economic burden upon both the community as a whole and its individual members. Yearly monetary loss to individuals due to robbery, burglary, auto theft, white collar crime and organized crime is too staggering to comprehend. Further, the taxpayer's bill for law enforcement activities adds significantly to the total cost.

Cost to the individual due to personal injury caused by crimes such as assault, robbery and rape result in substantial economic loss to the victims for time lost from work, medical bills and other incidental expenses. Willful or malicious destruction of property is another widespread and costly offense. Institutions, businesses and individuals report extensive damage due to vandalism. In order to deal more effectively with burglary and vandalism, many businesses are forced to install sophisticated security systems and hire large security staffs at great cost.

While the amount of money allocated by federal, state and local law enforcement agencies is directly related to a reduction in crime, this is not always the case. Federal outlays for law enforcement programs have greatly increased in recent years yet crime has not diminished. The 1973 federal law enforcement budget is in the neighborhood of 2.5 billion dollars. The problem of law enforcement includes the inadequate criminal justice system.

The criminal justice system, as it now operates on both the federal and local level, is overburdened and ineffective. In part, because of arrest quotas and the enforcement of victimless crime statutes, court calendars are needlessly bogged down. Since historically, both the federal and local criminal justice systems do not receive sufficient effective operational funds, the required number of judges and court personnel are not employed. In this clogged atmosphere, plea bargaining has become the rule instead of the exception. A poor defendant often stays in jail for months until his case goes to trial while the members of organized crime backed by the resources and legal talents of the syndicate are dealt with lightly.

Organized crime may be loosely compared to legitimate business operations. It employs and involves thousands of professional criminals working in highly organized and well structured operations that are engaged in supplying both illegal and legal goods and services. The most profitable of these illegal goods and services include gambling, narcotics and prostitution.

Many law enforcement officials agree that gambling is the greatest source of income for organized crime. It is, in fact, estimated that organized crime derives twice as much revenue from gambling as all other types of criminal incomes combined. Gambling revenue for organized crime has been estimated to be approximately $20 billion dollars annually with a profit of $6 to $7 billion a year. This estimate of annual profit is equivalent to the total annual profit of the nation's twelve largest corporations.[1]

Those in the lowest income brackets provide organized crime with the bulk of illegal gambling revenue. In slum areas throughout the United States, there is a highly organized and efficiently operated illegal gambling enterprise. These smoothly run operations are basically concerned with numbers betting, although horse racing and sports betting comprise a fair share of the total.

Illegal gambling's cost to legitimate society is not the total of illegal bets placed, but rather that amount of the total which is retained by the operators of the system. In economic terms, the bettors pay the bookmakers a fee to have money redistributed back to the bettors. That fee is the cost to society and it includes the bookies' profit as well as operating expenses such as graft, telephone expenses and runners. In essence, this fee is an addition to the resources of organized crime and represents a loss of revenue to the legitimate sector.

Since the numbers game entices scores of poor and un-

---

[1] L. J. Kaplan, "Economic Implications of Organized Crime in Gambling," *Proceedings of the John Jay College Faculty Seminars*, Vol. 1 (1967-1969), p. 4.

educated people with an opportunity to make a great deal of money with minimal risk, it serves a unique function. Most of those employed by numbers operations could not achieve commensurate success in the legitimate sector. The application is somewhat similar to the innovation adaptation in the *Social Structure and Anomie* paradigm.[2]

All those who earn their livelihood in the numbers game: the writer, the pick-up man and the banker, deal in a service that is in constant demand. The services of the bookmaker are also in constant demand by millions of the nation's citizens. State and local governments have been looking to the concept and possible implementation of legalized gambling as a means of gaining millions of dollars of needed revenue. Legalized gambling is seen by many as a harmless mechanism for raising funds that will lighten the burden of hard pressed taxpayers. A handful of states have legalized state lotteries and these lotteries are basically geared to raise funds for educational purposes.

Another aim of those who support legalized gambling is to damage the economic base of organized crime. There is, however, certainly no guarantee that legalized gambling would decrease the profits of organized crime sufficiently to affect its widespread operations. If the history of the legalized gambling experience in Nevada is a chronicle of the manner in which organized crime moves in on a legalized gambling operation, there certainly leaves much to be desired.

Organized criminal operations continually funnel profits from gambling operations into both legal and illegal areas. One of the most profitable of all illegal services is loansharking. Loansharking is usually defined as loaning money at higher rates than prescribed by law.

It has been estimated that loansharking is a yearly multibillion dollar operation. Lenders provide a sorely needed service to those who are in need of an unusually large sum of cash in a short period of time. Those who are most vulnerable to a loanshark are compulsive gamblers, businessmen who are in-

---

[2] Robert K. Merton, "Social Structure and Anomie," *American Sociological Review*, Vol. 3 (October 1938), pp. 672-682.

volved in a high risk venture and many professional criminals who often require "emergency funds."

The loanshark's relationship with professional criminals imposes a great burden upon the public. When a professional criminal expects his illegal activity to be extremely lucrative, he will approach a loanshark for seed money and fully expect to be able to pay the loanshark's usurious interest rates. If, however, the criminal's planned venture is not a complete success, other crimes must be committed in order to meet the loanshark's payments.

The loanshark provides a service that is regulated by consumer demand. The demand is huge in the high-risk business sector. The garment center, in particular, produces a disproportionate number of loanshark customers. In the garment center, a fortune can be gained and lost with the coming and going of a single season.

Prohibitive interest rates work in favor of the loanshark. The legal reins placed upon the ability of lending institutions to meet high-risk loans significantly adds customers to the loanshark's rolls. Individuals who already have loans outstanding or those with criminal backgrounds are often unable to secure a needed loan from a financial institution. The loanshark supplies the illegal service that these individuals need.

In recent years, there has been a massive infusion of organized crime manpower and money into the legitimate business sector. Law enforcement officials agree that organized crime has infiltrated nearly every commercial industry and profitable field.

Ownership of legitimate business creates an aura of respectability for the organized crime member. Further, through constant reinvestment in legitimate business, the illicit profit of organized crime is perceptively utilized to earn more money. Illicit money, once converted into legitimate business, is nearly impossible to trace. Despite the efforts of law enforcement agencies, underworld takeover of legitimate business is spreading rapidly. Not surprisingly, businessmen are still reluctant to turn over evidence of organized crime threats and infiltration.

Many underworld figures enjoy their connection with legitimate business, for it provides these men with the appearance of a legitimate source of income. The income derived from reputable corporations provides a legitimate cover for income tax purposes.

Moreover, a legitimate business connection solidifies one's standing in the community which can be further stretched into additional dollars and influence.

Some of the small businesses that organized crime prefers include motels, night clubs, vending machines, trucking companies and private sanitation collection.

A great deal of the profits gained from these businesses are used to set up other companies usually under false fronts or by proxies. Certain syndicate-controlled businesses and corporations have branches and extensive interests in Latin America and Europe.

Labor racketeering is another area where organized crime is well entrenched in the legitimate business sector. This often involves threatening of employers by organized crime members with labor troubles or property destruction unless under the table money is paid. Other organized crime members make great profits by offering their services in the settling of labor disputes. The negotiation of these labor disputes usually includes the promise of service contracts for the underworld contractors in return for strikebreaking efforts.

The narcotics traffic in the United States is a huge business which is controlled by organized crime. A major portion of the heroin that finds its way to the United States is grown in Turkey. Turkish farmers produce the crop and it is then refined in Syria and Lebanon. From the Middle East, the morphine base is smuggled into European countries, usually Italy or France, where it is converted in hidden laboratories into heroin and then smuggled directly into the United States. Southeast Asia is another significant source for heroin. Cocaine, a drug which has recently gained great popularity, is smuggled into the United States from the western coast of South America.

The importing and distribution of narcotics takes a great deal of money. Fortunes are lost when a huge narcotics shipment is confiscated. For those who are willing to risk imprisonment and loss of a great deal of money, the profits are huge.

Inevitably, the financing of smuggling operations has fallen to organized crime members.

The heroin business has grown signicantly in the last few years. "The number of addicts is believed to total more than half a million people. Often driven to criminal activity for support of their costly habits, heroin addicts clearly have contributed disproportionately to the steep climb that has been occurring both in crimes of violence and crimes against property."[3] The growth of the heroin business will not suffer for lack of manpower. Because of the profits involved in the smuggling and street dealing of heroin, individuals will always be found who are willing to take the consequent risks.

There has been an ongoing debate concerning the merits of various proposals dealing with the heroin epidemic. Many individuals and legislators feel that the legalization and decriminalization of the drug would be an effective means of dealing with the problem. Furthermore, decriminalization would save the public millions of dollars of lost personal property formerly coveted by addicts. The advocates of methadone maintenance point to the success of the current program. Yet, the costs of methadone maintenance are high and the degree of success of the program both medically and economically have been seriously questioned. It is apparent to everyone, however, that the narcotics problem imposes costs that transcend the purely economic.

The costs of white-collar crime in the nation run into billions of dollars. White-collar crimes may be loosely defined as those crimes that people commit in the course of their occupation. Included in this definition are antitrust violations and tax fraud. All indicators point to the fact that white-collar crime is pervasive in our society and causes enormous economic and social harm. First, it may and often does cause serious financial losses to individuals, businesses and the entire public. The exact financial loss to the government caused by tax fraud is difficult to determine but undoubtedly enormous. Some of this tax fraud

---

[3] The Morgan Guaranty and Trust Company, *The Economic Aspects of Crime* (April 1972).

is inadvertent, but a good deal of it is deliberate criminal evasion. The financial loss to the public caused by a single conspiracy in restraint of trade may be untold millions in extra costs paid ultimately by the buying public.

While no reliable estimates can be made of the financial deficits produced by white-collar crime, they probably are far greater than those produced by traditional theft offenses such as robbery, larceny and burglary. Moreover, white-collar crime may also result in physical harm.

Death or serious injury may result from tainted products merchandised in violation of the Pure Food and Drug Act or local health laws or misconduct by doctors. Building code violations may cause fire or other serious health hazards. Although offenses involving such risks constitute a small proportion of the total amount of white-collar crime, the potential number of victims of such conduct may be very high.

White-collar crime also does serious damage to our social and economic institutions. These crimes such as bribery and violation of conflict of interest statutes strike deeply at impartial government. The damage done by a conspiracy of twenty-nine electrical equipment companies to fix prices is not limited to the extra costs paid by their unsuspecting buyers. More broadly, white-collar crime affects the whole moral climate of American society. Misconduct by corporations and their managers, who usually occupy leadership positions in their communities, establish an example which tends to erode the law and provide an opportunity for other kinds of offenders to rationalize misconduct.

The great number of taxpayers in our society make criminal tax fraud a unique white-collar crime. Criminal tax fraud is not limited to those in the limelight. The average citizen is the person most often prosecuted for tax fraud. Tax fraud is the crime that almost all individuals, rich and poor alike, have engaged in at one time or another. The great number of tax fraud cases further contributes to a climate that is conducive to illegal acts.

The growth of the huge financial empire of organized crime,

is due, in large part, to the demand of millions of citizens for the illegal goods and services the underworld has to offer. Organized crime controls and provides gambling, narcotics, usurious loans, a cheap supply of labor and a score of other criminally related services.

> By joining hands, the suppliers of illicit goods and services (1) cut costs, improve their markets, and pool capital; (2) gain monopolies on certain of the illicit services or on all of the illicit services provided in a specific geographic area, whether it be a neighborhood or a large city; (3) centralize the procedures for stimulating agencies of law enforcement and administration of justice to overlook the illegal operations; and (4) accumulate vast wealth which can be used to attain even wider monopolies on illicit activities, and on legal business as well. In the long run, then, the 'small operation' corrupts the traditional economic and political procedures designed to insure that citizens need not pay tribute to a criminal in order to conduct a legitimate business.[4]

In essence, the public is not troubled greatly by the empire of organized crime. There is however, an increased concern about the problem of crime in general, and greatly aroused fears of being victimized. This fear leads many people to give up activities they would normally undertake. The costs of this fear are not only economic but constitute a serious infringement on an individual's social life. In the long run, the loss of human interaction and the consequent depersonalization is the larger cost to society. As the federal goverment allocates more and more money for crime prevention, crime rates remain largely unaffected or in fact continue to rise. With these facts in mind, it appears that both the incidence and cost of crime will continue to rise both economically and socially.

---

[4] D. Cressey, *Theft of the Nation* (New York, Harper and Row, 1970), p. 74.

CONTENTS

	Page
Contributors	vi
Preface	vii
Introduction	ix

Chapter

1. THE ECONOMIC ASPECTS OF CRIME
   Introduction 3
   The Economic Aspects of Crime
      The Morgan Guaranty Survey 4
   The Economics of Crime: An Introduction to the Literature
      Richard F. Sullivan 15
   What is Organized Crime? 24
   An Un-American Success Story
      Charles Grutzner 25
   Bibliography 28

2. THE ECONOMICS OF GAMBLING
   Introduction 35
   Gambling and Crime
      Rufus King 36
   Crime as a Business
      Ralph Salerno and John S. Tompkins 46
   Existing Gambling
      New York State Commission on Gambling 55
   Bibliography 57

3. THE ECONOMICS OF HORSE RACING AND
   SPORTS BETTING
   Introduction 63
   The Bookmaking Racket
      Michael J. Murphy 64
   How the Horseplayers Got Involved with the Urban Crisis
      John McDonald 73

Chapter   *Page*

    Betting on Sports

        The Fund for the City of New York 88

    Bibliography 100

4.   THE ECONOMICS OF THE NUMBERS GAME

    Introduction 103

    The Economics of the Numbers Game

        Lawrence J. Kaplan and James M. Maher 104

    Computation of the Winning Number

        The Fund for the City of New York 124

    A Model for a Legal Numbers Lottery in the District of Columbia

        Carl R. Fogelberg 126

    Bibliography 138

5.   LEGALIZATION OF GAMBLING

    Introduction 142

    Which Forms of Gambling Should be Legalized?

        The Fund for the City of New York 143

    The Feasibility of the Major Forms of Possible

        Legal Gambling 148

    Fiscal Issues 155

    Arguments For and Against Various Forms of Legal Gambling ...157

    Organizational Issues 163

    Summary, Conclusions, and Recommendations

        New York State Commission on Gambling 164

    Legalized Off-Track Betting in Other Places

        Lawrence J. Kaplan and Leo C. Loughrey 166

    Bibliography 174

6.   THE ECONOMICS OF LOANSHARKING

    Introduction 177

    The Economics of Loansharking

        Lawrence J. Kaplan and Salvatore Matteis 178

    The Economics of Usury Laws

        Douglass C. North and Roger Leroy Miller 193

    The Impingement of Loansharking on the Banking Industry

        Richard B. Miller 198

    Bibliography 210

Chapter *Page*

7. THE ECONOMICS OF NARCOTICS

Introduction 212

There Are People Who Say, 'Well, Business is Business'

Forbes 213

The Economics of Heroin

Roy A. Feigenbaum 220

The Socio-Economic Effect of Drug and Victimless
    Crime Prosecution

Dennis Kessler 236

Wholesale and Retail Costs of Common Drugs in the
    New York Metropolitan Area

Narcotics Police 239

Bibliography 241

8. CORRUPTION AND CRIME IN LABOR UNIONS

Introduction 245

Demand, Supply, and Profit

Donald R. Cressey 246

Racketeering and Labor: An Economic Analysis

Paul A. Weinstein 251

The Continuing Problem of Labor Racketeering

The Editors 269

Bibliography 271

9. INFILTRATION INTO LEGITIMATE BUSINESS

Introduction 275

How Criminals Solve Their Investment Problem

U.S. News and World Report 276

Areas of Business Enterprise Infiltrated by Organized Crime,
    The Kefauver List

U.S. Senate Report 277

How to Lock Out the Mafia

Charles Grutzner 283

Bibliography 307

10. ECONOMIC IMPLICATIONS OF PORNOGRAPHY
    AND PROSTITUTION

Introduction 311

How Big is the Smut Industry?

Chapter   *Page*

  U.S. News and World Report 312
  Hard-Core Grows Fashionable—And Very Profitable
   Ralph Blumenthal 314
  The Porno War
   Pete Hamill 323
  The Economics of Prostitution
   The Editors 325
  Bibliography 330
11. FINANCIAL OPERATIONS OF ORGANIZED CRIME
  Introduction 334
  Swiss Banking Services—Everything for Anybody
   Leslie Waller 336
  Turning Cash Into Credit
   Michael Dorman 344
  The Utilization of the Numbered Swiss Account by
   Organized Crime
   Matthew W. Raffa 348
  Bibliography 364
12. CONCLUSIONS
  Introduction 366
  Economic Analysis and Organized Crime
   Thomas C. Schelling 367
  Bibliography 399

Index 403

AN ECONOMIC ANALYSIS OF CRIME

THE ECONOMIC ASPECTS OF CRIME

INTRODUCTION

In THIS FIRST introduction to the readings, the stage is set for an explanation of crime through both an economic and sociological perspective. Literally billions of dollars have been spent in recent years to combat crime, yet the problem persists. In fact, as increased expenditures are funneled into crime control bureaucracies, virtually all classifications of crimes are on the increase. Even more distressing than the official figures are the results of a recent Law Enforcement Assistance Administration study of April 1974 which indicated that the crime problem is, in reality, a great deal worse than that shown in official statistics. According to that study, less than one half of the crimes actually committed are reported to the police. Yet, amid the overwhelming amount of crime in the United States and its obvious impact on the economic system, economists have, until recently, neglected to analyze or offer solutions.

In this chapter, the first article, prepared by the Morgan Guaranty Trust Company of New York speculates on the crime problem from an economic vantage point. In its analysis, crime is viewed as a direct cost to business and consequently to the consumer. The study indicates how business firms are attempting to cope with the ubiquitousness of crime and the concomitant result of higher consumer costs. The article also considers legalizing the sale of heroin, taking the profit out of the operation, and assigning regulation of its use to the medical profession.

In the second article, the author, an economist, believes that

3

a more cogent analysis of the crime problem can be achieved by defining crime as a rational enterprise. He questions such popular penal criminological conceptions as punishment, prevention, and deterrence, and concludes that in some circumstances it would be irrational for an ex-convict not to return to crime.

The third selection answers the question, "What is organized crime?" It concludes with a definition which was developed in 1965 and still is considered the best. Finally, the author of *An Un-American Success Story* traces the evolution of organized crime from the Prohibition Era to its current status, and labels it as the *perfect conglomerate*.

THE ECONOMIC ASPECTS OF CRIME*

Ever since the statistical invention called gross national product (GNP) made its appearance in this country some four decades ago, economists have argued off and on about whether the output measure ought to include the estimated market value of illegal goods and services—such as bootleg liquor. The "nays" have won out, with the consequence that statisticians make no allowance at all for illegal transactions when they estimate GNP. It is by no means inconceivable that figures on total output would be as much as $50 billion higher than they are if this were not the case.

Perhaps deterred by this tradition, economists have devoted relatively little effort to analyzing either crime problems or illegal markets. This neglect may be coming to an end, however, for it is becoming increasingly difficult for anyone to ignore the fact that crime is imposing heavy costs on U.S. society. The apparent eruption recently of old style gangland warfare in New York City hints rather strongly that large stakes may be involved.

It has been estimated that just on illicit wagering the American public may be spending upwards of $20 billion annually. Outlays on heroin are believed to be running at about $6 billion a year, with those for marihuana, although indeterminable, obviously also very large. Huge money flows are thus being diverted

---

* Reprinted from *The Morgan Guaranty Survey,* April 1972, published monthly by Morgan Guaranty Trust Company of New York. Used with permission.

from legitimate uses to the enrichment and expansion of the criminal sector. The heroin business in particular has grown extremely rapidly in recent years, with especially pernicious effects. The number of addicts is believed to total more than half a million people. Often driven to criminal activity to support their costly "habits," heroin addicts clearly have contributed disproportionately to the steep climb that has been occurring both in crimes of violence and in crimes against property.

Astonishingly, the losses business firms alone suffer from property offenses of the "ordinary" variety—such as robbery, burglary, shoplifting, and employee theft—were put by a recent Commerce Department study at $12 billion a year. The range of valuables involved cover everything that's movable—from securities to stereos. And the Commerce figure clearly understates the actual impact, for the study included estimates only for offenses reported to the police. These are thought by authorities to be far out-numbered by unreported instances of commercial loss, perhaps by as much as three to one. Attempts to assess the impact of theft from individuals run into statistical problems as well, for as in the case of business many offenses go unreported. Even so, it can be taken as a certainty that aggregate losses from ordinary property theft far exceed the $12 billion figure placed on property losses suffered just by business. Most stolen goods, of course, are not lost as far as consumption goes, but in many instances they obviously are used in a way that significantly modifies normal consumption patterns. The willing or unknowing buyer of "hot" merchandise often benefits at someone else's expense—with the criminal parties taking a cut in the process. It's hard to imagine any less desirable form of "income redistribution."

Attempting to get a handle on the impact of such other crimes as swindles or consumer frauds is an even more esoteric exercise, which rapidly carries estimation to the realm of speculation. Strikingly, however, some criminologists believe that victims' losses from such "white-collar" offenses may be larger than those associated with ordinary property crime.

Ordinary offenses, however, obviously entail costs over and above those occasioned by losses. In some high crime areas premium rates for insurance against theft loss have skyrocketed.

In Washington, D.C., for instance, rates for liquor store burglary insurance have more than tripled during the past decade and in the Bronx they have quadrupled. Private expenditures on guards, protective devices, and other deterrents also have soared. One study found that business outlays for crime prevention totaled almost $3.5 billion in 1969, a 150 percent increase over 1960. Altogether, private outlays for prevention may well be in the range of $6 billion a year.

None of this includes a host of intangible costs related to the loss of confidence in public safety that has occurred in many cities in recent years, as muggings and other violent crimes against the person have proliferated. In many places, people simply don't venture out at night but remain instead at home behind bolted and chained doors—often with a gun handily located. The effect on shopping and entertainment in some major cities has been enormous, with the closing of many restaurants and nightclubs in particular directly traceable to peoples' unwillingness to leave their homes. Even in daylight hours, countless people today go about the cities in taxicabs rather than subways, for fear of potential attack. Crime, in short, has drastically circumscribed individual freedom and mobility, and that in the ultimate sense is its largest cost.

Although precise measurement of the rise in personal and property offenses is not possible, virtually all analysts agree that most forms of crime, and especially property crime, are increasing considerably faster than the population. In light of this disproportionate rise in crime, public response—in terms of resources devoted to crime control—was surprisingly low-key during the past decade. To be sure, state and local governments did increase spending on police, courts, and correctional institutions from $3 billion in 1960 to $6.2 billion in 1969. But this rise of 104 percent was not in proportion to the increase in other budgetary outlays. State and local expenditures for all goods and services climbed 125 percent during the period. With the addition of somewhat more than $500 million in federal expenditures on law enforcement in 1969, the grand total of such outlays amounted to $6.7 billion—or just a little more than the country spent on the space program at its peak.

An Overburdened System

This relative neglect of crime deterrence in the scale of national priorities has left as a legacy a vastly overburdened system of criminal justice. This is evidenced by the fact that a smaller proportion of offenders is being caught each year. Only one in five reported "serious" crimes resulted in an arrest in 1970, compared with one in three in 1960* The actual number of such arrests has risen rapidly, however, contributing to mounting congestion in the court system.

In an effort to clear calendars officials frequently resort to plea bargaining, with the result that felony suspects often get off with pleas to a lesser offense than the original charge. In the relatively few cases ultimately brought to trial, months or even years often have elapsed since the arrest. This gives rise in numerous instances to repetition of criminal acts while suspects remain at large. Voicing the frustration of many law enforcement officials, the Police Commissioner of New York City has described the situation thus, "In the first ten months of 1971 our robbery arrests were up 31 percent, our burglary arrests were up 19 percent . . . Many of the criminals involved we have already arrested three, four, and five times so far this year."

At the other end of the criminal-justice "funnel," the correctional institutions, there are also serious problems. Many facilities are filled beyond capacity. Moreover, high rates of recidivism—with one study indicated that three quarters of those released from prison were rearrested within four years—point up the lack of success of correctional procedures.

With growing recognition that crime control efforts have been underfinanced, Washington has been in the process the past few years of both enlarging its own anticrime programs and stepping up the flow of federal aid to financially hard pressed states and localities. Federal outlays for "crime reduction" have nearly quadrupled in the past four years to $2 billion in the current fiscal year, and the budget for fiscal 1973 calls for an increase to $2.3 billion. Of the $2 billion being spent this year, about 36

---

* Serious crimes are defined by the Federal Bureau of Investigation as: homicide, forcible rape, aggravated assault, robbery, burglary, larceny of $50 or more, and automobile theft.

percent is going to aid state and local governments in mounting crime-reducing efforts across a broad front—from a variety of preventive programs through improvements in the criminal justice system.

Crackdown on Heroin Traffic

The Federal government's own anticrime efforts are being focused heavily on attacking the drug traffic, which former President Nixon called the "highest priority" of his Administration. A new nationwide thrust inaugurated in 1972 will bring stepped-up enforcement efforts against heroin pushers at the street level, and an expansion of prevention and rehabilitation programs for addicts. Underpinning the treatment aspects of the program, a law signed by Mr. Nixon authorized a budget of $1 billion through 1975 for the Special Action Office for Drug Abuse Prevention, a new agency charged with coordinating and supplementing antidrug programs of a dozen federal agencies.

The street-level thrust supplements greatly increased efforts in recent years on the part of the federal government to cut off heroin supply lines outside the U.S. and to suppress the trade domestically. Reflecting these intensified enforcement efforts, the manpower and budgetary authority of the Bureau of Narcotics and Dangerous Drugs—which has primary responsibility for curbing the drug traffic—have undergone very rapid expansion. The Bureau's budget for fiscal 1972 exceeded $64 million, up from $18.5 million in 1969.

Officials can point to some progress from the suppression approach. Under an agreement with Turkey—whose poppy fields are believed to feed a large part of U.S. heroin imports—that country has undertook to ban poppy cultivation after that year. Washington also has enlisted the cooperation of French authorities in efforts to curb heroin processing and transit operations in the south of France, and the U.S. Ambassador to France recently stated that the tide is turning. In 1972, in one of the largest captures on record, French officials seized nearly half a ton of heroin, embedded in concrete in the hold of a shrimp boat. Moreover, domestic and international seizures by U.S. agents rose markedly in 1971. The Bureau of Narcotics and Dangerous

Drugs reported capturing more than twice as much heroin in 1971 as in 1970 and the Customs Bureau said its seizures were up about threefold, for about two and a half tons. This is equivalent to about three months' estimated consumption in this country.

Despite these undoubted accomplishments, the traffic clearly is going to be extremely difficult to halt. Large amounts of opium are produced in countries other than Turkey, and the economics of the trade provide strong incentives for traffickers to devise alternate transit routes. On the streets of New York, for example, one kilogram of heroin grosses more than $225,000—a more than 600-fold markup from the cost of the raw opium from which it was processed. Once heroin reaches U.S. channels the difficulties of detection and control multiply rapidly. The initial importing and wholesaling seems to be concentrated in a limited number of criminal rings, but subsequent distribution involves literally thousands of independent dealers. The new thrust against street pushers—which officials expect will lead to information about higher-ups in the traffic, as well as reducing availability of the drug—is tacit acknowledgment that attempts to curb heroin imports have produced insufficient results.

An alternative approach often has been discussed, of course—that of taking the profit out of the heroin trade by legalizing the drug's sale and assigning regulation of its use to the medical profession. The discussion doubtless will receive fresh impetus from a report issued by the American Bar Association's Special Committee on Crime Prevention and Control. The report recommended that governments at all levels adopt a policy toward addiction control which places "primary emphasis on the treatment of addiction," with law-enforcement efforts to be concentrated on the upper levels of the distribution system. The committee stressed the need for widespread programs offering traditional treatments such as detoxification or methadone maintenance, but it also advocated experimenting with the radical departure of using heroin to lure addicts into treatment. While the Bar group's ideas certainly deserve consideration, it is difficult at present to fault the Administration's strategy in trying to make heroin unavailable.

Striking at Organized Crime

Another major target of Washington's efforts is breaking up the operations of organized criminal groups, with special emphasis on gambling and the corruption of public officials. Strike forces—teams of Justice Department lawyers and agents from other agencies who are sent into cities to investigate the syndicates for violation of federal statutes—have grown from a single unit a few years ago to eighteen. They have had significant success in developing evidence resulting in indictments. The Justice Department returned indictments against more than 2,100 defendants in organized crime cases during 1971, compared with 1,000 in 1970.

The campaign against gambling reflects the fact that this activity provides a major source of income for organized criminal groups. By drying up revenue from this source—or sizably lessening its flow—law-enforcement officials hope to achieve beneficial spin-off effects in impeding other syndicate ventures—such as loansharking and infiltration of legitimate business. These activities generate a good deal of associated crime, with loanshark victims sometimes pressured into facilitating hijacking or burglaries, for instance, and "legitimate" firms serving as conduits for distribution of stolen merchandise.

Governmental efforts to curb illicit gambling seem likely to be further strengthened. Interestingly, the Organized Crime Control Act of 1970 provided for the creation of a high-level review Commission at the beginning of 1973 for the purpose of evaluating policies toward gambling at federal, state, and local levels. Many states already are well advanced in reevaluating policy in this area, spurred mainly by interest in augmenting revenues but also by the view that extension of legalized gambling could have an appreciable by-product value in undercutting organized crime's heavy domination of wagering. New York State among others have moved some distance in this direction, with legalization of off-track betting on horse races and with the establishment of a state lottery.

The lottery was originally designed for $1 tickets and drawings once a month. It has been modified to provide for fifty-cent tickets and weekly drawings. And a bill currently before the legislature would lift New York's constitutional ban on various other forms of gambling, opening the way for the legislature to legalize such things as football and baseball bets and numbers games. There is even some talk in New York of legalizing prostitution but, as yet, no concerted push for that step. A definite momentum, however, toward "decriminalizing" heretofore proscribed activities is building.

No one imagines that the task of displacing the existing illegal gambling apparatus, or that of other illicit activities, is going to be easy. In the case of gambling, habit, the convenience of door-to-door runners, the privacy which winners enjoy from the tax collectors' eye, and the availability of credit all are powerful pluses for the syndicates. Indeed, any serious effort at displacement would probably rcqiure the exemption of winnings from taxation. Yet it is significant that a start is being made. The stakes are high. New York City's Off-Track Betting Corporation built up to a daily "handle" of nearly $1.5 million in its first year. From the economic point of view, the case for ending the virtual monopoly of gambling services which criminal elements now have in many locales is compelling. Besides filling underworld coffers, prohibition of gambling is a drain on police and court resources, and a major source of public corruption.

Aid from LEAA

Meanwhile, as noted earlier, the federal government has been cranking up crime control aid to state and local entities. The principal vehicle of aid is the Law Enforcement Assistance Administration (LEAA), a Justice Department agency which began operations in 1969. Its budgetary appropriation has grown more than tenfold since then, from $63 million the first year to almost $700 million in 1972. Altogether, in the agency's first four years of operation, it received some $1.5 billion.

The major part of LEAA's funds—about $1.3 billion in the fiscal 1969-72 period—has been earmarked by Congress for "action" grants to states and localities for carrying out law-enforcement plans devised by them. Such plans have encompassed projects ranging from the hiring of additional policemen and the training of correctional personnel to treatment of addicts.

Just how effective the LEAA grants are proving in reducing crime is as yet in doubt. The program has generated considerable criticism, much of it centering on charges that agency spending has lacked focus and that LEAA has failed to devise ways of evaluating the impact of its grants. The program is still evolving, however, and some recent steps taken by the agency recognize a need for sharper definition of priorities. In 1972, for instance, LEAA appointed a National Advisory Commission on Criminal Justice Standards and Goals, assigning it the task of producing a "blueprint" of priorities and performance standards for crime-reduction programs. In January 1972, the agency announced a new "high impact" program under which eight cities have been selected for special efforts to curb burglaries and street crime—including stepped-up prosecution and rehabilitation efforts—with the stated goal of reducing these offenses by 5 percent in two years, and 20 percent in five years. In addition, LEAA has called for a shift in state and local planning priorities to place greater emphasis than heretofore on improvements in the courts.

The question of priorities is one that needs much closer scrutiny than it has had in the past. Traditionally, state and local governments have tended to focus separately on the different components of the criminal-justice system, only rarely considering it in its entirety. One result is that courts and correction have often taken second place when it came to the allocation process, giving rise to imbalances in resources available to these facilities. Yet there is a growing body of opinion that spending additional dollars in these areas may be the most productive use of resources.

The Criminal Justice Coordinating Council of New York City, for instance, has noted that the Police Department's total cost per policeman, including support services, is approximately $24,000 a year. Thus, with an expenditure of $240,000 ten policemen could be added to the force and collectively, according to the averages, they would make thirty felony arrests a year, with one offender being sent to state prison and nine others to local jail for a short time. As an alternative, the Council estimates $240,000 would pay the annual cost of eight additional prosecutors and their support services, or the cost of three months of correctional services for 120 offenders. "Each of these alternatives," the Council concluded, "would probably do vastly more to improve public safety than the addition of ten policemen."

Such tradeoffs abound, and it is important that criminal justice as a system receive more of this kind of analysis. Improved allocation of resources as between police, courts, and correction is a prime requisite of significant progress in reducing crime. A related need is for improved management within the separate elements of the system. Some of what is wrong with the judicial machinery, Chief Justice Burger has stated, is the failure to apply the techniques of modern business to the purely mechanical operations of the courts, such as handling movement of cases. Citing the need for court administrators to relieve judges of management duties, as hospital administrators relieve doctors, the Chief Justice observed, "We are almost half a century behind the medical profession in this respect."

Reducing the Crime Burden

Even with a better financed and managed system, however, there will be limits to how far the criminal-justice dollar can be stretched. This suggests that a really hard look ought to be taken at the possible desirability of diverting some kinds of offense from the criminal-justice system. The start that has been made with decriminalizing gambling in New York State is very promising, and as an experiment of potentially important lesson value it deserves close attention. If gambling is more widely legalized, of course, expenditures for this purpose will blow up the gross national product just as repeal of the prohibition amendment has resulted in higher GNP figures owing to inclusion of consumer spending on alcoholic beverages—estimated at nearly $24 billion in 1972. This will be the case as well if federal and state laws are modified to legalize private possession of marihuana for personal use, as was recommended last month by the National Commission on Marihuana and Drug Abuse.

Drunkenness could very well be the next candidate for major experiment with decriminalization. It accounts for nearly a fourth of all arrests and for a large part of the jail population in many cities. Indeed, drunkenness arrests nationwide exceed those for "serious" crime—such as homicide, rape, burglary, robbery. But there are clear indications that the criminal-justice system is an inappropriate and ineffective vehicle for dealing with inebriates, except perhaps in instances when drunkenness unleashes aggressive behavior of a sort to justify incarceration. This has in fact received increasing recognition in recent years. Several states have repealed drunkenness statutes, and some cities have experimented with alternatives to arrest—such as persuading inebriates to go to detoxification centers. Overburdened police forces often play down arrests in instances of drunkenness, but so long as the statutes are on the books, periodic efforts at enforcement have to be made. This deflects much cumulative police, court, and correctional time from coping with activities that are criminal in the sense of causing harm to the person or property of others.

This country now has a criminal-justice system overburdened with tasks and hence unable to maximize the prevention and control of really serious crimes. It is a system, moreover, handicapped by lack of effective control over the proliferation of hand guns. The National Commission on the Causes and Prevention of Violence estimated in its 1969 report that civilians possessed as many as twenty-four million hand guns and that sales of these weapons were running at two and a half million a year, four times the volume in the early 1960s. This plainly has added immensely to public danger from homicide, robbery, and other crimes of violence. The joint actions of progressively decriminalizing so-called victimless offenses and of effectively restricting access to hand guns on the part of criminals could be worth literally billions of additional crime control funds.

Slowly but encouragingly public policy is beginning to respond in the right ways—namely, toward concentration of detection and arrest efforts on truly criminal offenders, speedier trials, and more effective correctional procedures. The distance to go is still very long, but at least the old directionless stumbling that was mostly devoid of any sense of priorities in the use of resources is gone. A weighing of cost tradeoffs is now widely evident in official thinking. The need now is for perseverance in the new efforts to use crime-control resources more efficiently and more tellingly.

Those efforts can be potent revenue producers. This is true not only in the case of creating legal gambling facilities. It can be so as well if crime-reduction efforts contribute to an environment characterized by less wastage of human life and property. To the extent that the country does a better job of controlling crime, and thus reducing its costs to society, the payoff in terms of real income benefits ought to be substantial—probably disproportionately so for lower-income groups who often are victimized especially cruelly by criminal activities.

THE ECONOMICS OF CRIME: AN INTRODUCTION TO THE LITERATURE*

RICHARD F. SULLIVAN

The recent onrush of academic economists into the field of criminology may be expected to increase our understanding of how criminal laws and sanctions function in our society and to explain the motivations and goals of criminals. In the short run, however, the picture is not quite so promising.

At one extreme, economists are saying that most concepts taught by schools of criminology are irrelevant and that individuals planning careers as probation officers, parole officers, or institutional correctional officers, with the intention of "rehabilitating" criminals, are suffering from delusions. According to economists, the intervention skills that these individuals are learning will largely fail because they are being implemented by the *wrong* people against the *wrong* people and for the *wrong* reasons. In other words, some economists seem to be saying that society would be better off if criminology students packed up their bags, went home, and urged elected representatives to do two things: (1) reallocate law enforcement expenditures to increase the probability that a criminal will be caught and (2)

* Reprinted from the National Council on Crime and Delinquency. *Crime and Delinquency*, April 1973, pp. 138-50. Used with permission.

increase the severity of punishment to make prisons less pleasant places to live in.

Economics for Criminologists

Until very recently, economists generally ignored the field of crime and law enforcement. They now contend, however, that their explanation of criminal behavior is superior to psychological or sociological explanations. The implications of this development for criminologists are profound. For the past generation, economic analyses and predictions on a wide variety of issues have been extremely useful to government policymakers. Furthermore, of all the social scientists, the economists have been most successful in selling the idea that they are the most scientific: their methods of building models, their adaptations of mathematical and statistical analyses, and their procedures for testing hypotheses more closely approximate those of the physical sciences, and where they do not, economists design analytic and predictive techniques that facilitate our understanding of how society works and of how government policies should be changed to achieve specific goals. As a result, economic researchers have always been able to obtain a very large share of foundation grants and government research money.

Academic economists are beginning to swarm into the field of criminology. Their publications and studies on this subject are growing. Most of the latter will appear in print over the next eighteen months. More importantly, large numbers of economists and nearly all of the larger economic research centers are importuning foundations and governments for research funds to conduct a wide variety of criminological studies. They will probably be successful in obtaining them. This means that in the next few years economic studies dealing with criminology will receive a great deal of attention both because of their volume and their novel approach to the field and because many professional criminologists will feel compelled to refute or elaborate on these explanations.

Although I have had experience in both worlds—as a probation officer and, more recently, as an academic economist—a short time ago I learned just how naive I had been. In a lecture I stated that "an economist would be well advised to ignore the case of the man who murders his wife in a drunken, jealous rage and should leave sadists and revolutionaries to psychiatrists and political theorists." I had underestimated the skills of my new colleagues. That week's mail brought a manuscript written by an economist of international reputation in which he claimed that he could explain all three cases *and* point out how to control them.*

Adam Smith, Jeremy Bentham, Beccaria-Bonesana, Karl Marx, and William Bonger wrote about economics and crime, but their observations have been largely ignored by recent generations of economists. Before 1968, some academic criminologists in North America and England adapted economic techniques to the study of criminology. This was also true of some civil servants working within various branches of the criminal justice system. But the current interest in the economic approach to criminology began in 1968 with the publication of a major article by Gary S. Becker in the *Journal of Political Economy*.[1] Since then, the stage has been set for a vigorous academic dialogue with far-reaching policy implications.

Becker's article is important because it is the first major statement on crime by the current generation of economists. It has not been refuted in print or seriously modified and has provided the model for a rash of econometric studies and will continue to do so. Consequently, it has been responsible for the shifting of scarce research money from other types of criminological studies to those having to do with the economics of crime. This article may have considerable influence on government policy-makers, although some important criminologists believe it to be, if not outright wrong, terribly oversimplified. Understandably,

---

* This may be an extreme interpretation of the paper by Gordon Tullock, "Two Hypotheses on Crime," presented at the meeting of the Southern Economics Association, Savannah, Ga., November 1971, and his forthcoming "The Economics of Repression" and "The Paradox of Revolution."

[1] Gary S. Becker, "Crime and Punishment: An Economic Approach," *Journal of Political Economy* (March-April 1968), pp. 169-217.

† A subdiscipline that utilizes mathematical techniques in testing and applying economic theories.

these criminologists are apprehensive about the potential influence of this particular school of economics. Important modifications are beginning to be formulated. The work done by Carr-Hill, Stern, and their associates in England should prove particularly helpful in this regard.

THE ECONOMISTS' VIEW SIMPLIFIED

Becker states that "a useful theory of criminal behavior can dispense with special theories of anomie, psychological inadequacies, or inheritance of special traits and simply extend the economist's usual analysis of choice" and that "the general criterion of social loss is shown to incorporate as special cases, valid under special assumptions, the criteria of vengeance, deterrence, compensation, and rehabilitation that historically have figured so prominently in practice and criminological literature."[2]

Becker is saying that for a broad range of criminals everything we have been told—that they are sick, abnormal, deviant, or deprived—is wrong. Criminals are relatively simple, normal people like the rest of us, and any attempt to treat them as abnormal or deviant or to "rehabilitate" them is doomed to fail.

Traditional explanations of criminality have applied the concepts of depravity, insanity, deviance, abnormality, and deprivation. Economists maintain that criminals are rational and normally calculating people maximizing their preferences subject to given constraints. This is a psychological explanation that economists prefer over nearly all other explanations of criminal behavior.

Opportunity Cost

Economists use the term *opportunitiy cost* to refer to whatever it is that must be sacrificed to acquire something else. The opportunity cost of war is peace; of the constraints of marriage, the freedoms of being single; of the earnings in one career, the earnings in another; of choosing legally obtained income, obtaining illegal income. In accordance with this reasoning, a heroin addict is no more abnormal or deviant than a nicotine addict. Through

---

[2] Becker, *op. cit.*, p. 170.

a historical accident, the act of possessing heroin has been declared criminal while the act of possessing the dangerous drug nicotine has not. The nature of the addictions is not so very different, in that, given our present knowledge, the heroin user is no less rational than the nicotine user. The law has simply driven up the price for the heroin addict's article of consumption, and, as a result, has often forced the addict to resort to illegitimate earnings. Change the law and the behavior of many heroin users would become similar to that of many nicotine addicts. They court death in different ways but otherwise lead normal lives—giving lectures, driving trucks, raising children, running governments—obliviously smoking or shooting away.

All of us have insatiable desires that we cannot accommodate because of our limited wealth and incomes. Within these constraints of wealth and income, we try to maximize our satisfaction in keeping with our preferences and tastes. Preferences and tastes differ among individuals, and constraints vary according to levels of wealth and income. We choose occupations that can provide us with the highest income or at least the greatest combination of monetary income and nonmonetary rewards. For some, the occupation itself has satisfaction features. All men are not born equal in regard to genetic endowments or social and economic opportunities. From the outset some individuals have more choices than others.

To avoid complications, I will restrict the discussion to various forms of theft. According to the economic explanation of criminality, the individual calculates (1) all his practical opportunities of earning legitimate income, (2) the amounts of income offered by these opportunities, (3) the amounts of income offered by various illegal methods, (4) the probability of being arrested if he acts illegally, and (5) the probable punishment should he be caught. After making these calculations, he chooses the act or occupation with the highest discounted return. To arrive at a discounted return he must include among his cost calculations the *future costs* of going to prison if he is apprehended. It is in this sense that the criminal is understood to be a normal, rational, calculating individual.

Parents, police, probation and parole officers, and judges are always saying, "If you keep it up, you will end up in jail (or in jail again)." Economists believe that this kind of admonition is irrelevant. The individual knows perfectly well that he will probably end up in jail, but he still reasons that he will be better off than were he to go "straight." He has already calculated the costs and benefits. If he is not caught or sent to jail, so much the better. But even if he pays the cost of a stretch in jail, he is still ahead of the game—according to his own calculations. His calculations are not assumed to be accurate: he may overestimate the income to be received or he may underestimate the costs— just as many graduate students in recent years overestimated the material benefits of graduate study.

The "amateur" criminal who overestimates the pay-off from a certain job or underestimates the probability of being apprehended and thus the cost to himself may be considered "irrational" and short-sighted. Many of the individuals who come through our court systems can be characterized this way. But their miscalculations are no more irrational than those of the consumer who gets too much in debt, the worker who does not save in anticipation of layoffs, the man who squanders a week's pay on a whim, or the businessman who goes bankrupt. In all of these cases, there has been a miscalculation in the discounting of future costs. The basic economic assumption does not maintain that people do not make mistakes but rather that they do their best given their reading of present and future possibilities and given their resources.

Since criminals calculate costs and benefits, the economist concludes that we must increase the cost to them by increasing the probability that they will be caught or by increasing the punishment if they are caught. Most of the evidence so far— if it can be called evidence—seems to indicate that criminals are more responsible to the probability of apprehension than to the extent of the punishment. This is not encouraging since it is highly doubtful that the proportion of solved crimes will dramatically increase given our scarce resources, the state of technology in the field of criminology, and the constraints of the law.

ECONOMETRIC STUDIES

Many econometric studies adhere too simplistically to the Becker model. The relations postulated are too simple—they relate the number of petty thefts to the length of prison terms for petty theft, the number of burglaries to the jail sentences for burglary—and rely primarily on global statistics, statistics for an entire state or an entire nation. Some economists, contrary to their training, are ignoring in their studies the long-run social costs of some of these relations.

To estimate the costs of crime and our methods of combating it, we must devise a method of relating the present sentences for petty theft to the future incidence of grand larceny, armed robbery, and murder. The economists should include in their studies the sociological variables, such as age, race, education, and social history, used by criminologists to develop their predictive techniques.

AN ECONOMIC VIEW OF RECIDIVISM

If it is valid, the economic explanation of criminality has profound implications not only for all our correctional institutions but for our entire society and, in particular, for every employer. If a man goes to prison, he goes there after making a rational choice. He has surveyed all his opportunity costs and has chosen this path. In most prisons he serves dead time or, if anything at all, acquires additional criminal skills. And when he is released from prison, he faces rational employers who are understandably reluctant to hire him because of the high recidivism rate among ex-convicts.

The high recidivism rate makes perfect sense to an economist. A man made a rational choice before he went to prison, acquired further criminal skills in prison, and faced rational, hostile employers when he was released. Given these circumstances this man would be irrational if he did *not* return to crime.

Academic criminologists and practitioners have initiated a strong movement for prison reform. The economic view should reinforce drastic reform of prison education programs, and it should argue for a social insurance system that would guarantee reimbursement for any financial loss incurred by hiring an ex-convict. This would be a minimal guarantee and there could be many variations on such a scheme.

The economist believes that the criminal is a rational human being making rational choices according to his constraints, opportunities, and preferences. To alter his calculations we must change his opportunities, increase his opportunity costs, and teach him to discount the future more realistically. Consequently, any "rehabilitative" program that assumes the criminal is abnormal, deviant, inadequate, irrational, or characterized by anomie is doomed to failure.

The economist takes tastes and preferences for granted and assumes that an individual maximizes satisfaction subject to constraints of wealth given his reading of his opportunities. The noneconomist might assert that it is not enough to change an individual's opportunity costs or to teach him to read or discount his future costs more realistically; his "tastes" or "preferences" must be changed by effective programs of "rehabilitation" or "punishment."

OTHER ECONOMIC CONTRIBUTIONS

The current economic approach to criminology has reopened the question of deterrence by seeming to make a stronger case for deterrence than has been made before. This question, however, is far from settled and should be the subject of many rigorous econometric studies within the next few years.

Economic analysis is a general equilibrium system with all parts accounted for according to certain principles called marginal rules. In regard to government policy, a simplified version of these rules is the following: Any government policy should be pursued until the marginal benefit of the policy equals the marginal cost. Marginal means *extra* or the *last in dollar terms*. This means that the benefits from spending the last dollar on a policy should equal exactly one dollar. Beyond this point, a program should not be pursued.

Not everything can be translated into dollar terms, but

economists maintain that policy makers frequently act as though nothing can be translated into meaningful dollar terms. Everyone in the field of criminology knows that policy makers ignore the high costs of some programs and the lower costs and higher benefits of alternative programs. Many of these costs and benefits can be objectively measured and should be.

How is this accomplished? One useful way is to assume that society has a single goal: the minimization of social costs. This one-dimensional view has been repeatedly rejected, but in operational terms it makes sense. In program budgeting terms for sentencing and correctional policy, concepts such as deterrence, prevention, rehabilitation, punishment, and retribution are considered alternative programs (not goals).[3] In these terms, the criminal law is simply one more program to be manipulated to achieve this goal.

The minimization of social costs is simply "protection of society" translated into operational terms. Any law that states that its goals are to protect society *and* to rehabilitate the offender is illogical inasmuch as it has elevated a program (rehabilitation) to a goal.[*]

Academic criminologists and practicing civil servants have preceded any economist into what would seem to be an economic preserve.[†] Nonetheless, there have been no rigorous cost-benefit studies or fully quantified systems analyses in the field, although some are now under way. There are many ways for the properly trained economist to contribute to the field of criminology, including making a strong case for the modification of the criminal code itself. The arguments and evidence presented by economists may effectively buttress criminologist's arguments for basic reform, both in the law itself and in administrative practices. It is certain that a closer cooperation among several disciplines is imperative for solving the problems of criminology.

---

[3] Robert Hann and Richard Sullivan, *Economic Analysis in the Department of the Solicitor General—A Framework for Evaluation of Specific Correctional Services, Case One: Psychiatric Services in Special Treatment Centres*, unpublished report, Department of the Solicitor General of Canada, Ottawa, 1972.

[*] Such a statement can be found in the California Probation Subsidy Law.

[†] Leslie T. Wilkins has been a leader in this regard.

WHAT IS ORGANIZED CRIME?*

CHARLES GRUTZNER

Organized crime in the United States involves about 5,000 hard-core members and at least 50,000 associates and employees operating multifarious enterprises across the nation and reaching often overseas.

The hard-core membership, known as the American Mafia or La Cosa Nostra, consists exclusively—according to its rigid rules—of those of Italian birth or descent through both parents. The 5,000 are organized in twenty-four criminal "families" or borgatas in principal cities from which their rackets and captive legitimate businesses spread out in a nationwide network.

The 50,000 associates and employees are drawn from almost every ethnic and national group represented in the population of the United States. Meyer Lansky, the former street hoodlum turned bootlegger and now a "money mover" on an international scale, carries as much weight in the top councils of the Syndicate (as the broader organization is known) as the most powerful of the Mafia bosses. The Jewish associates play such important roles in the Syndicate that the Mafiosi sometimes refer to them as the Kosher Nostra.

A criminal act is not necessarily part of organized crime just because its execution requires organized effort and planning. For instance, a bank robbery carried out by four or five participants acting in concert is not an act of organized crime unless it is part of the ongoing operation of the Syndicate. Nor are the operations of a neighborhood gang of sneak thieves and shop-lifters considered part of organized crime just because a receiver of stolen goods has arrangements for handling their loot.

Neither the size nor the kind of criminal act determines whether it is organized crime. As seemingly insignificant an infraction of the law as the collecting of fifty cents on a "number" is usually part of a multimillion dollar gambling operation controlled by organized crime. As simple an act of vandalism as

---

* Reprinted from *Harvard Business Review* (March-April 1970). Copyright 1970 by the President and Fellows of Harvard College. All rights reserved. Used with permission.

pouring sugar into the gas tank of a truck is almost always part of an organized crime scheme to cut into a legitimate business or to ruin a competitor. On the other hand, a $2 million theft of jewelry is not organized crime if the thief is an independent operator. It may, however, come into the organized crime orbit if the thief has to enlist the help of the Syndicate in disposing of such a valuable haul.

In 1965, forty law enforcement officials, university professors of criminology, sociologists, systems engineers, and other experts from coast to coast spent an entire day wrestling over a definition of organized crime and came up finally with the following, which is still accepted as the best:

> Organized crime is the product of a self-perpetuating criminal conspiracy to wring exorbitant profits from our society by any means —fair and foul, legal and illegal. Despite personnel changes, the conspiratorial entity continues. It is a malignant parasite which fattens on human weakness. It survives on fear and corruption. By one or another means, it obtains a high degree of immunity from the law. It is totalitarian in its organization. A way of life, it imposes rigid discipline on underlings who do the dirty work while the top men of organized crime are generally insulated from the criminal act and the consequent danger of prosecution.[4]

AN UN-AMERICAN SUCCESS STORY

The Prohibition Era provided the training grounds and generated the capital which enabled organized crime to scale the walls of legitimate business.

Even before the turn of the century, the Black Hand and other extortionists had been exacting tribute from small merchants, especially in the immigrant enclaves of cities. And well before World War I, gangsters had made alliances with some industrial managers by hiring themselves out as strikebreakers. But it was a long way from such scattered incidents to the organized infiltration of the economy at executive levels, which occurred more recently.

---

[4] See Ralph Salerno and John S. Tompkins, *The Crime Confederation* (New York, Doubleday, 1969), p. 303.

When the Volstead Act dried up legal liquor sales, the flood of bootleg booze lifted many lowly criminals to higher and richer ground as rum runners, moonshine distillers, brewers, distributors, and speak-easy operators. Shoestring gamblers, smugglers, extortionists, skullcrackers, and armbusters were drawn into business organizations which, while illegal then, required executive abilities and the professional skills of accountants, lawyers, transportation experts, chemists, and salesmen.

The end of Prohibition left the racket bosses with disciplined organizations, vast amounts of capital, and considerable business know-how. They became the owners or partners in legalized distilleries and breweries, importing companies, licensed liquor stores, and restaurants and night clubs. From this beachhead it was an easy step into such related industries as trucking, linen supply, food purveying, and waste removal.

During the renewed labor-management struggles of the 1930s over the issue of unionizing the garment industry, organized crime along the waterfront rented its goons and assassins to both sides. From the shop-owners the mob demanded and got partnerships in some companies. And from the unions it wrung an agreement to exempt racket owned shops from labor contracts. That is why there remains today some Mafia-controlled open shops in areas where the closed shop is almost universal.

To facilitate its black marketing during World War II, organized crime bought into companies dealing in sugar, shoes, meat, gasoline, automobiles, and other products in short supply.

On the basis of estimates by the Federal Bureau of Investigation, the Internal Revenue Services, the Securities and Exchange Commission, and other law enforcement and regulatory bodies, I would say that organized crime today owns or has decision-making influence in *50,000 commercial or industrial companies.* These companies represent a very wide and impressive variety of industries. It would be harder to think of businesses in which organized crime is not represented than businesses in which it is represented. And the "money movers" are constantly searching for new areas susceptible to the investment of their increasing profits from illicit and legitimate businesses.

In *The Crime Confederation,* the authors state: "The corporate giant of crime annually enjoys a profit greater than General Motors, Standard Oil, General Electric, and U.S. Steel combined. Its gross business is larger than that of all American automobile companies put together. . . .

"With a wide record of diversification, acquisitions and mergers, this perfect conglomerate will never be investigated by the Federal Trade Commission. Freely employing restraints of trade and widely utilizing monopolistic practices, it need not fear the Antitrust Division of the Department of Justice."[5]

What would an operating statement look like for this "perfect conglomerate?" Opinions vary widely, as might be expected. A very conservative estimate, based on necessarily inexact information from federal agencies, puts the annual revenue of organized crime at more than $30 billion, with the net profit between $7 billion and $10 billion. The profit rate is higher than in straight business operations because of the advantages organized crime enjoys through income tax cheating, "sweetheart" labor contracts with racket unions, hijacking of merchandise, skimming of profits off the top, and other outlawed practices.

The $30 billion estimate is for revenues from illegal and "legitimate" ventures. Law enforcement officials who are privy to nationwide intelligence reports are generally of the opinion that gambling and loan sharking are the top income producers, with the take from legitimate business a close third and moving up fast. A few officials privately hazard the guess that the profits from underworld investments in legitimate business already exceed those from gambling and loan sharking.

For a less conservative estimate, Dante B. Fascell believes the gross revenue of organized crime in the United States, from its legitimate businesses and illicit rackets, to be "at least $60 billion."[*] The Florida Congressman, who is Chairman of a House Government Operations subcommittee, says this estimate is based on the latest information from government and business sources.

---

[5] *Ibid.*, p. 225

[*] Address to the Second Organized Crime Training Conference of the U.S. Department of Justice, October 28, 1969.

BIBLIOGRAPHY

Background Books and Reports

Bloch, Herbert A.: *Crime in America.* New York, Philosophical Library, 1961.

Bonger, Willem: *Criminality and Economic Conditions.* Bloomington, Indiana, Indiana University Press, 1969.

Clark, Ramsey: *Crime in America.* New York, Simon and Schuster, 1970.

Lundberg, Ferdinand: Crime and wealth. *The Rich and the Super-Rich.* New York, Lyle Stuart, Chap. 3, pp. 113-154, 1968.

President's Commission on Law Enforcement and Administration of Justice: *The Challenge of Crime in a Free Society.* Washington, D.C., Government Printing Office, 1967.

Rogers, A. J., III: *The Economics of Crime.* Hinsdale, Illinois, The Dryden Press, 1973.

Rottenberg, Simon (Ed.): *The Economics of Crime and Punishment.* Washington, D.C., American Enterprise Institute for Public Policy Research, 1973.

U.S. National Commission on Law Observance and Enforcement: *Report on the Cost of Crime.* Publication No. 12, 1931.

U.S. National Commission on Law Observance and Enforcement: *Report on Police.* Publication No. 14, 1931.

U.S. President's Commission on Crime in the District of Columbia: *Report.* 1966.

U.S. Senate: Committee on the District of Columbia: *Investigations of Crime and Law Enforcement in the District of Columbia.* Senate Report No. 1989, 82nd Congress, 1952.

Background Articles

Becker, Gary S.: Crime and punishment: An economic approach. *Journal of Political Economy, 76*:169-217, 1968.

Coase, R. H.: The problem of social cost. *Journal of Law and Economics, III*:1, 1960.

Fooner, Michael: Some economic factors in crime, delinquency. *New York Law Journal, 161*:46. March 7, 1969.

Grutzner, Charles: What is organized crime? *Harvard Business Review,* 47, March-April 1970.

————: An un-American success story. *Harvard Business Review,* 49, March-April 1970.

Hann, Robert G.: Crime and the cost of crime: An economic approach. *Journal of Research in Crime and Delinquency,* 12-30, January 1972.

Hoover, John Edgar: What does crime mean to industry. *In Depth,* National Association of Manufacturers, September 21, 1964.

Kessel, Reuben: Economic effects of public regulation of milk markets. *Journal of Law and Economics, X*:51, 1967.

Martin, J. P.: The cost of crime: Some research problems. *International Review of Criminal Policy* (U.N.), 23.

Martin, J. P.: Problems in cost of crime analysis: Some aspects of police expenditure in England and Wales. *International Review of Criminal Policy* (U.N.), 25.

Martin, J. P. and Bradley, J.: Design of a study of the cost of crime. *British Journal of Criminology, 4*:6, 591-603, 1963-64.

McGrath, W. T.: Compensation to victims of crime in Canada. *The Canadian Journal of Corrections, 12*:1, 11-24, January 1970.

Morgan Guaranty Trust Company of New York: The economic aspects of crime. *The Morgan Guaranty Survey,* 4-10, April 1972.

Porter, Sylvia: The cost of crime. *New York Post,* May 17, 1967 and May 18, 1967.

Rottenberg, Simon: The social cost of crime and crime prevention. In McLennan, Barbara N. (Ed.): *Crime in Urban Society.* New York, Dunnellan, 1970.

Scaduto, Anthony: The mob: A new look. *New York Post,* 42, June 7, 1968.

Schelling, Thomas C.: Economics and criminal enterprise. *Public Interest,* 61-79, Spring 1967.

Stigler, George J.: Private vice and public virtue. *Journal of Law and Economics, IV*:1, 1961.

Sullivan, Richard F.: The economics of crime: An introduction to the literature. *Crime and Delinquency,* 138-150, April 1973.

Tullock, Gordon: An economic approach to crime. *Social Science Quarterly,* 59-71, 1969-70.

Organized Crime

Books

Allen, Edward J.: *Merchants of Menace: The Mafia.* (Organized Crime in Youngstown, Ohio). Springfield, Thomas, 1962.

Alongi, Guiseppe: *La Maffia.* Turin, Biblioteca Anthropologica Giuridica, 1886.

Chamber of Commerce of the United States: *Deskbook on Organized Crime.* Washington, D.C., 1969.

Clark, Ramsey: Organized crime: The limited empire. *Crime in America.* New York, Simon and Schuster, 1970, Chap. 5, pp. 51-67.

Combating organized crime. *Annals of The American Academy of Political and Social Science,* May 1963.

Conferences on Combating Organized Crime: *Combating Organized Crime.*

(Sponsored by the Office of the Counsel to the Governor of New York, The School of Criminology and Criminal Justice of the State University of New York, and Police Department of the City of New York.) Oyster Bay, New York, 1965.

Cook, Fred J.: *The Secret Rulers*. (Mafia: Historical Background and Current Information). New York, Duell, 1966.

Cressey, Donald R.: *Theft of The Nation: The Structure and Operations of Organized Crime in America*. New York, Harper and Row, 1969.

Demaris, Ovid: *Captive City*. (The Mafia in Chicago's Politics). New York, Lyle Stuart, 1969.

Drzazga, John: The Mafia. *Wheels of Fortune*. Springfield, Thomas, 1963, Chap. 2, pp. 16-51.

Feder, Sid and Joesten, Joachim: *The Luciano Story*. (Some background of the Mafia in the U.S.) New York, McKay, 1954.

Goddard, Donald: *Joey*. (Gallo). New York, Harper and Row, 1974.

Hobsbawm, Eric J.: Mafia. *Primitive Rebels*. New York, Praeger, 1963, Chap. III, pp. 30-56.

Ianni, Francis A. J.: *Black Mafia*. New York, Simon and Schuster, 1974.

Kefauver, Estes: *Crime in America*. Garden City, New York, Doubleday, 1951.

Kennedy, Robert F.: Organized crime. *The Enemy Within*. New York, Harper, 1960, Chap. 12, pp. 239-265.

Landesco, John: *Organized Crime in Chicago*, 2nd ed. Chicago, U of Chicago Pr, 1968.

Lewis, Norman: *The Honored Society*. (History and present position of Mafia in Sicily, and relationships with organized crime in U.S.) New York, Putnam, 1964.

Maas, Peter: *The Valachi Papers*. New York, Putnam, 1968.

McConaughy, John: *From Cain to Capone: Racketeering Down the Ages*. New York, Brentano's, 1931.

Messick, Hank: *Lansky*. New York, Putnam, 1971.

Messick, Hank: *The Silent Syndicate*. (Growth of organized crime from pre-Prohibition days.) New York, Macmillan, 1967.

Messick, Hank: *Syndicate Wife: The Story of Ann Drahmann Coppola*. New York, Macmillan, 1968.

Moquin, Wayne and Van Doren, Charles: *A Documentary History of the Italian-Americans*. New York, Preager, 1974.

Morris, Norval and Hawkins, Gordon: *The Honest Politician's Guide to Crime Control*. Chicago, U of Chicago Pr, 1970.

Pasley, Fred D.: *Al Capone: The Biography of a Self-Made Man*. New York, Garden City Publishing, 1930.

Peterson, Virgil W.: *Barbarians in Our Midst*. (Organized Crime in Chicago.) Boston, Little, 1952.

Ploscowe, Morris (Ed.): *Organized Crime and Law Enforcement*. American Bar Commission on Organized Crime. New York, Crosby Press, 1953, 2 vols.

President's Commission on Law Enforcement and Administration of Justice: *Task Force Report: Organized Crime*. Washington, D.C., Government Printing Office, 1967.

Reid, Ed.: *Mafia*. New York, Random House, 1952.

Reid, Ed.: *The Shame of New York*. New York, Random House, 1953.

Reid, Ed: *The Grim Reapers: The Anatomy of Organized Crime in America*. Chicago, Regnery, 1969.

Salerno, Ralph and Tompkins, John: *The Crime Confederation: The Cosa Nostra and Allied Operations in Organized Crime*. New York, Doubleday, 1969.

Sann, Paul: *Kill the Dutchman: The Story of Dutch Schultz*. New Rochelle, New York, Arlington Hse, 1971.

Schiavo, Giovanni: *The Truth About the Mafia*. (Aims to expose "The myth of the Mafia in America.") New York, Vigo, 1962.

Smith, Alson J.: *Syndicate City*. (Development of organized crime in Chicago and its tremendous control of the Chicago Area.) Chicago, Regnery, 1954.

Sondern, Frederick, Jr.: *Brotherhood of Evil; The Mafia*. New York, Farrar, 1959.

Turkus, Burton B. and Feder, Sid: *Murder, Inc.* New York, Farrar, 1951.

Tyler, Gus (Ed.): *Organized Crime in America, A Book of Readings*. Ann Arbor, Michigan, U of Mich Pr, 1962.

U.S. House of Representatives. Committee on Government Operations: *Federal Effort Against Organized Crime: Report of Agency Operations*. House Rep. No. 1574, 90th Cong., 1968.

U.S. Senate. Committee on the Judiciary: *The Attorney General's Program to Curb Organized Crime and Racketeering: Hearings on S. 1653*. 87th Cong., 1961.

U.S. Senate. Special Committee to Investigate Organized Crime in Interstate Commerce: *Interim Report*. Senate Report No. 2370, 81st Cong., *Second Interim Report*. Senate Report No.141, 82nd Cong., *Third Interim Report*. Senate Report No. 307, 82nd Cong., and *Final Report*. Senate Report No. 725, 82nd Cong., 1950-51.

Varna, Anthony: Mafia. *World Underworld*. London, Museum Press Limited, 1957, Chap. 4.

Wolf, George, and DiMona, Joseph: *Frank Costello, Prime Minister of the Underworld*. New York, Morrow, 1974.

Organized Crime

Articles

Apalachin, New York gangsters conference, November 15, 1957. *New York Times,* 13, January 3, 1958.

Apalachin roundup. *Newsweek, 53:* June 1, 1959.

Boom in the underworld. *Business World,* August 15, 1953.

Brean, H.: How the big roundup was run: Apalachin gang. *Life, 46:* June 1, 1959.

Brennan, R.: New Mr. Big in crime. *Look, 17:* July 28, 1953.

C. Grutzner series on internal organization of Mafia. *New York Times,* 1, May 8, 1967.

Chamberlin, Henry B.: Some observations concerning organized crime. *Journal of Criminal Law, 22:* January 1932.

Cook, F. J.: Apalachin decision. *Nation, 191:* December 17, 1960.

Cook, F. J.: Riesel mystery. *Nation, 183:* September 29, 1956.

Cook, F. J.: Rise of Gallo brothers in Brooklyn underworld. *New York Times,* 37, October 23, 1966.

Cressey, Donald: Organized crime. *New Republic, 163:* July 18, 1970.

Crime syndicate and the way it works. *U.S. News and World Report, 55:* August 19, 1963.

Dembitz, Nanette: The Apalachin conspiracy. *Record of the Association of the Bar of the City of New York, 16:* January 1961.

F.B.I. director Hoover says organized crime costs public $22 billion a year. *New York Times,* 22, January 30, 1960.

Federal grand jury probe of New York City 5 Cosa Nostra families that control rackets in New York City area. *New York Times,* 1, February 13, 1964.

Federal narcotics bureau aide Cusack tells New York State legislature watchdog committee that Apalachin conference was Mafia grand council session. *New York Times,* 1, January 10, 1958.

Fraenkel, Osmond K.: The Apalachin case. *Law in Transition, 21:* Spring 1961.

Geis, Gilbert: Violence and organized crime. *The Annals of the American Academy of Political and Social Science,* March 1966.

Interstate organized crime. *Notre Dame Lawyer,* Symposium, Notre Dame, University of Notre Dame, 1963.

It pays to organize. *Time, 57:* March 12, 1951.

J. Edgar Hoover reports. *American City, 67:* June 1952.

Lahey, E. A.: Gangs go legitimate. *New Republic, 124:* May 15, 1951.

The Jewish underworld: Kosha Nostra. *Daily Forward,* February 29, 1967.

Johnson, E., Jr.: Organized crime: Challenge to the American legal system. *Journal of Criminal Law, Criminology and Police Science,* December 1962-June 1963.

Kefauver, Estes: Crime in the United States. *Saturday Evening Post, 223*: April 7, 1951.

Kennedy, Robert F.: Robert Kennedy defines the menace. *New York Times Magazine,* January 26, 1964.

Lindesmith, Alfred R.: Organized crime. *The Annals of the American Academy of Political and Social Science, 217*: September 1941.

Mafia, a hidden power that rules the deadly rackets? *Newsweek, 50*: November 25, 1957.

McLain, L.: Mafia, secret empire of evil. *Coronet, 45*: November 1958.

Mob: Empire of organized crime; its power structure, tactics. *Life,* September 8, 1967.

Moley, R.: After Kefauver, what? *Newsweek, 37*: April 9, 1951.

Mortimer, L.: Underworld confidential: Virginia Hill's success secrets. *American Mercury, 72*: June 1951.

Moynihan, Daniel P.: Crime: a $20,000,000 bill for Americans. *Senior Scholastic, 79*: November 15, 1961.

Nagler, B. and Helfand, J.: My battle with the fight mob. *Saturday Evening Post, 228*: June 2, 1956.

New Yorkers pay $50 million racket tax yearly: Illegal payments to racketeers raise retail prices at least 5%. *New York Times,* 38, April 21, 1956.

New York State police and federal agents round up and eject group of 65 from Apalachin, New York. *New York Times,* 1, November 15, 1957.

Organized crime; Selected articles. *Crime and Delinquency, 8*: October 1962.

Partners in crime. *Colliers, 128*: December 12, 1951.

Peterson. V. W.: Rackets in America. *Journal of Criminal Law, 59*: March-April, 1959.

Report to Harriman on Apalachin convention. *New York Times,* 1, May 2, 1958.

Rice, R.: Business of crime. *Saturday Review, 39*: December 22, 1956.

Rise of dishonesty. *U.S. News and World Report, 31*: November 31, 1951.

Sellin, T.: Organized crime: A business enterprise. *Annals of the American Academy of Political Science, 347*: May 1963.

Senate committee reports at least two major crime syndicates exist. *New York Times,* 1, March 1, 1951.

Shadoan, G.: Behind the crime scare. *Nation, 200*: May 10, 1965.

Slater, S.: My life inside the mob. *Saturday Evening Post, 236*: August 24, 1963.

Smith, Sandy: Mobsters in the marketplace: Money, muscle, murder. *Life Magazine, 63, 10*: September 8, 1967.

Sollazzo, S. and R. Rice: Annals of crime. *New Yorker, 31*: March 5, 1955.

Twenty-two seized as members of crime school for youth set up by leading mobsters to recruit members for crime syndicate. *The New York Times,* 1, August 11, 1960.

Uncle syndicate. *Newsweek, 38*: October 17, 1951.

U.S. attorney Morganthau reports all major crime in New York City is controlled by underworld families. *New York Times,* 29, January 6, 1965.

Velie, L.: Man to see in New Jersey. *Colliers, 128*: August 25, 1951.

Walsh, Lawrence E.: Organized crime. State Conference of Mayors, Los Angeles, July 15, 1959.

Warshafsky, F.: Father Clarke's underworld parish. *Coronet, 49*: February 1961.

Way big crime operates in U.S. *U.S. News and World Report, 55*: October 7, 1963.

What has happened since Kefauver; Reports from six key cities. *Life, 31*: October 1, 1951.

Your land is hoodland: Cosa Nostra families. *Life, 63*: September 1, 1967.

CHAPTER 2

ECONOMICS OF GAMBLING

INTRODUCTION

THE ECONOMIC ROLE of organized crime in our society can be understood best by citing a few figures. Estimates of annual gross revenue from all forms of gambling in the United States range from $7 billion to $50 billion a year. Many law enforcement officials use the figure of $20 billion a year which includes illegal betting on horse races, other sporting events, such as football, baseball, and basketball, and the numbers game.

Evidence gleaned at public hearings indicates that organized crime's profit from illegal gambling runs as high as one third of gross revenue. Using the $20 billion a year gross figure, organized crime's profit is $6 billion to $7 billion a year, reported in the President's Commission on Law Enforcement and Administration of Justice, *Task Force Report on Organized Crime*. The role of illegal gambling in organized crime had been substantiated previously by the Kefauver Committee after its lengthy investigation. The Committee concluded that illegal gambling is the principal source of income for organized criminal gangs in the United States.

A profit of about $7 billion a year from illegal gambling operations is equivalent to the total profit of the twelve largest industrial corporations ranked according to sales. These companies include General Motors, Ford, General Electric, the largest oil companies, U.S. Steel and International Business Machines. The $7 billion profit for the twelve largest companies with sales of about $100 billion is about an 8 percent return. A

$7 billion profit on a $20 billion volume of illegal gambling is a 35 percent return.

Rufus King in *Gambling and Organized Crime,* the first reading in this chapter, traces the relationship between gambling and crime from the nineteenth century to the present. He clearly indicates the power of money as a corruptor of law enforcement and ultimately local governments and government at even higher levels. Salerno and Tompkins in *The Crime Confederation* discuss crime as a business indicating that loansharking runs gambling a close second as a moneymaker for organized crime. After gambling and loansharking, other income producing illegal activities include importing and wholesaling of narcotics and other activities including extortion, labor racketeering, hijacking, securities fraud, cigarette smuggling and bankruptcy fraud.

The third reading in this chapter reports on the current status of both legal and illegal gambling in New York State. The gross volume of gambling in New York State is estimated at $4 billion annually, excluding personal betting, of which about $900 million is actually lost by bettors.

GAMBLING AND CRIME[*]

Rufus King

Until the middle of the nineteenth century, gambling in America was seldom associated with crime at all. Both in the rugged tradition of our frontiers and on the more sophisticated Eastern seaboard, local gambling operations flourished unchecked, while lotteries had been widely employed from colonial times in the promotion of worthy causes. The earliest criminal enactments had to do with cheaters and crooked gambling operators who offended society by using the cloak of gambling games to cover what was in effect outright larceny. Public reaction against all forms of gambling commenced early in the

---

[*] Reprinted from Rufus King, *Gambling and Organized Crime,* Public Affairs Press, 1969, pp. 23-25. Used with permission.

nineteenth century, was inflamed by a series of national scandals involving crooked lotteries, and resulted in various antigambling prohibitions enacted by the legislatures of nearly every state in the post-Civil War era.

But the people who defied these laws, the gambling promoters of the late nineteenth and early twentieth centuries, were seldom identified with the "hard" criminal elements of their day. Some illegal gambling operations were organized in the sense that they were conducted on a large scale and involved the participation of many people, e.g. "policy," which grew out of the suppressed lotteries, and the nationwide slot machine industry which flourished despite repressive laws after 1900, but there was little evidence of organized criminal activity in the syndicate style. Gambling was intimately associated with shabby local politics and corrupt police forces rather than with violent crime. No excesses of the gambling fraternity before World War I could be said even to have approached the viciousness of the organized prostitution rings which led to enactment of the federal White Slave Act of 1910.

The modern phenomenon of organized crime—which is essentially merely a projection of the ancient offense of criminal conspiracy, committed over an extended period by an identifiable criminal group—did not truly make its appearance on the American scene until the 1920s. The urban "gangster" was a product of Prohibition who soon expanded his operations from hijacking and bootlegging into other new fields opened for him by our efforts to prohibit the use of narcotic drugs under the Harrison tax law, and by violent dissension in the labor movement. But though illegal gambling did not produce the gangster, and was perhaps not an important factor in his early rise, it proved to be an activity well suited for him to take over and develop, along with extortion, prostitution, organized pilfering, and fencing. The speakeasy and the hoodlum-guarded roadhouse casino soon prospered together, both often protected by the same "muscle" and immunized from official harassment by the same "arrangements."

Slot machines and other coin-operated gambling devices likewise lent themselves to the building of gang-controlled empires, with their own dismal chapters of savage warfare over territories, intimidation tactics to build lucrative operators' routes, and corruption of public officials. Organized criminal groups also began to move into local clandestine lottery operations and to enlarge the ubiquitous neighborhood "numbers" games. By the time the Wickersham Commission made its report to President Hoover in 1931, it could be estimated that the revenues from illegal gambling were somewhere near $500 million per year, as compared with an estimated two to three billion from bootlegging, and perhaps another $500 million from the drug traffic and other less lucrative sources.

With repeal of the Eighteenth Amendment in 1933 the picture changed abruptly. Except for the significant number of erstwhile bootleggers who managed to move over into the legalized production and distribution of alcoholic beverages, the so-called crime syndicates found themselves depending primarily on the proceeds of gambling to hold their empires together. (If Narcotics Bureau estimates are accepted, the illicit drug traffic has remained almost constant in volume, and thus impliedly in the revenues it produces, from the early 1920s to the present—with only a brief hiatus when World War II choked off virtually all smuggling.) As a result gangster muscle and gangster money produced a runaway expansion of illicit gambling activities in the 1930's. One careful observer of the period claimed that, excepting only unpopulated Western ranges, some kind of gambling institution, casino, horse parlor or numbers bank, was established within thirty miles of every home in America. Police departments, entire city governments, and one small Western state (Nevada went "legal" in 1931) were virtually captured in the onslaught.

Nor is it without significance that this was the era in which state after state allowed the opening of horse and dog tracks, with pari-mutuel betting. Horseracing, "the sport of kings," traditionally attended by pools, stakes and side-wagering, had become a popular pastime in this country as soon as horses appeared in the colonial settlements. In the post-Civil War era, track racing emerged as a popular sport, with local races at county seats all over the nation and major meets held each year at New York's famous Saratoga and in Maryland, Kentucky, and Louisiana. But in the seemingly inevitable pattern uncontrolled gambling at these events soon began to go sour: The bookmakers who dominated betting shortened their odds, defrauded their customers, skipped town when they lost too heavily, caused a series of major scandals by bribing trainers and riders, and were sometimes exposed racing their own horses under false colors—all of which eventually produced a strong wave of popular reaction and new antigambling legislation.

By the turn of the twentieth century, racing and bookmaking had been generally outlawed in all states except Maryland, Kentucky, and New York; and in 1910 New York prohibited track betting (trying for some years thereafter a strange scheme wherein wagers could only be accepted by notation, provided the bookmaker took no money and settled with his patrons through a system of adjusting balances on a succeeding day). In the predepression twenties only five states officially acknowledged horseracing with state controls in the form of regulatory laws. But in the period between 1930 and 1940, the number of states with regulated tracks jumped to eighteen, and in the following decade, to twenty-five.

The ostensible reason for this about-face by state lawmakers was the desperate need of state governments for new sources of revenue in the aftermath of the Great Depression. Other possible reasons, perhaps the real reasons, lie in a shadowland of ill-concealed pressures around virtually every state capital involved, crude patronage deals, flashy lobbying, stock handouts to legislators, and persistent rumors of outright bribes on so lavish a scale that the "black bag" economies of not a few state legislative chambers have allegedly been permanently inflated as a result. And though gangsters have seldom turned up inside the track enclosures (horseracing has long been policed to an appearance of remarkable purity by one of the most efficient private "protective" organizations in the country), it is indisputable that the legalized tracks provided the essential foundation for what soon became gangland's largest single illegal enterprise, the organization and management of off-track bookmaking.

The key to control of the bookies was the notorious race wire services. Beginning in the early twenties on a small scale, these leased-wire networks (which flashed odds, scratches, and results to bookie joints) ultimately became so powerful that one of them was disclosed, in the tax evasion trial of Moe Annenberg in 1940, to have become the *fifth largest customer* of the American Telephone and Telegraph Company.

With elaborate organizations to gather information by clandestine observation at the tracks, vast networks of their own telephone and telegraph lines, and "drops" in every major population center, the wire services furnished a structure almost literally analagous to a great spider's web blanketing the nation. They even had a convincing façade of legality, for they served as bonafide "news" agencies for some bonafide sports editors and variously mob-connected racing sheets (and let no man lay a clumsy hand on anything even remotely related to the touchy prerogatives of the Fourth Estate under the First Amendment unless he is looking for trouble!).

Following the murder of James E. Ragen of Continental Press in 1946, into the center of this spider's web moved Tony Accardo and "Greasy Thumb" Guzik, the heirs of Al Capone from Chicago, with satellite gang overlords joining them from every crime center in the country—the Dutch Schultz heirs and the Costello and Adonis interests in New York, Jack Dragna and Mickey Cohen from the West Coast, Carlos Marcello in New Orleans, the Binaggio forces in Kansas City, and so on through the whole evil roster.

To attribute half the gang killings and mob violence of the forties and fifties to battles over control of this gambling empire would be a very conservative speculation. Whoever controlled the wire service "drops" in a town became the master of gambling activities there. And more often than not he also controlled— the word is responsibly chosen, controlled—the community's local law enforcement agencies. No one could run a substantial book without the wire service, or in competition against it: First, because the competitor who had results instantly flashed to him by the service could wipe out the man without them by the simple tactic of slipping in bets on horses which had already won their races; second, because the bookmaker himself depends for profits on a skillful balance of his bets, and the use of "lay-offs," and "come-backs," which requires him to follow odds changes; and third, because the real horse player wants continuing "action"—he will not waste time on one-shot bets if someone provides him with an opportunity to diversify his play and parlay as the results come in.

Regarding the assertion about controlling law enforcement (I acknowledge an obligation to define "lay-offs" and "come-backs," but we will reach that in the discussion of pari-mutuel betting in the next chapter), it is obvious that no bookmaking operation, or lottery or numbers game or casino, for that matter, can be run on a basis substantial enough to make it profitable without becoming well known in the community. The gambling promoter must find his patrons in some segment of the public, and he cannot reach out very far without coming to the attention of those charged with responsibility for enforcing the law. So, disregarding Nevada and a few scattered spots where experiments have been made from time to time with legalization, wherever gamblers operate there is *always* some degree of official corruption.

In this aspect, gambling is uniquely vicious. The little man at the end of the line who takes a few $2.00 bets, writes some numbers, has a slot machine or two for the amusement of his patrons, etc., is simply not much of a challenge to the cop on the beat or the lieutenant in his precinct headquarters. Often he is an established and accepted member of the community, drawing beer or jerking sodas or welcoming chilly patrolmen in his warm shop when the temperature drops. Or he will be in humble and familiar contact with his clientele—around Washington, D.C. the place to find the "action" in federal buildings, not excluding the F.B.I. section of the Department of Justice, is among the elevator operators and messenger and driver pools.

And gambling money is not "dirty" money. Even if the officer does not like to take an occasional flier on the numbers or the horses himself, it is not hard for him to accept the first ham at Christmas, the first case of whiskey, or a few dollars here and there in return for overlooking what is going on under his nose.

But once you have the patrolman—and his lieutenant and his captain and the Chief—taking bribes from your organization for "protection" of a harmless little gambling enterprise, *you have got them for all purposes*. And once the front is breached, whether the men on the street hear rumors that the Chief is getting rich, or whether the senior officers start coming down the line for a cut of the good thing their men have found, law enforcement efforts will fall apart very rapidly.

This was the clear finding of Attorney General McGarth's Conference on Organized Crime, convened in February 1950, and of the Kefauver Committee Investigations which followed (and perhaps undeservedly outshone it). This is why the big time mobsters fought so bitterly for control of gambling, and especially for the wire services. And this is what gave rise to the truly organized, phenomenally powerful "crime syndicates" of recent decades. With the insidious entering wedge of gambling, local law enforcement was universally impaired and sometimes totally corrupted. And outward, along the strands of the web from its evil center, into communities invaded by the bookie and captured by the gang, came organizers of real racketeering and hard crime—drugs, blackmail, extortion, usury, prostitution, burglars, robbers, hired killers and the rest.

Widely in the last three decades and occasionally today, the gambler-gangster has managed to hit an even higher target: Instead of corrupting and capturing local police forces he has been able to gain control of local governments. As one eminent scholar in the field stresses, people who aspire to careers as city and county office holders are not always our most upstanding citizens; sometimes, especially in the ward politics of large cities, such aspirants may even tend to be somewhat opportunistic. Not only have the gambling interests controlled astronomical amounts of money (the lifeblood of political organization and campaigning), but, again particularly in urban ward politics, they have been able to provide substantial manpower for party work and even to deliver significant blocs of votes.

A narrative history of the working partnerships between gamblers, brothel lords, modern hoodlums and the "in" groups of local politics in this century would expand this study into something like the Five Foot Shelf. From Bathhouse John Coughlin and Hinky Dink Kenna in Cook County, through the regimes of Boss Tweed and Tammany in New York, Blonger in Denver, Curley in Boston, Crump in Tennessee, and New Orleans under Huey Long, and back to the Jimmy Hines scandals which launched Thomas E. Dewey on his career as a crimebuster, the sordid pattern is always and everywhere the same. The Wickersham Commission observed that at the time of its studies (1931) gamblers were in full control of Los Angeles, San Francisco, Detroit and Kansas City. The American Municipal Association, complaining of racketeer influences in municipal governments in 1949, cited Los Angeles, New Orleans and Portland, Oregon, as captive cities.

Currently, Seattle, New Orleans, Baltimore and most of Illinois and South Carolina, among others, are being run by "tolerance" regimes which permit the open operation of gambling pinball machines (faster and "hotter" gambling devices than the old one-armed bandit); there is not an urban concentration in the country without numbers writers; and even some segments of the old wire services are believed to be back in operation. When the cozy arrangements in Seattle were threatened by a reform movement, the Washington Legislature, allegedly responding to pressures generated by a combination of gamblers and union leaders, slipped through a law to protect the machines, touching off a comic opera sequence that ended in someone's stealing a truckload of referendum petitions directly out of the official safe of the Secretary of State in Olympia. In Baltimore, I.R.S. records show year after year that there are more federal gambling-device tax stamps issued for Baltimore City and County (where gambling devices are absolutely illegal) than for all of the four Maryland counties where slot machines have until recently been operating under the sanction of special legalizing ordinances. When Kentucky closed out coin-machine gambling in 1966 by a new state law, the gamblers made so strong a comeback in the next session of the General Assembly (under a new Governor and with new faces in the State House in Frankfort) that only a spirited press campaign coupled with rumors that bribes had reached a choking seven figure aggregate, enabled antigambling forces to effect a cliff-hanger rescue of the new law.

The Kefauver Committee exposed patterns like this in small cities such as Covington, Kentucky, and Pennsylvania's Wyoming Valley (Scranton and Wilkes-Barre) which it chose almost as random samples; Buffalo, New York, has recently been rocked by a gambling scandal involving its entire city government; Biloxi, Mississippi, and Hot Springs, Arkansas, have survived for decades as famous gambling meccas; while in the District of Columbia a Senate committee, investigating crime and law enforcement in 1952, found that the sacrosanct Metropolitan Police Department of Washington, D.C. was directly running much of the illegal gambling in the District—and most of the narcotic drug traffic besides. President Johnson's Crime Commission turned out to be more conservative than any of its predecessors about naming real names or actual places, but its mythical "Wincanton" is a skillful composite of conditions it presumably saw around the nation and endorsed as typical in 1966. There is nothing anonymous about the interplay of gambling and corruption reported at all levels in this official community of Wincanton and appraised as a dominant influence in its public affairs.

It would be hard indeed to find a city or county government anywhere in the United States that does not have some suggestion of scandal, involving gamblers' money, somewhere in its recent history. It might even be hard to find a local government whose *present* office holders do not include in their numbers anyone who—for sure—owes anything whatsoever to the gambling and vice rackets right now. And it is not easy to rule out—with certainty—the possibility that some of the lines of influence reach upward through tawdry city halls and county courthouses to much higher levels in our state and national governments. After all, even those whose political careers are crowned by a reserved seat in the Senate Wing or the Oval Room usually made their starts working for their party in some seamy Wincanton; and it takes vastly more money and more supporting cronies, not less, to reach for the big prizes in American politics.

Before the foregoing generalizations are dismissed as reckless, let consideration be given to the consensus of informed speculation about the resources commanded by those who control illegal gambling in the United States today. As with any clandestine activity, exact figures are not available and approximate figures are not perfectly defensible by those who offer them. However, there seems to be general agreement that the total sum spent annually by Americans in all forms of illegal gambling (the yearly "handle"), runs in the range of $15 to $25 billions. Some reputable estimators double those figures. But let us say $20 *billions!* If the "take" of the gambling promotor amounts to one third of this (and the patron in illegal gaming assuredly gets no breaks), the income shared by those who control this form of criminal activity would be between $6 billion and $7 billion.

In various investigations, interviews with convicted gamblers who have repented or reformed, and estimates given by knowledgeable people willing to "level" with their interrogators, it has been established that the direct and indirect costs of protection in the form of bribes, political contributions, blackmail, etc., works out to something above one third of the "take." So rounding off again to be conservative, it can be responsibly asserted that no less than $2 *billions per year* is sponged up by public officials and law enforcers as the price exacted for letting the gambling promotor and the gambling syndicates carry on their enterprises in our society.

If that figure were cut, and cut again, and then divided a few times, it is still a breath taker! It is the amount of dollars, the same kind of dollars you and I work for and try to save and pay our taxes with, that disappear each year into the pockets of the police, the administrators, the judges and the lawmakers who are supposed to be running our governments and protecting our common welfare and well-being. And it must be remembered that virtually all this flow enjoys the enhancing value of moving in cash, unaccounted for and outside the reach of any taxing authority. No wonder the federal campaign fund laws noted a few pages back, supposed to prevent any individual from giving any candidate for federal office more than $5,000, and corporations and unions from giving him anything, are such a joke!

No wonder our worthy lawmakers, from town councils to the halls of Congress, do so much backing and filling when anyone around them talks seriously about putting teeth in campaign expenditure disclosure laws! Americans seem neither puzzled at the conspicuous opulence of some of their lifelong public servants, nor much shocked when, occasionally, the screen slips a little so they can catch a glimpse of the inner workings of their elective system. Yet even without the current confirmation of Congressman Gallagher's alleged mob connections and the antics of Bobby Baker and his friends at one end of the scale, and the non-enforcement of gambling laws on virtually every Main Street in America, at the other, it would be hard to believe that office holders whose need for money is insatiable and favor seekers whose supply of money is virtually inexhaustible would *not* be widely linked in arrangements having obviously great mutual benefits.

So we have arrived at the paradox which troubles everyone who undertakes to study illegal gambling. The activity itself, in terms of the small patron and even the small promoter, is relatively inoffensive; yet in another inseparable aspect, it is at the very root of the grievious problem we describe as organized crime. It corrupts officials who would otherwise be incorruptible. It arms our most vicious criminals with a power far more menacing than the bombs and Tommy guns of the twenties—the power of money. And to an alarming extent it has directly undermined the structure and functioning of local government itself—even, possibly, of government at higher levels.

CRIME AS A BUSINESS*

RALPH SALERNO AND JOHN S. TOMPKINS

We're bigger than U.S. Steel.

Meyer Lansky

Mr. Lansky was being modest. In 1967, the United States Steel Corporation had assets of $5 billion, $600 million and sales

---

* Reprinted from *The Crime Confederation*, Doubleday, 1969, pp. 225-235. Used with permission.

of $4 billion on which its profits after taxes were $172 million $500 thousand. Unless Lansky was talking only about his own activities, he understated the actuality. On the most conservative basis, the Confederation's gross from illegal activities alone is $40 billion a year, or ten times as much as U.S. Steel. And net profits, of course, are proportionally much, much higher because the Syndicate groups do not pay taxes on their illegal income, though payoffs and other overhead expenses do cut heavily into the gross.

The corporate giant of crime annually enjoys a profit greater than General Motors, Standard Oil, Ford, General Electric, and U.S. Steel combined. Its gross business is larger than that of all American automobile companies put together.

If the profits from one division alone (gambling) had been invested for the past seventeen years (since the Kefauver investigation) so as to earn only 5 percent on the principal, the sum today would be sufficient to purchase *every single share* of common stock in the ten largest corporate complexes in the United States (as listed in *Fortune* magazine) and the small change left over would buy up American Tel & Tel.

With a wide record of diversification, acquisitions and mergers this perfect conglomerate will never be investigated by the Federal Trade Commission. Freely employing restraints of trade and widely utilizing monopolistic practices, it need not fear the Anti-Trust Division of the Department of Justice.

Security regulations and the need to avoid jealousy and temptation make income figures within the Confederation a closely guarded internal secret. Only those with the need to know are privy to the income from any particular operation. Any numbers banker, loanshark, or narcotics pusher can give the dimensions of his own business, but he will not know anyone else's figures. He may not even know who else is in the same business.† There is no overall consolidated balance sheet or

---

† Several years ago, New York police bugged the office of a man who controlled a numbers bank. He had been trying to find out the identity of another big banker in the same area, but the insulation of organized crime is such that he was always frustrated:

"The front line has to be friends. Therefore if a worker is in the front, they have more respect for the worker, when they don't know the boss. You know

profit and loss statement for even one Cosa Nostra family let alone the entire Confederation.

Aside from security, the main reason for the lack of overall financial statements is that organized crime is not a single corporate entity with many subsidiaries and uniform accounting. It is more like a public market with many individuals occupying booths and stalls under the same roof. As long as they pay rent for their space, the owner of the market has no interest in the volume or profits of each entrepreneur. When a Cosa Nostra Boss gets tribute from his men, he does not know exactly how much their profits are; he depends on fear and respect to insure that his cut is proportionate.

Many criminals' *legal* business investments are unlikely to be known to their associates. Such separate activities, even as his home life, are kept distinct from illegal operations. Joseph Valachi told one of the authors (Salerno) that he had not known of most of the legal activities of the leaders of his own Cosa Nostra family until he heard them described to the hearings by the police.

Because of the lack of reliable statistics, estimates must be arrived at by deduction and extrapolation from known samples and benchmarks.

Gambling is the largest single income producer. The number of dollars bet illegally vastly exceeds the nearly $7 billion wagered in Las Vegas casinos, at the pari-mutuel tracks, and in the several state lotteries. The main reason for this is convenience. People who do not have the time or money to go out to the track, much less fly to Nevada, can bet over the phone, or hand a quarter to a man who comes around every day. Experts on gambling, such as John Scarne, have estimated that seven dollars are bet illegally

---

how long it took us to find Max. Maxie, he was a plainclothesman. He was a phantom. He was a guy that was a partner with a plainclothesman. He was the detective from the DA's office. We never could find out who this ....ing guy was . . .

"You could ask God. You could ask a dozen people. We went to Mike and Lefty. We went to this guy. We went to that guy. We went to the branchmen. We could never find out who Max was. He always operated with some- body in front of him. I never met the same ....ing guy twice. And that's. the way he operated for years, Pete, for years."

for every dollar bet legally. And a five or four-to-one factor is considered conservative. (The various estimates are based on interviews with bookies, numbers bankers, and gamblers plus the actual sample data gleaned from gambling operations that the police have raided.)

In the late 1950s, William P. Rogers, President Eisenhower's Attorney General, estimated the total gross of organized crime at $20 billion a year, half of it from gambling. Around the same time, J. Edgar Hoover put the total at $22 billion, with $11 billion coming from gambling. Then, Milton Wessel, who headed a special Justice Department group that looked into the Apalachin meeting, studied the problem and came up with a figure of $47 billion a year—*from gambling alone*. This reflects Scarne's seven-to-one ratio.

President Johnson's Commission on Law Enforcement and Administration of Justice also tackled the problem. Rufus King, a Washington lawyer, who had served as aide to Senator Kefauver during his crime hearings in the early 1950s, made his own study. Trying to be conservative, King decided to leave Nevada out of the legal total and use a three-to-one ratio of illegal to legal betting. His estimate is $20 billion a year gross, with a net income to organized crime of $6 billion to $7 billion. King also estimates that $2 billion of the illegal gambling is spent on the corruption of public officials, including police.

Not generally appreciated is the fact that loansharking runs gambling a close second as a moneymaker for organized crime, and it is growing much faster. The annual take is now running about $10 billion on an investment of $5 billion in working capital, and most of the income is net income. One New York Boss invested $500,000 with his lieutenants in loansharking in 1959. By 1964 his money had been pyramided to $7,500,000. In 1965, a New York investigation identified Nicholas ("Jiggs") Forlano and his partner Charles ("Ruby") Stein as running the biggest loanshark operation in the city with up to $5 million on the street (loaned out) at any one time. It was calculated that at an average 2 percent a week return, the two were taking in at least $100,000 a week.

Loansharking has proved an almost perfect medium for the

investment of funds thrown off by gambling. In fact, having access to big time loansharking as an investment is one of the advantages that Syndicate gamblers have over those who are still independent. Consider the case of "Newsboy" Moriarity, a Jersey City numbers racketeer who operated on a large scale, but managed to avoid being absorbed by any organized crime group. His independence may have been profitable and personally satisfying, but Moriarity found it impossible to do anything with the cash his business generated. He couldn't invest it fast enough without connections, he couldn't put it in banks, he couldn't even move it very far without help. So, Moriarity had to hide it and he did just that. In July 1962 $2,500,000 in cash was found crammed into his garage in Jersey City.

Not only is loansharking a high return investment, it is also a simple business to operate. A loanshark needs nothing but money and borrowers. He does not have to have an office. Most loansharks meet their clients in restaurants and nightclubs. He needs no employees for he can call on his Syndicate backers for enforcers to help in collections. No special equipment is involved, and he does not require any particular skill or training in subtle intimidation or violence. Unlike gambling, the business has no odds or set rates or rules except for one: The borrower must pay.

The interest charged is, literally, whatever the traffic will bear. On a weekly basis rates have ranged between 1 percent and 150 percent, according to the relationship between the lender and the borrower, the intended use of the money, the size of the loan, and the ability of the customer to pay. Much of the time, the lender is more interested in perpetuating interest payments than in collecting the principal, so he will try to set the size and terms of the loan so that it is slightly more than the borrower can afford to carry.

Bankers like to talk about the power of compound interest, pointing out that money deposited and left to grow at 5 percent will double in fourteen years and three months. By loanshark standards this is not just standing still, it's moving backward. For in addition to the huge interest charges, the loanshark does what banks do: He puts each dollar repaid back out to work for him with another customer. A poor Negro workman in a Midwestern city borrowed $10 from a loanshark and agreed to pay $1 interest on it every week. At the end of nearly sixty weeks when the loanshark was arrested the workman had still not paid any of the principal, but had paid 600 percent interest. During that time the loanshark found several other customers for the money he had got back from the first borrower, thus pyramiding his capital investment constantly.

Confederation members are often wholesale loansharks, lend-their money at 1 percent a week to associates who relend it at 2 percent or 2½ percent to sidewalk operators who have to get 5 percent or 6 percent a week and often much more. The "six-for-five" man is getting 20 percent weekly for small loans. For instance, the wholesaling within one Syndicate operates this way:

> The Boss invited ten of his trusted lieutenants to a Christmas party at his home. After an excellent dinner he had a suitcase brought into the dining room and counted out $100,000 in cash for each of the ten men. He said, "I want 1 percent a week for this. I don't care what you get for it. But I want 1 percent a week."
>
> He did not record any names; they were all old friends. He did not have to record the amount given out. His only problem at the next party will be finding more good men to lend out the money that he will earn during the year.

Each of the lieutenants found places to put the $100,000 and earned for themselves at least as much as the $1,000 a week they paid their Boss. On the third tier, the retail loansharks probably earned even more. So, an original $1,000,000 investment produced $2,500,000 to $3,000,000 a year in earnings.

After gambling and loansharking other income producing illegal activities pale into relative insignificance, though they add up to a gross of $7½ billion to $10 billion a year. This area includes the importing and wholesaling of narcotics, and activities involving extortion, labor shakedowns and racketeering, counterfeiting, hijacking, cigarette smuggling, securities fraud, and bankruptcy fraud.

The Classic Pattern

In following the pattern of organized crime as a business (see Table 2-1) we have to separate two different kinds of violations of the law. The first are strategic and tactical crimes designed to create a state of mind: an acquiescence, a willingness of a victim or competitor to cooperate in whatever the Confederation wants him to do. These crimes are arson, assault, blackmail, bribery, coercion, extortion, mayhem, murder and sabotage.

Such crimes do not and are not intended to, produce an immediate economic gain for the Syndicate using them. They are called on for short term or long term gains. In this context, for example, arson might involve the burning out of a restaurant which would not install a Confederation jukebox or take its liquor supply or have its laundry done by a member firm. The arson is used as a form of warning or punishment. This kind of extortion is getting something of value (here, business for a service company) through the use or threat of force or fear— the value being one of future potential rather than immediate cash income.

Through the use of strategic and tactical crimes, organized crime has been able to enter, dominate, and even control to varying degrees, all kinds of illegal businesses and activities. Arson is, of course, also used for fraud, as when a business is intentionally burned out after most of the inventory has been removed and the insurance money for the full value is collected from the insurer. Extortion is also used tactically for immediate economic gain, through "protection," where payments of cash are demanded for the right to continue in business without harm.

All of the violent crimes can contribute to a strategy: taking over the garbage collection business in a city, seizing control of independent bookmakers, dominating the restaurant supply industry in an area.

As a result of operating illegal businesses, the Confederation began to gather in huge profits. Each of these activities has its own peculiar attraction or advantage to the men engaged in them. Gambling over the years has brought in the most money because of the volume of bettors; loansharking is extremely attractive because of the high yield on investment compared with the small legal penalties and the difficulty of conviction; and narcotics was attractive for the quick turnover and high return on investment, at least until the penalties became severe.

TABLE 2-I

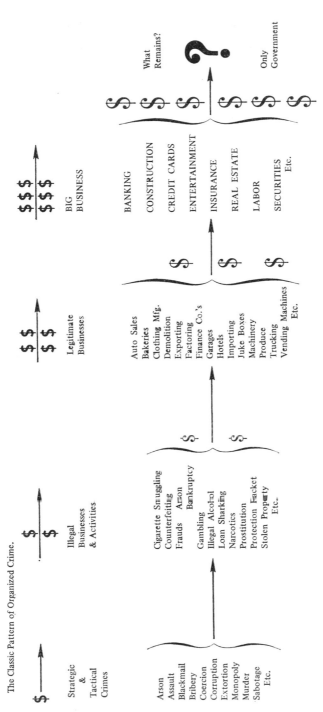

The Classic Pattern of Organized Crime.

Strategic & Tactical Crimes	Illegal Businesses & Activities	Legitimate Businesses	Big Business	What Remains?
$ $	$ $	$$$ $$$	$$$ $$$	$ $ $ $ $ $
Arson	Cigarette Smuggling	Auto Sales	BANKING	Only Government
Assault	Counterfeiting	Bakeries	CONSTRUCTION	
Blackmail	Frauds Arson Bankruptcy	Clothing Mfg.	CREDIT CARDS	
Bribery	Gambling	Demolition	ENTERTAINMENT	
Coercion	Illegal Alcohol	Exporting	INSURANCE	
Corruption	Loan Sharking	Factoring	REAL ESTATE	
Extortion	Narcotics	Finance Co.'s	LABOR	
Monopoly	Prostitution	Garages	SECURITIES	
Murder	Protection Racket	Hotels	Etc.	
Sabotage	Stolen Property	Importing		
Etc.	Etc.	Juke Boxes		
		Machinery		
		Produce		
		Trucking		
		Vending Machines		
		Etc.		

The Confederation takes these profits and couples them with further strategic and tactical crimes and uses both to penetrate legitimate businesses. While such businesses are themselves legal per se, they are run in such a way that the advantages of Syndicate membership can be used to move ahead of competition and make them even more profitable. Competitors can be intimidated by tactical crimes, and bribery and corruption can be used to cause them labor problems and higher operating costs. Having entered legitimate business, the Confederation seeks always to reduce free competition and establish monopoly whenever possible. The result is added profit, and a minimum of fuss.

It should be understood that throughout the progression from simple extortion and mayhem to the penetration and control of sophisticated larger businesses there is never an abandonment of illegal enterprises. In organized crime a man never goes completely "legit," though he may well move out of direct operation of illegal businesses. These will probably be run directly by lesser associates or even employees, with the higher ranking member giving only enough of his personal time and attention as is absolutely necessary. In addition to the increased profits to be gained from legitimate business, there is the added benefit of paying *some* taxes (from legal income) which helps to create a more convincing picture of legitimacy.

The main reason for entering legitimate business, though, is to make more money. It is a myth that proper taxes will be paid on all of the income of the legal business, or that respectability is the primary motive. The profits from legal and illegal businesses are melded so as to be indistinguishable. The Confederation man does not think in terms of "clean" money or "dirty" money. To him it is all money. He does use legal and financial advisers who tell him how much income he has to report on his tax forms to explain his standard of living.

The combined profits of legal and illegal business are now so substantial that the only place they can be invested is in big business and large industries. Once again, entry is made, operations safeguarded, and control effected by the use of strategic and tactical crimes. At this stage there will be less extortion, murder, arson, and assault, but much more blackmail, bribery, and coercion. The result is the same. The real danger of the Confederation invasion of big business is not that profits will go on to reach astronomical heights, but the fact that such enterprises have proved to be defenseless against penetration despite their large resources and educated managements.

What remains after the Confederation is solidly entrenched above ground? Like all other major industrialists, it will have lobbyists, favorite candidates for public office, and preferences in future legislation. In addition to the resources that legitimate industry normally uses with government, the Syndicate men will again have a competitive edge: strategic and tactical crimes. It is not ridiculous to conclude that the only area left to conquer will be the government itself.

EXISTING GAMBLING*

Legal gambling in New York State includes the lottery, on which about two thirds of all adults bet, horse race betting with something like sixteen million visits to the tracks annually and twice as many visits to OTB parlors, and bingo with twenty-six million players (including repeaters) last year. This betting amounts to over $2 billion a year, over 90 percent on horse racing. In addition, New Yorkers gamble legally by betting among themselves on a noncommercial basis and by going to Nevada, the Caribbean, or elsewhere to play in casinos.

Altogether, legal gambling produces about $200 million of revenue for the State and local governments, $44 million for the charities running bingo games, and most of the support for the racing industry.

The huge volume of legal gambling is nearly matched by illegal gambling, which may be engaged in by as many as a quarter of all adults. The most popular illegal game is the numbers (policy) on which perhaps two million New Yorkers bet as much as $600 million a year. A smaller number of New

---

* Reprinted from *Increased Legal Gambling in New York: A Policy Analysis.* State of New York, Executive Department, New York State Racing and Wagering Board, Report of the Commission on Gambling, 1973, pp. 1-3. Used with permission.

Yorkers, perhaps half a million, bet perhaps twice as large a sum with bookies each year on sports and horse races. A much smaller amount, perhaps $40 to $100 million, is bet on sports pool cards, mostly football cards. Other forms of illegal gambling, such as floating crap games, do not amount to much.

Illegal gambling is the principal livelihood or a major source of income for perhaps 25,000 people, and it generates on the order of $50 million of net profits, a great part of which goes to members of organized crime families and organizations.

Illegal gambling also spends on the order of $30 million a year in bribes, payoffs, political contributions and other techniques for securing political power and protection against law enforcement. Corruption efforts designed ostensibly or primarily

SUMMARY OF EXISTING GAMBLING IN NEW YORK
(Estimated—Millions of Dollars)

LEGAL	1. *Gross Volume*	2. *Amount Lost by Bettors*	3. *Net Amount Received by Government, Charities, or Operators*
Horse Tracks	1,600	290	170
Off-Track Betting	300	54	18*
Bingo	150	57	44
Lottery	80	50	35
Total Legal**	2,130	451	267
ILLEGAL			
Numbers	600	300	30-50
Sports Betting (including horses)	1,200	120	30-60
Sports Pool Cards	50	25	10
Total Illegal	1,850	445	95
Grand Total— Approximate	4,000	900	360

(The difference between Column 1 and Column 2 is the winnings paid back to the bettors. The difference between Column 2 and Column 3 is the expenses of operating the gambling activities, including commissions.)

---

* This number is difficult to define, is changing, and is not significant in the total.

** Excludes private betting and card playing which probably involves a gross transfer of over a billion dollars per year among private citizens. This also does not include that part of stock market and commodity exchange speculation which is essentially a form of legal gambling.

to protect illegal gambling are the largest single components of corruption in the criminal justice system.

Altogether, therefore, New Yorkers probably bet something over $4 billion a year (excluding personal betting) and lose, we estimate, about $900 million of this. About 30 percent of the bettor's losses go to government or to charities. The State's share provides about 3 percent of State revenues. The almost $1 billion of gambling expenditures by individuals, that is, their net losses, represent about 1 percent of personal income in the State and compares with $10 billion spent on food or $3 billion on other recreation. Table 2-II on the following page summarizes the existing gambling estimates for the State.

BIBLIOGRAPHY

Books

Adams, Harland B.: *The Guide to Legal Gambling*. New York, Citadel Pr, 1966.

Allen, David D.: *The Nature of Gambling*. New York, Coward-McCann, 1952.

Allen, Edward J.: *Merchants of Menace—The Mafia*. Springfield, Thomas, 1962.

Asbury, Herbert: *Sucker's Progress*. New York, Dodd, 1938.

Ashton, John: *A History of Gambling in England*. London, Duckworth, 1898.

Bergler, Edmund: *The Psychology of Gambling*. New York, Hill & Wang, 1957.

Blanche, Ernest E.: *You Can't Win: Facts and Fallacies About Gambling*. Pub Aff Pr, 1949.

Brennan, Bill: *The Frank Costello Story*. Derby, Connecticut: Monarch Books, 1962.

Chafetz, Henry: *Play the Devil: A History of Gambling in the United States from 1492-1955*. New York, Potter, 1960.

Chamber of Commerce of the United States: *Deskbook on Organized Crime*. Washington, D.C., 1969.

Coggins, Ross: *The Gambling Menace*. Nashville, Broadman, 1966.

Cole, Gordon H. and Margolius, Sidney: *When You Gamble You Risk More Than Your Money*. New York, Public Affairs Committee, 1964.

Committee for Economic Development: *A Fiscal Program for a Balanced Federalism*. New York, Government Printing Office, June 1967.

Cook, Fred J.: *The Secret Rulers*. New York, Duell, 1966.

Cressey, Donald R.: *Theft of a Nation*. New York, Harper and Row, 1969.

Davis, Clyde B.: *Something for Nothing*. Philadelphia, Lippincott, 1956.

Demaris, Ovid: *Lucky Luciano*. Derby, Connecticut, Monarch Books, 1960.

Drzazga, John: *Wheels of Fortune*. Springfield, Thomas, 1963.

Dubins, Lester E. and Savage, Leonard J.: *How to Gamble if You Must*. New York, McGraw-Hill, 1965.

Feder, Sid and Joesten, Joachim: *The Luciano Story*. New York, McKay, 1954.

Fortune Directory: *The 500 Largest U.S. Industrial Corporations*. New York, *Fortune Magazine*, June 15, 1967.

Fraley, Oscar: *4 Against the Mob*. New York, Popular Library, 1961.

Goulart, Ron: *Line Up Tough Guys*. Los Angeles, Sherbourne, 1966.

Herald, George W. and Radin, Edward D.: *The Big Wheel: Monte Carlo's Opulent Century*. New York, Morrow, 1963.

Herman, Robert D. (Ed.): *Gambling*. New York, Harper and Row, 1967.

Jacoby, Oswald: *Jacoby on Gambling*. New York, Hart, 1963.

Jennings, Dean: *We Only Kill Each Other*. Englewood Cliffs, Prentice-Hall, 1967.

Katcher, Leo: *The Big Bankroll*. New York, Harper, 1958.

Kefauver, Estes: *Crime in America*. New York, Doubleday, 1951.

King, Rufus: Gambling and Crime. *Gambling and Organized Crime*. Washington, D.C., Pub Aff Pr, 1969, pp. 23-35.

Knapp Commission: *Report on Police Corruption*. New York, Braziller, 1973.

Lewis, Oscar: *Sagebrush Casinos: The Story of Legal Gambling in Nevada*. New York, Doubleday, 1953.

MacDougall, Ernest D.: *Speculation and Gambling*. Boston, Stratford, 1935.

MacDougall, Michael: *Gamblers Don't Gamble*. New York, Greystone, 1939.

MacKenzie, W. Douglas: *Ethics of Gambling*. New York, Doubleday, 1928.

Martin, Raymond V.: *Revolt in the Mafia*. New York, Duell, 1963.

Marx, Herbert L. (Ed.): *Gambling in America*. New York, Wilson, 1952.

McClellan, John L.: *Crime Without Punishment*. New York, Duell, 1962.

Messick, Hank: *Syndicate in the Sun*. New York, Macmillan, 1968.

Messick, Hank: *Syndicate Wife*. New York, Macmillan, 1968.

Messick, Hank: *The Silent Syndicate*. New York, Macmillan, 1967.

Mockridge, Norton and Prall, Robert H.: *The Big Fix*. New York, Holt, 1954.

Mullady, Frank and Kofoed, William H.: *Meet the Mob*. New York, Belmont Bks, 1961.

Newman, David (Ed.): *Esquire's Book of Gambling*. New York, Harper and Row, 1962.

New York State Commission of Investigation: *Syndicated Gambling in New York*. New York, February 1961.

Peterson, Virgil W.: *Gambling . . . Should It Be Legalized?* Springfield, Thomas, 1951.

Prager, Ted and Moberley, Leeds: *Hoodlums, New York.* New York, Retail Distributors, 1959.

President's Commission on Law Enforcement and Administration of Justice: *The Challenge of Crime in a Free Society.* Washington, D.C., Government Printing Office, 1967.

President's Commission on Law Enforcement and Administration of Justice: *Task Force Report: Organized Crime.* Washington, D.C., Government Printing Office, 1967.

Quinn, John P.: *Gambling and Gambling Devices.* Montclair, N.J., Patterson Smith, 1969.

Reid, Ed. and Demaris, Ovid: *Green Felt Jungle.* New York, Trident, 1963.

Reid, Ed: *The Grim Reapers: The Anatomy of Organized Crime in America.* Chicago, Regnery, 1969.

Rice, Robert: *The Business of Crime.* New York, Ferrar, 1956.

Rishell, Paul W.: *Why Take a Chance?* Syracuse, N.Y., The New York State Council of Churches, Inc., 1966.

Rubner, Alex: *The Economics of Gambling.* London, Macmillan, 1966.

Salak, John: *Dictionary of Gambling.* New York, Philos Lib, 1963.

Salerno, Ralph and Tompkins, John S.: Crime as a business. *The Crime Confederation.* Garden City, N.Y., Doubleday, 1969, pp. 225-235.

Scarne, John: *Scarne's Complete Guide to Gambling.* New York, Simon & Schuster, 1961.

Smith, Alson, J.: *Syndicate City.* Chicago, Regnery, 1954.

Starkey, Lycurgus Monroe: *Money, Mania and Morals: The Churches and Gambling.* New York, Abingdon, 1964.

State of New York: *Existing Gambling. Legalized Gambling: Report to Honorable Nelson A. Rockefeller, Governor and the Legislature.* Albany, Commission on Gambling, 1973, pp. 1-3.

Sullivan, Edward D.: *Rattling the Cup on Chicago Crime.* New York, Vanguard, 1929.

Surface, William: *Inside Internal Revenue.* New York, Coward-McCann, 1967.

Turner, Wallace: *Gamblers' Money: The New Force in American Life.* Boston, Houghton, 1965.

Tyler, Gus (Ed.): *Organized Crime in America.* Ann Arbor, U of Mich Pr, 1962.

U.S. House of Representatives: Committee on Interstate and Foreign Commerce. *Gambling Devices: Hearings on H.R. 3024.* 87th Cong., 1962.

U.S. House of Representatives: Committee on the Judiciary. *Prohibiting Certain Acts and Transactions Involving Gambling Materials: Hearings on H.R. 7975.* Serial No. 20, 83rd Cong., 1954.

U.S. Senate: Committee on Government Operations. *Gambling and Organized Crime.* Senate Report No. 1310, 87th Cong., 1962.

U.S. Senate: Interstate and Foreign Commerce Committee. *Transmission of Gambling Information: Hearings on S. 3358.* 81st Cong., 1959.

U.S. Senate: Special Senate Committee to Investigate Organized Crime in Interstate Commerce (The Kefauver Committee), *Final Report,* 82nd Congress, 1st Session, Report No. 725, 1951.

Varna, Anthony: *World Underworld.* London, Mus Pr, 1957.

Vaus, Jim: *Why I Quit Syndicated Crime.* Los Angeles, Scripture Outlet, 1951.

Wilson, Allan N.: *The Casino Gamblers Guide.* New York, Harper, 1965.

Wykes, Alan: *The Complete Illustrated Guide to Gambling.* Garden City, Doubleday, 1964.

Zeiger, Henry A.: *Sam the Plumber.* New York, Sig Nal, 1970.

Articles

Astor, G.: Your friendly neighborhood betting shop. *Look, 34:* July 28, 1970.

Betting the point spread: how the bookies beat the odds; football betting. *Newsweek, 74:* September 15, 1969.

Blanche, Ernest E.: Gambling odds are gimmicked. *Annals, 269:* May 1950.

Bill to ban shipment of interstate gambling devices approved. *New York Times,* 18, July 27, 1961.

Brooklyn rackets grand jury charges gambling has become foundation of nationwide organized crime. *New York Times,* 1, February 27, 1959.

Carey, Bernadette: Two bit bet: financing a crime empire. *Look,* 131-132, December 14, 1965.

College-trained bets. *Newsweek, 37:* April 2, 1951.

Cook, F. J.: Gambling, Inc. *Nation, 191:* November 5, 1960.

Cook, F. J.: $50 Billion Dollar Window. *The New York Times Magazine,* November 5, 1961.

Federal Regulations of Gambling: Betting on a Long Shot. *Georgia Law Journal, 57:* February 1969.

Governor Hughes Orders Drive on Illegal Gambling. *The New York Times,* 11, July 2, 1962.

Grafton, S.: Illegal Gambling Casinos in the U.S.A.: Where the Law Ends. *Look, 28:* October 20, 1964.

Gramont, Sanche de: How to Play a Lottery. *The New York Times Magazine,* Section No. 6, May 7, 1967.

Hill, G.: Why they gamble: A Las Vegas survey. *The New York Times,* August 25, 1957.

In Britain, gambling is a growth industry. *Business Week,* September 14, 1963.

IRS agents hold 18 in raids on betting headquarters, reportedly part of nation-wide syndicate. *The New York Times,* 16, April 20, 1956.

Jacoby, Oswald: The forms of gambling. *Annals, 269:* May 1950.

James, T. F.: Gambling boom in America. *Cosmopolitan, 145:* July 1958.

Kaplan, Lawrence J.: Economic implications of organized crime in gambling: Possibilities of gaining revenue and eliminating corruption through government ownership and operation. *Proceedings of the John Jay College Faculty Seminars, I:*1967-1969.

Kennedy, Robert F.: The baleful influence of gambling. *The Atlantic Monthly,* April 1962.

Laxalt, R.: What has wide-open gambling done to Nevada? *Saturday Evening Post, 225:* September 20, 1952.

Lawrence, Louis A.: Bookmaking. *The Annals of the American Academy of Political and Social Science,* May 1950.

Murtagh, Judge, John M.: Gambling and police corruption. *Atlantic Monthly,* November 1960.

Negotiable instruments: Licensed gambling establishments and California's public policy. *University of San Francisco Law Review, 4:* October 1969.

Nevada gaming commission probe alleged *skimming* of casino profits and underworld influences. *New York Times,* 14, August 9, 1966.

Number 11 off the boards: Valuable man to Costa Nostra in the field of betting on college and professional athletics. *Time, 95:* March 2, 1970.

Ploscowe, Morris and Lucas, Edwin (Eds.): Gambling. *Annals of the American Academy of Political and Social Science,* May 1950.

Recovery of gambling losses. *University of Florida Law Review, 5:* Summer 1952.

Reynolds, Q.: Crimes that pay. *Saturday Review, 44:* June 3, 1961.

Ross, A. Franklin: The history of lotteries in New York. *Magazine of History, V:*3, March 1907.

Scaduto, Anthony: The mob: A new look. High stakes in the gambling business. *New York Post,* Magazine Section, June 7, 1968.

Senate committee offers bills to require annual federal license for interstate transmission of betting data. *The New York Times,* May 30, 1951.

$7 billion from illegal bets and a blight on sports, Cosa Nostra involvement. *Life, 63:* September 8, 1967.

Sheehan, Neil: Crooked deals in Swiss accounts aided by inaction of banks. *The New York Times,* December 1, 1969.

————: Thousands linked to Swiss deposits. *The New York Times,* December 5, 1969.

Sherman, E. F.: Feds sharpers and politics in Nevada. *New Republic, 55:* October 29, 1966.

Smith, Sandy: Mobsters in the marketplace: Money, muscle, murder. *Life*, *63*:10, September 8, 1967.

Stevenson, A. E.: Who runs the gambling machines? *New Republic*, *126*: February 18, 1952.

Sullivan, Ronald: New Jersey's proposed lottery. *The New York Times*, October 17, 1969.

Syndicate open in Westchester; took in $2.5 million yearly in bets. *The New York Times*, 34, July 21, 1956.

The urban poor and organized crime: A report by twenty-three Republican House members. Washington, D.C., August 29, 1967.

Underwood, J.: True crisis; corruption in sports. *Sports Illustrated*, *18*: May 20, 1963.

U.S. attorney Morgenthau reports IRS has smashed $11 million-a-year bookmaking ring run by Mafia. *New York Times*, 44, November 23, 1967.

U.S. attorney Morgenthau says gambling and other evidences of organized crime are widespread in Westchester county. *The New York Times*, 1, June 21, 1967.

U.S. attorney says the 'Mob' has bought control of Jersey. *The New York Times*, November 30, 1969.

Van Gelder, Lawrence: States push hunt for added taxes to meet demands. *The New York Times*, July 7, 1969.

Velie, L.: Las Vegas: The underworld's secret jackpot. *Readers' Digest*, *75*: October 1959.

Where legal gambling doesn't pay—enough. *U.S. News and World Report*, August 28, 1967.

Wyden, P.: How wicked is Vegas? *Saturday Evening Post*, *234*: November 1, 1961.

The Lottery

Danks, P. K. L.: How to run a lottery. *Criminal Law Review*, 1957: September-October 1957.

Ezell, John Samuel: *Fortune's Merry Wheel: The Lottery in America*. Cambridge, Harvard University Press, 1960.

Gramont, Sanche De: How to play a lottery. *The New York Times*, Magazine Section, No. 6, May 7, 1967.

Rockefeller signs lottery bill. *The New York Times*, 1, April 19, 1967.

Ross, A. Franklin: The history of lotteries in New York. *Magazine of History*, *V*:3, March 1907.

Sullivan, Ronald: New Jersey's proposed lottery. *The New York Times*, October 17, 1969.

Williams, Francis E.: *Lotteries, Laws and Morals*. New York, Vintage Press, 1958.

THE ECONOMICS OF HORSE RACING AND SPORTS BETTING

INTRODUCTION

H ORSE RACING, AS one form of gambling, is more than 6,000 years old. Inscriptions on tablets found in Asia Minor that date from 1,500 B.C. prove the existence of chariot racing. The first formal mounted race of record took place in the Thirty-third Olympiad in Greece in 624 B.C.

Organized racing began in England in 1174, during the reign of Henry II. In 1665 horse racing was started in America. The site of the first race track was the Newmarket course on Hempstead Plain, Long Island, not far from the present location of the Belmont Park race track which opened in 1905.

Pari-mutuel, on-track, betting, legal in six states at the close of the 1920s, was legal in twenty-one states at the close of the 1930s, and is legal in more than half the states today. The race tracks in those states where pari-mutuel betting is legal attract more than sixty million people a year who bet almost $5 billion annually. Revenue to the states is more than $350 million a year.

In New York State pari-mutuel, on-track, betting was approved by the electorate in November 1939. Starting in about 1950, New York City began its annual appeal to the State's Legislature to legalize off-track betting. Success was finally achieved in April 1970. Since then, New York City through its Off-Track Betting Corporation is operating a legal off-track betting system which is tied into the pari-mutuel, on-track computers. New York City is first in the nation to have the opportunity to experiment with this type of activity. Other states, cities, and municipalities are carefully evaluating New York's ground breaking effort.

The first article in this chapter, "The Bookmaking Racket," provides an outline of various techniques employed in the conduct of illegal betting operations. The article's introductory comments cite the New York State Penal Code as the model for enforcement and the recent court decisions that restrict police behavior.

In the second selection, "How the Horseplayers Got Involved with the Urban Crisis," the heart of the issue of legalization and the role of the Off-Track Betting Corporation are analyzed. It describes in detail the evolution of the OTB system which has emerged into a viable business entity. The intricacies of the operation are explored from its precarious beginnings as a political football to its eventual economic success feeding needed funds into the coffers of the urban budget.

In the selection entitled, "Betting on Sports," the results of a comprehensive study on the betting habits of football, basketball, and baseball enthusiasts are examined. The article describes in detail the extent of sports betting, how bets are made, and explains how point spreads operate.

THE BOOKMAKING RACKET*

Michael J. Murphy

Section 986 of the Penal Law, which is the basic provision of law prohibiting bookmaking, makes it a misdemeanor for any person to accept wagers on any event based on chance. Traditionally, the principal source of revenue of the bookmaker has come from betting on horse races and more recently on sporting events such as basketball, baseball, and football. The law has

---

* Reprinted from *The Gambling Situation, 1964*. A Report by Police Commissioner Michael J. Murphy on the Status of Illegal Gambling and Gambling Enforcement in New York City to The Select Legislative Committee on Off-Track Betting, February 27, 1967. Used with permission.

not seen fit to punish the bettor but rather concentrates on the person engaged in the business of accepting bets and those who would aid and abet him in his operation.

In order to make out a *prima facie* case against the bookmaker, the arresting officer must be able to spell out all the elements of 986 Penal Law. The best way of doing this would be to have the officer place bets directly with the bookmaker or, in the absence of this, to observe the transaction taking place in his presence.

In 1960 the Legislature made it a violation to possess knowingly records of bets made by persons engaged in bookmaking (Section 986-b P.L.).

In the same year Section 986-c P.L. was enacted making it a felony to accept bets in the amount of more than $5,000 in any one day.

Recent legislation provides for mandatory jail sentences upon second, third or subsequent convictions for bookmaking. Necessary legal action was also taken to permit photographing and fingerprinting of violators of this section. The decision in *Mapp vs. Ohio* had far-reaching effects on the work of police officers in the enforcement of gambling laws making this task much more difficult. However, some recent legislation has helped to lessen the burden of the police officer in this area without infringing upon the private rights of the individual concerned.

Former Modes of Bookmaking Operation

In order to show the present situation in bookmaking it will be necessary to go back a few years to show the effect of law enforcement on the pattern or mode of operation of the bookmaker.

Horse Room

The ideal setup is a so called "horse room" with odds and entries posted on the wall, clerks sitting at desks ready to accept bets either from the bettor in person or over the telephone, direct wire services with current racing data and other auxiliary services. This type of room has been out of business for many years in New York City.

Street Bookmaking

At one time, not too many years ago, it was not uncommon to have a bookmaker operating on the public streets of New York City. An air of public apathy prevailed and his activities were carried on with little interference. The responsibility for the enforcement of the gambling laws at that time was strictly within the province of a limited number of plainclothes officers. The duty of the uniformed police officer, if any, was to report a condition so that necessary action could be taken by plainclothesmen. In the last twenty years, consistent enforcement has reduced the street bookmaker to a rarity.

Retreat of the Bookmaker

Inside Rooms

With the demise of the horse room and the elimination of fixed outside spots, the bookmaker had to resort to less convenient and less lucrative methods in plying his trade. He began to set up his business in pool rooms and billiard parlors, bars and other locations where bettors might be likely to congregate. These locations were ideal since the bettors would always know where to find the bookmaker. However, with increased pressure from law enforcement this pattern was soon to change. The proprietor of a bar or a pool room placed his license in jeopardy by permitting a bookie to operate in his premises, even though it meant increased business to have this convenient service available to his customers. Arrests were made in volume in such cases and forced an end to this type of bookmaking.

Due to enforcement, Police Department arrest figures show a steady decrease of *inside* arrests since 1959 when 2,092 such arrests were made. In 1963, there were only 1,005 such arrests made.

"Walking" Handbooks

Because of these factors, the walking handbook or "stroller" came in to more prominence. He has his selected bettors in various spots in the neighborhood. The stroller is usually a male in his forties with a background of several arrests for bookmaking. He is cagey and cautious and is always looking back to make sure he is not being tailed by a police officer. He is quite familiar with all of the buildings in his territory and not infrequently will go in the side door of one building and out the front door of the same building and even will backtrack in order to avoid being tailed. Knowing that the mere possession of bookmaking records is grounds for an arrest, not infrequently the stroller will pick up a few bets and frequently without even making a notation as to those bets, go to a telephone and call the bets into a wireroom.

The responsibility for the apprehension of gamblers operating inside premises is primarily that of members assigned to plain-clothes duty. However, in the case of the stroller the responsibility for suppression is now shared with members of the force in uniform. Because of the attention given, the arrests for book-making outside of premises decreased from 1,496 arrests in 1958 to 509 arrests in 1963.

The Wire Room

The wireroom operator is the most difficult type of bookmaker to apprehend. Holed up in a small office or apartment many floors above the ground, moving furtively in and out without causing any attention to be drawn to him, he represents the last major stronghold of illegal bookmaking. Generally speaking his method of operation is as follows:

> The bookmaker operating through a wireroom first finds himself a location with a telephone. This location may be one room in a downtown financial section, in the garment area, or a small apartment within the suburban city limits. Telephone service is then obtained, frequently under a ficticious name, and one or two phones installed. The telephone number is then given to the players or bettors, often with a code or lead line supplied so that the person answering the phone will know that the caller is a bonafide customer. The player will then place his bets and will "settle up" with the bookmaker at some predetermined point, frequently a bar, candy story or neighborhood gathering spot. It will be noted that in settling up nothing but money passes between the bookmaker and the bettor, making the problem of detection that much more difficult.
>
> The person answering the telephone is often referred to as a sheet writer or clerk. He is again usually a male in his forties or fifties with several prior bookmaking arrests. He is a skilled artisan

and is aware of all the tricks and pitfalls of his trade. His salary may range anywhere from $100 a week to $250 a week depending upon his skill and frequently he is able to bring the clientele with him. Normally his hours of work are between 11:00 A.M. and 4:00 P.M. and not infrequently he returns for an additional two hours between 6:00 and 8:00 P.M. particularly during the season of the trotting races. In cases where the action in the wirerooms is exceptionally heavy, a pickup man will be assigned to go to the wireroom and bring the slips or "work," as it is called, to another location which is known as the "figure room." The reason for this practice is twofold. One, to avoid having the slips seized in the event of a raid and two, to decrease the amount of volume so as to stay outside the felony provisions of the bookmaking law. At the end of the day's work the sheet writer and often the bookmaker himself, will sit down in the figure room and tally the work, figure the wins and losses and make up a figure for each player.

The foregoing represents what is called a "straight in" wireroom. The difficulty of apprehension in these cases is increased by the use of such devices as backstraps, cheese boxes, alarms and codes.

Backstraps

The backstrap is an illegal extending of wires of the telephone from the place of the original installation to another location which may be within the same building or which may be several blocks distant. The telephone is removed from its orginal installation point and the connecting wires are run out of the room through a window, door, or dumbwaiter to another floor and often to the roof of the building. Not infrequently the wire is further strung through a maze of other wires, down the side of a building and often through brick walls to a new location where the telephone is then set up in another room and the bookmaker or sheet writer commences operation from this point. Thus, arresting officers or investigating officers, who may be fortunate enough to come into possession of the telephone number over which the bookmaker is operating will get a listing from the phone company and go to the location where the telephone was installed, as is indicated in the records of the telephone company. This is normally where the telephone should be located and where the bookmaker should be operating. Many times where the so-called backstrap is utilized by the bookmaker it is accompanied by the use of an alarm or signal installed in the room where the original telephone installation was made by the telephone company so that anyone entering the room would set off an alarm which would tip the bookmaker off at his new location that the premises was being entered. The alarm wires usually run alongside the backstrap telephone wires.

Cheese Boxes

Another auxiliary secretive service utilized by the wireroom operator is a so-called cheese box, the title so derived because it was originally set up in an empty cheese box. The cheese box can be best explained in the context of a practical example of usage. The bookmaker employing this device rents an apartment or room and then goes to the telephone company and has two separate phones with different numbers installed. He then disconnects the instruments from the telephone wires and attaches the wires to separate ends of the cheese box. This has the effect of connecting the two phones. The bettor is then given one of the telephone numbers to call and place bets. The bookmaker sitting at a different location "opens" up the cheese box each day by calling the other number and when the players call they are automatically connected. Officers investigating suspect numbers will usually go to the location of the telephone as listed in telephone company records. There they will find only the cheesebox. Frequently the cheese box has an alarm which is attached to it and which will warn the bookmaker when the room is entered.

The task of apprehending the wireroom operator is further complicated by the use of codes, thus the bettor in calling the wireroom will be given a certain code such as "Joe for 44" or some similar designation. In addition, the sheet writer is frequently instructed to answer the telephone in a certain manner so as to indicate to the player that he is a bonafide sheet writer and not a police officer raiding the premises.

The principal tool used in connection with the apprehension of wireroom operators is legal wire tapping. When information is obtained in connection with a suspect number, application is made to the Supreme Court for an order permitting interception of conversations over the bookmaker's telephone. At the outset it should be noted that many judges are reluctant to issue wire tap orders in connection with bookmaking because of recent decisions in the Federal Courts which have created a cloud as to the interception and divulging of telephonic communications. Even where the tap is authorized by State law and court order it is a practice of the district attorneys within the City of New York not to use wiretapping evidence in the prosecution of gambling offenses. Therefore the use of the wiretap is reduced to that of supplying information which it is hoped will lead to the apprehension of the bookmaker through other methods.

Because of the increased pressures on bookmakers operating inside and outside of premises the use of the wirerooms has increased. The figures of the Police Department indicate that in 1956 there were 291 arrests for wireroom bookmaking. This number has steadily increased. In 1962, 813 such arrests were made. The number of arrests in 1963 dropped to 777 because of concentrated and continuing effort on the part of the police against wirerooms. This has been successful to a considerable extent as indicated by the bookmaker switching to use of the telephone answering service to avoid detection.

One of the most ingenious operations ever encountered by members of this department involved the use of a cheese box, backstrap and alarm. It extended from New York County to the Bronx.

In December of 1961, members of the Police Commissioner's Confidential Investigating Unit obtained information that gambling was being conducted over telephone number LO 9-2325, listed to a subscriber located at 21 Broadway Terrace, Apartment 3C, in upper Manhattan. In the course of the investigation, one of the officers dialed the number from a public phone, heard a clicking sound and his dime was returned. This was an indication to the experienced officer that this was a cheese box operation, the returning of the coin being the one give away of an otherwise clever device used by the bookmakers to avoid detection.

With the cooperation of the New York Telephone Company, the task was begun of tracking down the bookmaker who was sitting on the other end of the cheese box. Where would he be?

Somewhere in the confines of the city or perhaps in Westchester or Nassau? After several hours of tedious labor on the part of the telephone company's security men, it was finally learned that the bookmaker was calling the cheese box from Apartment 3G at 1833 Bryant Avenue, in Bronx County, using telephone number DA 9-3249. Discreet observation of the apartment indicated that there was no one inside. This meant that the room must have been backstrapped, that is, the telephone extended out to some other location. However, an examination of the terminal boxes and the installation showed no irregularities to indicate a backstrap.

Officers and telephone agents then began the tedious task of tracing the cable. About a block away from the place where the phone should have been, a large cut into the telephone cable was discovered and a line was found running to premises 1777 Bryant Avenue, Apartment 3B.

Having reasonable grounds to believe a felony was being committed by the illegal cutting into telephone lines, officers entered the apartment and therein found and arrested four men, each of whom had several prior arrests for bookmaking.

Officers seized over $7,900 in U.S. currency, a large quantity of slips bearing wagers on horses and various other gambling paraphernalia. A total of five telephones were also seized. Officers also found an electronic warning device which would have gone off had the officers entered the apartment at 1833 Bryant Avenue, where the suspect telephone was originally installed.

The extent to which these bookmakers went to avoid detection is indicative of the police pressure that is being brought to bear to stamp out illegal gambling.

THE MOVEMENT INTO ANSWERING SERVICES

The telephone answering service is used by bookmakers to relay messages from the player to the bookie. This service may range from the large commercial answering services to the suburban housewife working for the small bookmaker.

Our experience has been that the large commercial answering

services shy away from the bookmaker as clients and as a result the bookie is forced to set up his own service. Here he uses mostly females although males can be found to be doing this work. Usually, the bettor or player is given the number of the service and calls using a predetermined code, and leave his own number for the bookmaker to call back. The message may be a terse: "Have Mr. Jones call me at BX 4-3109." Thus the person in the service may have no knowledge of the nature of the operation. When Mr. Jones (the bookmaker) calls the service, the operator gives him the telephone numbers of all the players who have called. The bookmaker then calls the players and takes the action. The bookmaker is hiring the person to sit in the telephone answering service may pose as a salesman or other businessman and simply take the name and say that his customers will call and the service shall simply take the name and number of the caller. Usually, he pays $50 a week and up in cash or in money order. From the foregoing it can be seen how difficult it can be to establish guilty knowledge on the part of the person answering the phone.

During 1963, the Confidential Squad reported 106 cases in which it was alleged that a telephone was being used as an answering service to aid and abet bookmakers.

These cases were all thoroughly investigated and in over 50 percent arrests were made, or the telephone seized, or the condition was suppressed. In some cases, the most that could be done would be to tell the subscriber that he or she was aiding and abetting bookmaking. The subscriber would indicate innocence (feigned or real) and would agree to discontinue the practice. Follow-up investigations were conducted to determine whether in fact the practice was discontinued; if not, appropriate action was taken.

The answering service or call back system is not too well liked by the bookmaker because it cuts down on the amount of play. Many bettors are reluctant to have their home or office telephone numbers supplied to the bookmaker for the necessary call back. The transactions are very time consuming. In addition, three telephone calls are required as compared with one for the "straight in" wireroom. The fact that the bookmaker is resorting to the use of the answering service is clearly indicative of the effect of the gambling laws. The bookmaker would much rather have his "straight in" room where the players can call direct. Further, the call back system is not conducive to replay of money won by the bettors in earlier races.

For the past two years, this Department has tried unsuccessfully to have legislation enacted which would allow some measure of control over the answering services. The effect of the proposed legislation will be to license any answering service or any person who sets himself up in the business of relaying messages. Provision would also be made for the inspection of the records of such businesses to determine whether the business is legitimate or illegitimate. Violation of the licensing provisions of the act would be a misdemeanor on which the police could take action.

HOW THE HORSEPLAYERS GOT INVOLVED WITH THE URBAN CRISIS*

JOHN MCDONALD

New York City's Off-Track Betting Corporation, which opened the first of its betting shops two years ago in Grand Central Station and now has over sixty of them scattered around the city, has been billing itself in ads as "The New Game in Town." There's no doubt that it's quite a game; citizens eager for action are already pushing over $1 million a day through OTB betting windows, and this figure might well double over the next year or so as the corporation acquires more shops (forty are expected to open within the year) and gains more control over its computers (whose persistent breakdowns have prevented thousands of those eager citizens from getting in their bets). OTB hopes for a betting handle of $1 billion in its 1973-74 year.

In a sense, however, the Off-Track Betting Corporation has brought to town an even bigger game than the one it is now advertising. The big new game is one in which New York State, New York City, the New York Racing Association, New York

* Reprinted from *Fortune Magazine*, April 1972. Published by *Time, Inc.* Used with permission.

harness tracks, the unions of track employees, and the breeders and owners of horses are among the contestants. All of them have been fighting for a larger share of the bettors' money. And since quite a lot of money is bet on races in the U.S.—about $4 billion a year on the thoroughbreds, about $2 billion more on the trotters—the outcome of the contest in New York is naturally a matter of great interest elsewhere. Some thirty states now have horse races on which betting is legal, and every one of them, it seems safe to say, would be delighted to find a way to divert more of the bettors' money into the public treasury. Which is, of course, precisely what OTB was designed for. Its ultimate sources of strength are the urban crisis—or, more precisely, the growing tax pressures on state legislatures and near-bankrupt cties—and the fact, known to all state legislators, that gambling taxes are lucrative and acceptable to the public.

Off-track betting seems almost certain to spread into other states in the next few years. Connecticut, which does not yet have any racetracks, is thinking about starting some; meanwhile, it has passed a bill providing for off-track betting on races in and out of the state. Maryland is ready to pass a bill of its own. OTB legislation has been introduced in nine other states. Although it still looks esoteric to most Americans, off-track betting has been established for years in other parts of the world— France, England, Australia, New Zealand, and Japan, to name a few.

The Problems of Success

It has certainly been a smashing success at those off-track windows in New York. Even its problems, which are considerable, are in good part the problems of success, i.e. they arise from OTB's popularity with the bettors. Its popularity has been reducing attendance at the tracks; the N.Y.R.A. scheduled some employment cutbacks attributed to that decline, and the mutuel clerks' union thereupon struck at Aqueduct, the state's most important racetrack. The strike cost the State of New York some $300,000 a day in lost tax revenue. In the crisis that followed, it is noteworthy that OTB's opponents were directing their efforts, not at trying to kill off-track betting, but at trying to get control of it.

OTB was created over the opposition of the powers that be in racing, and set up in the town that has long been the citadel of the sport in the U.S. New York offers the biggest betting market in the country. The Jockey Club, which runs the studbook that certifies the thoroughbred breed, has its headquarters in New York and its finger on the pulse of New York thoroughbred racing. It has supplied the trustees of the quasi-public New York Racing Association, which puts on the top thoroughbred racing show at its three great plants: Aqueduct, which is within the city limits, Belmont, which is just outside them, and Saratoga, which is upstate. New York also has the two largest harness tracks in the country, Roosevelt Raceway and Yonkers Raceway, operating at night under lights that glow in the sky as brightly as those of Las Vegas and together generating close to half the public revenue from the nation's harness tracks. Those five tracks accounted for the great bulk of the $1.6 billion that was bet at New York tracks in 1971; $170 million of that amount went to the state.

All those powerful forces are affected by OTB. First, it competes with the tracks. Like most U.S. racetracks, New York's have been favored with the right to run the only (legal) game in town, and their owners and operators are naturally upset about losing that monopoly. Since OTB started taking bets, nearby harness and thoroughbred tracks have suffered declines in attendance and betting. Second, there is the effect of these declines on the purses paid to horse owners. Since purses mainly come out of money bet at the track, any decline in track business is translated fairly soon into smaller purses for horsemen; and the rewards of winning, placing, or showing in New York thoroughbred races did in fact decline substantially late last year. And since smaller purses leave the owner poorer, they translate eventually into smaller fees to trainers and lower prices for breeders. Thus all horsemen—breeders, owners, and trainers—are registering outrage over OTB these days. Some have traveled from the horse states, notably Kentucky, to join New York horsemen in the struggle with the monster. The harness and thorough-bred people, who heretofore have never been especially friendly with each other, are even meeting together. OTB's gathering enemies are insisting that, as presently constructed, it is doing more harm than good and will not realize its aims.

Birthdays and Other Systems

Horse racing, pure, simple, and entrancing, is a game of chance. Breeding horses is a game of genetic chance. Skill in breeding the best sires to the best dams refines this chance: The best way to get a winner of the Kentucky Derby, Preakness, or Belmont Stakes is to breed a champion or champion-producing mare to the winner of one of those classics or their foreign equivalents. Racing a horse entails some random chance or untoward events: stumbling, brushing, bumping, lack of racing room, getting a horse's tail caught in the gate, a horse's indisposition, and a thousand other chance events affect races. Conditioning a horse well for a race brings it up to its best chance, and winning races reveals the great unknown—which horses are the best.

Betting is a game of horseplayer against horseplayer. A racing fan may bet his favorite number or numbers associated with his children's birthdays. A handicapping horseplayer will try to get away from blind chance by predicting, from data on past performance, how the race will be run; as a bettor, he may compare his own judgment about a horse's chance of winning with the consensus on the odds board. Owners and trainers will make some tactical calculations in deciding which horses to enter in which races; jockeys make all sorts of judgmental decisions during the running of a race. Yet the rational view is that racing is a game of chance.

The sport also has some uniquely attractive qualities in its color and romance, the myths associated with horses, the traditions of sportsmanship for groom, trainer, jockey, and owner, the suspense of animal and man in a race. It is a special racetrack world with special and indefinable appeals to horsemen and horseplayers alike.

A New Player in the Game

When all that is said, it also remains true that the horse-racing business is a game of strategy, in which many different parties, each seeking to maximize his own advantages, find their interests to be intertwined. Indeed, horse trading itself is a synonym for bargaining; and the horsemen bargain with each other over the sales of horses and the marketing or bartering of stallion and mare services. Beyond that, they bargain with the racetracks, threatening to go to one track instead of another for a better deal, and joining in boycotts to get the purse level up. Racetracks, governors, the legislatures of the racing states—all these, too, negotiate and bargain in their peculiar way with the horsemen and one another. (A peculiarity of the bargaining done by the states is that, while they are in principle concerned with the well-being of the sport on which their revenue depends, they typically construe their interests as being short-run, getting what they can here and now and shrugging off the future.)

One characteristic of a strategic game is that, when a new player sits in, it becomes a new game. And when New York City cut itself in on the benefits of horse-race gambling, it introduced a radically different kind of player into the game. The old players —horsemen, racetracks, and the states—had been dividing the spoils in a game whose rules had become standardized over thirty-odd years.

There was one element of instability in that agreement, however, and it was fairly important. The economy of racing is based on the "takeout"—the percentage deducted from the betting handle before the winning bettors receive their payoff. Some of it goes to the state, some to the industry. Arguments about who gets how much have tended to be accompanied by much tugging and hauling, boycotts, factional conflicts, splits among the horsemen, and lobbying by the tracks. But when one or another participant in this process succeeds in getting more for himself, it is usually *not* at the expense of another participant. The extra money is provided, instead, by increasing the total takeout. Or, stated another way, the money is provided by the horseplayers. Since they are themselves nonstrategic players, they have nothing much to say about what percentage they are charged for the privilege of gambling. They are stuck with a take-it-or-leave-it proposition.

Until the mid-1940s, the takeout on thoroughbred racing was 10 percent, with the state taking 5 percent, the track the other 5. In 1946, Mayor William O'Dwyer got local governments into the game and the takeout was raised to 15 percent, a hike that horseplayers bitterly dubbed "the O'Dwyer bite." But O'Dwyer and his successor did not have the political power to hold on to the extra 5 percent, and in a few years had to yield it to the state—which thus wound up doubling its share from 5 to 10 percent. This division remained stable until 1967, when dissatisfied thoroughbred horsemen, under pressure of rising costs, demanded higher purses, and struck—more precisely, they shut down Aqueduct by refusing to enter any horses. N.Y.R.A. said it couldn't pay more out of its 5 percent share and remain solvent. The state, refusing to yield any of its 10 percent, resolved the impasse in 1968 by raising the total takeout to 16 percent and allotting the extra percentage point to the horsemen and track.

The state, one might notice, wears two hats when it participates in these discussions: It is a player with an interest in the game—and the arbiter of the game. As player it kept its interest intact; as arbiter it transferred an additional payment from horseplayers to the industry. This division of spoils proved unstable, however. In the spring of 1971 the state again resolved a crisis at the track by raising the takeout. This time it went to 17 percent.

An additional hidden tax on horseplayers has been levied in recent years under the euphemism "breakage." This term originally referred to the fact that the track would not pay out odd pennies, which were declared to be a nuisance. The tracks now pay out only at prices divisible by twenty cents, and "break" to the lower amounts. With betting tickets sold at a minimum of $2, a payoff of $2.39, for example, will break back to $2.20; thus about half the horseplayer's winnings are kept from him. On ordinary win, place, and show betting, breakage averages out to about one percentage point, making the total takeout about 18 percent. Each percentage point in New York State as a whole in recent years has been worth about $16 million. As matters stood in thoroughbred racing before OTB, the state was taking out 10 percent, the track 4 percent, the horsemen 3 percent, with special arrangements for dividing the breakage. (The harness tracks' split is made along roughly the same lines.)

The last two percentage points seem to have been a factor in a decline in traditional betting. The racing industry worried that it had gone beyond the maximum that it was prudent to charge the horseplayer. Collectively, of course, all horseplayers must lose. Still, there is a question about how fast they are willing to lose and still come back.

In the efforts to extract more from the horseplayer, the racing industry was also approaching another limit of sorts. Tracks in Metropolitan New York, in common with many elsewhere that are under continuous pressure from the state, had increased the *quantity* of racing nearly to its limit in races run per day and racing days per year. The harness tracks run all year round except for a brief rest at Christmas. The thoroughbred tracks, in the longest season in their history, closed December 15 and reopened March 1, 1972. Some of the horsemen would like to continue year round but many others believe that to be unsound; as it is, the number and quality of thoroughbreds in action drastically decline late in the season.

With the takeout apparently as high as it could go, and the racing season about as long as it could go, neither the state nor the industry could discern a way to get substantially more revenue from racing. Indeed, the increasing economic pressures on the racing industry left many horsemen persuaded that the state might have to take *less* than its 10 percent. But the city had a way to raise racing revenue by going outside the tracks.

Filling the Budget Gap

Actually, New York City had been trying for some years to get off-track betting, on the grounds that it would enlarge the betting market and take it away from illegal bookmakers, relieve the city's strained budget, and reduce its need to call upon the state for revenue aid. The city's budget analysts had dreamed of taking in $200 million a year from off-track gambling revenue.

The racing industry had for years opposed the city, and was confident that it had done so successfully again in 1970.

But then, in the last days of the 1970 legislative session in Albany, the lawmakers came under especially heavy pressure to aid the city, which was projecting a budget gap of $630 million. With scarcely any warning, the legislature passed the city-supported bill to make off-track betting legal. The law also gave other municipalities in the state the right to set up their own off-track betting agencies under certain conditions. In New York City itself, OTB would be run by a new public-benefit corporation with a board of directors appointed by the mayor. All the traditional equilibrium between horsemen, racetracks, and the state was suddenly shot to pieces.

The racing industry was horrified by the new rules. They provided that the city would have a takeout of 17 percent on off-track betting—betting, the industry noted bitterly, on *its* races. Part of the 17 percent was allocated to horsemen and racetracks, but their slices were far thinner than those they were used to getting from on-track betting. Specifically, 0.5 percent of the OTB handle went to the state, 1.5 percent to the tracks and horsemen. The remaining fifteen percentage points could cover the OTB corporation's operating costs and profit. The first $200 million of profit would be divided roughly eighty-twenty between city and state; beyond that point the split would be fifty-fifty. Furthermore, although the law provided compensation to the industry for damage "on account of" OTB, it offered no way of gauging the extent of OTB's responsibility.

The percentages were bad enough, in the industry's view, but its deeper grievance was the mandate that the OTB corporation had to act as a separate player. OTB was not just another device to extract money from horseplayers. It was the operator of a betting business specifically designed to maximize the city's interest, even where that collided, as it surely would, with the interests of the horsemen and tracks. All this was hard enough to take—and then came Howard Samuels.

A Baggies Man for OTB

Mayor John Lindsay found in Samuels a man who would not be bashful about exercising the new player's prerogatives.

Samuels had managed to lose some New York political campaigns and still emerge looking like a comer in politics; in the 1970 primary he was narrowly beaten out by Arthur Goldberg for the Democratic nomination for governor. Many politicans thought it was folly for him to take on the job of running a "bookmaking" operation—he was soon nicknamed Howie the Horse; but after a year of making the front pages, he observes, with a winner's smile, that he has become one of the three best-known political personalities in New York (along with Governor Nelson Rockefeller and the mayor).

Samuels' appointment was not simply an exercise of political patronage. He had solid business credentials as the founder of Kordite Co., which among other things developed Baggies®. He and his brother Richard started the company in 1946 on $25,000 of borrowed capital; eventually it was sold to Mobil Oil, with a payoff of several million dollars for the brothers, and Howard for a time was a vice-president of Mobil.

Samuels had long advocated the infusion of modern business practices into public-sector enterprises and made it clear that he meant to bring such practices to OTB. But doing so hasn't been easy. OTB's critics can point to high operating costs, which have chewed up about ten percentage points of the takeout, leaving only 5 percent for profits; Samuels replies that after the start-up year is past the profits are golden. The persistent computer breakdowns are admittedly a "disaster"; in his own defense, Samuels observes that the deal with Computer Sciences Corp. was largely determined by the city administration. The breakdowns have restricted OTB's capacity to take bets, raised costs, and created dissatisfied customers. And yet, despite all the difficulties of starting from scratch in a new kind of business, OTB's volume in March 1972 ran at an annual rate of $400 million, and Samuels expected $800 million in 1973.

For all his own aggressiveness, Samuels cannot push the other players in the game too hard, for in the last analysis all the players are interdependent. Samuels, the horsemen, the racetrack owners and operators, and the state itself—all have choices that are limited by the others' choices and all must bargain to attain their economic objectives. Samuels needs not only horse races but also the cooperation of horsemen and the tracks; in particular, he needs some revision of standard racing procedures. For example, a good many OTB customers place their bets on the way to work, i.e. at eight or nine in the morning. But at these times some information critical to horseplayers— for example, on entries, scratches, jockey changes—is unavailable. Most of all, Samuels needs televised races, which have proved to be tremendous bet producers. In addition to needing cooperation from the tracks and horsemen, Samuels has to be careful not to hurt them to the point where his own gambling wheel, the racetrack itself, is hurt.

The tracks and horsemen have some bargaining counters that Samuels cannot ignore. Racing plants, for example, often have considerable value for alternative real estate uses, and *in extremis* a track operator may just decide not to make his annual application for a racetrack license. Horsemen can take their stables elsewhere; and racetrack unions actually do strike. The tracks and horsemen might also retaliate against OTB in court, or in the state legislature where they still have a fair amount of influence.

Acknowledging the inequities in the original bill and wanting to stave off an industry coalition against him, Samuels tried to bargain separately about the takeout with spokesmen for the different tracks and the horsemen. But from their point of view, more than a new division of the takeout was at issue. The very presence of the intruder, with his special priorities and independent powers, limited the traditional powers of the industry, and forced them to deal with him about the entire economics of racing. By now they were reconciled to off-track betting as a new way of life—except for the harness tracks' taking one last shot at OTB in court, in an effort to get the basic law declared in violation of New York State's constitution. But their preference was to get rid of the new player and resolve the economic issues of off-track betting among themselves. With this in mind, the major branches of the industry began to meet quietly in August 1971.

A Preference for the Old Game

Meanwhile, however, one part of the racing industry, the New York Racing Association, was exploring the possibility of coming to terms with OTB. The N.Y.R.A. is a nonprofit corporation (technically, it seeks to make enough to pay for capital improvements) whose purpose is to foster thoroughbred racing and, in the process, provide public revenue. It was finding the going tough even before OTB appeared; its handle had been growing but attendance was trending downward, and with increased costs and heavy debt service charges, it lost money in 1969, 1970, and 1971. After building the great new Belmont plant in the mid-1960s at a cost of $31 million, it was unable to meet horsemen's demands for larger purses, the upshot of which was the state's intervention to hike the takeout by two percentage points.

It seems evident, in retrospect, that N.Y.R.A. was deluding itself in recent years in thinking that it could build Belmont, maintain its August race meet at Saratoga (the mecca of thoroughbred racing despite the normally lower attendance and handle of an upstate track), raise horsemen's purses, and at the same time avoid a still higher takeout. The association plainly needed additional income from some such source as off-track betting. If N.Y.R.A. had sponsored off-track betting itself several years ago, it might easily have secured control of the game. Now it will have trouble gaining control and its future is further compromised by the threat of "encirclement" of its metropolitan tracks: prospective new tracks to the north in Connecticut and to the west, across the Hudson River in the Jersey Meadows, and perhaps to the east in Long Island. Clearly N.Y.R.A. needs a deal of some kind.

In the midst of its growing difficulties, the association recently got a new chief executive in Alfred G. Vanderbilt, a dedicated racing man who has long been a force for change in racing in the councils of the Jockey Club and the N.Y.R.A. itself. He has been exploring ways to make racing more attractive to the ordinary fan; but thus far, at least, his management has not come up with anything that has the potential of state-wide off-track betting with televised races—a huge new market, still virtually untapped by thoroughbred racing. Recognizing the accomplished fact of off-track betting, and not sure whether the new player would be overthrown, Vanderbilt's posture toward it has been ambivalent.

Squeezing Out the New Player

There was a time in November of 1971 when N.Y.R.A. appeared to have found common ground with Samuels. Its vice-president, Jack Krumpe, came out of an executive session at a convention of the Thoroughbred Racing Association (the national organization of thoroughbred racetracks) saying that N.Y.R.A. expected to reach an agreement in principle with OTB "within three weeks," and was hopeful that the two could together take a package to the legislature. But this alliance never developed. Instead, the alternative efforts—to bring the industry together and squeeze out OTB—began to gather momentum. Last month the conflict between the racing industry and OTB exploded with the sudden appearance in Albany of an industry-supported bill proposing that a new *state* operating board take over off-track betting and also proposing a new set of payoffs for all parties.

The board envisaged in this bill, made up largely of racing-industry people, would run off-track betting throughout the state. It would have the power to determine the number and location of a municipality's betting shops, the system's communication and transmission systems, the kinds of wagers permitted and their minimum and maximum amounts, the race meetings on which wagers would be accepted, off-track business hours, the conditions for televising races, and the like.

One result of this arrangement would be that the industry, through the board it would dominate, could divide the betting market along whatever lines it saw fit. For example, it could decide to limit betting away from the track to exotic bets—the kind that appeal especially to lottery-minded players. Exotic bets, which have become an important fixture of off-track betting, and increasingly of on-track betting as well, have taken the form of the Triple or the Superfecta, in which either three or four horses are picked in order of finsh.

All parties, including Samuels, are agreed on promoting this kind of betting and applying a 25 percent takeout to it—the idea being that the bettor won't notice the deeper gouge because the winning payoffs are so large. (Superfecta winners at New York's harness tracks have been paid $10,000 or more for $2 tickets.) There is also talk of taking $1 bets on races of this type and attracting the numbers players. Here, more than anywhere, there is a prospect of finding *new* money to divide. But whereas Samuels now takes all kinds of racing bets (he would even like to expand to all-sports betting), the industry appears to want to limit OTB to exotic bets alone—with the traditional win, place, and show bets accepted only at the track. The industry hopes thereby to keep the regular racing fans coming to the track. (Samuels does not rule out OTB's eventually specializing in exotic bets, but would rather consider the matter after he has more off-track experience.)

The industry-supported plan would also change the pay-offs to all the players—the municipalities, the state, the tracks, and the horsemen—and would allot the municipality a specific share rather than the profit it receives under the original OTB bill. The proposal assumes that the takeout would remain at 17 percent on standard bets and assigns 6 percent to the state operating board for its own expenses. All other pay-offs would vary with the kind of racing and the volume of business. Assuming Samuels' projected volume for 1972 to 1973, the tracks and horsemen of N.Y.R.A., who now receive a total of 1.5 percent, would be allotted double that, split fifty-fifty; and the state and participating municipality would divide the remaining 8 percent, 3.2 to 4.8. That 4.8 percent contrasts with 7.6 percent that New York City would be getting now (and 1.9 percent that the state would be getting) if its own OTB brought operating expenses down to 6 percent. So the city would be a substantial loser under the proposed rules.

Samuels is looking for a compromise. He would like the city to retain control of OTB but he would be willing to revise the scheme of payoffs to make them more favorable to the racing industry. The extra money would be generated mainly by those high-takeout exotic bets. In addition, Samuels proposed a sliding scale: On standard bets at N.Y.R.A., for example, on next year's estimated OTB volume it would average out to about 2.5 percent for tracks and horsemen—not too far from the industry's own proposed figure. He also told the thoroughbred horsemen that, if they and N.Y.R.A. cooperated with OTB, it would guarantee them $2 million more in purses in 1972 than they got in 1971. And he did not overlook the state itself, offering it a 1972 guaranteed minimum payoff equal to about 1 percent, paid monthly.

It was not clear in mid-March 1972 whether any such compromise with the industry could be pulled off. The only group that had responded at all sympathetically to Samuels was an organization of owners and trainers of thoroughbreds. ("We try to keep all the avenues open," was the cryptic report of its New York president, Eugene Jacobs.) With the industry supporting a specific alternative to New York City's OTB, Samuels countered by taking his proposals directly to the legislature. The conflict had escalated to a battle and the scene had shifted to Albany.

More Visions of Sugarplums

Why have the on-track and off-track forces, agreed as they were in principle that the payoffs had to be revised, nevertheless split into two camps? It is certainly true that the two sides differ as to the payoffs they would like to arrange, but that alone does not explain why they failed to bargain out their differences. One basic problem may be their widely different perceptions of the real prospects of gambling revenues—on-track and off-track. Samuels saw OTB, working in cooperation with the racing industry, gathering in greater total revenues than the industry had ever envisioned. Racing has stagnated, in his view. Just think— he will urge anyone willing to listen—of the phenomenon of professional football, a sport "made" by television and yet played to full stadiums. Think then of a system in which horse-players could easily bet in city shops or by telephone, then sit home in the evening or on weekends, including Sundays, watching televised races, such as the Kentucky Derby and other great classics of racing—or, if they chose, continuing to bet at the track (like those football fans who still like their action live). Think of exotic lottery-like betting "specials," attracting tens of thousands of new bettors and yielding enormous revenues to government and the racing industry. Samuels, thinking enthusiastically of all these prospects, sees a wide new public of racing fans rolling up the biggest betting handle in racing history, with greater payoffs for all parties.

It is true, of course, that this vision cannot be proved out unless someone is willing to take some risks and experiment. Samuels is asking the racing industry to do just that—to yield some of its tangible advantages now to aid in the realization of these visions of sugarplums. What the racing industry is looking for, meanwhile, is a riskless way of finding out how much reality there is to the vision. Most of the industry at times has appeared willing to cooperate if it had ironclad guarantees from OTB that the "experiment" could be conducted with no losses. The industry is clearly bemused by notions of a vast bonanza out there, and some of its members have taken some halting steps to cooperate with Samuels. He was able for a while to televise harness races from Monticello, New York, during the Christmas and New Year's holidays, with impressive results; and he has had a deal to take bets on Maryland races, with Saturday afternoon television rights to two races at Bowie. But when it gets down to brass tacks, the industry is still fearful that the bonanza might not materialize.

A Difference of Perceptions

Meanwhile, their long-term anxieties about OTB's effects are being colored by the business it is presumed to be taking away from the racetracks here and now. Samuels admits he is hurting attendance; the question is by how much. Again, there are different perceptions of the problem. The horsemen and tracks say OTB is the sole or principal source of their lower attendances and betting handles. Samuels admits only that OTB is one of several causes of the declines. How much, he asks, rhetorically, was also due to the soft U.S. economy; how much to the problems that already beset the New York Racing Association, including that last rise in the takeout; how much to the higher cost of attending the racetracks; how much to scandal at the scandal-prone Yonkers track; how much to possible other causes; and how much to OTB? Samuels gets some support from one unexpected source. The New York State Racing Commission attributes a 1971 nationwide decline in attendance and wagering primarily to the increased takeout, i.e. the higher cost of betting.

It is scarcely surprising that Samuels and the racing industry have not seen eye to eye on the impact of OTB, or on its prospects for future payoffs. Nor is it surprising that an ancient sport and business, which throws off revenue to the state, should get its back up when confronted by a brash new entity like OTB. But it would be very surprising indeed, considering what might ultimately be involved for money-starved municipalities all around the U.S., if those differences are not somehow resolved in the next year or two.

BETTING ON SPORTS*

According to police estimates based on known gambling operations, New York City bookmakers accept about $1 billion a year in sports bets and another $150 to $200 million on horses. The Quayle poll, which was limited to City residents, found that New Yorkers annually wager some $428 million on sports with bookmakers.† The discrepancy in the figures may be explained by the fact that the total bookmaking handle includes a large volume of bets by commuters and other nonresidents.

The Quayle survey found that New Yorkers who bet on sports with bookmakers are slightly more likely to be white and upper income than the city's population as a whole. Among respondents to the Quayle survey, baseball is the most popular sport for betting. Eighteen percent of adult New Yorkers wagered on baseball, compared with 15 percent on football and 13 percent

---

* Reprinted from *Legal Gambling in New York*, November 1972. Released by The Fund for the City of New York. Used with permission.

† The Quayle survey was also limited to betting on the three major sports: football, basketball, and baseball.

on basketball. However, of bets made with bookmakers, the most money is bet on football—$189 million, compared with $118 million on basketball and $122 million on baseball. Another $35 million is bet each year on pool cards—$25 million on football games and the remainder split evenly between baseball and basketball. Almost three out of four bettors on football and basketball gambled most or all of the time on professional games. The others divided their wagers about equally between professional and college contests.

Although most *bets* are made directly between acquaintances, the vast majority of *money* wagered is bet with bookmakers. The bookie handles larger bets that cannot be made comfortably between friends. His role is that of a broker between those who want to bet on one team and those who want to bet on the other. For this service, he takes a commission on the total amount wagered.

The bookmaker's goal is to equalize the amount bet on each side, so that the losses of one set of customers will cover the winnings (less his commission) of the other. To attract the same amount of money to each team, he employs either (in the case of baseball) betting odds or a point spread (football and basketball).

The point spread is a handicap for the stronger team. If the Jets are listed as a seven-point favorite over the Vikings, Jet backers win only if their team wins by more than seven. If the Jets win by exactly seven points, it is a betting tie and all wagers are returned. To avoid this wasted effort, spreads are frequently given in half points. Since the point spread is intended to attract backing equally to each side, it must reflect bettors' impressions of the contestants as well as the bookmaker's assessment of their relative strengths.

Many bookmakers subscribe to a national handicapping service that provides detailed information, including field conditions and weather outlook, the physical and even the psychological well-being of the players. A list of point spreads can also be purchased, and some games may be checked as suspicious to warn the bookmaker about accepting bets on it.

Bookies distribute printed point spreads of their own at the beginning of the week. These are usually close to the point spreads that appear in the mass media during the week. Bookmakers, however, change their spreads as betting develops to encourage backing for a team that is being inadequately played. A sophisticated bettor can sometimes make bets on both sides of a game at different spreads that give him an opportunity for large winnings at virtually no risk.

To illustrate, assume that Minnesota is favored over Chicago by seven points early in the week, but that later the spread increases to ten. If a bettor wages $10 on Minnesota at the seven-point spread and later puts $10 on Chicago at the ten-point spread, here are his possibilities: If Minnesota wins by seven or ten, he wins one bet and ties the other, if Minnesota wins by eight or nine, he wins both bets. In any other case, he splits his bets and is out only his commission on one bet.

This situation works to the disadvantage of the bookie, of course. Suppose for example, that the opening spread brought in $1,000 in bets on Minnesota and none on Chicago. After the spread was widened to ten points, however, $1,000 came in on Chicago and no other bettors backed Minnesota. The bets have now been equalized, but the bookmaker is in danger. If Minnesota wins by eight or nine points, he loses all the bets. In the terminology of the trade, he has been "middled."

As the foregoing examples make clear, it is vitally important to the bookmaker that the initial point spread be as accurate as possible and that changes be minimized. If the point spreads are faulty, the bookmaker will find himself risking his own money on the outcome of the game. He will be gambling, in other words, instead of brokering.

Point spreads are ultimately set by a kind of supply and demand process. But in general they appear to conform closely to the outcome of the games. A comparison of the Friday point spread printed in the *The New York Times* with the later results shows that a bettor on the underdog would have won about half of the time. A bettor who could pick fifty-five games out of every 100 would have a 5 percent edge on the bookmaker. The fact that bookmaking continues to thrive demonstrates that point spreads are effective in equalizing the bets.

The use of point spreads increases the fear of some sports fans and officials that games might be fixed. It is easier, they reason, to persuade an athlete to slacken his efforts and win by less than the point spread than to lose the game outright. Many observers have remarked on the behavior of some spectators at games whose winner is already decided but whose betting outcome is still in doubt because of the point spread. Such spectators sometimes appear to be more interested in the contest as a gambling vehicle than as a sporting event.

Because of their reluctance to see gambling emphasized at the expense of interest in the competition, as well as their fear of attempted fixes, professional sports officials strongly oppose legalized gambling on their sports. Under the present illegal system, the bookmaking enterprise defends against fixed games. Not only would the bookmaker be a probable loser on a fixed game, but revelations of a fix could permanently damage business—as it has already done to betting on college basketball and professional boxing.

If the point spread (or uneven odds, in the case of baseball) fails to equalize bets on a given game, the bookmaker can simply refuse to accept any more wagers on the favored team. He does this unwillingly, because it offends customers and reduces his handle and potential profit. But he may resort to closing his book when a sudden change in the outlook for a game, e.g. an injury to a key player, throws the point spread and the betting pattern seriously awry. He may also refuse bets that he senses are unusual or large bets that he is unable to layoff.

The layoff process in bookmaking is considerably more complicated than in the numbers game. It may take several steps to complete, working all the way through a national system before equilibrium is established in the money bet on each team. For example, in a game between the New York Knicks and the Los Angeles Lakers, local fans might bet heavily on the home team regardless of the point spread. Rather than change the spread or close their books, bookies in the two cities can trade off their excessive bets through the layoff system or through individual arrangements known as "marriages."

The larger a layoff system's volume, the greater its capacity to even out imbalances at lower levels. But if faulty point spreads skew the betting pattern across the country, layoff bets may be accepted only at a high premium—sometimes not at all. If a bookmaker cannot layoff excess bets, he faces the unpleasant choice between gambling or curtailing his own business.

A bookmaker's success depends on his ability to generate balanced business. He must be able to accept risks in the short run. Over the long haul, if he is skillful, he is likely to come out ahead. The greater his ability to survive losing periods, the more business he can accept. A bookmaker who is an agent of a larger organization can expand more easily because of his access to the layoff and emergency financial backing.

If his books are in balance, the bookmaker keeps 4.5 percent of his total football and basketball handle as his commission. The bettor must put up $11 to win $10. With one bet on each team, the bookie will take in $22 and pay back $21. His commission on the transaction is $1 or 4.5 percent of the $22 handle.

His percentage on baseball bets is more complicated to calculate. Suppose that the odds on a game between Baltimore and Cleveland are 7½ to 5. The bookmaker will list the game as 7-8 Baltimore favorite. This means that the bettor on Baltimore must risk $8 to win $5. A Cleveland backer must bet $5 to win $7. With one wager on each side, the bookmaker takes in $13. If Baltimore wins, he pays out $13; if Cleveland wins, $12. Assuming the odds are accurate and Baltimore wins three of five games, the bookmaker takes in $65 (5 x $13) and pays out $63. His commission over the five games is $2 or 3.1 percent.

In this example, 8 to 5 equals $1.60 to $1.00 and 7 to 5 equals $1.40 to $1.00. The difference is twenty cents; these odds are known as the 20-cent line, the line that is offered in New York. On large bets, or when taking layoff bets from other bookmakers, the bookmaker may offer the 10-cent line, in which his percentage is correspondingly smaller. The most favorable game for the baseball bookmaker is the even game. Under the 20-cent line, the bettor must wager $5.50 to win $5.00 betting on either team. This yields the same percentage of 4.5 as the 11 to 10 bet in football and basketball. The advantage is lower on games that are not evenly matched. On the whole, the percentage for the bookmaker is less on baseball than on the other two sports.

Bookmakers also offer a variety of complicated combination bets, some of which can yield him as much as 16 percent of his handle.* But they take more time to record and tabulate than normal bets, and are not encouraged. On most of his sports betting volume, a bookmaker normally makes only about 4.5 percent on sales.

Horse race betting is far more profitable. The bookmaker pays track odds. But the track, the owners and the state keep almost 17 percent of the pari-mutuel handle. So that if the bookie's bets are distributed in the same proportion as those at the track, he retains that same high percentage. In terms of profit to the bookmaker, $1 bet on horse racing is worth $3.80 wagered on football or basketball.

These figures are important in any consideration of legalizing sports betting. The higher profit potential in bookmaking—legal or otherwise—is in horse race betting, which OTB has already preempted. To clear $1,000 after expenses, the sports bookmaker must handle from $50,000 to $100,000. OTB, to make the same profit, need take in only about $10,000 and the state lottery a mere $2,000.

A typical small to medium-sized bookmaking operation in New York City currently is organized and operates roughly as follows:

---

* Combination bets include parleys, round-robins, "if" bets, and "reverse" bets. In a parley, the player bets $6 and chooses a team in each of two games. If both win, he receives $20.20, but loses his bet if either team loses. The probability is that one parley of four will win. The bookmaker will retain $3.80 for each $24 handled, about 16 percent. The round-robin is a three-team bet which is really three two-team parleys. The bettor takes three teams and bets $18. If all three win, he has won three parlays of $6; he receives $60.60. If two teams win, he wins one parley, loses two, and receives $20.20. If only one of his teams win, he loses his $18. The percentage for the bookmaker is the same as in a single parley. In an "if" bet, the bettor bets $11 on Team A at the normal odds and, say, $11 on Team C at the normal odds, but the latter bet becomes effective only if Team A wins. If Team A wins, but Team C loses, the bettor gets back his $11. A reverse bet combines the "if" bet, "Team A if Team C." In the if and reverse bets, the favorable percentage of the bookmaker is also 4.5.

The office manager is either a low-level member of a diversified criminal organization or an independent entrepreneur. If he is an agent of organized crime, he will be paid a salary and a share of the profits. An independent will pay tribute to a criminal organization based on the size of his operation.

If the office is equipped with a protected telephone, it will be manned by a salaried "writer" to transcribe bets. A "tabber" keeps track of the bets and decides when to change lines or spreads and when to lay off bets. The manager may well act as tabber. A salaried figure man keeps the accounts. In an office that has no protected phone, communication of bets is slower and more round-about. It may require a call-back phone, an answering service or some other intermediary. The speed and skill of a writer is not needed. Instead, a clerk or two perform the duties of writer and tabber.

A typical office like the one described might have twenty-two runners who take bets from clients directly or provide them with telephone access to the office by use of a code word. Bets are recorded with the code word of runner and bettor. The runner may be regarded as the bookmaker by his clients. Indeed, some independent bookmakers who have been "organized" actually function as runners. A runner keeps one half of his customers' losses. If, in a given week, his customers are net winners, the runner is in the red to the office and must clear his debt before he begins to collect his share of the profits again.

On the average, runners for such an office may collect $750 a day in horse racing bets and $3,500 a week in football wagers. If there is no other action, the office handles $99,000 on horse racing and $77,000 on football a week. If all bets are in balance, the office retains about $16,500 from its horse racing action and $3,500 from football—a total of $20,000. Half of this goes to the runners, who average about $450. (There are wide variations in income among runners. Some may have expenses, such as gratuities to good customers who are heavy losers.)

The office has a weekly payroll of roughly $1,500, including the manager's salary. Rent and phones cost about $200. Another $1,000 may be set aside for such contingencies as arrest expenses. The rest (less protection money) is profit—less than 5 percent of sales. The office we have described has a far heavier horse racing business than the average estimated by the police. If its $176,000 handle were divided according to that estimate, only one fifth ($35,000) would come from horse racing and four fifths ($141,000) from football. Commissions would be $6,000 from the former and $6,500 from the latter. The income of the runners and revenue of the office would be reduced correspondingly. Runners would average about $300 a week. Office expenses would still be $2,500 to $3,000, so that profits would be cut to $3,500 or about two percent. If all the handle were sports betting, net profits would be less than one percent.

In *Theft of a Nation,* Donald R. Cressey describes the organization of bookmaking as a franchise or sharecropper system, in which there are advantages to the sharecropper. In the late 1950s, he says, bookies in Suffolk County were "organized" by a criminal organization that demanded 50 percent of their profits to forestall violence. But the bookmakers soon discovered six advantages:

1. "A 'sportsman' or two provided absolute backing for all bets so that the independent operator no longer needed to gamble or to reinsure his bets through a 'layoff' operation."
2. "This backing permitted each independent operator to handle more bets, with the result that each bookmaker actually made a bigger profit."
3. "The bookmakers no longer found it necessary to do so much running around the streets taking bets. They merely provided regular bettors with New York City telephone numbers. After the bettors had called in their bets and had them recorded in a rather elaborate set of books, the bookmaker needed only to go around and collect the money or, in a minority of instances, to pay off."
4. "The bookies themselves no longer had to handle many telephoned bets, thus making it more difficult for the police to determine by wire tapping what was going on."
5. "The bookies had legal services and men with 'connections' available to them, so that the risk of conviction, even when arrested, was decreased."
6. "Squabbles with other bookmakers were minimized—under the new arrangement, each man was assigned exclusive rights to a territory."

Some theorists hold that the independent bookmaker is the victim of organized crime because, as an illegal operative, he cannot turn to the police for protection from threats of violence. But the structural organization of bookmaking, as Cressey's account indicates, is based on economic logic as well as underworld power relationships. Certainly it is doubtful that a simple repeal of the laws against bookmaking would undo the organizational ties that now exist.

Poolselling

The most popular form of poolselling in New York City is the football card, on which $25 million is bet annually. Another $5 million each is wagered on baseball and basketball cards. The games are not truly pools, but parlays in which many games are chosen and the payoff does not keep pace with the multiplying odds against winning.

In British soccer pools, a fixed percentage of the pooled wagers is returned to the winners. It is theoretically possible for an American poolseller to have to pay out more in prizes than he collects in bets. But this is highly improbable in view of the very low payoff odds.

Football cards are distributed weekly during the season at such places as factories, offices and schools. Each card typically lists about ten professional games and twenty college contests, each with a point spread. A bettor picks at least three (sometimes four) games and turns in a numbered stub showing his selections and the amount of his wager.

If any of the player's chosen teams loses *or ties*, he loses his bet (except for consolation prizes). Pool card point spreads are slightly, but significantly different from those set by bookmakers for single game action. The cards never list half-point spreads, and are usually fixed at the most frequent margin of victory, e.g. 3, 4, 6, 7, 10, 13. The purpose is to bring about tie games and add to the seller's advantage.

Completed sets of football pool cards were not available for this study, but a review of the point spreads printed during the season by *The New York Times* showed that they brought about ties in six games out of 182—an edge for the poolseller of 5.4 percent.

Table 3-I below demonstrates the enormous advantage to

KICK-OFF   N⁰ 13370

4 out of 4....10 Points	8 out of 8....75 Points
5 out of 5....16 Points	9 out of 9....100 Points
6 out of 6....30 Points	10 out of 10..250 Points
7 out of 7....40 Points	9 out of 10....20 Points

ALL TEAMS MUST WIN-TIES LOSE
Any game played before noon on date of ticket,void
NEWS - MATTER - ONLY

1 TULANE	2 GEORGIA TECH	+3
3 UCLA	4 CALIFORNIA	+3
5 GEORGIA	6 KENTUCKY	+3
7 HARVARD	8 DARTMOUTH	+4
9 ARMY	10 HOLY CROSS	+6
11 ILLINOIS	12 IOWA	+6
13 MISSOURI	14 COLORADO	+6
15 TEXAS TECH	16 SMU	+6
17 STANFORD	18 WASHINGTON ST	+7
19 WASHINGTON	20 OREGON	+6
21 TEXAS A&M	22 BAYLOR	+6
23 PENNSYLVANIA	24 PRINCETON	+7
25 PENN ST	26 WEST VIRGINIA	+7
27 MICHIGAN ST	28 PURDUE	+7
29 YALE	30 CORNELL	+7
31 KANSAS	32 IOWA ST	+10
33 NORTH CAROLINA	34 SOUTH CAROLINA	+10
35 WISCONSIN	36 INDIANA	+14
37 PITTSBURG	38 NAVY	+14
39 MARYLAND	40 NO CAROLINA ST	+14
41 FLORIDA	42 DUKE	+14
43 TENNESSEE	44 CLEMSON	+14
45 VIRGINIA	46 WAKE FOREST	+17
47 NEBRASKA	48 OKLAHOMA ST	+17
49 NOTRE DAME	50 MIAMI	+17

PRO-FOOTBALL

51 ST LOUIS	52 WASHINGTON	+3
53 KANSAS CITY	54 SAN DIEGO	+3
55 DETROIT	56 GREEN BAY	+6
57 PHILADELPHIA	58 NEW ORLEANS	+7
59 DENVER	60 CLEVELAND	+7
61 MINNESOTA	62 NEW ENGLAND	+7
63 DALLAS	64 GIANTS	+10
65 BUFFALO	66 CHICAGO	+10
67 LOS ANGELES	68 JETS	+12
69 OAKLAND	70 SAN FRANCISCO	+13
71 MIAMI	72 BALTIMORE	+17
73 CINCINNATI	74 HOUSTON	+17

CIRCLE SELECTIONS

N⁰ 13370

```
        1   2   3   4   5   6   7   8   9  10  11
   12  13  14  15  16  17  18  19  20  21  22  23
   24  25  26  27  28  29  30  31  32  33  34  35
   36  37  38  39  40  41  42  43  44  45  46  47
   48  49  50  51  52  53  54  55  56  57  58  59
   60  61  62  63  64  65  66  67  68  69  70  71
   72  73  74  75  76  77  78  79  80
```

Amt. ....

Figure 3-1.   A football pool card.

the seller in every betting situation. The payoff schedule is shown in Column 2 and the true odds in Column 3.

The poolseller offers consolation prizes to those who bet on ten or more games and correctly pick the winners of all but one. In spite of these bonuses, which are designed to induce a player to pick more games, the odds against the bettor rise rapidly as he adds selections. Assuming that each game is an even proposition, the poolseller who takes in $65,536 from bettors picking 16 games will pay $5,000 to one winner and sixteen consolation prizes of $200 each. He will keep $57,336 or 88 percent of the handle. For the player, the best strategy is to pick four games. This cuts the poolseller's probable share to 37.5 percent.

The effect of tie games, which is not shown in the table or the example cited, can be important. If ties occur once in twenty games, almost fifteen of every 100 three-team bettors, twenty of every 100 four-team bettors and half of all ten-team bettors will lose because of a tie among their picks.

The game's very high profit margin greatly simplifies the poolseller's operations. Rarely if ever does he need to lay off bets. He is unconcerned about fixed games. Even if a player knew the outcome of one game, the odds would still be against him on all but a four-team card. In that situation, the bettor's edge would not justify fixing a contest. The probabilities are that the fixer would have to bet $100,000 to win $5,000.

Two columns in the table indicate the effect of skill in picking football card winners. A player who could correctly choose 55 percent of the games would still lose from nine to 55 percent of his wagers, depending on how many games he selected (plus whatever losses were caused by ties). A player who could pick 60 percent of the winners would still lose if he consistently bet the three-for-three card, but he would be a net winner on other cards (ties not considered). The seller's tie advantage would offset the bettor's skill on cards of four, five and six games and would reduce the bettor's winnings on the others. It is true, however, that an extremely skillful football handicapper can win playing football cards—a fact that helps account for its attraction.

TABLE 3-I

ODDS AND PAYOFFS OF FOOTBALL CARDS

Number of Games Played	(1) Payoff on $1	(2) *Odds Against Winning	(3) Probable Percentage Retained by Operator	(4) **Odds Against Winning	(5) ***Odds Against Winning
3 out of 3	$4	8-1	50%	6-1	4.66
4 out of 4	$10	16-1	37.5%	11-1	7.78
5 out of 5	$15	32-1	43%	20-1	12.99
6 out of 6	$25	64-1	61%	36-1	21.69
7 out of 7	$50	128-1	61%	66-1	36.22
8 out of 8	$100	256-1	61%	120-1	60.49
10 out of 10 (9-10)	$250 ($15x10)	1,024-1 (1,024-10)	80%	398-1	168.70
12 out of 12 (11-12)	$500 ($25x12)	4,096-1 (4,096-12)	80%	1,334-1	470.49
15 out of 15 (14-15)	$2,000 ($100x15)	32,768-1 (32,768-15)	90%	8,043-1	2,191.29
16 out of 16 (15-16)	$5,000 ($200x16)	65,536-1 (65,536-16)	88%	14,638-1	3,659.45

---

 * The advantage to the Operator of winning tie bets is not included. Assumes each game is a 50-50 proposition.
 ** Assumes the skills of the players allows them to pick 55 winners in 100 games.
 *** Assumes the skill of the players allows them to pick 60 winner in 100 games.

Very little is known about poolselling organizations. Operators are believed to be organized; certainly they operate with the sanction of organized crime. They receive their printed sheets from a central publishing agency. Poolselling has a lower status in the illegal gambling hierarchy than bookmaking. It is, in fact, disdained by police and bookies alike. Bettors are regarded as suckers in the same class as numbers players, and sellers as small-time operators. Bookmaking records seized by the police reveal no evidence that bookies engage in poolselling, and there is a feeling among some bookies at least, that selling pool cards would be beneath their dignity.

In the aggregate, however, poolselling is a lucrative business. The Quayle study found that football bettors make pool bets regularly. Only 28 percent bet a single three or four-game card per week. Most bet cards with more picks which offer odds on which the seller retains an average of 53 percent to 90 percent of the bets. It is reasonable to estimate that a poolseller's markup is between 60 percent and 80 percent of the $35 million spent on pool cards by New Yorkers each year. That amounts to $21 million to $28 million, before expenses.

BIBLIOGRAPHY

Books
Buck, Frederick S.: *Horse Race Betting.* New York, Arco, 1962.
Caillois, Roger: *Man, Play and Games.* New York, The Free Press of Glencoe, 1961.
Chenery, J. T.: *The Law and Practice of Bookmaking, Betting, Gaming, and Lotteries.* 2nd ed., London, Sweet & Max, 1963.
Cohen, Ira S. and Stephens, George D.: *Scientific Handicapping.* Englewood Cliffs, Prentice-Hall, 1963.
Cook, Fred J.: *A Two-Dollar Bet Means Murder.* New York, Dial, 1961.
Cressey, Donald R.: *Theft of the Nation.* New York, Harper & Row, 1969.
Drzazga, John: Bookmaking, pari-mutuel betting. *Wheels of Fortune.* Springfield, Thomas, 1963, Chaps. 3 and 4, pp. 52-115, 116-125.
Fabricand, Burton P.: *Horse Sense.* New York, McKay, 1965.
Kaplan, Lawrence J. and Loughrey, Leo C.: *The Ins and Outs of On-Track and Off-Track Betting on Horse Races.* New York, Gould, 1970.
Maas, Peter: *The Valachi Papers.* New York, Putnam, 1968.

Malloy, Michael T.: Racing today. *The National Observer*, Silver Springs, Md., 1968.

Marx, Herbert L.: *Gambling in America.* New York, Wilson, 1952.

O'Hare, John Richard: *The Socio-Economic Aspects of Horse Racing.* Washington, D.C., Cath U Pr. 1945.

Palmer, Joe H.: *This Was Racing.* New York, Barnes and Noble, 1953.

Reid, Ed: *The Grim Reapers: The Anatomy of Organized Crime in America.* Chicago, Regnery, 1969.

Robertson, William H. P.: *The History of Thoroughbred Racing in America.* Englewood Cliffs, Prentice-Hall, 1964.

Scarne, John: *Scarne's Complete Guide to Gambling.* New York, Simon and Schuster, 1961.

Scott, Marvin B.: *The Racing Game.* Chicago, Aldine, 1968.

Reports

New York City: Mayor's Citizens Committee on Off Track Betting. *Final Report.* New York, February 6, 1959.

New York City: Mayor's Citizens Committee on Off Track Betting. *A Plan for Legal Off-Track Betting in the City of New York.* Part I, A Plan, December 30, 1963. Part II, *Electronic Equipment and Other Operational Matters,* January 8, 1964, New York.

New York City: Office of the Mayor and Office of the Comptroller. *Report of Survey of Off-Track Betting in New Zealand, Australia, England and France,* by Albert Margolies and James A. Cavanagh. New York, October 17, 1963.

New York Racing Association, Inc.: *An Introduction to Thoroughbred Racing.* Jamaica, N.Y., 1968.

New York State Assembly: *Pattern for New York? A Report on Off-Track Betting in England,* by Henry D. Paley and John A. Glendinning. Albany, N.Y., January 1964.

New York State Commission of Investigation: *Syndicated Gambling in New York.* Albany, New York, February 1961.

New York State: Joint Legislative Committee to Study All Laws, Rules and Regulations Relative to Horse Racing in New York State. *Final Report.* Albany, N.Y., Legislative Document No. 45, 1954.

New York State: Select Bi-Partisan Committee on Off-Track Betting. *Report.* Albany, N.Y., Legislative Document No. 32, March 19, 1964.

Articles

Annual Report of the New York City Police Department, 1963. New York, April 1964.

Bill making it federal crime to use telegraph wires or telephones in interstate operations passed. *The New York Times,* July 29, 1961, p. 17.

Come into the parlor: Off-track betting in New York. *Newsweek, 62:* November 4, 1963.

Cope, M.: Profile of a bookmaker. *Saturday Evening Post, 236:* April 27, 1963.

Court rules anyone not a track patron placing pari-mutuel bets and getting gratuity when bet is cashed is guilty of bookmaking. *The New York Times,* 1, December 15, 1952.

Day, John I.: Horse racing and the pari-mutuel. *The Annals, 269:* May 1950.

Flaherty, Joe: Frank Carlin, the bookie. *The New York Times Magazine,* Section No. 6, April 2, 1967.

Fox, Philip G.: A primer for chumps. *Saturday Evening Post,* December 11, 1959.

Fund for the City of New York: Betting on sports. *Legal Gambling in New York: A Discussion of Numbers and Sports Betting.* New York, November 1972, pp. 35-48.

Grutzner, Charles: Survey on the operation and organization of policy. *The New York Times,* 1, 17, June 26, 1964.

Havemann, E.: Great trotting scandal. *Life, 35:* November 16, 1953.

Lawrence, Louis A.: Bookmaking. *The Annals of the American Academy of Political and Social Science, 269:* May 1950.

Maxwell, J. A.: Minor league Las Vegas in the blue grass state. *Reporter, 16:* January 10, 1957.

McDonald, John: How the horseplayers got involved with the urban crisis. *Fortune,* 94-97, 133-135, April 1972.

Murphy, Michael J.: The bookmaking racket. *The Gambling Situation, 1964. New York, Police Department,* February 27, 1964, pp. 32-38.

Senate subcommittee urges federal government dry up organized gambling profits by curbing horse race wire services. *The New York Times,* 29, March 29, 1962.

Stump, A.: Racing's hidden crime. *Coronet,* 44: May 1958.

Three owners of two horse-racing tip sheets held under new federal anti-racketeering law. *The New York Times,* 9, March 13, 1962.

Toperoff, S.: Mafia at Saratoga. *Sports Illustrated, 29:* November 11, 1968.

Yonkers doodle: Harness racing scandal. *Time, 62:* October 5, 1953.

THE ECONOMICS OF THE NUMBERS GAME

INTRODUCTION

ORGANIZED CRIME FINDS the numbers game the ideal criminal activity. The reasons are many. The numbers game is easily organized. It is popular with the public. There is a guaranteed, built-in margin of profit for the operators. And, while detection by the police is relatively easy, punishment for those who are occasionally arrested is mild, and consequently does not serve as a deterrent.

Millions of dollars are squeezed out of the nation's inner city slums each year by organized crime. The individuals involved in these organized crime activities are not limited to the Mafia, but include Blacks, Puerto Ricans, Cubans, and other ethnic minorities. The Chairman of the New York State Joint Legislative Committee on Crime once commented that the flow of money from the ghetto to organized crime is so great that there can be little meaningful economic improvement in New York City's ghettos until it is stopped.

The 1972 study, *Legal Gambling in New York*, estimates that illegal gambling operations in New York City gross more than $1.7 billion a year and that one out of four New Yorkers play the numbers game. The $100,000 report by the Fund for the City of New York concluded that the State Legislature should legalize the numbers game in order to force organized crime out of this exceptionally profitable business and at the same time reduce corruption of law enforcement personnel and government officials.

Recently, The New York City Off-track Betting Corporation presented a detailed plan for an OTB takeover of the numbers game that would disable organized crime and siphon millions of dollars into New York City's communities for financing schools, hospitals, and other socially necessary projects. The proposal suggested that OTB would run the numbers game as it is now operated and that past arrest records for numbers writing would not be a bar to employment. The proposal is under consideration by the Legislature.

The first reading in this chapter "The Economics of the Numbers Game" provides an historical background of the numbers game, an analysis of the operation of the game, its economic aspects, conclusions and recommendations; the second selection outlines the technique for computing the winning number; and the third selection provides a model for a legal numbers lottery. Even though it was designed with specific reference to the District of Columbia, the model may be applied to other core areas of cities.†

THE ECONOMICS OF THE NUMBERS GAME*

LAWRENCE J. KAPLAN AND JAMES M. MAHER

INTRODUCTION

The problems that exist in the underprivileged areas of the nation have been studied and analyzed by social scientists in the hope that understanding their background may help supply some solutions. All too often, however, the analysis reveals a chain of events that proves difficult, though not impossible, to follow. One of the problems that falls into this category, a product of the hopelessness and emptiness prevalent in the lives of people living in the slums, is that of illegal gambling. The purpose of this article is to analyze just one aspect of that problem: the economics of the numbers game.

Millions of dollars of federal money are poured into urban

---

* Reprinted from *The American Journal of Economics and Sociology.* Copyright 1970, pp. 391-407. Used with permission.

† The State of New Jersey initiated a three-digit numbers game on May 22, 1975, the first legal numbers game in the nation.

areas to be spent on welfare, employment, and training. In turn, the poor divert millions from their incomes into illegal gambling, primarily into the numbers game; into the purchase of narcotics; and into paying exorbitant interest rates to loansharks. Directing and controlling all these activities is the organized criminal syndicate. If America is concerned with poverty, then it must also be concerned with organized crime for the urban poor who are the principal victims of it. Indeed, organized crime is the major beneficiary of the misery of the slums.

Today, the primary source of funds for organized crime is through illegal gambling. Gambling profits finance the other major interests of organized crime, including narcotics, prostitution, loansharking, bootlegging, and labor racketeering. The most popular form of illegal gambling is the numbers game, which, with its lure of a possible 600-to-1 payoff, has surpassed horse race betting and other gambling activities.

ORGANIZED CRIME IN THE GAMBLING BUSINESS

The President's Commission on Law Enforcement and Administration of Justice defines organized crime as:

> . . . a society that seeks to operate outside the control of the American people and their governments. It involves thousands of criminals, working within structures as complex as those of any large corporation, subject to laws more rigidly enforced than those of legitimate governments. Its actions are not impulsive but rather the result of intricate conspiracies, carried on over many years and aimed at gaining control over whole fields of activity in order to amass huge profits.[1]

The President's Crime Commission and the Kefauver Committee, which reported its findings in 1951, are in agreement that organized crime—also known as the crime syndicate, the Mafia, or Cosa Nostra—controls almost all of the illegal gambling in the United States.[2] Since basic statistics on the magnitude of the

---

[1] President's Commission on Law Enforcement and Administration of Justice, *The Challenge of Crime in a Free Society* (Washington, D.C., Government Printing Office, 1967), p. 187.

[2] United States Senate, Special Senate Committee to Investigate Organized Crime in Interstate Commerce (the Kefauver Committee), *Final Report*, 82nd Congress, 1st Session. Report No. 725 (1951), p. 88.

illegal gambling business, by their very nature, are not knowable, it is necessary to make estimates, using the few sources available.

A widely used estimate of organized crime's annual gross revenue from gambling is $20 billion a year, of which the major portion comes from wagers in the numbers game.* Evidence gleaned by the President's Crime Commission indicates that organized crime's profit from gambling alone runs as high as one third of gross revenue, or $6 or $7 billion a year, about a 35 percent return. This annual profit is equivalent to the total profit of the twelve largest industrial corporations in the United States in 1966 ranked according to sales. These twelve companies had sales of 86.3 billion in 1966 in order to earn their $7 billion profit, about an 8 percent return based upon sales.[3]

The underworld is gradually finding its way into the upper-world. The leaders of the syndicate understand well a basic law of economics. Money is worth nothing unless it is put to work. And so, the millions, perhaps billions, of dollars which are shipped to Swiss banks for safekeeping or which are hidden privately in the United States ultimately are invested in many sectors of our economy. The "dirty" money of the syndicate thus becomes clean. Examples of legitimate businesses which are being infiltrated by the syndicate include: bakeries, motels, night clubs, trucking companies, laundries, service stations, catering establishments, jukebox and vending machine businesses and meat wholesaling.[4]

A common characteristic of these businesses is that they involve heavy flows of cash.

The Syndicate tends to choose cash businesses to invest in, to win room for maneuver in reporting income for tax returns.[5]

But, the Syndicate also chooses businesses that complement other activities. For example, Syndicate bosses go into plastic

---

* Based upon ranges suggested in the Crime Commission's report.

[3] The *Fortune* Directory, *The 500 Largest U.S. Industrial Corporations.* (*Fortune,* June 15, 1967).

[4] Sandy Smith, "Mobsters in the Marketplace: Money, Muscle, Murder," *Life,* Vol. 63, No. 10 (September 8, 1967).

[5] Bernadette Carey, "Two Bit Bet: Financing a Crime Empire," *Look* (Dec. 14, 1965), pp. 131-132.

manufacturing which gives them access to chemicals used in converting raw opium into heroin, another illicit operation.[6]

The legitimate business ventures often turn out to be convenient adjuncts for the racket.

> The junkyard may contain an auto-crushing machine through which they pass an automobile containing a disobedient gang member which flattens both into what looks like a thick piece of dirty metal; the garage may turn out to be a paint shop for hot cars; and the print shop may do church programs at a discount, but it may also turn out tally sheets for the operation of the numbers bank.[7]

Organized crime finds the numbers game the ideal criminal activity, and the reasons are easy to understand. A former New York City Police Commissioner states the case succinctly:

> The numbers game is easily organized; it is popular with the public; there is a guaranteed, built-in margin of profit; detection, because of the protection and security offered by the laws of search and seizure, and by recent court decisions, is difficult; and punishment is mild and hardly a deterrent.[8]

Historical Background

The numbers game is probably a variation of the Italian National Lottery which was started in 1530, and is still operating.[9] This lottery is based upon a selection of numbers from one to ninety coupled with the selection of one of ten Italian provinces where the drawings are held. Unlike the numbers game, the lottery is a once a week operation.[10] The Italian lottery is not

---

[6] *Ibid.*

[7] Fred Powledge, "Pick a Number from 000 to 999," *The New York Times Magazine* (Dec. 6, 1964), p. 156.

[8] A Statement by Michael J. Murphy, a former Commissioner of the New York City Police Department, quoted by Charles Grutzner, "Survey on the Operation and Organization of Policy," *The New York Times* (June 26, 1964), p. 17.

[9] John Scarne, *Scarne's Complete Guide to Gambling* (New York, Simon and Schuster, 1961), p. 164.

[10] John Drzazga, *Wheels of Fortune* (Springfield, Thomas, 1963), p. 150.

too different from the numbers game as it is known in the United States.[11]

The origin of the numbers game may also be traced to the London Lottery shops during the first half of the eighteenth century. They sold an insurance or policy ticket which brought gambling within reach of those who could not afford to purchase a lottery ticket. For a small sum, a player selected one or more numbers which he believed would appear on the winning lottery ticket. The amount of his winnings was predicated on odds that were quoted for the number of correct choices.[12] In point of similarity it would appear that the London Lottery was the direct forbear of the numbers game as we know it today.

In the United States, through the colonial period, the numbers game was similar in its operation to the London Lottery. But, the reputation of the game was low. In 1819, a Committee on Lotteries in New York City, after a study of that city's sixty lottery shops, discovered various types of fraud, particularly manipulation of winning numbers.[13] As time elapsed, one state after another legislated these lottery shops out of business.

At this point, the numbers game began to operate and it was dominated by groups who made enduring alliances with the political groups of the era. The game was big business, profits were large, and it gradually expanded to twenty other cities across the young nation. The "Policy Kings," as they were called, increased the moneymaking possibilities of the game by insuring that only numbers that were not played won. Some of the operators were finally jailed and by 1915, the nineteenth century numbers game was no longer an important part of the scene in the United States.[13]

The idea of the numbers game, however, was not dead. In 1921 a group of Negro lottery salesmen selling treasury tickets, a form of lottery, added a policy ticket, and the game was started up again.[14]

Organized crime became interested in the numbers game

---

[11] Charles Grutzner, *op. cit.*, p. 17.
[12] Herbert Asbury, *Sucker's Progress* (New York, Dodd, 1938), pp. 89-90.
[13] *Ibid.*, pp. 90, 156.
[14] John Scarne, *op. cit.*, pp. 168-171.

when Prohibition was voted out. Bootlegging was no longer profitable and the personnel and capital of the underworld sought greener pastures.

> Dutch Schultz (Arthur Flegenheimer) was the first white hoodlum to discover that there were huge profits to be earned in the ghettoes through the numbers game. At the time he was a bootlegger. He finally moved in and took it over. The Syndicate exiled him to New Jersey. later had him executed, and has been operating the game ever since.[15]

The numbers game is also known as "policy." The term "policy" first came into American usage around 1885. It was derived from the Italian word *polizza* which means voucher or receipt.[16] Another view of the origin of the term is the following:

> Policy is a form of lottery usually based on horseracing results. The name derives from its earliest days, when poor people used for betting money the nickels and dimes saved to pay insurance-policy premiums.[17]

Operation of the Numbers Game

THE GAME: A numbers player selects three digits from 000 to 999. Between 000 to 999 are 1,000 three-digit numbers, and only one of them wins. The various forms of play are termed:

    a. Straight (three digits)
    b. Combination (of any three digits)
    c. Front bolita or boleda (first two digits)
    d. Back bolita or boleda (last two digits)
    e. Single action (any one digit)[18]

a. *The straight bet* is one on any three-digit number; for example, 753. The chances or probability of winning are 1 in 1,000, or the odds are 999 to 1 against the player. Each player has an equal chance of winning, and the odds remain the same every day. The payoff odds are 600-to-1 generally.

---

[15] Bernadette Carey, *op. cit.*, p. 134.

[16] D. Wakefield, "Harlem's Magic Numbers," *Reporter* (Feb. 4, 1960), p. 25.

[17] Bernadette Carey, *op. cit.*, p. 134.

[18] Frederick W. Egen, *Plainclothesman* (New York, Greenberg, 1952), pp. 66-70.

b. *The combination bet* increases the probability of winning. The player is betting on all arrangements of the three-digit number, which is known as a six-way combination. For example, if the number is 753, the bet is on all six of the following: 753, 735, 573, 537, 357, and 375. This reduces the payoff to one-sixth so that the 600-to-1 payoff is reduced to 100-to-1.

c. *The front bolita* or *boleda bet* is one in which the player selects a two-digit number, for the first two of the three digits. For example, the player selects 75, 7 for the first slot and 5 for the second, as follows:

$$| 7 | 5 | X |$$

(Structure 1)

In this type of bet, the payoff is 60-to-1. Variations exist among the different games.

d. *The back bolita* or *boleda bet* is one in which the player is betting only on the middle and last numbers. For example, he may bet 53 in the following manner:

$$| X | 5 | 3 |$$

(Structure 2)

The payoff odds are the same as in the *front bolita* or *boleda bet*, 60-to-1, with possible variations among the different games.

e. *The single action bet* is one in which a "bank" permits a player to bet on a single digit in any one of the slots. For example, the bettor may wager that a 7 will appear in the first, second, or third slots:

$$| 7 | X | X | or | X | 7 | X | or | X | X | 7 |$$

(Structures 3, 4, 5)

On *the single action bets*, the payoff is 6, 7, or 8 to 1, depending upon the bank.

THE ODDS. On a straight bet, the chances of winning are 1 in 1,000, or the odds are 999 to 1 against the player. While the payoff odds are 600-to-1 generally, in some games the odds are 550-to-1, 500-to-1, or even 450-to-1. For example, lower bids prevail in Brooklyn than in other boroughs of New York City, because the Syndicate is more tightly operated there.[19]

---

[19] Fred Powledge, *op. cit.*, p. 147.

POPULAR NUMBERS. Some examples of popular numbers are 111, 125, 222, 711, or 325 in various combinations. There are other popular numbers.

Payoffs on these numbers is less, so that a bank does not get hit too hard. The popularity of certain numbers may be attributed to superstition.[20] Some numbers represent life, some death, some sudden wealth, and some are derived by observing the license number of a passing car. Payoff odds are lower, possibly 500-to-1 or 450-to-1, depending upon the game's operators. The lower odds seek to discourage widespread play on them, and possible ruination of the "bank" if the number should win for the day.

Some game operators depend upon a "layoff" system to reduce the pressure of heavy betting on a particular number. Usually, the Syndicate stands ready to support a particular numbers game operation.[20] The "banker" pays a premium for this service but the layoff system insures the business by preventing bankruptcy if a number with a large play wins.[21]

SIZE OF BETS. Bets used to be pennies and nickels. In today's affluent society, a quarter is generally considered a minimum bet. Typical players bet fifty cents or a dollar. Middle income players are joining the fun with $5 and $10 bets, and even more.

In Manhattan, straight play is the usual method, and is often called New York policy.[22]

PLACING A BET. The seller of bets usually has a piece of paper on which he records the number selected by the bettor, the amount of the bet, and identifying initial of the bettor, as follows: "753—50¢. J." The amount of recorded information is a minimum. No receipt is given to the player.

In some locations and in some cities where the pressure of law enforcement officers is not too great, additional paperwork may be involved. The seller of bets may carry a small paper pad about half the size of a bank check. Each bet is recorded on the first sheet which has two carbon copies underneath. The collector takes the fifty cents, tears off the top sheet,

---

[20] Anthony Scaduto, "The Mob: A New Look," *New York Post* (June 7, 1968), p. 42.

[21] John Drzazga, *op. cit.*, p. 143.

[22] Fred Powledge, *op. cit.*, p. 35 ff.

and gives it to the bettor. The two carbon copies remain in the pad. The seller retains one copy and turns the money and second copy over to the pick-up man.[23]

PAYOFFS. If a player makes a *hit* on a *straight bet*, he is paid at the 600-to-1 odds, but receives only 540-to-1. If the player had bet $1, he gets $540, not $600, because the collector, who pays off the winner, retains 10 percent, or $60, as his tip or commission.

Another element of the game which is a hazard to the potential winner, is the rule: *Not responsible for arrested work*. If the collector is arrested, and the records are either destroyed, lost, or taken into custody by the police, no payoffs are made to the unlucky players.

DETERMINING THE WINNING NUMBER. The numbers game depends upon the payoff odds used to pay winning bettors at the local horse racing track. Usually, a particular track is designated for the determination of the winning number. These odds are determined by the pari-mutuel machine. While variations exist, it has been estimated that 95 percent of numbers game operators derive the winning number from pari-mutuel race results, also known as the *Manhattan way* for computing the winning number.[24]

To compute the three digits which make up the winning number for the day, the following system is used.

For the first number, the six money winnings figures, or *mutuels*, for each of the first three races are added together. That is, the amounts that $2 bets would have won are summed. These bets cover the one horse that won, the two which placed and the three which showed. The last digit to the left of the decimal in the total is taken as the first digit of the Manhattan Number. Similar operations for the first five races give the middle digit and for the first seven races the third digit. The eighth and ninth races do not figure in the determination.[25]

A less complex method also used is called the Brooklyn number. It is derived from the pari-mutuel handle of the day

[23] John Scarne, *op. cit.*, p. 177.
[24] Charles Grutzner, *op. cit.*, p. 17.
[25] John Scarne, *op. cit.*, p. 171.

(the total amount of money bet at the track that day). The three numbers to the left of the decimal is the winning number. For example, on July 17, 1968 the pari-mutuel handle was $2,614,790. The Brooklyn number for the day was 790.[26]

Generally, the game's operators accept bets on the Manhattan number. Some operators, however, will accept bets on the Brooklyn number if the player specifies this when placing his bet.

Some numbers players find the need for additional action after the first number becomes available. The operators fulfill this additional service. When the trotting races are in season, a second three-digit number is figured in the same manner as the Manhattan number, but based upon the pari-mutuel results from the trotting tracks. Because the results are not known until late at night, it is called the night number.[27]

Other systems are available for computing winning numbers:

A few banks, chiefly in East Harlem, take play also on the number that comes up in the legal weekly lottery in Puerto Rico. In Italian neighborhoods, there is still some play on numbers in the daily treasury reports of 10 provinces in Italy. There is even a Chinese policy game, based on daily drawings in Chinatown, which involves colors as well as numbers.[28]

Most numbers players, prefer the *Manhattan way* for computing the winning number, because it employs a randomizing process based upon the laws of chance, and is thus secure from human manipulation.

Economic Aspects of the Numbers Game

Of an estimated annual gross gambling revenue of $20 billion, the authors figure there is a national numbers game handle of between $10 and $12 billion a year. This is big business! In New York City alone it is believed tha the numbers game grosses two million dollars a day.[29] Another estimate for New

---

[26] Charles Grutzner, *op. cit.*, p. 17.

[27] *Ibid.*

[28] *Ibid.*

[29] John Scarne, *op. cit.*, p. 177.

York City states that: More than 500,000 daily players pour at least $200 million a year into this city's policy banks.[30]

Exact figures on the operation are not available. However, the amount is so huge that, even allowing for error, the number of players and the amount of money involved in the numbers game are tremendous. To operate a big business requires careful management, efficient organization, and an alert group of specialists.[31]

ORGANIZATION OF THE NUMBERS BUSINESS. The numbers game business begins with the player who wishes to place a bet. He represents a foundation block in a giant pyramid. The individual who accepts the bet is the *collector*. In the larger banks he is usually a full-time employee, and in the hierarchy is at the bottom level of the numbers game business. In smaller operations, the *collector* may be a storekeeper, a newsstand operator, an elevator operator, barmaid, a pizza seller, or a fellow employee in a plant or company, and works in the numbers business as a part-time employee to supplement his income.

On the level above is the *controller*. He operates as a branch manager or area manager. He is responsible for tabulating daily collections, maintaining the records of a large number of *collectors*, and making payoffs with money from the bank. A *controller* may operate out of an apartment or a private house. The location is changed hourly or daily in order to avoid detection. The place is referred to as a *drop*, because this is where the pick-up men drop off their money and slips. Thousands of these *drops* are in operation in a large metropolitan area.

At the top of the pyramid is the *bank*. Often referred to as the *Big Drop*, it is the headquarters which collects the daily receipts of the various *controllers*. The *bank* operator is referred to as *banker*. In this capacity he serves as the administrative head of the operation. The authorities estimate that between fifteen and twenty banks operate in New York City.[32] One numbers game operation, headed by a bank, may employ as many as 400 people, which includes about 300 collectors. Payoff money is

---

[30] Charles Grutzner, *op. cit.*, p. 1.

[31] "Bigness and Badness," *Time* (Jan. 13, 1967), p. 64.

[32] Fred Powledge, *op. cit.*, p. 147.

paid by the *bank* to the *controllers* who in turn pass it on to the *collectors* who in turn make the payoffs to the winners. The *banker* manages the operation, hires the specialists and workers, and determines the area where they will work.[33]

The *banker* reports to a member of the Syndicate who probably never sets foot in the *bank* which is only one of his many enterprises. The overlords of the numbers game ". . . are mixed up in every sort of illegitimate activity and vice. Its profits are used to finance traffic in dope, abortion rings, loansharking, prostitution, extortion, hijacking, smuggling, and murder."[34]

Organized crime is firmly entrenched in the numbers game. Several of the overlords ". . . are retired practitioners of violent ventures who have invested in the numbers racket some of the money amassed from bloodier enterprises."[35]

A *pick-up man* operates as liaison between the *collectors* and the *controllers*. A different *pick-up man* operates between *controllers* and the *bank*. Generally, the money and betting records travel different routes to prevent total loss and to reduce evidence available to police in case of arrest. The *pick-up man* is salaried. Other staff members include lookouts, tabulating machine operators, bookkeepers, bail bondsmen, accountants, and lawyers.[36] Accountants, lawyers, and bail bondsmen perform their normal professional services to maintain an efficient operation.

The entire operation, while well organized, is decentralized to prevent disruption by the police. The lookout man may spot a law enforcement officer and warn a collector but this is not always possible. However, in addition to employing lookouts, the operators of the game pay graft to police officers to allay arrest or for promising that they will be tipped off if a raid were planned.[37]

The employees in the numbers game know that if they are arrested, the bail bondsman and attorney of the Syndicate will

---

[33] Thorsten Sellen, "Organized Crime: A Business Enterprise," *Annals*, Vol. 346 (May 1963), p. 7.

[34] Bernadette Carey, *op. cit.*, p. 132.

[35] Charles Grutzner, *op. cit.*, p. 17.

[36] *Ibid.*

[37] *Ibid.*

be down to get them out. If they are convicted, fines may be imposed, but jail terms are short.[38]

DIVISION OF THE PROCEEDS OF THE GAME. *Collectors* receive commissions on the numbers they bring in from players. Commissions are 25 percent, and if the collector desires to make a personal bet of a dollar, he gets the dollar bet for 75 cents. If a collector takes in $100 a day in bets, he turns over $75 to the controller and keeps $25.

The *controller,* after rounding up all the bets from the collectors, deducts 10 percent for himself as commission. He then turns the money and slips over to the bank.

The *bank* receives 65 percent of the money wagered. Out of this, the bank pays off the hits as well as the overhead of the operation including rent, graft, salaries to inside workers, bail bondsmen, lawyers and accountants.[39] The bank's lawyer is responsible for springing arrested collectors and pick-up men. Incidental expenditures of the bank includes handouts to hard-up players; entertaining players, collectors, and pick-up men at bars and restaurants; and contributions to charities.[40]

The profit which goes to the member of the Syndicate who owns the game is estimated at between 5 and 15 percent.[41] If the New York City gross is estimated at $200 million a year, then the profit is $10 to $30 million a year. If the national numbers game handle is estimated at $10 to $12 billion a year, a 5 to 15 percent profit would yield between $500 million to $1.8 billion to organized crime from this single enterprise.

EMPLOYMENT AND EARNINGS. The numbers game is a major factor in the economics of ghettoes all over the country.[42] Employment opportunities for the unskilled Negro in a ghetto are either limited or not available. The numbers game offers a poor boy the opportunity to earn a livelihood. He could start as a collector. If he knew some arithmetic and could operate an adding machine, he could be a controller. And if he had some administrative

---

[38] Fred Powledge, *op. cit.,* p. 156.
[39] D. Wakefield, *op. cit.,* pp. 25-26.
[40] John Scarne, *op. cit.,* p. 178.
[41] Fred Powledge, *op. cit.,* p. 147.
[42] Bernadette Carey, *op. cit.,* p. 134.

skill, perhaps he could be a banker. In the words of a numbers game operator in Harlem: "Harlem was the place with the heaviest concentration of numbers players. . . . Numbers is a way of life in Harlem and many, many people there make their living this way."[43]

One estimate for numbers game employment in New York City is 10,000 jobs.[44] Another estimate places the number of jobs at 100,000.[45] The true figure probably lies somewhere in-between but thousands of people earn their livelihood in the numbers game. An end to the numbers game would certainly mean a wave of unemployment.

Earnings estimates of the various classifications of personnel vary. Collectors have the largest proportion of jobs in the operation of the game. Collectors' incomes range from about $50 to $200 a week depending on the season (holidays are best); on the amount of regular trade built up; and on whether they are part-time or full-time on the job.[46] In a Ford plant in Detroit, a $100 a week employee earned another $1,000 a week soliciting numbers bets.[47]

The wife of a Syndicate leader who ran a numbers bank for her husband testified at a separation hearing that her husband drew between $1 million and $2 million a year out of it. She spoke freely about her husband's interests in narcotics, liquor, extortion, night clubs, and dog tracks he owned.[48]

One student of the operation in Harlem estimated that the criminal syndicate takes out $300,000 a week, or more than $15 million a year.[49] Another estimate places the money flow out of Harlem into the Syndicate as a result of the numbers game at $1 million a week.[50] Certainly, some part of the poverty of

[43] Quoted by Jack Roth, "Gamblers Operate Numbers Game in Open," *The New York Times* (May 7, 1967), p. 80.

[44] D. Wakefield, *op. cit.*, p. 25.

[45] John Scarne, *op. cit.*, p. 172.

[46] D. Wakefield, *op. cit.*, p. 25.

[47] John Scarne, *op. cit.*, p. 173.

[48] *Ibid.*, p. 42.

[49] Thomas A. Johnson, "Legality is Urged for Numbers Play," *The New York Times* (Dec. 18), 1966.

[50] Bernadette Carey, *op. cit.*, p. 134.

the slums is the result of an unfavorable balance of payments with more money leaving than coming in. The source of these monies is salaries, pensions, and relief checks of slum dwellers.

Lone operators of the game who die suddenly leave huge sums of cash. In February 1964, an effort to total a decedent's cash took shifts of officers twenty hours. They finally arrived at a figure of $763,233.30! In Jersey City, N.J., a few years ago, $2,400,000 in cash was found in the trunk of a car. After long debates on how to dispose of this money, in July 1965 it was decided to turn it over to the Internal Revenue Service.[51]

An estimate of the division of the national numbers handle is as follows:[52]

Item	Percent
Prize money to players	54
Salaries and operating expenses	36
Graft for politicians and police	5
Profit	5
Total	100

Taxes to the federal and state governments on the billions involved in the numbers game are zero.

Evaluation of the Numbers Operation

Several basic ideas must be considered in evaluating the numbers operation:

1. Illegal gambling flourishes because the *good* citizens support these activities. The national attitude has not changed since Prohibition days when the demand for liquor was supplied illegally.

Even though the numbers game is illegal in every state, including Nevada, the individual who wants to bet can always find a collector. In New York State, it is illegal to *accept* bets, but not to place bets.[53]

2. The billions of dollars generated by the numbers game

---

[51] Bernadette Carey, *op. cit.*, p. 132.
[52] John Scarne, *op. cit.*, p. 165.
[53] State of New York, *Revised Penal Law*, "*Gambling Offenses,*" Article 225, pp. 127-129, effective Sept. 1, 1967.

and controlled by the Syndicate are bypassing the nation's tax flows and legitimate channels of investment. The members of the Syndicate and the employees of the game who receive their wages and salaries from this illegal source do not report such income, and pay no income taxes, thus increasing their relative incomes and decreasing government revenues, making taxes higher for income-earners in legitimate activities.

3. A significant share of numbers game money is used to bribe dishonest policemen and dishonest politicians. This corruption and compromise of the principles of clean government destroys respect for law and order, encourages juvenile delinquency, and undermines the foundations of our democracy.

4. Enforcement of laws against illegal gambling, particularly the numbers game, requires large expenditures of public funds. Hundreds of policemen are required daily to combat the game. To this cost must be added the cost of police supervisors, administrative costs of city, state, and federal agencies concerned with this problem, court costs to prosecute offenders, and costs for incarceration when required. Government costs amount to tens of millions of dollars in a venture which is not entirely successful.

5. The operators of the numbers game use the tremendous profits for other criminal activities. The cash generated by this illegal game finds its way into many other illegal activities including narcotics and loansharking. In addition, the huge earnings are infiltrating legitimate businesses which, like contracting, could still result in cheating the public. For example, inferior materials may be used. Some syndicate truckers are known to have eliminated competition and then raised rates.

6. The numbers game has been legislated against as an evil. As such, this interpretation is contrary to the desires and beliefs of the people who play the game. It is a conflict between what man is and what some people believe he ought to be.

The attitude of the poor people who participate in this daily source of hope may be summed up in the following: "Nobody bothers about the rich racetrack guys or the big shots who play the stock market. They call them sportsmen and financiers. They are *society*. When we bet on something, we're criminals."[54]

---

[54] Quoted by Bernadette Carey, *op. cit.*, p. 134.

7. The thousands and thousands of ordinary, decent people who play the numbers game are often unaware and unconcerned that the bets they place support a Syndicate consisting of some, of the worst elements in American society. The average American is amused by the existence of the underworld, and does not think of it as a blemish on American culture.

The President of the National Council on Crime and Delinquency pointed out recently that if we retain the anti-gambling laws ". . . organized crime will, in ten or fifteen years, amass at least one half a trillion dollars."[55]

A. U.S. Justice Department attorney stated:

> All the country's rackets are organized. They are run by Syndicates . . . the top criminals in the country who have some agreement as to territory. They are connected. They cooperate with each other in carrying on their illegal activities and unify against forces of the law. Policy helps finance it all.[56]

STATUS OF GAMBLING IN THE UNITED STATES. New York State and about twenty-five other states have legalized pari-mutuel betting at racetracks. New York State voters approved pari-mutuel betting at racetracks in November 1939.

New York State and some other states have legalized bingo, while some states tolerate the game even though it is illegal under antilottery laws. The voters of New York State approved bingo games in November 1957 for ". . . religious, charitable, and similar non-profit organizations."

Two states have legalized lotteries to raise revenues for educational needs, New Hampshire since 1964, and New York since June 1967 after approval by the voters in November 1966.

In New York State, in addition to current efforts to legalize off-track betting, an Assemblyman from Harlem, Charles Rangel, proposed a bill in the State Legislature which would authorize a study of the feasibility of legalizing the numbers game. The Assemblyman claims that legalization would, first, stop what he calls police-criminal collusion in slum areas, and, second, provide needed revenue for community improvement. Mr. Rangel said:

---

[55] Carl M. Loeb, Jr., "Anti-Gambling Laws Opposed," (Letters to Editor), *The New York Times* (July 14, 1968).

[56] Quoted in Bernadette Carey, *op. cit.*, p. 134.

". . . the profits could be made to work for the good of the community in hospitals, for nursing homes, and educational centers."[57]

Several gambling laws were approved in New York State by the 1970 session of the Legislature and signed by Governor Nelson Rockefeller.

1. New York State's 1966 lottery law was amended to stimulate lagging sales. The amendments permit the state to operate the lottery more frequently than once a month; to increase the prize pool; to reduce the $1 ticket price to as low as twenty-five cents; to sell tickets through vending machines; and permit sales of lottery tickets in bars and liquor stores.

2. In another action, New York State legalized off-track betting. Two laws were approved. One creates the New York State Off-Track Pari-Mutuel Betting Commission whose function is to regulate the local option plans of participating municipalities, or to directly operate the local plan through its own employees and facilities if a municipality requests it. The law requires a referendum in localities planning to set up the betting system. Since a November 1963 referendum in New York City approved the principle of legalizing off-track betting by a 3 to 1 margin, New York City is allowed to proceed with its plans without conducting a new vote.

The second off-track betting law creates a public benefit corporation known as the New York City Off-Track Betting Corporation to be administered by a board of directors consisting of five members appointed by the Mayor. In early July Mayor John Lindsay appointed Howard J. Samuels as chairman of the city's new Corporation and named the four other members. These positions are unsalaried. The Corporation planned to open at least 1,000 off-track betting windows in 100 wagering parlors within a year. Wagers accepted from patrons are recorded and transmitted by computers to the pari-mutuel pools at harness and flat tracks in New York State as well as at some tracks outside New York State.

Revenues for both the state and city will be derived from a 17 percent tax on harness track bets and a 16 percent tax on thoroughbred track bets. The city will receive 80 percent of the

---

[57] Thomas A. Johnson, *op. cit.*

tax money and the state 20 percent. When the city's revenues go over $200 million, the split will be 50-50.

3. Another law established a New York State Quarter Horse Racing Commission which has been authorized to set up pari-mutuel betting at licensed quarter horse race meetings. Quarter horses are a cross between the American mustang and the thoroughbreds. They are well-known for their ability to run a quarter-mile at high speed, 21 or 22 seconds. Quarter horse races are held on a quarter-mile straightaway.

A spot check of players, collectors, and policemen has resulted in a consensus that the illegal numbers game will remain un-affected by the state's latest efforts. Those individuals who play the numbers game apparently are seeking daily action at low cost; enjoy the convenience of having the collector seek out the player to pick up the daily bet; and prefer the nontaxable nature of winnings.

STATUS OF GAMBLING IN OTHER COUNTRIES. France, Britain, Sweden, other European countries, Australia, New Zealand, and Puerto Rico have government-operated gambling services. Some have lotteries that are very similar to the numbers game. In France, for example, a system of off-track betting, called *Tierce,* was initiated in 1954. Bettors must pick the win, place and show horses in a designated Sunday race at one of the French tracks. Bets are placed in government-operated off-track pari-mutuel booths. In 1966, the French spent $680 million on *Tierce* of which the French Treasury's share was $160 million. The earn-ings of *Tierce* are equal to two thirds of the earnings of the Renault automobile works, indicating the popularity of the game with the average Frenchman.[58]

The statement of the head of the French lottery is relevant. He says:

> "Traditional morality condemns gambling. It is not the function of the State to exploit its citizens' taste for gambling. But on a practical level, a State which prohibits gambling will see it taken

---

[58] Sanche de Gramont, "How to Play a Lottery," *New York Times* Magazine (May 7, 1967).

over by organized crime. Thus, the State is forced to control and participate in this most culpable form of gain."[59]

Conclusions and Recommendations

Conclusions

1. In the last analysis, gambling thrives because a large proportion of people enjoys betting of all kinds. These people see no harm in gambling, and do not regard it as immoral even though our society has declared it illegal. As long as this attitude prevails, and there is no reason to expect it to change, effective enforcement of antigambling laws is impossible.

2. Government operation of gambling would make a significant inroad into the economic resources of organized crime. The government's entry into gambling would cut the Syndicate's profits which today are unreported and therefore untaxed.

3. Antigambling laws and their resultant, organized crime, have created a major source of bribery, political corruption, and evasion of law.

4. Government operation of gambling would pose many new technical and administrative problems, but these must be isolated and solved, since today's illegal gambling in our nation is not being successfully curtailed.

Recommendation

Government should organize and operate the numbers game as a public service, and should compete with the Syndicate by offering better odds. If the odds of the game are 600-to-1 for a straight number, the government should offer 750-to-1. The profits of the operation could be used to provide a variety of projects and services in the nation's slums which provide the primary source of income for the game. While government operation and control may eliminate a significant portion of corruption, it may bring in its wake a host of new problems.

Perhaps a thorough study and evaluation of foreign experience could help to pinpoint the problems and discover those areas of operation which may be adjusted to fit American requirements.

[59] *Ibid.*

COMPUTATION OF THE WINNING NUMBER*

In the numbers game's most popular form, a player chooses any three-digit number from 000 through 999. The player thus has one chance in 1,000 of winning. In New York City, a winner is paid off at advertised odds of 500 to 1 in some games, 600 to 1 in others. *Betting* on numbers is not an offense under the penal law, but the *operation* of a numbers game is.

The winning number is determined by betting totals or payoff odds on selected races at horse racing tracks. Belmont or Aqueduct results are used during their season. At other times of the year, those of Florida's Hialeah or Maryland's Pimlico and Bowie are used. Since the tracks are closed on Sunday, numbers are played six days a week.

Two systems are used to determine the winner. The "Brooklyn" number is simply the last three digits of the track's total pari-mutuel handle for the day.

The more widely used "New York" number is more complicated and combines the payoff odds for win, place and show horses in the first seven races. The first digit is calculated after the third race, the second after the fifth race and the last after the seventh. For this reason, betting the New York number is sometimes called playing "3-5-7" (See Fig. 4-1).

The New York number was introduced because bettors feared that operators might be able to fix the simpler Brooklyn number. But the New York number also makes possible two variations of the standard bet:

Bolida, a wager on the first two or the last two digits of the final winning number.

Single Action, a separate bet on each digit as it is calculated.

---

* Reprinted from the Fund for the City of New York in its report, *Legal Gambling in New York: A Discussion of Numbers and Sports Betting,* 1972, pp. 20-21. Used with permission.

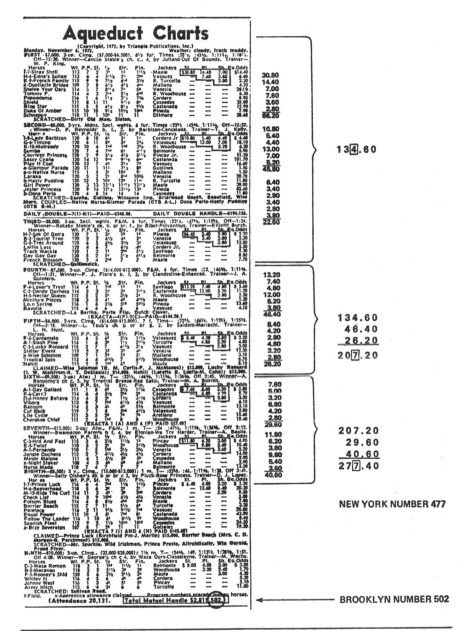

Figure 4-1. The winning number is based on horse race results.

A Model for a Legal Numbers Lottery in the District of Columbia*

Despite information available from the police and other sources on the structure and operation of illegal numbers, designing a legal game that can successfully compete is problematic. Legal numbers exists nowhere, and without an operating model to watch and evaluate, any design for a legal game must be tentative and experimental.

Nevertheless, the case for experimentation is strong. The flow of great profits from illegal gambling to criminals grows each year and the cycle of official corruption continues. The prohibitionist policy, aimed at moral evil, and a psychology of excess has fostered more wickedness and error than ever derived from gambling itself.[60] A new approach should be given a chance.

> No more prohibitions should be made than are absolutely necessary. . . . As a general principle the criminal law must not be lightly invoked; and the evils which result from any prohibition, however desirable the object aimed at, must be set in the balance against the evil which it is sought to diminish. *Final Report: Royal Commission on Lotteries and Betting*, p. 68 (1933).

Fortunately, the experiment proposed need not be a shot in the dark. Two recent events will help avoid imprudent choices. The State of New Jersey now operates a daily lottery with fifty cent tickets. Although this game differs in some important respects from the illegal numbers lottery, its design and its experience will be helpful in modelling a legal numbers lottery. The second event of importance is the publication of a study by the Fund for the City of New York† which proposed a model

---

* Reprinted from the Washington Lawyers' Committee for Civil Rights Under Law in its report, *Legalized Numbers in Washington*, Carl R. Fogelberg, Project Director, 1973, pp. 46-64. Used with permission.

[60] Noting that experiments with prohibition have often brought the law into disrepute and multiplied the evils the law sought to control, the 1932 Royal Commission on Lotteries and Betting warned against the continuation of the policy:

† The Fund is a tax-exempt foundation established in 1968 by the Ford Foundation. It operates independently of Ford and of the City of New York to which it provides a consulting service on questions of public importance.

for a competitive legal numbers game to be run in New York City. Again, despite some important differences between numbers in New York and Washington, the Fund model, a product of a careful and extensive (and expensive) analysis, will provide an excellent reference for our efforts.

First purposes will determine the design of the game. States that operate lotteries do so to raise badly needed revenues,[61] not to attack organized crime. Their prize structure, frequency, ticket prices, and system of distribution look nothing like the games people are playing illegally. The state-run games exist beside illegal operations; one does not affect the other. For example, a market analysis done for the New Jersey Lottery Commission describes their lottery customers as white, middle-income and middle-educated, i.e. high school or above. Business has not been good where numbers is popular.[62] Thus, the decision to run a lottery as a revenue raiser meant new bettors and little impact on the illegal game.[63]

There are strong reasons for adopting other first purposes. The chance that a legal numbers lottery may seriously damage the profitability of the illegal game and reduce the social costs attributed to it, instructs another design.

A General Outline

The D.C. lottery should be a daily game. It should allow players to select their own number and bet small amounts; a fifty cent ticket would be a good starting point. Betting locations should be numerous and convenient to the game's players, and

---

[61] *Council of State Governments*, p. 1. Demand for public services and taxpayers' resistance to higher levies, have encouraged many states to examine the revenue-raising potential of lotteries. "State government expenditures exceeded revenue from all sources for the first time in more than a decade in 1971 according to the U.S. Bureau of the Census." *Ibid.*

[62] This information is derived from a *Market Analysis Summary of the New Jersey State Lottery, 1971-72*, prepared by the Automated Wagering Division of Control Data Corp. (1973).

[63] In addition, many states have been dissatisfied with the revenue raising powers of their lotteries. Few have met the levels of profits predicted for them. *Report of the New Jersey State Lottery Planning Commission*, p. 3 (1970) and *Council of State Governments*, pp. 16-17.

payoffs should be made promptly. These are the essential and most appealing features of the illegal game. To compete with it and to damage it, the D.C. lottery must either duplicate them or offset their appeal with attractive features of its own. All that can be done without much difficulty, as will be explained shortly. But the key to successful competition will be the size of the legal game's payoffs.

The Payoff

The illegal game returns in prizes only about half of what it takes in bets.* A D.C. lottery can do much better; it could return 80 percent or more in payoffs, i.e. payoff winners at the rate of $800 for each $1 bet.† The failure of the illegal game to return more to players derives not only from the greed and inefficiency of its operators but from the necessity to cut heavily played numbers and to protect itself by bribing public officials. A legal game would not cut numbers; payoffs would be fixed at 800 to 1.[64]

> At an annual value of $100,000,000, 68 percent of the time the payoff will be between 71 percent and 79 percent of the handle; 95 percent of the time the payoff will be between 67 percent and 83 percent of the handle; 99.7 percent of the time the payoff will be between 62 percent and 88 percent of the handle and only once in 20 years would the government expect to have to return more than 90 percent (break even) of the money wagered. Section IV.

Even if estimates of the illegal take are only 50 percent accurate, this means that a D.C. lottery, for every 10 percent

---

* Payoff rates vary for a variety of reasons. Heavily played numbers may be "cut" i.e. the payoff is reduced by an operator who fears great losses should such a popular number also win. Some players with special or friendly relationships with the game's operator may get higher payoffs—as high as 800 to 1 have been reported. But this is rare. The economics of the illegal game dictate lower payoffs.

† The *Fund Report* argues that an 825 to 1 payoff is feasible for a legal game.

[64] A report by the New York City Off-Track Betting Corp. entitled *Legalized Numbers: A Plan to Operate a Legal Numbers Game Now* (1973), hereinafter "OTB Report." The OTB Report, Section IV, provides a mathematical analysis explaining the fixed odds payoff and the probabilities assumed by the free selection of numbers:

of the illegal business it can seize, could return well over $3 million per year more than the illegal game.*

These calculations discuss only the return in prizes, or payoffs to the community of bettors. Where profits go is also of interest. It is estimated that a legal lottery, paying off at 800 to 1, and operated as will be described, can achieve about 10 percent in profits.† Rather than financing other criminal activity, as profits from illegal gambling often do,‡ profits from the legal game can be applied to projects of importance to the community.[65]

High payoffs will also help offset a major attraction of the illegal game. Numbers winnings are seldom reported on the tax return of the game's customers. The 800 to 1 payoff promised by the legal game would offer players bigger prizes than the illegal game, *even after taxes.*** Under federal law, players

---

* Assuming this 50 percent accuracy, the gross receipts for the illegal game would total $183 million. While an illegal game, paying off at 600 to 1 would return $109 million in payoffs, a legal lottery that totally supplanted the illegal game and paid off at 800 to 1, would return $145 million to players. Hence, for every 10 percent of the illegal business the D.C. lottery can take away, about $3.6 million more would be returned by the legal one. Since the illegal game cuts numbers and deducts 10 percent from winnings, the 600 to 1 rate used here is too high, meaning the $3.6 million figure is at least 10 percent too low.

† The Fund model, paying off at 825 to 1, estimates profits at 7 percent while the Hudson Institute and OTB models predict 10 to 15 percent profits with slightly lower payoff odds.

‡ Law enforcement officials note that an interdependence exists among rackets. An individual arrested on gambling charges, for example, was found to be free on an appeal bond from a major narcotics trafficking conviction in another state. In another case, a large narcotics wholesaler was also participating in gambling operations.

[65] The legislation creating the New Hampshire and New York lotteries directs expenditure of profits on state education. The New Jersey Lottery Act earmarks its profits for state education and state institutions, e.g. prisons. Massachusetts law provides for the return of profits to communities in the form of municipal grants for special projects. Pennsylvania lottery profits are allocated exclusively for property tax relief to the elderly *Council of State Governments,* pp. 17-18. It has also been suggested that the profits from legal numbers be used to combat another source of organized crime's wealth—loansharking. Numbers profits would be used to fund a "community based low interest high risk loan facility" to compete for the business of the usurer. Ianni Testimony, Appendix D, p. 32.

** This was checked out by accountants for individuals in various tax brackets.

determine tax liability on the gambling activity by subtracting their losses from their winnings. A positive difference during the tax period is counted among the player's taxable income for that period. The *Fund Report* demonstrated that players in a legal numbers game, "who diligently report their winnings, would usually realize a higher net prize after taxes in the legal game than (they) now do in the untaxed, illegal game." In fact, the *Fund* added, "Only for a player earning taxable income of more than $25,000 does the present game offer an advantage over a legal one."[66]

Illegal numbers, contrary to popular mythology, is not a very efficient business. Its illegality dictates expenditures which would not be duplicated by the legal game. Costs relating to the protection† an illegal game must have, and the 35 percent commissions paid to the runners and collectors would not be incurred by a legal operation. The promise of higher profits in a legal game can be fulfilled, but it is a promise that must be kept if the legal lottery is to undermine the appeal and success of the illegal game.

Paying off at a fixed rate of 800 to 1 leaves open the statistical possibility that the legal game could lose money during any given period.‡ But this possibility should not deter the experiment. There are numerous methods of insuring against losses, and legislative hearings can produce the technical information necessary to decide which would best serve the purposes of the

---

[66] *Ibid.* It should also be noted that the federal tax laws require a report to IRS on payments of over $600. The *OTB Report* points out that, since the maximum payoff in a legal game would be well under $600 on a single bet (a fifty cent ticket in a legal game would return $400 where the payoff was 800 to 1), there would be no need to file a report with the IRS.

† These include not just payments to corrupt officials but the cost of protective devices from flash paper to safes and weaponry. The *Fund Report* estimates that illegal profits are reduced 25 percent by the cost of protection. See Kaplan and Maher, *Economics of the Numbers Game.* The authors estimate a 50 percent reduction in profits for this reason.

‡ The *Hudson Report* states that some Las Vegas casinos "have had gambling losses for as long as a month." But, says the Institute: "The legal system should be permitted to use any actuarially sound and safe game even if it is not guaranteed to win each and every day (or every event). The betting authority ought to be allowed to rely on the law of averages." pp. 14-15.

legal game.§ It is stressed, however, that the maintenance of fixed odds payoffs as a competitive feature is an important goal. Especially at the outset, when the legal game is seeking customers from the illicit numbers market, the straightforward fixed odds payoff would not confuse bettors or be looked upon with suspicion as might a more complicated but statistically safer method.

After this initial period when competition with the illegal game will be most intense, experiments with more complex prize structures and payoff systems could be undertaken. For example, intermediate prizes might be awarded to those who pick two out of three winning numbers, and payoffs might be made pari-mutuelly.[67] But a legal lottery designed to compete with the game run by criminal organizations must not only offer better payoffs, it must satisfy the customers' demand for entertainment and convenience.

Number Selection

The power to select the number on which to bet is like the power to touch the wheel of fortune, the power to manufacture luck—or so it seems. You pick not just any number. You think about it, worry on it, consult sources. A legal lottery in the District, if it is not merely to create a new class of bettors, must incorporate this feature of the numbers game.

The legal game should also offer the same betting opportunities. Bettors should be able to play one, two or three numbers, or any of the combined and exotic bets accepted by the illegal game.[68] That's entertainment. And if the legal game doesn't provide it, the criminal organization will.

---

§ The *Fund Report*, p. 64, discusses four possibiilties:

1. Establish an upper limit to total payout, with prizes fixed pari-mutuelly when that limit is exceeded.

2. Fix an upper limit, but pay winners the excess (up to the normal prize) in scrip that can be used for future wagers.

3. Purchase insurance from commercial insurers.

4. Set aside a reserve fund large enough to serve as a self-insurance pool.

[67] *Hudson Report, op. cit.,* pp. 13-14.

[48] In the illegal game, players can bet on the first digit (this is called "single action"), on the first two digits (called "bolida") or bet on any combination of the three digits. For example, a player may choose 456 as the

There is also good reason to determine the winning number in the same manner as the illegal game. A study of the present system has affirmed its randomness; no unnecessary risk would be assumed.[69] The community of bettors would also be less likely to view the legal game with suspicion. They can continue to check the winning number in their newspapers, and more easily contrast the payoffs in the legal game with those in the illegal one. In addition, by continuing to determine the winning numbers from the betting on horse races a federal excise tax of 10 percent on gross receipts can be avoided.*

The Price

Surveys of the betting habits of New York City residents have reported that the most popular numbers bet is between fifty

---

winner and bet on any combination of those numbers. The payoff odds for each type of bet vary, of course, with the probabilities each bet faces. See Lasswell and McKeena, *op. cit.* A design for a manually completed lottery ticket is suggested in the *OTB Report*, Appendix B, Figure 2. It would be printed on "mark sense" paper, and thus allow the completed form to be recorded by a computer terminal equipped with an optical reader. Once the bet is transmitted to the computer, a ticket would be automatically printed by a machine connected to the terminal. A less sophisticated but cheaper system could be devised on the basis of the French Tierce pari-mutuel tickets which are sold by licensed retailers. Bets are made by punching holes in the ticket through the number of the horse or horses selected. A hole punch also indicates whether the bet is straight or in combination. Tickets are sold during the morning hours on the day of the race. Copies of the completed forms are then delivered to a central location, and there, after the results of the race are known, winers are determined manually by passing the tickets over spindles which sort out the losing tickets.

---

[69] *OTB Report*, Section IV.

* The Internal Revenue Code requires payment of a 10 percent excise tax (26 U.S.C. § 4401) on all wagers accepted by a legal lottery, if the game does not come within one of the Code's exemptions. (See, 26 U.S.C. § 4402). The Code exempts lottery wagers where "the ultimate winners . . . are determined by the results of a horse race." (26 U.S.C. § 4402(3)(b)). This section has been construed to exempt lottery bets dependent upon the amount of money wagered on horse races as well as the results of the races. The New Jersey lottery and others take advantage of this construction and utilize the betting totals on horse races in the selection of their winning tickets.

cents and one dollar.[70] There is no similar study on local betting habits, but D.C. police officials, familiar with the local numbers scene, have stated to the Lawyers' Committee that the results of these New York surveys could be duplicated in Washington.

The experience of the New Jersey lottery instructs that low minimum bets are to be preferred. Not only has the New Jersey's games' popularity spread since the introduction of the fifty cent ticket, its revenues have soared and some lottery officials are now claiming that inroads into the illegal numbers market are being made.[71]

Frequency

The head of the Justice Department's Organized Crime Strike Force in New England has commented that "a lottery to have any substantial impact on the illegal numbers business would need a drawing every day."[72] The illegal game opens for business Monday through Saturday. The legal game should do the same.[*]

Distribution System

It is easy to bet a number. The shop steward comes around before the coffee break; the secretarial pool keeps a line open

---

[70] The *OTB Report* concluded that "The typical numbers player currently wagers on the game between two and four times a week. Market research shows that the average daily wager on numbers is $.90." *OTB Report*, Section II. An Oliver Quayle survey done for the *Fund Report* concluded that the most popular bet per day was one dollar. "Relatively few (19%) say they usually bet less; nearly half report they usually bet more than a dollar on the days they play." *Fund Report*, Appendix, p. 16.

[71] Even before the introduction of the fifty cent New Jersey Lottery ticket, Ralph Batch, director of that State's Lottery, estimated a 15 percent drop in illegal numbers receipts statewide, with a 40 to 50 percent reduction in the illegal business in some locations. *New York Times*, September 22, 1971, p. 94.

[72] *The Washington Post*, November 25, 1972, p. A-3.

[*] This does not appear to be too difficult to do. The New York, Pennsylvania and New Jersey lotteries sell their fifty cent tickets daily, except Sunday. *Council of State Governments, op. cit.*, p. 14. However, these state lotteries do not involve daily lottery drawings, but rather daily sales of weekly lottery tickets. The size of the District of Columbia, the relative homogeneity of its numbers playing public, and the ease with which the illegal numbers operators can meet their deadlines, suggest that a legal game in D.C. could reproduce the same operation. Throughout France, collections of wagers, made in Le Havre to Corsica, are delivered to central locations for processing within a few hours.

until the first race; add a dollar to your bill at the local grocer's. In all, there are probably two to three thousand people in D.C. who will write down any three digit number you want to bet. The illegal game is convenient to its players. The attraction of high payoffs may make it unnecessary for the legal game to provide equal convenience, but its services must be competitive.

The systems of distribution in use, by both legal and illegal gambling operations, can quickly be outlined:

a. Licensed Retailers—

Most of the state operated lotteries rely upon this system. New Jersey, for example, licenses small retail store owners, who receive a 5 percent commission on the tickets they sell.† N.J. Lottery tickets are available throughout the state at counters in over 3,000 news stands, supermarkets, restaurants, bars, etc. Winning tickets are presented to N.J. motor vehicle offices where a claim form is completed and forwarded to the state lottery office for final validation and payment.

b. Machine Outlets—

Although no automated vending machines, allowing players to select their own number, are currently available, plans for such a system are being developed by OTB in New York.‡ New Jersey is using over 500 computer-linked vending machines to sell its fifty cent lottery tickets but these are not equipped to permit number selection by the players.[73]

c. Lottery Offices—

The Off-Track Betting Corporation in New York City utilizes this system. It has established over 100 offices throughout the city, each connected to a central computer which records all bets and validates winning tickets.

d. Runners—

A legal numbers game could adopt the system used by the illegal game and employ, on commission, its own runners or collectors.

---

† *Council of State Governments, op. cit.,* p. 14. Agents pick up their tickets for the week at over 700 commercial banking outlets throughout the state, pay for the tickets sold during the preceding week and receive credit for those unsold.

‡ *OTB Report,* Section IV. The Automated Wagering Division of Control Data Corporation will demonstrate, within a year, a computer terminal with a keyboard similar to that on touchtone telephones. The device will be equipped with a printout machine and will allow for the selection of numbers. Agents for the legal lottery would then purchase such a terminal, at a cost estimated between two and three thousand dollars.

[73] *Council of State Governments, op. cit.,* p. 14.

Discussion

The choice of system need not be exclusive; a combination of all four may upon further examination turn out to be the best. But, as an initial network, licensed retail stores would be easiest. Aside from their technical inadequacy, the cost of installing vending machines would be prohibitive especially during the games' early stages.** Likewise, separate lottery offices would mean the creation of large salaried staffs and larger overhead costs than a successful operation need allow. Without a rapid, probably computerized, system of collecting wagers, lottery offices might become crowded with impatient bettors who will return to the illegal game rather than wait in line.

It is also unlikely that lottery offices could come close to providing the number of betting outlets provided by the illegal game. In New York, it is estimated that between 10,000 and 15,000 persons are employed by illegal numbers, most of whom collect bets.[74] The legal game should be as available to its players as the competition.*

With regard to the adoption of the illegal system, i.e. employment of the present games runners and collectors, a few points should be emphasized. First, the legal game could not pay its runners and collectors the 35 percent commission received by their counterparts in the illegal game and still maintain the high 800 to 1 payoff.† Second, many runners are engaged in other criminal activities. They receive an income from numbers, but it is only a part of their earnings:

> One of the fundamental characteristics of the existing operation
> is the relationship of the runners to other types of criminal activity

---

** The necessary security and maintenance of the vending machines would also enhance the costs of this system.

[74] *OTB Report,* Section VII.

* There is no evidence that numbers will continue to be preferred by Washington people who play games. Numbers may be replaced just as it replaced the policy wheel. Establishing a network of offices to run a legal numbers game may award it more permanency than is warranted.

† The *OTB Report* suggests an alternative. Lower payoffs are to be awarded those who wish to bet with OTB runners rather than at an OTB office. The OTB runner would receive the 15 percent deducted from the winner's payoff. *OTB Report,* Section IV.

. . . Typically, the runner is the easiest contact with crime for ordinary citizens. An ordinary citizen who wants to use crime or the criminal organization may establish his contact by working through his numbers runner.[75]

The services provided by the runner-collector are exaggerated such that the legal game's higher payoffs may nullify their attractiveness. Surveys of numbers bettors and information provided by the police countradict the widespread belief that the runner-collector provides more than pick-up service for the illegal wagers. Credit is extended to few players, and other services, low interest loans, for example, are even more rare.[76]

D.C. police have estimated that there are at least 2,000 runner-collectors operating in the city. If legal numbers successfully competes with the illegal game, these runner-collectors will be out of their illicit jobs. Aside from the economic effects on a community which finds itself with 2,000 more persons unemployed, other negative consequences may follow. Some runner-collectors may transfer their attention to other criminal activities which may be more dangerous than numbers running—narcotics traffic, robbery, loansharking, for example. Some may choose to remain in the business and fight the legal competition with violence and intimidation.[77] To avoid such evils, legalization of numbers must provide for the runner-collector.

The use of runners and collectors in the legal game need not be ruled out. "To the extent that [they] are now providing a service to bettors . . . they will be able to sell such services after the legal game is established."[78] To the extent that they are employable elsewhere, the community should assist them in providing legitimate opportunities.

Licensing local retailers promise the least difficulty and offers some distinct advantages over other systems of distribution:

1. A network of outlets for the legal game could be quickly established without swelling government payrolls with a new kind

---

[75] *Hudson Report, op. cit.,* p. 11.
[76] *Fund Report, op. cit.,* p. 26.
[77] Lasswell and McKenna, *op. cit.,* p. 228.
[78] *Hudson Report, op. cit.,* p. 78.

of bureaucrat and without the enormous costs of setting up separate betting offices.

2. It would insure the return of an additional 5 percent of the games' revenues to the community in the form of commissions to local shop owners.*

3. The number of betting outlets, and so the convenience of the game to its players, would compare with the illegal system.

Control

A legal numbers lottery in the District could be run through private franchises or by public corporations or by the city government itself. The history of privately run lotteries is scandalous (see Chap. 1, above); that mistake should not be repeated. Between the public corporation and the city government, the choice is more difficult and less guided by experience. Nevertheless, the state lotteries and OTB in New York provide examples of each choice.

State lotteries are controlled by state agencies. The New Jersey Lottery Commission is a division of that State's Department of the Treasury. In New York, the lottery is run by its State Department of Taxation and Finance. New Hampshire's, Connecticut's and Maryland's lotteries are run by independent agencies. A bipartisan lottery board or commission, with a policy-making role, is usually appointed by the governor or legislature or both. Day-to-day operations are left to salaried directors and staff.

Off-track betting in New York City is controlled by a tax-exempt "public benefit corporation" whose officers are appointed by the Mayor.[79] OTB possesses all the powers of a private

---

* The 80 percent return in payoffs to bettors, plus this 5 percent commission to local licensers, far outdistances the illegal game's return of dollars to the community. In addition, the 10 percent profit from the legal game would be returned to the community, to support educational, housing and medical improvements or, as suggested above, to fund a "community based low interest high risk loan facility."

[79] OTB has a Board of Directors composed of five unsalaried members, each appointed by the Mayor, "two of the five may be public officers of the city and serve at the Mayor's pleasure; the other three are appointed by the Mayor for six-year terms and are removable by the Mayor for cause." *Council of State Governments*, p. 22.

corporation, but it is required to report to the Comptrollers of the State and City governments on its operation.

Since the primary purpose of legalizing numbers is to damage or destroy the profitability of the illegal game, the organization of the legal numbers lottery should reflect its competitive purposes. It must not only inspire the trust and confidence of people who now bet with the illegal game, but it must also succeed as a business in a highly competitive market. A public corporation can best meet these standards. Its officers would be selected by public officials,* its books open to and reviewed by government auditors, but more important, it would act as a private corporation, quickly and with a flexibility unfamiliar in government.† A public corporation will also be more remote from city hall politics and the danger that its law enforcement purposes might be subverted by other political considerations. Finally, a public corporation, unlike a government agency, could disappear —go out of business—if the public's appetite for lotteries subsided at some time in the future.**

BIBLIOGRAPHY

Books

Allen, David D.: *The Nature of Gambling.* New York, Coward-McCann, 1952.

---

* The implementing legislation should require a bipartisan board which represents a variety of private and official points of view, from those of the police to those of the community of bettors. Popular election of some or all of the board members might also be considered.

† Prior to the New Jersey experiment, state lotteries disappointed many of their supporters with unexpectedly low profits. Most of the blame has been attributed to the governmental rather than businesslike approach of their administrators. The enabling legislation for the New Jersey Lottery took account of this problem and awarded decision-making powers which rival those of private corporations to its lottery commission.

** It is not unrealistic to suppose that the public might lose interest in this form of entertainment. The New Jersey Lottery was selling tbout six million tickets per week during its initial phases; it is now down to about three million per week. In this connection, we suggest that the legislation establishing the legal lottery provide that the legislation establishing the legal lottery provide for its disappearance. Once its law enforcement objectives have been accomplished and public support for lotteries wanes, the legal lottery should be prohibited by its enabling legislation from promoting itself in perpetuity.

Allen, Edward J.: *Merchants of Menace.* Springfield, Thomas, 1962.

Asbury, Herbert: *Sucker's Progress.* New York, Dodd, 1938.

Bell, Daniel: *The End of Ideology* (Rev. ed.) New York, Free Press, 1962.

Bergler, Edmund: *The Psychology of Gambling.* New York, Hill, 1957.

Block, Herbert A.: *Crime in America.* New York, Philos Lib, 1961.

Danforth, Harold R. and Horan, James D.: *The D.A.'s Man.* New York, Crown, 1957.

Dineen, Joseph F.: *Underworld U.S.A.* New York, Farrar, 1956.

Drake, St. Clair and Cayton, Horace R.: Policy: Poor man's roulette. *Black Metropolis.* New York, Harper, 1962, Vol. II, Chap. 17, pp. 470-494.

Drzazga, John: Policy or numbers game. *Wheels of Fortune.* Springfield, Thomas, 1963, Chap. 6, pp. 138-162.

Egen, Frederick W.: *Plainclothesman.* New York, Arco, 1959.

Elliot, Mabel A.: *Crime in Modern Society.* New York, Harper, 1956.

Frasca, Dom.: *King of Crime.* New York, Crown, 1959.

Horan, James D.: *The Mob's Man.* New York, Crown, 1959.

Ianni, Francis A. J.: *Black Mafia.* New York, Simon & Schuster, 1974.

The Kefauver Committee Report on Organized Crime. New York, Didier, 1951.

Lasswell, Harold D.: *The Impact of Organized Crime on an Inner City Community.* New York, The Policy Sciences Center, Inc., 1972.

Lerner, Max: *America as a Civilization.* New York, Simon & Schuster, 1957.

Martin, Raymond V.: *Revolt in the Mafia.* New York, Duell, 1963.

New York City Off-Track Betting Corporation: *A Plan to Operate a Legal Numbers Game Now.* New York, 1973.

New York State Commission of Investigation: *Syndicated Gambling in New York.* Albany, New York, February 1961.

Peterson, Virgil W.: *Gambling—Should It Be Legalized?* Springfield, Thomas, 1951.

President's Commission on Law Enforcement and Administration of Justice: *The Challenge of Crime in a Free Society.* Washington, D.C., Government Printing Office, 1967.

Reiss, Albert J., Jr.: *The Police and the Public.* New Haven, Yale U Pr, 1971.

Rubenstein, Jonathan: *City Police.* New York, Farrar, 1973.

Scarne, John: *Scarne's Complete Guide to Gambling.* New York, Simon and Schuster, 1961.

Turkus, Burton B. and Feder, Sid: *Murder Inc.* New York, Farrar, 1951.

Tyler, Gus (Ed.): *Organized Crime in America.* Ann Arbor, Mich., U of Mich Pr, 1962.

United States Senate: Special Senate Committee to Investigate Organized Crime in Interstate Commerce (The Kefauver Committee). *Final Report, 82nd Congress, 1st Session, Report No. 725,* 1951.

Van Cise, Philip S.: *Fighting the Underworld.* New York, Houghton, 1936.

Articles

Bigness and badness need to be studied. *Time,* January 13, 1967.

Blanche, Ernest E.: Gambling odds are gimmicked. *Annals, 269:* May 1950.

Brooks, T. R.: Numbers the game that only mobsters win. *Reader's Digest, 91:* September 1967.

Cook, Fred J.: The Black Mafia moves into the numbers racket. *The New York Times Magazine,* Section 6, April 4, 1971.

Carey, Bernadette: Two bit bet: Financing a crime empire. *Look, 25:* December 14, 1965.

Day, John I.: Horse racing and the pari-mutuel. *Annals, 269:* May 1950.

Five seized in raid on Anastasia's ILA Brooklyn headquarters on charges of participating in $500,000-a-year numbers and bookmaking racket. *New York Times,* 21, May 20, 1961.

Fogelberg, Carl R.: A model for a legal numbers lottery in the District of Columbia. Washington, D.C., Washington Lawyers' Committee for Civil Rights under Law, 1973, pp. 46-64.

Fund for the City of New York: Computation of the winning number. *Legal Gambling in New York: A Discussion of Numbers and Sports Betting.* New York, 1972, pp. 20-21.

Gage, Nicholas: Organized crime in city bleeds slums of millions. *New York Times,* 1, September 9, 1970.

Gramont, Sanche de: How to play a lottery. *New York Times* (Sunday Magazine, Section 6), May 7, 1967.

Grutzner, Charles: Survey on the operation and organization of policy. *The New York Times,* June 26, 1964.

House committee votes special 10 percent tax on gross business of bookmakers and policy operators. *The New York Times,* 1, May 17, 1951.

Jacoby, Oswald: The forms of gambling. *Annals,* 269: May 1950.

Johnson, Thomas A.: Numbers called Harlem's balm. *The New York Times,* 1, March 1, 1971.

Kaplan, Lawrence J. and Maher, James M.: The economics of the numbers game. *The American Journal of Economics and Sociology,* October 1970.

Kihss, Peter: Lumbard on state drive to control crime. *New York Times,* May 7, 1967.

Loeb, Carl M., Jr.: Antigambling laws opposed. (Letters to the Editor). *The New York Times,* July 14, 1968.

Mayfield, J.: Numbers writer: A portrait. *Nation, 190:* May 14, 1960.

Mayor Wagner reports $1 million-a-year numbers racket broken as a result of anonymous letter to special P.O. complaint box. *New York Times,* 1, May 2, 1961.

McFadden, Robert D.: State will offer daily lottery plan as an experiment. *The New York Times,* 1, June 16, 1974.

Multi-million-dollar policy ring broken. *The New York Times,* 64, April 3. 1958.

Police raid 2 policy banks in Harlem. *The New York Times,* 58, November 25, 1956.

Plescowe, Morris: The law of gambling. *Annals, 269*: May 1950.

Powledge, Fred: Pick a number from 000 to 999. *The New York Times,* (Magazine Section), December 6, 1964.

Redding, J. Saunders: Playing the numbers. *North American Review,* December 1934.

Roth, Jack: Gamblers operate numbers game in open. *The New York Times,* May 7, 1967.

Scaduto, Anthony: The mob: A new look. *New York Post,* June 7, 1968.

Sellen, Thorsten: Organized crime: A business enterprise. *Annals, 346*: May 1963.

Smith, Sandy: Mobsters in the marketplace: Money, muscle, murder. *Life Magazine, 63*:10, September 8, 1967.

State of New York: Revised Penal Law. Gambling Offenses. Article 225, effective September 1, 1967.

Three indicted members of multi-million dollar policy operation. *The New York Times,* 21, February 20, 1965.

Treaster, Joseph B.: Jersey planning 3-digit lottery. *The New York Times,* 1, December 29, 1973.

Wakefield, Dan: Harlem's magic numbers. *Reporter,* February 4, 1960.

Woetzel, Robert K.: An overview of crime: Mores vs. morality. *Annals, 346*: May 1963.

LEGALIZATION OF GAMBLING

INTRODUCTION

THE AMERICAN PEOPLE are moving rapidly to accept legalized gambling as a fact of life. Legislators in many states are advocating lotteries, horse and dog racing and even casino gambling as a means of raising new revenues to meet increasing demands for more tax money. In spite of moral, political and practical objections against gambling in this country, states are beginning to recognize that billions of dollars siphoned out of the economy by organized crime, completely untaxed, are a potential source of revenue to provide for improved public services. The public feels overburdened with taxes and yet the public is clamoring for better schools, better transportation, improved health and welfare systems, and decent housing.

The first selection, "Which Forms of Gambling Should Be Legalized," analyzes numbers and sports betting and the various forms in which each could be legalized. After carefully reviewing the arguments, it concludes for many reasons that the best vehicle for legalization is the numbers game. If a government numbers game proves successful, then it might be worthwhile to move into the legalization of sports pools.

The second selection is a partial reprint of a report to former New York State Governor Rockefeller and the Legislature of the State of New York in 1973 by a Commission on Gambling. Five of the seven sections of the report are included. The first section expands in some detail the argument of the previous selection in its analysis of "The Feasibility of the Major Forms of Possible Legal Gambling." The second, "Fiscal Issues," examines the revenue potential of numbers, sports betting, casinos, and wide-open gambling. The third section analyzes the "Arguments For and Against Various Forms of Legal Gambling." These are considered in the context of the proposed areas for legalization. The fourth section analyzes the "Organizational Issues," and the fifth is the "Summary, Conclusions, and Recommendations."

The final reading analyzes legalized off-track betting in Great Britain, France, New Zealand, Australia, Puerto Rico, and Nevada. In Nevada, all gambling was legalized in 1931. Casinos provide the major activity of the gambling business there while horse race betting is a very minor part of the total gambling picture.

WHICH FORMS OF GAMBLING SHOULD BE LEGALIZED*

In the Introduction to this report, we argued that gambling should be legalized only as a means of denying its present illegal revenues to organized crime and corrupt officials. Our reasoning is that legalized gambling—in a form acceptable to the public—can contribute little to solving the problem of official corruption until the control of organized crime is broken. We also believe that legalized gambling cannot produce expected amounts of public revenue without sacrificing the improvements in payout to winners that are needed to give it a competitive edge over the present illegal game.

It follows that only those forms of gambling should be legalized that can compete successfully with their illegal counterparts. In this section, we shall review the reasons why we believe that:

1. *Bookmaking* is inappropriate for legalization because there is little prospect that it can be operated either by the government or by private licensees on a profit margin as low as that of illegal bookmakers.

---

* Reprinted from Fund for the City of New York in its report, *Legal Gambling in New York: A Discussion of Numbers and Sports Betting*, 1972, pp. 49-54. Used with permission.

2. *Poolselling* could readily be legalized, would pose few mechanical problems and would have reasonable prospects for competitive success. But the profits of the present game are not an important source of income for organized crime. Neither does poolselling appear to contribute significantly to the problem of police corruption. Therefore, legalizing poolselling at this point would not be of significant social value.

3. *Numbers* are the best vehicle for an experiment to test the proposition that legalizing gambling can have an impact on organized crime and can, in the long run, help to reduce official corruption.

Sports betting could be legalized in four forms:

1. Government operation (for example OTB).
2. Private operation, government-regulated and tax (pari-mutuel betting at horse racing tracks).
3. Government operation of central functions with franchised or licensed private sales outlets (the state lottery).
4. Private operation subject to no more government supervision than any other legitimate business.

In our opinion, the fourth is neither advisable nor acceptable to the public and its elected representatives. As a practical matter, the best way to legalize any form of gambling is to design a game that can be authorized by the state legislature under a pending amendment to the New York State Constitution. That amendment, approved once by concurrent resolution of the State Senate and Assembly, must be approved once more by the next Legislature and then by the voters in a popular referendum.

The amendment permits the legislature to authorize gambling "operated by the state or a public benefit corporation created for the purpose of operating such activities." This limitation clearly rules out privately run sports betting, whether supervised by the government or not. That leaves only some form of direct government operation.

But the state cannot become a bookmaker, if only because it cannot take the risks of losing. It cannot gamble with taxpayers' money. In pari-mutuel betting or the lottery, the state takes no risks. It cannot lose. Prizes cannot exceed a fixed percentage of receipts—and this percentage can be set at any level the operators choose, since there is no effective competition to force a higher payout to bettors.

Bookmaking has no such protection. Over the long haul, as we have explained, the skillful bookmaker is likely to turn a profit. But there is always the chance that he will lose, and some do. Even the bookie's long run success depends in many cases on his access to the nationwide layoff system and other devices that would not be available to a state run bookmaking system.

A government bookmaking operation would face other serious competitive disadvantages. Illegal bookies are remarkably efficient, apparently thriving on a commission of 4.5 percent for sports betting. Their commission charges compare favorably with those of stock exchanges, which perform a similar function of balancing buyers and sellers by means of shifting prices. The experience of OTB suggests that the cost of a state run betting activity would be considerably above those of the illegal operation.

Unless it could pay its costs with less than 4.5 percent of its receipts, a government bookmaking operation could not increase the payout to bettors and therefore could hardly hope to compete even if all other conditions were equal. In fact, they would not be. Unless bets were accepted and winnings paid on a pari-mutuel basis, all wagers would be subject to the 10 percent federal excise tax. In any case, legal winnings would be subject to federal income taxes. And it is unlikely that the government operation could accept bets on credit, as illegal bookmakers habitually do.

Pari-mutuel bookmaking on sports would overcome some of these problems. It would make the game financially secure and would eliminate the federal excise tax. At the same time, however, it would raise other difficulties. Bettors accustomed to fixed odds would probably not be attracted by a wager in which the ultimate payoff is not known until all betting closes. Such a pari-mutuel operation would not compete directly with illegal bookmaking as it is currently practiced, and therefore could not displace it.

Our conclusion is that bookmaking on sports cannot successfully be run as a government operated or controlled enterprise. Under present and any prospective law, it cannot be legalized for private operation under government regulation. Competitively successful legal bookmaking could cut off large revenues from organized crime, but we see no practical way to accomplish this. If bookmaking is to be curbed, it will require a massive law enforcement effort. Legal bookmaking schemes that are technically feasible would be of little or no assistance.

Poolselling presents none of the problems of operating efficiencies that make bookmaking such an unlikely candidate as a government enterprise. Profits now are so outlandish that the government could sell pool cards offering the bettor far higher returns and still retain most of the receipts to pay expenses and provide public revenue.

There are a few obstacles. It would have to be converted to a pari-mutuel system, or a maximum payout established, in order to assure that the government could not lose money in a given week. Neither of these alternatives is impossible. Bettors typically are relatively unsophisticated about odds or they would not play the present game. And they could be offered a much more attractive deal than they now have in either case. Nor does the federal excise tax tip the scales heavily in favor of a pari-mutuel operation, since the present margin could easily accommodate an additional 10 percent in cost. Cards sold in $1 or $2 denominations, moreover, would rarely pay winners more than $600, so that the government would not be required to report winners to the Internal Revenue Service.

The mechanics would be simple. It is conceivable that college games would have to be removed from the cards, since some officials or citizens might find government sponsorship of gambling on college contests distasteful. But point spreads could simply be taken from the line published in the mass media, and cards could be sold through retail outlets as are lottery tickets.

But if there is no particular reason why poolselling *should not* be run by the government, neither is there any compelling reason why it *should*. As we have noted, poolselling is not taken seriously by law enforcement officials, and there is no evidence that it contributes seriously to corruption. While it is likely that some of its profits ultimately enrich organized crime, the sums involved are small compared to these provided by numbers and bookmaking.

Even from a revenue-raising standpoint, government poolselling would be disappointing. The state, to run a competitive game, would have to pay substantially higher prizes. Thus, government revenues would be considerably under the current profit, even if the legal game captured the entire market.

The best argument for government poolselling is that a fairer proposition would be offered to customers. Little or nothing would be accomplished toward solving the problems of organized crime and corruption associated with illegal gambling, and it would be misleading to promote government poolselling on that basis.

Perhaps most important, in our opinion, there is available a much better vehicle for legalization—one that could accomplish the primary objective that we seek.

Numbers is far more important by every measure: volume of business, profits to organized crime and the burden on the police. It can be legalized almost as readily as poolselling. Its customers are also relatively unsophisticated bettors of small amounts. Its handle is substantial and steady. It is played six days a week at an almost unvarying pace. While it is more complicated to operate than poolselling, it is by no means as difficult as bookmaking. Finally, its current payout level is low enough that a legal game could improve it sufficiently to achieve a competitive advantage. If a government numbers game proves successful, it might be worthwhile to move into legal operation of the less important sports pools.

There are three major obstacles to a legalized numbers game. The first is design of a mechanism to protect the game against loss, an essential feature of its legal viability. The others are limitations on a legal game's competitiveness: the current federal income tax laws and the resistance of black and Puerto Rican residents to government operation of an enterprise in which they perceive a strong community interest. These problems can be overcome.

THE FEASIBILITY OF THE MAJOR FORMS OF POSSIBLE LEGAL GAMBLING*

Numbers

We define numbers as a daily lottery, in which the bettor is allowed to select his own number and make bets as small as fifty cents. In a numbers game the bulk of the prize money goes to payoffs in the range of $600 for a $1.00 bet, unlike the State lottery where most of the prize money is paid out in much larger sums at much higher odds.

The right of the bettor to choose the number he is betting on is absolutely critical to the appeal of this game. Many bettors feel that the number they choose has some particular significance. Others like to have "their own" number, which they will play every day for as much as a year. Without bettor selection there is probably no hope of taking away the customers from the illegal game.

It is clear that a numbers game could be operated by the state or by PBC's.† It is not clear, however, how widely distributed a numbers game can be established offering true daily action.

The basic operating problem in providing daily action is the difficulty in getting the betting slips or other recording of the bets into central headquarters each day before the winning number is selected (in order to prevent false winning numbers being put into the system). Increasing the number of outlets in order to increase convenience to the bettor makes the task of getting all the betting slips in each day more difficult. This problem is eliminated if the betting information is originally entered into machines with secure communication to central computer facilities. However these machines are moderately expensive, and require fairly high volumes of usage before they are economically justified. Thus, while it seems clear that the

---

* Reprinted from the State of New York, Executive Department, New York State Racing and Wagering Board, from the report of the Commission on Gambling, *Increased Legal Gambling in New York: A Policy Analysis,* 1973, pp. 5-13, 15-18, 23-29, 31-32, and 33-34. Used with permission.

† PBC is the abbreviation for Public Benefit Corporation.

costs would be low enough and the usage high enough to justify at least a modest number of machine parlors providing real daily action, the exact number of such parlors that could be opened is very difficult to estimate until cost and usage are better known through experience or detailed study.

If there is to be a legal numbers game, we recommend that the first phase combine real daily action in a limited number of parlors (on the order of 50 to 200) and by telephone, and "pseudodaily action" through something like 10,000-20,000 retail outlets. "Pseudodaily action" means that a winning number would be chosen each day, that winners will be able to collect the following day, and a bettor can place a separate bet each day, but there is a lag between the day the bet is placed and the day the number is picked.

Pseudodaily action would work as follows: The bets would be taken by authorized agents working much as the state lottery agents do today. The betting slips would be collected Friday and Saturday night and processed by the central facilities before the first winning number was picked the following Monday afternoon. Winning numbers would be picked each afternoon. The player could either go in each day and bet on the winning number for the next week (that is on Tuesday he could buy next Tuesday's number, etc.), or he could wait until Saturday afternoon and buy numbers for each day of the following week, or he could visit or telephone one of the parlors providing true daily action and bet on the number that will be chosen the same day.

Such a system is feasible to operate and would cost about five to ten cents a bet.* The real question is whether the system can attract existing players away from the illegal numbers game. There are a number of reasons why a legal numbers game would have difficulty in competing, even if it offers better prizes than the illegal game. Probably the strongest reason is that many players will feel that they don't have to pay taxes on the winnings from the illegal game, but that they would have to on legal winnings. This is not completely true. Legal numbers winnings

---

* The lottery is now operating at 7.5 cents total cost including commissions for fifty cent tickets.

would have to be reported by the state to IRS only where winnings on a single bet are over $600.00. This would not happen on a fifty cent ticket, and might or might not happen on a one dollar ticket. Furthermore, only net winnings are taxable. All winners will have substantial losses to deduct from their winnings and many will have no net winnings on which tax would be due. As a practical matter, it is possible that many numbers winners at the legal game will not pay more income tax than they do when they win the illegal game, although this is a difficult matter to understand and requires more study.

Despite the tax problem and others, we believe that if something like 75 percent out of the amount bet is returned to the bettors in prize money, the legal system described here combining "pseudodaily" and true daily action can take away most of the business from the existing illegal operators and return approximately 10 to 15 percent of the amount bet to the government. Most bettors bet to make money and the attraction of more winnings we believe will dominate other issues if the game is intelligently promoted and the prize money well "packaged."

We believe that if this system were operated it would not significantly increase the number of people betting on lotteries— legal and illegal—although it would increase the total *amount bet* on legal and illegal lotteries somewhat, perhaps by a factor of two and conceivably substantially more. Bettors' losses would not be increased nearly as much as the total amount bet because the proposed numbers lottery would only take 25 percent whereas the existing lotteries take out much more.

Sports Betting

There are two major kinds of sports betting. Either could feasibly be operated by the state or PBC's. The most important kind is betting on single events (head-to-head betting); the other kind is sports pools or pool card betting, in which the bettor picks the winner of a number of events and is paid only if a specified percent of his selections are correct. Depending on how they are set up, pool cards can either be somewhat similar to head-to-head betting or quite different from it.

Head-to-Head Betting

The operational problem with head-to-head betting is that most events are more or less even money bets (or are made so by a handicapper) and thus the bettor cannot afford to give a big percentage to the operator. In fact, this group of bettors probably now loses only 8 to 12 percent of all the money they bet.* This 8 to 12 percent must cover all costs and profits of the betting operation. Since the operating costs are the same for any size bet, the problem of keeping operating expenses to a low percent of the bet can be solved by having high minimum bets. This is the way most of the bookmaking business is done. A better way for the state to operate would be to have a fixed service charge on all bets to cover all selling and operating expenses. This charge would be about forty cents per bet.

The other problem of the state in conducting a betting operation is to make sure it does not lose. This can be solved simply by using a pari-mutuel system under which the winners are paid a percent of all the money bet, as in horse race betting. If this is to be done we recommend that a sports handicapping "line" be used to try to make all contests as close to an even bet as possible.

If the state is going to set up a legal sports betting operation, we would recommend a distribution system similar to that proposed above for the numbers. The system would include widely dispersed selling agents operating on a weekly basis† and a limited number of betting parlors providing daily action. As with the numbers, which could use the same betting parlors, we would recommend starting out with a fairly small number of parlors—50 to 200 statewide. Experience would then show how strongly people preferred daily action to the weekly or pseudo-daily action available in widely distributed locations, and it

---

* The nominal percent of gross profit on a balanced book is 4.5 percent for large bets (over $50). This is decreased by the risk of being "middled" if the line is shifted as described in the Report. However, it is increased on small bets, most combination bets, horse race bets, and by any net winnings of the bookie when he takes a position on events.

† This would work very well for football and less well for other sports. Other compromises between daily action and wide distribution might be worked out for other sports.

would also show what the cost would be of creating more parlors so that they would be conveniently available for more people. On the basis of the experience with the dual system, it might also turn out to be desirable to develop a compromise system involving fairly widely distributed machines located in public facilities of some kind rather than in betting parlors. This would provide daily action on a fairly widely distributed basis, e.g. several thousand outlets.

For sports betting—like numbers—the real question is not feasibility but competitiveness (and desirability). We believe that although sports bettors are now used to betting on a fixed odds basis, the game described here could take a substantial share (conceivably as much as half of the existing bookie betting business), if the pari-mutuel takeout (including breakage) were limited to two or three percent. The federal 10 percent excise tax would not apply. As at the race track, winners would have to fill out federal income tax reports (Form 1099) only if they win over $600 at more than 299 to 1 odds.

Pool Card Betting

Pool cards now serve two purposes: providing a cheap way to bet on many games, and giving an opportunity for the sports bettor who likes to try for a high odds payoff. The existing pool card business is believed to be fairly small, probably about $50 to $100 million a year (although possibly more). Because profit margins and distribution costs are now extremely high it would be easy to take the bulk of the business away from the illegal operators, and probably to add substantially to the total volume. This is now mostly a weekly business and therefore easy to distribute through a lottery-type distribution system.

If, as we believe, head-to-head betting is thought to be undesirable, pool card betting could also be used as a kind of compromise which can be made to come reasonably close to head-to-head betting. This is achieved by letting the pool card bettor bet on a relatively small number of games, and by providing payoffs in cases where the bettor is correct on a fairly low majority of his bet, e.g. four out of six.

Pool cards should also be operated on a pari-mutuel basis

where they will be used to imitate head-to-head betting, but either fixed odds (which would include the payment of a 10% excise tax) or pari-mutuel payoff is suitable for providing high odds betting opportunities.

Casinos

It is not practical for the state to operate casinos itself, but a PBC could effectively operate casinos. PBC casinos would almost cerainly not be as attractive to gamblers as private casinos, but this would not prevent them from being popular and profit-able as long as they would not have to compete with private casinos.

New York could build up a casino capacity big enough to handle all the business currently being done in Nevada with thirty casinos or less. This number of casinos could be opened over a period of ten to twenty years. Sufficient experienced staff could be recruited so that the casinos could be operated efficiently and securely, although this certainly would require paying some salaries higher than civil service (each casino would probably require a manager in the $60,000 to $75,000 range and about three to six other executives earning over $30,000).

Since about three quarters of Nevada gamblers come from California, it is reasonable to think that the potential market for casinos in New York is 50 to 100 percent of the Nevada industry, if the New York industry were operated more or less the same way, appealing to all income levels. This assumes that in the long run the number of out-of-staters attracted to New York by casinos will be partly balanced by New Yorkers or potential New York visitors attracted to casinos in other eastern states.

If New York were one of the first states in the East to start casino gambling, it probably would at first attract more out-of-staters to New York than New Yorkers who would be going out-of-state. For long-range planning it is prudent to assume that other states would have attractions comparable to New York, and New York would not have a substantial competitive advan-tage over other states on the basis of casino gambling. (If other states authorized private casinos they could have a competitive advantage over New York casinos.)

On the basis of the Nevada-California experience it is reasonable to assume that if there is a full-scale casino industry in New York (even without casinos in or near New York City) the amount of casino gambling done by New Yorkers would increase many fold (perhaps 5 to 10 times).

The primary feasibility question for casinos is not whether they can be operated profitably, but whether they will help the economy of the state. It seems clear that casinos can help the economy of the immediate localities where they are located (although they may well produce some costs and negative consequences for these localities as well). In general, however, economic benefits to the localities where the casinos operate will be more or less matched by losses to the rest of the state. For example, casino gambling might well hurt race tracks, and it will take business away from other parts of the entertainment business and other competitors for the consumer's dollar. Basically, most of the casino business and business stimulated by casinos will not be new money for the state, but will be money transferred from some other activity in the state.

If a casino industry is started in the state, the state will retain some part of the money now being spent by New Yorkers on gambling trips out of state. However, a big gambling industry in New York will almost certainly stimulate some New Yorkers who do not now make gambling trips to Nevada or the Caribbean to do so. So the amount of New York money going out of state to Nevada or other distant casino centers on gambling trips will not be reduced to zero, and might not even be substantially reduced.

It is theoretically feasible to operate casinos in such a way that people with low incomes represent a much smaller percent of the players than they do in Nevada. It is not possible to say how well a policy of discouraging small or poor bettors would work. There would be a substantial chance that the restrictions designed to do this would tend to erode over time as a result of pressures to make more money, or to be more "democratic." If small bettors were discouraged, the total volume in profits would be much lower than it would be with "Nevada-style" casinos, probably less than half as large. (Most casino winnings in Nevada come from small bettors.)

FISCAL ISSUES

Revenue Potential
Numbers

A legal numbers game returning 75 percent of the amount bet to the bettors in the form of winnings is likely to attract an annual volume between $500 million and $1 billion a year, beginning with the second or third year of operation. This should produce a net income of $50 to $150 million a year. We regard the prospects of profits above the level of $100 million as highly speculative.

Sports Betting

Head-to-Head Betting

It is reasonable to estimate that a sports betting program along the lines described herein would be able to do between $300 million and $1 billion worth of betting a year, although it might take a few more years to seize a large share of the existing bookie business than to take over the numbers. Profits should be figured at about 3 percent which means that the state could reasonably expect to make about $10 to $30 million a year from head-to-head sports betting. After perhaps ten years the total volume of legal sports betting could rise to the $1 to $2 billion range.

Sports Pool Cards

Pari-mutuel sports cards, along the line of the British, German, and many other foreign pools, or fixed-odds pool cards like the illegal ones, probably could develop a volume of at least $50 or $100 million, and perhaps much more, appealing to sports fans who like to take a small chance on winning a large amount of money. The fixed-odds card probably would make a more effective competitor than pari-mutuel cards (even with the 10%

excise tax which would be paid by the betting agency), but either one would be a reasonable choice. Most of the objections to head-to-head betting do not apply to these pool cards. The percent profit to the state should be set so that the state game is clearly superior to the illegal cards. We believe that an average takeout of about 30 percent would be reasonable (high enough to be safe but low enough to be competitive and not exploitative) —with most of the money coming from the high odds bettors. This would net $10 to $20 million after expenses.

Casinos

If New York State provides for casinos, we would propose opening large casinos to economize on management skills. Each of such large casinos, operated by PBC's, should be able to earn $1 to $5 million profit per year if operated Nevada style. This would mean total profits, after ten to twenty years of buildup, in the range of $50 to $200 million per year. If the casinos tried to exclude or discourage small bettors, profits would be perhaps two to ten times smaller, depending on how strongly the policy was followed.

Wide-Open Gambling

If New York tried to maximize its gambling income by providing for as many kinds of gambling as would be profitable, it could do such things as providing jai-alai, dog racing, mouse racing (as in Australia), widely distributed slot machines, gambling pinball machines and other low-skill gambling devices. All such other forms of gambling might be expected to net the state an additional $50 million to $200 million. As the number of forms of gambling increased, the problem of each one competing with the other would also increase.

Summary

We think that a prudently conservative estimate of total gambling revenues from a fairly broad but well-controlled program of increased legalized gambling would be within the range of $100 to $150 million a year without casinos and another $100 million with casinos. Any sound gambling program would probably involve a number of controls and restrictions. If the policies behind these are to be protected, it is important that the revenue concerns not become dominant.

One way to keep down excessive pressures for revenue, and to avoid the speculative aspects of gambling revenue, would be to adopt a policy of only budgeting the gambling revenues actually received in the previous year so that the gambling operators do not have pressure to meet revenue quotas.

The gambling enterprises would be self-supporting and after a brief time self-financing. (The gambling enterprises should be charged with the costs of their own regulation.) The only type of gambling that would make a substantial increase in other costs would be casino gambling which would bring large numbers of visitors to the casino locations. However, since these locations would be in the resort and tourist areas, which desire these visitors, that should not be thought of as a major additional cost.

The principal revenue dangers concern the possibility that new forms of legal gambling would reduce state revenue from existing legal gambling.

Since it is being extensively studied elsewhere, we have not looked into the question of the extent to which off-track betting reduces revenue from on-track betting.

On-track betting might well be hurt by legal head-to-head sport betting, or by casinos, but probably would be only marginally affected by legalized numbers.

Existing lottery revenue would probably be hurt by a legal numbers business. But lottery revenue could probably be maximized by having both medium odds (numbers-type) and jackpot-type lotteries available, as well as mixed games, on a daily basis. As will be discussed below, numbers and lottery should be operated together.

ARGUMENTS FOR AND AGAINST VARIOUS FORMS OF LEGAL GAMBLING

General

Objections to gambling are made on the following grounds:
1. It is immoral or bad for people's character because it

involves getting something for nothing.

2. It is bad on practical grounds, because people spend money on it that they should more appropriately spend on other things, and/or because gambling leads to undesirable associates and other undesirable activities.

Many people would disagree with each of these arguments, and the issues are not resolvable by analysis.

Even if the moral, practical, or social undesirability of gambling is accepted, a major practical problem remains. There is now a tremendous amount of legal and illegal gambling. Theoretically New York could shut off the legal gambling, but that would be politically impossible. So far it has not shut off the illegal gambling. Most people including the authors, think it is not possible to do so without providing more legal alternatives. Therefore, a realistic decision concerns the question of the balance between legal and illegal gambling. They are now about equal in dollar volume, and the question is, would it be a good idea to reduce the amount of illegal gambling and increase the amount of legal gambling?

Another major argument against increasing the amount of legal gambling is that doing so will increase total gambling. However, it is unlikely that the total number of persons who gamble *can be* substantially increased, because it already includes about two thirds of the population (if playing the lottery is counted as gambling). The maximum possible increase in the dollar volume of gambling by further legalization of gambling is probably not as much as 50 percent, unless casinos were opened. Casinos, on the other hand, could almost double the amount of gambling now going on in the state.*

Another argument against increasing the amount of legal gambling is that given the social and political situation we are now in, every small reduction in controls by society is a step in

---

* If a full-scale casino industry were opened in New York, the amount bet would probably be over twice as much as all gambling now going on, but since most casino games have a relatively small advantage for the house, the net amount lost by the bettors to a big casino industry would only be about half as much as is now being lost in all legal and illegal betting.

the wrong direction, which should be resisted even if it is not important of itself.

The general arguments in favor of increasing the amount of legal gambling are:

1. Gambling is an innocent form of entertainment, widely enjoyed by societies throughout history, which produces much entertainment and pleasure for New Yorkers.
2. If there are moral objections to gambling, they are a matter of individual conscience and it is not appropriate for the state to attempt to enforce them.
3. While gambling will lead some people to be imprudent with their money, it is either not right or not practical for the state to try to decide and enforce how individuals should spend their money. (The millions of dollars spent gambling might be spent in worse ways if they were not being spent on gambling.)
4. Increasing the amount of legal gambling would not significantly increase the number of "compulsive gamblers." Because of the typical character structure and behavior of compulsive gamblers, it is reasonable to think that most of them are already gambling, either legally or illegally.
5. If people are going to gamble, it is better to have them gambling legally.
6. Reducing the amount of illegal gambling will reduce the amount of police corruption and the amount of profits for organized crime.
7. Increasing legalized gambling would produce money for the state which is otherwise going to criminals.
8. Increasing the amount of legal gambling would reduce the gambling losses of the state's citizens because the legal games would provide better returns to the bettor, at least in some cases.

Numbers

If these is to be any increase in legalized gambling the strongest case is for providing a legal numbers game. There is already a legal lottery. While some people may regard the numbers as more pernicious, because people get more interested in their number bet, it also provides more entertainment. Numbers is also the place where providing a legal alternative will (1) have the most impact on organized crime and corruption, (2) give the bettors a substantially better break than they are now getting, and, (3) where (apart from casinos) the most money is to be made. (All of this is on the assumption the legal game will return something like 75% of the amount bet to the bettors.)

Sports Betting

Head-to-Head Betting

Legalized head-to-head sports betting presents a much more doubtful case, because it will make small profits for the state, because it is likely to make a smaller dent in its illegal competitor, and, most important, because of its involvement with sports. Many associated in a formal way with organized sports, both amateur and professional, will oppose legal sports betting. They feel that it is bad for a sport to become known as a betting game, and that legal betting will increase and emphasize the danger of fixed games. However, a very large number of sports fans now bet on games, either legally with each other, or illegally with bookies. The amount of betting would scarcely double (although it is possible that the number of bettors might double) if legal, commercial betting were established.*

Although opponents of legal sports betting argue that it will increase the danger of fixed games, we think that the tendency in this direction is probably rather weak. We think that it is the responsibility of sports to protect their own events, rather than call upon society to force people to bet illegally in order to protect the games. We also do not think that the general viability of sports as a form of mass entertainment is threatened seriously by danger of increased fixes because of more legal gambling. Many sports do very well despite the knowledge of occasional fixes. Many people, however, legitimately prefer to be very

---

* The Quayle survey indicated that in New York City something like half of all sports bettors bet only privately, and about 25 percent of all adults are now betting on sports.

cautious in this direction. We believe the questions of this kind justify a study in much greater depth before a decision is made to go ahead.

We don't believe that legal head-to-head betting is justified by its usefulness in fighting bookies, corruption, and organized crime. First we believe that most of the value for this purpose can be achieved by the two kinds of pool cards described above. Second we are skeptical that a sufficient attack on illegal gambling will be mounted to accompany the legal competition. Without such an attack legal head-to-head betting will not be sufficient to make a decisive difference in the role of illegal sports-betting. We would start with the pool cards; if experience indicated that head-to-head betting would make a critical difference, then that would be the time to decide to go into head-to-head betting.

Sports Pool Cards

Whether or not legal head-to-head betting is established, there is a good case for selling pool cards, in which the bettor is given a chance to pick the winner of ten to twenty games and get a large prize if he is correct on all of them. This is an almost unobjectionable way for people to make small bets on sports and appeals to people who like big jackpots. (There is not much basis for objecting to it.) It does not provide a good opportunity to profit from fixing games. It does not seem to have caused bad results in England, Germany, or the other countries with such games. It would take a profitable business away from illegal gamblers, give the bettor a better break, and make some tens of millions of dollars for the state.

If head-to-head betting is not legalized it probably would be a good compromise to experiment with pari-mutuel pool cards designed to simulate head-to-head betting. (There could be a top limit of, say, $100 on a single card.) These would be less objectionable than straight betting, would take some of the bookie business away (many bettors, relatively few dollars), and would be fairly simple to operate, although they would not be very profitable.

Casinos

While it is quite feasible for New York to operate casinos profitably, and reasonably cleanly, we believe that it would be a mistake for the state to do so for the following reasons:

1. "Feasible" does not mean "easy." Most other types of gambling should be easier to develop and administer.
2. Even with reasonable management, revenues accruing to the state would not make a significant difference in the tax burden.
3. The general economic impact of casinos would be mainly money transfers within the state. Most of the business created by casinos would be matched by other business lost as a result of money being spent on casinos, rather than other things.
4. In the long-run, New York State could not expect to bring in much more outside money with casinos than the New York money that would go out of state. In fact, New York PBC casinos would be inferior attractions to private casinos in other states (although the private casinos represent a greater danger of corruption and political influence).
5. If New York opened casinos it is likely that a number of other states in the East will and it seems better for the country if casino gambling remains restricted.
6. Casinos are a particularly dangerous form of gambling because their fast action tempts people to bet more than they can afford and more than they intend.
7. While it is quite possible to keep casinos and their surroundings reasonably clean and uncorrupt, there are a number of ways in which controls over casinos can break down. There is a real risk that casino operation will have poor results or undesirable by-products, and that the state would ultimately regret that it had begun a casino program. Once such a program had built up momentum, it would be hard to reverse.

Some people argue that New York ought to provide for casinos because New Jersey is about to do so, and New York should try to get there first. Similar arguments are being made in New

Jersey. If casinos are held to be undesirable, New York should take steps to avoid a "casino race." Such steps could include efforts by the governors of the various states to insure coordinated action, to jointly study the program, to agree not to act without warning the other states, etc. New York could also seek to get federal legislation which would inhibit casino operations in all states that do not now have casinos, or at least coordinate decisions about where or whether casinos should be opened. It is not clear whether this is practical, but the possibility should be explored.

ORGANIZATIONAL ISSUES

If there is to be more legalized gambling, the control of gambling in the state probably ought to be reorganized. In particular, off-track race betting, the lottery, the numbers, pool cards, and straight sport betting, if it is started, ought to be operated together. They should all use the same distribution facilities; a combination of lottery-type distribution through part-time commission agents, and betting parlors more or less like those established by New York City OTB.

The numbers and the lottery are two related but different products. Their distribution and marketing ought to be coordinated so that the customer is able to buy that in which he is interested.

We believe it makes sense to have the agency which runs the coordinated gambling enterprises (which would not have to include on-track betting) be a PBC rather than a state agency. We believe that a PBC would be more appropriate because it would have greater flexibility of operations, because the function is more nearly business than governmental in character, and because there is slightly less moral affront to those citizens who object to gambling if it is conducted not by their government, but by a separate nongovernmental agency (however, many of them will not care about this distinction). There are many detailed practical problems that would face the state government if it tried to conduct a variegated gambling enterprise itself, including provision for rapid and convenient payment of winnings, etc. While these problems are not insuperable, we see no particular reason to take them on. For these reasons we recommend the creation of a PBC to carry out the gambling program.

In terms of the division between local and state operation and control of the gambling PBC there are a great many possibilities, no one of which has outstanding advantages. It would be possible to have a single statewide PBC operating out of branch offices in each locality, which could provide for local control of some operating practices, locations, etc., through representatives of local government. Another alternative would be to have local PBC's in any locality that wishes to have legal gambling and a statewide PBC to establish the games, ensure necessary coordination, and provide centrally those services which the local PBC's did not want to provide for themselves.

The advantages of local control and of centralization, and the disadvantages of each, are well known from other state activities. Local option to exclude gambling, at least betting parlors or casinos, is obviously desirable.

SUMMARY, CONCLUSIONS, AND RECOMMENDATIONS

Conclusions

1. Legal gambling now involves about two thirds of the adult population and a little over $2 billion of betting. (Card playing and private betting are in addition to these numbers.)
2. Illegal gambling now involves perhaps a quarter of the adult population and probably a little under $2 billion of betting.
3. Casinos could double the amount of gambling in the state. But other new forms of legal gambling could probably not increase total gambling by as much as 50 percent, and would not substantially increase the amount of harm to "compulsive gamblers."
4. There is no substantial possibility of greatly reducing the amount of gambling in New York.
5. Therefore, except for casinos, the only real choice is whether to change the current 50-50 balance between legal

and illegal gambling in the direction of a higher percentage of legal gambling.

6. Profits of illegal gambling are a major source of income to organized crime.

7. Graft for protection of illegal gambling is a critical source of corruption of the criminal justice system, and other parts of the government.

8. The state could realize substantial revenues (perhaps $100 to $150 million) from a legal numbers game and/or from a casino program, but this would be only a few percent of the state budget and so would not noticeably reduce the tax burden.

9. The economic effect of casinos would be primarily to redistribute money; any *net* gain would not be large enough to be significant for the state's economy.

10. A legal numbers game with a high payout to the bettors could largely destroy the illegal numbers racket, and significantly reduce corruption.

11. A legal sport betting program could hurt the bookies but probably not enough to produce a very important impact on corruption or organized crime.

Recommendations

1. The extension of legal gambling should be directed more toward hurting organized crime and ending corruption than maximizing revenue.

2. Legal systems should be attractive as possible to customers of illegal systems.

3. A legal numbers system should be established with daily and pseudodaily action, small bets, bettor selection of number, many prizes, and a *higher* payoff than the illegal system.

4. A system of legal sports pool betting should be established using pool cards similar to the existing football cards—providing primarily high odds betting on many games. In addition it probably would be a good idea to experiment with low odds pool cards designed to take away some of the bookie business.

5. The introduction of legal sports pool betting should be accompanied by a major attack against bookies using primarily the civil law. (The criminal justice system is in such bad shape that it is not available as a significant tool against gambling.)
6. Legal head-to-head sport betting, while feasible, should not be started without further study and very careful consideration.
7. The new legal betting systems plus the lottery and OTB should be operated together by a single PBC structure (possibly using local as well as statewide PBC's).
8. N.Y. should not establish casinos and should work with officials in other states who are trying to prevent casinos from coming into this part of the country.

LEGALIZED OFF-TRACK BETTING IN OTHER PLACES*

LAWRENCE J. KAPLAN AND LEO C. LOUGHREY

Legal off-track betting has been in existence for many years in several parts of the world. In some foreign countries, off-track betting is provided by private licensees, in other countries it is wholly government operated, and in still others, it is operated by a combination of both the government and private licensees. In most of the countries, off-track betting is nationwide and not limited to provinces or states. The volume of off-track betting in the various places under review is a small fraction of the volume anticipated for legalized off-track betting in New York State.

Great Britain

1. Prior to 1960 bookmakers in Great Britain operated freely both on and off the racktracks, though unlicensed. Both cash and credit bookmaking† were legal at the tracks. Away from the

---

* Reprinted from *Ins and Outs of On-Track and Off-Track Betting* by Lawrence J. Kaplan and Leo C. Loughrey, Gould Publications, 1970, pp. 8-16. Used with permission.

† Credit betting requires predeposited money with the bookmaker.

tracks, bookmakers were legally permitted to handle only credit bets called in by telephone. Known as turf accountants, book-makers operated off-track in stores and offices. Cash betting was illegal off-track, but the same bookmakers accepted cash bets either personally or through street runners who picked up the bets for them.

2. In 1949, a Royal Commission was appointed to investigate these conditions. Its *Report* was issued in March 1951, recommending the licensing of betting shops where off-track bets could be legally made for cash. It offered the following reasons for the recommendation: first, to elminate the illegal bookmaker; second, to enable poorer people, unable to establish a credit rating, an opportunity to bet legally; and, third, to wipe out subterfuge and law-evasion.[1]

3. In 1960, Parliament enacted the *Betting and Gaming Act*, patterned after Ireland's law of 1926. The British law became effective in 1961. Under the terms of the new law, licensed off-track cash betting shops were legalized as privately-operated, profit-making enterprises throughout England, Wales and Scotland. The turf accountants who handled off-track credit betting were now authorized to accept both credit and cash bets in their betting shops.

4. The law of 1960 also legalized certain other gambling activities, such as *chemin de fer* and bingo. Since the effective date of the *Betting and Gaming Act* in 1961, about 15,600 licensed betting offices have opened, 2,200 of them in London, serving a population of over 3,000,000.[2]

5. The affluent age and the *Betting and Gaming Act* of 1960 have made gambling in Great Britain big business. It is estimated that gambling Britons bet between $3 billon and $4 billon a year. Some of the giant bookmaking and pool operators, such as the William Hill group, a public company, and Littlewoods, a private company, take in well over $100 million a year each.[3]

---

[1] Royal Commission on Betting, Lotteries and Gaming. *1951 Report* (London, H.M. Stationery Office, 1951).

[2] *New York Times* (October 7, 1967).

[3] "In Britain, Gambling is a Growth Industry," *Business Week* (September 14, 1963).

6. The British Government collects no tax on the money wagered. It derives revenue from license fees, income taxes from turf accountants and betting shops, as well as profits taxes. The Government, eager to get both more revenue and more control over gambling, is seeking to increase taxes, permit closer scrutiny of gambling clubs, and to limit the formation of new clubs. However, because of the fear of driving gambling underground, there is no present intention of trying to legislate a reduction in numbers despite all the talk of the social evils that the gambling craze has brought in its wake.[4]

7. A betting shop in Britain may be established by obtaining a license from the local magistrate. The only restriction relates to its location. A generally accepted rule is that it not be set up next to a bar. An individual must be at least eighteen years old and orderly to be admitted to a betting shop. The police do not permit loitering outside the shops, but no limit is set on the amount of time that one may spend inside.

8. An official evaluation of the economic and social consequences of the establishment of betting shops in Britain was made by two different American teams of investigators in 1963. Their conclusions on the impact of off-track cash betting in Britain are diametrically opposed to each other.[5] At the time of the studies, cash betting shops had been in existence for only two and a half years. A summary of the main issues and the position of the two teams is given below. (Table 5-I)[6]

Both teams agree that illegal bookmakers have been largely eliminated and that the police and the courts have been enabled to concentrate more of their efforts on more serious areas of law enforcement.

---

[4] *New York Times* (October 7, 1967).

[5] New York State, Assembly, *Pattern for New York? A Report on Off-Track Betting in England* by Henry D. Paley and John A. Glendinning (Albany, N.Y., January 1964), and New York City, Office of the Mayor and Office of the Comptroller, *Report of Survey of Off-Track Betting in New Zealand, Australia, England and France* by Albert Margolies and James A. Cavanagh (New York, N.Y., October 17, 1963).

[6] New York State, Assembly, *Ibid., p. VII et. al*: New York City, *Ibid.*, pp. 1-2, 9-14.

TABLE 5-I

Issue	*State Team*	*City Team*
1. Increase in horse betting	Massive. A four-fold increase	Estimate is invalid, because volume prior to legalization is unknown
2. Effect on retail sales	Sharp decline, because expenditures diverted to gambling	Significant increases in retail sales
3. Defaults on installment debt	Significant increase	No change
4. Number of people receive welfare assistance	Increase	No change

France

1. France has the longest history in the orderly control of off-track betting. Betting in general is a matter of respected tradition. The number of people betting and the amount of turnover are enormous.[7] Since the mid-eighteenth century, all bets on horse racing were private transactions between bettors and bookmakers. Because of a series of racing scandals in 1880, a law was approved eleven years later, 1891, which outlawed all bookmakers at the tracks, and required that nonprofit, civil societies be formed for this purpose, under government supervision. This law specifically prohibited off-track betting, and consequently illegal bookmakers expanded their operations.

2. In 1929, the government decided to eliminate illegal bookmaking, and channeled all off-track betting through a government-supervised agency. In 1931, another law extended on-track pari-mutuel betting to off-track betting. Bookmaking was made a crime, and both the bookmaker and the bettor were made liable to prosecution. Today, the volume of bookmaking in France is negligible.

3. Off-track betting in France is handled by Pari-Mutuel Urbain (P.M.U.), which, since World War II, is a nonprofit government agency. Tobacco shops handle 85 percent of off-track bets while cafes and similar establishments handle the remaining 15 percent. These establishments, referred to as

---

[7] New York City, *Ibid.*, p. 22.

bureaus, are licensed by P.M.U., and retain one percent of their turnover for expenses. The demand for these franchises is large because of their effectiveness in bringing in business to the shop. France has about 2,200 licensed betting shops of which 600 are in the Paris area.

4. With both daytime and night racing, these bureaus take bets seven mornings a week, 365 days a year. Bets may be placed every morning up to about an hour before the start of the first afternoon race. Since no results are given or posted at the betting bureaus, there is no problem of loitering. Bettors come in, fill out a betting form, pay their money, and leave. Winnings are paid out the following day.

5. The Pari-Mutuel Urbain opened twenty-one of its own betting agencies in 1950-51, five in Paris and sixteen in other large cities. These agencies accept bets in the afternoon as the races are being run. Bets are accepted up to post time, and winnings are paid out after each race. Liquor and tobacco are sold and consumed on the premises. The New York City team of investigators found these agencies unattractive, recommending that they not be used as the model for New York.[8]

6. The New York City team estimated that about 15,000 persons place bets in the bureaus and agencies of the P.M.U. on an average weekday in Paris. On Sundays, the figure is 600,000. Nearly all betting is cash. Telephone betting against predeposited accounts is permitted in the P.M.U.'s own agencies, but not in the bureaus. About 3,000 deposit accounts are in Paris, but only about 1,000 are active.[9]

7. In 1954, a new form of off-track betting was initiated in France. It is called *Tierce*, and today is the most popular form. In *Tierce*, a bettor must pick three horses in one race to finish in order for longest odds, or to finish as the first three at shorter odds. The Tierce amounts to 70 percent of the volume handled on a Sunday. As a betting form, it is provided only on Sundays and national holidays, and a bettor may wager not less than 60 cents.[10]

---

[8] *Ibid.*, p. 24.
[9] *Ibid.*
[10] *Ibid.*, Part II, p. 6.

8. *Parlay betting* is also available. Known as *report betting* in France, the bettor makes advance selections of horses in various races, and authorizes P.M.U. to wager his winnings successively on these selections. Win and place and daily doubles are also provided, as well as *couple* bets on win and place. In a *couple* bet, two horses are picked to finish one-two in a particular race.[11] In 1966, the French spent $680 million on *Tierce* which is an amount equal to two thirds the earnings of the Renault automobile works. The Treasury's share in 1966 was $160 million.[12]

New Zealand

1. Up to 1911, bookmakers in New Zealand operated freely both on and off the race tracks. In that year, all bookmaking was declared illegal. But they continued their operations illegally for thirty-five years. Growing public protest against bookmakers led the government to appoint a Royal Commission in 1946 to formulate a system of legal off-track betting. In 1951, as a result of this study, the government set up the Totalizator Agency Board (T.A.B.) through whose betting shops located around the country off-track bets are relayed to the tracks where they are collated with bets made on-track through totalizators to set the odds.[13] T.A.B. also supervises franchised agents who receive a fee based upon the volume of business. About 301 branches and agencies are in operation.[14]

2. Bets are accepted up to ninety minutes before post time for each race. Payouts to winners are made the following day. Bets are taken for win, place and double. The minimum off-track bet is 75 cents for doubles and $1.50 for win and place.

3. T.A.B. deducts 17.35 percent of its turnover. Of this, it keeps 7.50 percent, pays 9.35 percent to the government, and pays .50 percent to the racing association for the improvement of amenities. The remainder, 82.65 percent, is returned to the bettors.[15]

---

[11] *Ibid.*

[12] Sanche de Gramont, "How to play a Lottery," *The New York Times,* Magazine Section, No. 6 (May 7, 1967).

[13] New York City, *op. cit.,* Part I, pp. 2-7; Part II, pp. 1-2.

[14] *Ibid.*

[15] *Ibid.*

4. The atmosphere at the branches and agencies of T.A.B. is sedate and dignified, similar to the atmosphere of a bank. No police or private guards are on duty. People come in, study the programs of race meetings posted on the walls, and then go to one of the windows to place their bets.[16]

5. In New Zealand, legal off-track betting accounts for 51.9 percent of all legal gambling. On-track betting accounts for 39.6 percent, and the remainder, 8.5 percent, by two lotteries. About 90 percent of illegal bookmaking has been eliminated, because people prefer legal betting to illegal betting. Police officials believe that more advanced equipment for off-track betting tied in with the track totalizator could keep the betting shops open almost to post time, and this would probably eliminate the very few bookmakers still operating.[17]

Australia

1. The Australian state of Victoria, of which Melbourne is the principal city, approved a Racing Act in 1958. A Totalizator Agency Board, a government-controlled nonprofit organization, started operations in 1961.[18]

2. A comparison of Victoria's off-track betting procedures with those of New Zealand indicate the following differences (Table 5-II):

TABLE 5-II

Item	*Victoria, Australia*	*New Zealand*
Advance cash deposit required for telephone betting	$3.00	$6.00
Amount of time by which betting is stopped before post time	40 minutes	90 minutes
Broadcasts from the track after each race	Results only	Results and odds

3. Former illegal bookmakers estimate that 60 to 70 percent of the telephone bookies, handling larger bets, have been elimi-

---

[16] *The New York Times*, August 19, 1963, p. 14.

[17] New York City, *op. cit.*, p. 5.

[18] New York City, *op. cit.*, Part I, pp. 16-19; Part II, pp. 2-3.

nated since off-track betting was legalized. They also estimate that 100 percent of the smaller, or street, bookies have disappeared from Melbourne, a notable accomplishment because *street* bookies accepted bets from teenagers and even children.[19]

4. In the state government of Western Australia, controls on bookmakers were nonexistent prior to 1955. In that year, a licensing system was imposed on bookmakers, both on and off the tracks. In 1960, Western Australia approved a Betting Control Act, which set up a Totalizator Agency Board. Operations were started in 1961.[20]

5. The illegal bookmaker has gone and the race tracks are enjoying substantial benefits from T.A.B.'s annual contributions. In Western Australia, bets are taken up to three minutes before post time. Winners are paid in about fifteen minutes after each race. In addition, wagers are accepted for win and place on out-of-state tracks. T.A.B. also operates the daily double and quinella, maintaining its own pool and making its own odds. The system provides a form of parlay betting, known in Western Australia as *all-up* bets.[21]

Puerto Rico

1. Off-track betting on the island of Puerto Rico was legalized in 1913. More than $100 million a year is gambled in Puerto Rico of which about $25 million is on racing. Other government-approved forms of gambling are casino activity (dice, blackjack and roulete), weekly lotteries, and cockfights. It is estimated that 85 percent of the play is by tourists.[22]

2. The off-track pool is distinct from the pari-mutuel pool, and is under the supervision of the Racing Commission. At the off-track betting shops, payoffs are made on the following day. Racing in Puerto Rico is held only on Sundays, Wednesdays and Fridays.

3. The island's only track, El Comandante, is operated by a

---

[19] *Ibid.*, p. 17.

[20] *Ibid.*, Part I, pp. 19-21; Part II, pp. 3-4.

[21] *Ibid.*

[22] *New York Times*, December 15, 1963.

private corporation licensed by the government of Puerto Rico. This corporation grants permits to and supervises about 320 local off-track pool agencies which are located throughout the island.[23]

Nevada

1. In Nevada, all gambling is legal since 1931. Horse race betting, however, is a very minor part of the total gambling picture. Off-track betting is operated by bookmakers who are licensed by the Board of Gambling Control and the State Tax Commission. Six horserooms operate in Nevada, four in Las Vegas and two in Reno. The placing of bets by telephone is prohibited. A player who visits the horseroom gets a free racing sheet, coffee and doughnuts. Bookmakers may not be located in buildings where other types of gambling are located, and for the privilege they pay the state a 3 percent tax on gross winnings.

2. No pari-mutuel operations exist in Nevada, and at the present time the state has only one minor track which operates on weekends. The betting, therefore, is on out-of-state races. Payoffs are at track odds.[24]

Other Places

Other places where off-track betting is legal include Sweden, Western Germany, Ireland, and, behind the Iron Curtain, Poland and Czechoslovakia.[25]

BIBLIOGRAPHY

Books

Cole, Gordon H. and Margolius, Sidney: *When You Gamble You Risk More Than Money*. New York, Public Affairs Committee, 1964.

Cressey, Donald: *Theft of the Nation*. New York, Harper and Row, 1969.

---

[23] *Ibid.*

[24] New York City, Mayor's Citizens' Committee on Off Track Betting. *Final Report* (February 6, 1959), pp. 40-41. Also, William H. Rudy, "The Off-Track Scheme: Some Advice from Nevada," *New York Post*, Magazine Section (February 7, 1964), p. 1.

[25] *The New York Times* (August 19, 1963, and June 3, 1968).

Fund for the City of New York: Which forms of gambling should be legalized. *Legal Gambling in New York: A Discussion of Numbers and Sports Betting.* 1133 Sixth Avenue, New York, 1972, pp. 49-54.

Great Britain: Royal commission on betting, lotteries, and gaming. *Report, 1949-51.* London, H.M. Stationery Office, 1951.

Kaplan, Lawrence J. and Loughrey, Leo C.: Legalized off-track betting in other places. *Ins and Outs of On-Track and Off-Track Betting.* New York, Gould, 1970, pp. 8-16.

King, Rufus: *Gambling and Organized Crime.* Washington, D.C., Public Affairs Press, 1969.

New York State: The feasibility of the major forms of possible legal gambling; Fiscal issues; Arguments for and against various forms of legal gambling; Organizational issues; Summary, conclusions, and recommendations. *Legalized Gambling: Report to Honorable Nelson A. Rockefeller, Governor, and the Legislature.* Albany, New York, Commission on Gambling, 1973, pp. 5-13, 15-18, 23-29, 31-32, 33-34.

Peterson, Virgil W.: *Gambling—Should It Be Legalized?* Springfield, Thomas, 1951.

Tec, Nachama: *Gambling in Sweden.* Totowa, N.J., Bedminster, 1964.

Articles

Baus, J. W.: Legalized gambling approaches in Pennsylvania. *Christian Century,* 77: March 9, 1960.

Betting, Gaming and Lottery Act of 1963 (Act Eliz. II, 1963, c.2, sch.1). London, H.M. Stationery Office, 1964.

Bookmaking seen continuing even if legalized off-track betting plan is approved. *New York Times,* 4, October 26, 1958.

Cook, F. J. and Gleason, G.: Rackets and payoffs: off-track betting in New York City. *Nation, 189:* October 31, 1959.

Cragin, E. W.: Legalize gambling? *Rotarian, 78:* May 1951.

District Attorney O'Connor favors legalized off-track betting as means to curb bookmaking. *New York Times,* 28, March 22, 1965.

Fino, Paul A.: Let's legalize gambling. *Coronet, 39:* November 1955.

Gamblers, gangsters, and government: Should the federal government tax gambling? *Scholastic, 59:* October 10, 1951.

Gambling-the need for legislative reform. *Kentucky Law Journal, 57:* 1968-1969.

Government report links organized crime in U.S. to casino-in-study of tourism. (Puerto Rico) *The New York Times,* April 1, 1969.

Hammond, M. K.: Legalized gambling in Nevada. *Current History, 21,* September 1951.

How? Off track betting. *New Yorker, 35:* February 21, 1959.

Hungarians keep two state lotteries busy. *The New York Times,* March 6, 1966.

Kaplan, Lawrence J.: *Economic Implications of Organized Crime in Gambling: Possibilities of Gaining Revenue and Eliminating Corruption through Government Ownership and Operation.* Proceedings of the John Jay College Faculty Seminars, *I*: 1967-69.

Leonard, John: The big flutter. *The New York Times Magazine,* October 22, 1950.

Loeb, Jr., Carl M.: Anti-Gambling Laws Opposed (Letters to the Editor), *The New York Times,* July 14, 1968.

Macao-Hong Kong, China. *Newsweek,* January 28, 1962.

Mayor Lindsay asks legislative approval of off-track betting for New York City subject to November referendum. *The New York Times,* 1, May 4, 1966.

Neuberger, R. L.: No national lottery. *Christian Century,* 75: April 30, 1958.

New York State: Gambling offenses. *Revised Penal Law,* Article 225, effective Sept. 1, 1967, pp. 127-129.

Off-Track Betting: The outlook in New York, Nevada and Britain. *U.S. News and World Report,* 55: November 18, 1963.

Peterson, V. W.: Look at legalized gambling. *Christian Century,* 82: May 26, 1965.

Ploscowe, Morris: The law of gambling. *Annals, 269:* May 1950.

Puerto Rico warns of gambling scandal. *The New York Times,* 16, April 1, 1969.

Rockefeller and legislative leaders agree on lottery plan. *The New York Times,* 1, February 1, 1967.

Shuster, Alvin: Casinos in Britain face a new deal. *The New York Times,* 10, March 2, 1969.

State as bookie; legalized gambling. *Sports Illustrated, 22:* January 4. 1965.

Wessel, M. R.: Legalized gambling—the dreams and the realities: New York City's proposal to legalize off-track betting. *Nation,* 200: January 18, 1965.

Wisconsin lotteries—are they legal. *Wisconsin Law Review, 1967:* Spring 1967.

CHAPTER 6

THE ECONOMICS OF LOANSHARKING

INTRODUCTION

Loansharking, the lending of money at higher rates than the legally prescribed limit, after gambling is the second highest source of revenue for organized crime. Gambling profits often provide the initial capital for loanshark operations.

Usury is an interest charge in excess of a maximum established by law. The term *usury* is generally applied to any rate of interest considered to be unfair and unjust.

In the United States usury laws are under the jurisdiction of the states. The maximum legal limits range from 6 to 30 percent, although in many states the statutes do not apply to corporate borrowing. Penalties for breaking usury laws vary from forfeit of the excess interest to loss of the entire loan and/or jail sentences.

Borrowers who are willing to pay usurious rates of interest include gamblers who borrow to pay gambling losses, narcotics users who borrow to purchase drugs, and wage earners who may require a small loan until next pay day. It did not take long for members of organized crime to recognize the profit potential of these types of loans, and soon they dominated this business. The small, high-risk borrower is generally eager and willing to pay 20 percent a week to a loanshark, the standard interest charge. On the other hand, banks, small loan companies, or other legal lenders are not geared to handle a borrower with shaky credit. Consequently, the loanshark and the criminal syndicate have been extremely successful and have expanded their operations.

The first article, "The Economics of Loansharking," traces usury through the ages, usury in the United States, and analyzes the organization of the loanshark racket, and the business of loansharking. The article offers several recommendations made by the New York State Commission of Investigation at the conclusion of its public hearings. All of them are designed to curb loansharking.

The second selection, "The Economics of Usury Laws," analyzes usury from the point of view of the "money market." It indicates the effects of interest rate regulation on various economic groups, and concludes that restrictions on interest rates lead to curtailment of the supply of loans, with lower-income groups being most adversely affected.

The third selection analyzes "The Impingement of Loansharks on the Banking Industry." Although it appeared in 1966, the article is relevant currently.

THE ECONOMICS OF LOANSHARKING°

LAWRENCE J. KAPLAN AND SALVATORE MATTEIS

Introduction

Loansharking has become a major source of revenue for the underworld and a major route by which crime syndicates have infiltrated legitimate businesses. When taken over by the loan-sharks, these businesses are used to further other criminal enterprises. Since ancient times the moneylender has played a significant role in society. His sharp practices and hard heart have been highlighted in literature. The borrower in our modern day who is in some kind of financial difficulty is not too different from his counterpart of other eras. The pressure on the borrower to obtain a loan often means he cannot quibble over terms. This being the case, the moneylender is in a position to make the most of such a situation.

The numerous public documents and newspaper reports are

° Reprinted from *The American Journal of Economics and Sociology.* Copyright 1968, pp. 239-251. Used with permission.

replete with cases in which consumers have been charged an astronomical true annual rate of interest for a small loan. Interest rates charged by loansharks vary from 200 percent per year to 2000 percent per year, depending on the relationship between lender and borrower, the intended use of the money, the size of the loan, and the repayment potential. The classic "6-for-5" loan, 20 percent a week, is common with small borrowers. Payments may be due by a certain hour on a certain day, and a few minutes default may result in a rise in interest rates, or even more drastic action. In modern terminology, this type of lending operation has come to be known as "loansharking."

Loansharking is the lending of money at higher rates than the legally prescribed limit. After gambling, loansharking is the second highest source of revenue for organized crime.[1] Gambling profits often provide the initial capital for loanshark operations. Law enforcement officials suggest that the borrowers who are victimized by these activities include gamblers who borrow to pay gambling losses, narcotics users who borrow to purchase drugs, and wage earners who may require a small loan until next payday, or who may be employed in particular occupations dominated by labor racketeers who insist that workers borrow as a requirement for work, such as longshoremen.[2] Another outlet for loans includes some small businessmen who borrow when legitimate credit channels are closed. Bigger borrowers include individuals and corporations requiring large sums of money quickly, often for legitimate business activities.

This study is designed to investigate the historical background of usury through the ages, its contemporary status in the United States, including a case study of a loanshark operation, the business of loansharking, its source of funds, interest rates, business volume, and major areas of operation, including infiltration into legitimate business, summary, recommendations, and conclusions.

---

[1] *The Challenge of Crime in a Free Society*, a report by the President's Commission on Law Enforcement and Administration of Justice (Washington, D.C., U.S. Government Printing Office, 1967), p. 189.

[2] *Ibid.*

Usury Through the Ages

Usury, in its original concept, was synonymous with interest. In biblical times it referred to all returns derived from the lending of capital. The prohibition against usury or interest appears twice in the Old Testament.[3]

Antiusury laws appeared later in Greece and Rome. In Athens, the legislation of Solon limited the rate of interest in order to ease the financial burden of the agricultural population. In Rome, the Twelve Tables established a maximum interest rate of 10 percent. In 342 B.C. a law was passed prohibiting the taking of any payment for loans. The law, however, was never enforced, and wealthy individuals developed and flourished through "usurious" activities.

The attitude of the church was based upon the scriptural command of St. Luke, "Lend, hoping for nothing again."[4] This idea was gradually expanded so that by the Middle Ages all interest charges were defined as usury. Usury was no mere transgression of the law but a mortal sin punishable by excommunication. This rigid measure originally applied only to the clergy but was subsequently extended to all lay Christians.[5]

During the sixteenth and seventeenth centuries some writers began to distinguish between interest, which was considered a "fair" return on a loan, and usury, or an excessive charge for a loan. By the eighteenth century, under the impact of an emerging capitalism, the antiusury attitude of the church receded into the background, and moneylending became respectable. The problem which plagued the Romans once again came to the fore, namely, what is a usurious rate?

Early economists of the eighteenth century began to grapple with this problem. At that time the maximum rate generally prevailing was 5 percent. Jeremy Bentham, in his *Defense of Usury* in 1787, demanded the same degree of freedom for money trade as that prevailing in commodity trade. This was a right derived from the concept of personal liberty. The progress of

---

[3] *Leviticus* 25:36, and *Deuteronomy* 23:20.

[4] *Luke* 6:35.

[5] G. A. T. O'Brien, *An Essay on Medieval Economic Teaching* (London, 1920), p. 174.

economic liberalism in the nineteenth century gradually resulted in the repeal of antiusury laws. England removed its ban on usury in 1854, Holland in 1857, Belgium in 1865, and Prussia and the North German Federation in 1867.

The repeal of the antiusury laws in these countries created a flood of credit abuses. In the latter part of the nineteenth century many of the countries, therefore reenacted legislation designed to protect inexperienced or careless borrowers from the money-lender.

Historically, the attitude toward usury kept changing with the times. A transaction condemned in one historical period as usurious was recognized as a normal economic practice in another. And practices among countries varied. Practices outlawed and punished in one country were freely permitted in another. Thus, usury as an economic concept may be understood only in the light of the moral and legal norms prevailing in a particular period.[6]

Usury in the United States

Attempts to control charges on loans were made by usury laws. In the United States these regulations usually took the form of state usury laws. Generally, these limited the interest charged to 10 to 12 percent on a true annual rate. If a lender charged more than this stipulated amount, he was guilty of usury and subject to punishment.

In practice, usury laws did not provide the protection required by needy consumers. A small consumer loan is relatively expensive to process and administer. The legal limits on interest imposed by law discouraged respectable financial institutions from making consumer loans. However, the desperate need for money by low-income factory workers as well as high-income groups was ever present. The loanshark, recognizing the demand, sought to supply it. The loanshark operation was illegal under the law and so rates charged were as high as the traffic would bear. Borrowers were intimidated and often were made to remain

---

[6] W. J. Ashley, *An Introduction to English Economic History and Theory* (London, 1906-1909), 2 volumes. Vol. I, pt. 1, pp. 148-163; pt. 2, pp. 377-488.

perpetually in hock, and required to pay the exorbitant interest rates.

The Russell Sage Foundation undertook studies of these conditions early in the century.[7] Their studies concluded that small consumer loans represented a special area of finance which called for special legislation. The studies argued that making small consumer loans was too expensive for reputable institutions to handle, and therefore encouraged the illegal operations of the loanshark. The studies suggested that special legislation was required which would increase the legal limit on small loans so that legitimate financial agencies would find it profitable.

With the support and encouragement of the Russell Sage Foundation, Massachusetts passed the first small loan law in 1911. All the laws adopted elsewhere subsequently operate about the same. Financial institutions which make small consumer loans are licensed and are exempt from the usury laws. They are restricted to a sliding scale of interest charges ranging from 18 percent to 30 percent a year on the unpaid principal. They are also restricted to a maximum loan of $800.

In New York State, for example, the usury laws apply only to loans under $800 made to individuals. No criminal penalty applies to loans to individuals in excess of $800. Moreover, no criminal penalty attaches to loans made to corporations regardless of how onerous and unconscionable a rate of interest is imposed.

In 1928 the National City Bank of New York announced its entry into the personal loan field. This move was acclaimed by the press with such headlines as:

LOAN SHARKS DOOM SOUNDED BY BIG BANKERS.
USURY DEALT HEAVY BLOW BY BANK'S ACTION.
NATION'S BIGGEST BANK FIGHTS LOAN SHARKS.[8]

Up to that time large commercial banks stayed out of the consumer loan business. Since 1928 personal loan departments

---

[7] Arthur B. Ham, *The Campaign Against the Loanshark* (New York, Russell Sage Foundation, 1912).

[8] Richard B. Miller, "The Impingement of Loansharks on the Banking Industry," *Bankers Magazine,* 149 (Winter, 1966), pp. 84-91.

have grown to be a major part of modern banking. Still the loanshark has survived and has even expanded his operations. Various public hearings show that loansharks have infiltrated banks and many other legitimate businesses.[9]

Case Study of a Loanshark Operation

The typical loanshark operation is often called a "6-for-5" operation, because that is how it started.[10] In the following case study, "6-for-5" loans constitute a small proportion of the business. This illustrative case is a relatively small operation compared with similar operations in Las Vegas, Los Angeles, or even in factory cities such as New York or Pittsburgh. The loanshark in our case study—let's call him Joe—usually has between $50,000 and $75,000 outstanding. He employs nineteen runners who make actual contact with borrowers. All the runners are employed full-time in the four factories covered by his operation and enjoy extra earnings, averaging about $50 a week, working for him on a part-time basis. A few, with good connections, make more than $100 a week, but the job requires only two to three hours a week. Earnings are based upon straight commission.

Joe also employs five full-time, supervising bookkeepers at a straight salary of $200 a week each. Each full-time man keeps the records for three to four runners.

Like most businesses, loansharking is subject to seasonal variations. Activity increases at Christmas or during the horse racing season, spring and summer. A plant layoff increases activity. Those laid off can pay only the interest, which is acceptable to the loanshark. And more borrowers seek loans. If Joe is short, he goes to his downtown connection and borrows $10,000 for which he must pay a flat 1 percent a week, or $100 a week. The loan made to a factory borrower requires no collateral, no contract, no closing fees, no insurance fees, not even a signature. A man's word is all that is required. Interest is not deducted from the loan in advance, and when a man pays

---

[9] U.S. House of Representatives, *Investigation into Crown Savings Bank Failure* (Washington, D.C., U.S. Government Printing Office, 1966).

[10] "Confessions of a Six-for-Five Juice Man," *Burroughs Clearing House,* 49 (April, 1966), pp. 40-41.

off the principal, he gets no receipt. To obtain a loan from a legal source requires making application, a credit check, and possibly a cosigner. In loansharking, the runner carries a large roll of money and peels bills off for anybody at any time.

The rate of interest is lower on a larger loan than it is for smaller ones. An individual who borrows $5 until next payday pays back $6, a 20 percent interest charge. The person who needs the $5 does not object to the $1 charge. A borrower of $100 until next payday pays back $110, a 10 percent interest charge. And if the borrower has difficulty in repaying, he need only maintain the interest payments every payday.

The runners are usually keen in financial matters and often dispense advice free of charge. For example, a collection agency was hounding a longshoreman to settle his wife's doctor bills. He approached the runner for a loan, but was advised to discuss the problem with the doctor and to tell the doctor to be patient for a while longer. "After all," he was told to say, "you cannot repossess an appendectomy." Those engaged in loansharking know that a satisfied customer is good for business.

The loansharking business is particularly designed to dispense short-term loans, not long-term loans for home improvements or for purchase of furniture. A typical borrower may be a young man in one of the four factories who wishes to finance a Saturday night date. He borrows $50. A successful evening is worth $10 interest. Or a gambler hears of a poker game. Hoping for a winning streak, he borrows a few hundred dollars for a stake. The loanshark may also team up with a bookie and perhaps jointly hire a shill who serves up hot tips on the races. In this setup, the trio may collect a good sized proportion of the weekly factory payroll.

Joe occasionally has a bad debt problem. When a borrower refuses to pay back his loan the loanshark calls in the muscle squad. This is expensive. To have a man's legs broken used to cost $50, but inflation has doubled this cost. It is also not good business, because the borrower then cannot work and the possibility of repayment disappears. But if a man loses his job and cannot repay his loan, the loanshark may use him as an example for the rest and pay the muscle squad to rough him up.

Normally a finger deliberately slit open with a razor blade enables the borrower to stay on the job—while reminding him of the amount due next payday. Or a few teeth may be pulled out with a pair of pliers. Or, perhaps, a broken nose may serve the same purpose. Other tactics include street-beatings with bicycle chains or toy baseball bats. Muscle is only part-time work. In a well-functioning business operation, muscle is seldom needed for collections.

Joe is a solid member of the middle-class community. He pays taxes, lives in a quiet residential community, participates in civic projects, donates money to charitable organizations and to his church, and sends his children to select colleges. As a rule, the typical loanshark is no longer a crude, flashily dressed, fast-living character. Generally, the top-level syndicate leader wears ivy league suits. Sometimes he hires public relations firms to add luster to his image. While technically he is classified as a gangster, the loanshark considers himself in the money business, supplying an existing demand. And, incidentally, the work he does is legal in most other countries.

Organization of the Loanshark Racket

The usurious moneylending business operates successfully through existing underworld organizational structures. Three main echelons may be identified.[11] At the top level is the underworld boss. He supplies the money and directs the operation. The bosses distribute millions of dollars to the second echelon. These are the chief lieutenants or underbosses who serve the top echelon with absolute allegiance. The amount of money received from the top depends upon an under-boss's past performance and market demand for money. The only requirement is that the second echelon must pay 1 percent weekly for the money in use. This is a levy upon the second echelon's income derived from interest and penalty charges on usurious loans. The underworld term for interest and penalty charges is *vigorish*. Each under-boss is an independent contractor and knows that

---

[11] New York State Commission of Investigation, *An Investigation of the Loanshark Racket* (New York, April 1965).

the 1 percent return to the boss is mandatory, with no excuses for failure. The second echelon loans money to the third echelon. These are the "6-for-5" operators who deal with the "public," the victims of this underworld moneylending system (Table 6-I).

TABLE 6-I

INTEREST RATES CHARGED IN LOANSHARKING

| Echelon | Interest Rate Return (Percent) | |
	Weekly	Annually
First	1	52
Second	1.5—2.5	78-130
Third	5	260

The Business of Loansharking

The lucrative loansharking business is based upon the exorbitant rates of interest charged as the money flows from the top echelon to the borrower and back to the source.[12] Data collected by the New York State Commission of Investigation have revealed the pattern of interest rates shown in Table 6-I.

While the top echelon receives a weekly return of 1 percent, borrowers pay the third-echelon loanshark a weekly rate of interest of not less than 5 percent per week.

The pattern has a slight variation. Cases on record reveal second-echelon loansharks who handle their own loans. In New York City these are among the major loansharks who can loan $1 million at a time to a borrower without collateral. The lender makes clear to the borrower that "Your body is your collateral."

Of the five recognized criminal syndicates operating in New York City, testimony at the public hearings of the New York State Crime Commission revealed that 121 high-echelon members were engaged in the loansharking business. Usurious moneylending outside the syndicates is almost impossible. This is revealed by the case of a professional gambler who operated a numbers or policy racket in Jersey City and also operated as a loanshark. Unable to move his money into new areas of activity,

---

[12] *Ibid.*

he had to hide it. In July 1962, a hoard of approximately $2.5 million dollars in cash was found hidden in a Jersey City garage.[13]

The Profits of Loansharking

The loansharking business yields enormous profits. A syndicate boss may have a Christmas party at his home and invite ten trusted lieutenants. At the party he may distribute $1 million in cash, or $100,000 per man, with the request that each must return to him 1 percent per week, thus yielding $10,000 a week, or $520,000 a year. The gang leader's only problem is to find five more men at next year's Christmas party to lend out the $520,000 earned the previous year.

To carry this example to the third-echelon lender who charges a minimum of 5 percent weekly, $1 million at this level can produce $50,000 a week or $2.6 million a year. Of this amount, $15,000 to $25,000 a week—or up to $1.3 million a year—is passed up the line to underworld bosses.

It is almost impossible to estimate the volume of the loansharking operation in the United States. Based upon the operations of a single loanshark in New York City, according to official testimony, over a five-year period, $500,000 was pyramided to $7.5 million.[14] A conservative estimate would put the loanshark business in the United States in the $1 to $2 billion class.

Underworld Infiltration into Legitimate Business

Today criminal gangs exist in every sizable city in America. The U.S. Senate's Permanent Subcommittee on Investigations and the Federal Bureau of Investigation are aware of criminal activities in New York, Chicago, Philadelphia, Detroit, Cleveland, St. Louis, Boston, New Orleans, Pittsburgh, Buffalo, Kansas City, Miami, Tampa, Providence, and Las Vegas. Many of the richest gangsters of today made their millions in the old prohibition days. With the repeal of the Eighteenth Amendment on December 5, 1933, and the increase in prosecutions for income tax evasion by the Internal Revenue Service that era came to an end.

---

[13] *The New York Times,* July 4, 1962, p. 1, col. 2.
[14] New York State Commission of Investigation, *op. cit.*

Government law-enforcement officials currently recognize that the big money in crime is made in gambling, narcotics, and loansharking. These illegal activities provide the billions which the underworld is funneling into legitimate businesses. When a businessman falls behind on his payments to a loanshark, the gangster often simply takes over the business. This is a convenient vehicle for turning so-called "black money" into "white money," or legitimate funds.

The New York State Commission of Investigation points out that loansharks have constantly used corporate borrowers as a cover or concealing device for themselves and other hoodlums. Typical is the instance in which a loanshark took his weekly vigorish payments in the form of a salary check from an automobile dealer to whom he had loaned money. The gangster appeared on the corporate books as an outside salesman. He never sold a car. When questioned, he was able to claim legitimate employment as evidenced by his regular weekly paycheck.[15]

In another case an heir to a large sum of money in trust attempted to sell his inheritance rights for a usurious one-third the actual value of the trust fund.[16]

The Commission of Investigation also received testimony of an attempt by "the mob" to take over a bank, having as their objective the use of the institution as a cover for usurious money-lending operations.[17]

Organized crime appears to be infiltrating multimillion-dollar business enterprises. These include banks and Wall Street brokerage houses, big real estate syndicates, and large corporations which serve the public in numerous activities.[18]

In real estate, underworld investments run into "hundreds of millions," according to the U.S. Attorney. These investments are in hotels and skyscraper office buildings in all the major cities of the country.

---

[15] New York State Commission of Investigation, *Transcript of the Public Hearing* (New York, December 1964), p. 238.

[16] *Ibid.*, p. 233.

[17] *Ibid.*, p. 234.

[18] "How Criminals Solve Their Investment Problem," *U.S. News and World Report,* 56 (March 30, 1964), pp. 74-76.

In banks, enforcement officials affirm that criminal elements have purchased stock in many large institutions. One medium-sized bank in Detroit is owned outright by "the mob." It is known as the hoodlums' bank. Similar evidence has been collected in New York, Chicago, and Miami.[19]

In securities, official files reveal that organized criminals have infiltrated into brokerage firms. Several are "boiler room" operations which are set up to unload worthless stocks through high-pressure sales tactics.[20]

In the garment industry, especially in the dress manufacturing business, centered in New York, loansharks and racketeers play dominant roles. Many have become millionaires. The racketeers run nonunion shops by hiring killers and strong-arm men as "labor consultants." The loansharks supply unlimited amounts of cash quickly to assist the dress manufacturer through the production cycle. Inability to pay back the loan results in physical harm or a business takeover. One member of the underworld is said to own a string of dress factories.

In other businesses, the underworld has made serious inroads. The list of businesses dominated by criminal elements is long and includes firms in almost every type of legitimate business.

To counteract the growing infiltration of the underworld into legitimate business, the United States government has increased its investigations in this area. An intelligence unit has been established in the organized crime section of the U.S. Department of Justice. It draws on the resources of more than twenty-five federal enforcement agencies. These include the F.B.I., the Securities and Exchange Commission, and the Treasury Department including the Internal Revenue Service, Secret Service, Narcotics Bureau, and Customs.

Summary and Recommendations

Loansharking has grown to tremendous proportions, producing millions in revenue, victimizing many people, and bringing fear and violence into the community. A serious gap exists

---

[19] New York Commission of Investigation, *An Investigation of the Loanshark Racket* (New York, April 1965), pp. 66-77.

[20] *Ibid.*, pp. 57-67.

in the usury laws both at the federal and state levels of government. While traditional organized crime operations such as gambling, narcotics, and prostitution carry, to varying degrees, significant risks of prosecution and severe penalties, no comparable laws exist for the loanshark. Strong criminal laws against unconscionable usury are lacking. The underworld is aware that no criminal penalty attaches to usurious loans to corporations, or in the case of individuals, for loans in excess of $800.

In the case of New York State, law enforcement officials used to have available only two usury laws which carried a penalty. One was section 357 of the Banking Law, and the other, Section 2400 of the Penal Law.

Section 357 of Article IX of the New York State Banking Law, which regulated the small loan business, penalized as a misdemeanor unlicensed lenders making to individuals loans of $800 or less bearing more than the authorized rate of interest. This section was useful to some extent against the "6-for-5" type of loanshark. It was weak in that its violation constituted only a misdemeanor. Moreover, it provided no penalties against the top echelon bosses.

Section 2400 of the New York State Penal Law penalized usury as a misdemeanor only when tools, implements of trade, or household goods were taken as security. This section was ineffective, because loansharks did not normally require collateral.

The New York State Commission of Investigation offered five recommendations at the conclusion of its public hearings which are designed to curb loansharking. These recommendations were based upon suggestions offered at the commission's hearings by the New York County District Attorney's office, Kings County District Attorney's office, New York City Police Department, Waterfront Commission of New York Harbor, and the Suffolk County Police Department.

Recommendation (1)

Add a new section to the New York State Penal Law which would make the charging of interest at a rate greater than 25 percent a year on a loan to any individual, partnership, association, or corporation, the crime of "criminal usury," a felony.

Small loan companies which deal in high-risk, low-profit, small personal loans are permitted by present law to charge an effective rate of 21 percent. Commercial factors, lending on accounts receivable, also charge up to 21 percent. In loans of $100 or less, the permitted statutory rate for small loan companies is over 30 percent and would remain lawful under the proposal.

The 25 percent rate or less is generally accepted by the community. A rate greater than 25 percent is considered unconscionable. Declaring it such by criminal statute strikes the area dominated by the loanshark. Thus the creation of the crime of criminal usury is the basic recommendation. The other recommendations which follow implement and strengthen this basic recommendation for dealing with loansharking.

Under the law, conviction of a felony is punishable by imprisonment for a term not exceeding five years or by a fine not exceeding $5,000, or both.

Recommendation (2)

Add a new section to the New York State Penal Law which would make possession of loansharking records a misdemeanor.

This section would provide law enforcement officials with an additional effective weapon against the loanshark. First, loansharks must and do maintain records of loan transactions which identify borrowers, list principal balances, interest due and paid, and charges and penalties. These records are identifiable and susceptible to proof as such by expert testimony to the satisfaction of the court. The proposed section above is patterned after Section 975 and 986b of the New York State Penal Law which makes the possession of bookmaking or policy racket records unlawful.

Second, individual borrowers from loansharks are generally afraid to make formal complaints. With this section available, law enforcement authorities would be able to obtain information necessary to investigations and to seize loanshark records while protecting the identity of an individual complainant. The loanshark could be successfully prosecuted under this proposed section, without necessity of borrowers' testimony in open court.

Recommendation (3)

Add a new section to the New York State Penal Law which grants immunity to witnesses in criminal usury investigations.

This proposed section would aid law enforcement ofificials in reaching top echelon loansharks by means of the testimony of accomplices or borrowers who may seek to hide behind the privilege against self-incrimination. This proposed section is patterned after other immunity provisions of the New York State Penal Law.

Recommendation (4)

Amend Section 242 of the New York State Penal Law to include "roughing up" tactics of loansharks as felonious assult in the second degree.

Recommendation (5)

Add a section that would permit corporations to interpose the defense of usury in actions to collect principal or interest on loans given at interest greater than 25 percent per annum.

Loansharks make it a policy to loan to corporations. Individual borrowers often are required to incorporate before being granted a usurious loan. The above recommendation would prevent a usurer from recovering on a loan for which he could be prosecuted.

Recommendation (6)

The Legislature and appropriate agencies of the state should consider the licensing and regulation of all persons or business entities engaged in the moneylending business in New York State who are not otherwise licensed under existing provisions of law.

This recommendation would help the government identify and supervise the loanshark who may continue in the money-lending business by conforming his operations to the bare require-ments of the proposed recommendations 1 through 5 which would amend the State Penal Law.

On April 14, 1965, the Committee on Rules of the New York State Assembly introduced a bill which incorporated recom-mendations (1) through 5.[21] The bill was passed by the Assembly

---

[21] New York State Assembly Intro 5855, Assembly Print 6961.

on May 24, 1965, by the Senate on May 26, 1965, and signed into law by the Governor on June 6, 1965.[22]

Conclusion

It is evident that remedial action is required to curb loansharking and its ruthless methods of collection. Usury laws today are generally inadequate for dealing with the problem. They require strengthening. Primarily, the states should license individuals and businesses engaged in moneylending and thus be in a position to regulate this activity.

At the same time it must be recognized that loansharking is only one phase of organized criminal activity. The business of loansharking is the final stage in the process of earning profits through crime and then seeking profitable investments for these funds. Coordinated federal and state efforts directed toward the elimination of organized crime would be most effective in ferreting out the loansharking business.

THE ECONOMICS OF USURY LAWS*

DOUGLASS C. NORTH AND ROGER LEROY MILLER

Moneylenders have long been the targets for endless vituperative attacks as bloodsucking leeches on society. The stigma has been so great that dominant ethnic groups have historically shunned the occupation, leaving it to minorities to serve the borrowing needs of any given community, and consequently to endure victimization, purges, and bloodlettings when scapegoats were needed.

The Western world has certainly been no exception. The laws of the Church against usury were explicit, and it was left to the Jews to dominate the profession for many centuries. As happened with the Chinese in Malaysia and the Hindus in Africa in more recent times, they became a ready target for persecution.

[22] New York State Statutes, Chapter 328, Laws of 1965.

* Taken from "The Economics of Usury Laws," *The Economics of Public Issues*, 2nd ed., by Douglass C. North and Roger LeRoy Miller, 1973, pp. 44–49. Used with permission.

The concept of *interest* for money lent dates back to Roman times when, by law, the defaulting party to a contract had to pay his creditor a compensation. Medieval lawyers used the legal tactic of *damna et interesse* to extract such compensation. Thus *interesse* became a charge for the use of money (under the guise of indemnity for failure to perform a contract).

It would be convenient to think that the opposition to money-lending for *interesse* resulted from an ancient ignorance of economic principles. After all, why should someone be willing to give up the use of his own money unless he were paid? Man's modern enlightenment on this topic has not, however, completely changed the picture. In fact, the persistence of legislation affecting the lending of money makes it clear that a widespread suspicion still lingers that the moneylender possesses some unique, shady, and monopolistic influence. Many states have enacted laws setting maximum rates of interest on loans to consumers, and the federal government has legislated the maximum interest rates for various uses of money. What are the consequences? To find out, we must examine the so-called "money market."

The market for money is like any other market. The suppliers are individuals and institutions who are willing at a price (the interest rate) to forego present command over current use of goods and services; and the higher the price, the more money they will lend. The demanders are many: consumers wanting to buy goods now and pay later, investors undertaking some enterprise, and governments. And, as with other goods and services, the lower the price, the more will be demanded. So far, so good! But the money market in fact is composed of a lot of submarkets —those for consumer loans, commercial credit, and real estate, to name a few. Each submarket has its own institutions—consumer loan companies, finance companies, banks, savings and loan associations—which specialize in bringing particular classes of borrowers and lenders together. Moreover, the price of money is different in each market. For financing the purchase of an automobile, the effective interest rate may be 18 to 24 percent per year; yet a corporation may be able to borrow for 7 percent, and the federal government for 5 percent. These rates also fluctuate over time with overall changes in the supply and demand for loans.†

What concerns us, however, is an explanation of the variations in rates at any given moment in time. Several factors determine the differences, other things being equal. First is the length of the loan. The longer the time period involved, the less certain the lender can be about conditions at the time of repayment; consequently, he demands higher compensation. Second is the degree of risk. A lender who feels that a given loan is excessively risky will ask a high rate of interest. Finally, the cost of administering the loan must be considered. It frequently costs as much to handle a small loan as a large one; therefore, the "load" factor, or handling charge, is necessarily a much higher percentage of a small than a large loan. Since this is a charge added to the "pure" price, it implicitly shows up as a higher interest rate.

Each type of loan has its own characteristics. For example, automobile loans are more risky than most and impose a high handling cost. Corporate loans may be for a long or short period, and are subject to risk varying with the credit reputation of the company. Since they usually involve substantial amounts of money, the handling charges constitute a relatively small percentage of the total cost of such loans. The federal government issues short-term notes which are in effect riskless; because of the government's taxing power, they cannot be defaulted. They also involve substantial sums and therefore small handling charges per dollar involved. The net result of these factors is a relatively low rate of interest.

The suppliers of loanable funds can reasonably be expected to shift their funds from one submarket to another depending on where they can obtain the highest rate of return, adjusted for time, risk, and handling charges. However, they must have access to information on all of these possible outlets for their

---

† In addition, during periods of inflation these rates will go higher, reflecting the fact that suppliers are willing to loan money only at greater interest than before because when they are paid back the money will be worth less than it was when it was borrowed.

money. Since a wide variety of agencies and news media dispenses this information at very low cost, the overall capital market tends to be very responsive to changes which affect the rates of return to various suppliers.

To return now to the question of usury laws: Suppose a state legislates a maximum interest rate of 12 percent on consumer loans. If this is higher than the generally prevailing interest rate, it has no effect. However, this is an unlikely assumption. Even in the absence of inflationary tendencies, the going rate on run-of-the-mill consumer transactions is normally higher than 12 percent. What, then, is the effect of the restriction? At the lower rate, buyers will demand more money than the finance companies are willing to supply at that return. Lenders will begin by introducing service charges to cover "handling costs" which formerly were incorporated in the interest rate. Then they will move to some sort of rationing of the funds available for loans. Logically, they will attempt to eliminate the riskier loans; and since empirically the risk of default on loans is inversely related to the income of the borrower, the refusal of loans to the lowest income groups will offer the easiest course, i.e. the least costly procedure in terms of acquiring information about potential borrowers. The predictable outcome, therefore, is that loans will be made only to the higher-income groups and the would-be borrower whose income is low will face a closed door.

Before turning from state usury laws to federal analogies, we should investigate the allegations of those who support a ceiling on interest rates. The charges cover two areas: (a) that a monopolistic conspiracy exists among loan companies to maintain a high rate of interest; and (b) that the interest rate is too high because of legislation, presumably inspired by the loan companies, to restrict entry of new companies into the consumer-finance field.

No *a priori* judgment is possible on either contention without an examination of conditions in the consumer-loan market in each state. In any case, however, the solution to the problem of rates that are higher than the competitive level cannot be found in the fixing of an arbitrary ceiling, for the reason just described.

Rather, the solution must lie in vigorous prosecution of any conspiracy or in the repeal of laws unduly restricting entry into the field.

No usury laws exist at the federal level, but there are federal restrictions on the interest that commercial banks are allowed to pay for deposits. Just as restrictions on the interest rates for loans have been shown to exert certain economic effects, so, too, do restrictions on the interest payable by banks on deposits.

Commercial banks are forbidden to pay interest on the demand deposits (check accounts) that they hold. What is the effect of this restriction? It must be understood that banks benefit from holding your money in a checking account. The amount you leave on deposit can be used for investment either in loans to other customers or in stocks, bonds, and real estate, all of which yield income to the bank. Banks, therefore, would quite willingly compete for your profitable dollars.

A zero interest payment restriction simply leads banks to compete in some other way.* You are offered "free" checking if your balance is kept above $200, "free" overdraft provisions if your balance exceeds $500, and personalized printed checks with pleasant pictures of sailing clippers embossed on them, at no extra charge. You are, therefore, receiving a valuable consideration (interest) on your checking account because you are charged less than cost for certain services.

Restrictions also govern how much interest can be paid for time deposits (savings accounts). When competition for funds would normally induce banks to offer higher interest rates, they must instead resort to giving away "free" hairdryers, clocks, and pens to new customers. During our most recent inflationary episode, as interest rates climbed steadily for corporate bonds of impeccable quality, the banks were hard pressed to compete for funds. Regulations were even invoked to prevent free giveaways from gaining too much value. As a result, savings and loan associations suffered large outflows of funds during the

---

* The legal restriction actually grants all banks, taken together, a government enforced *monopsony* in the market for an input called "demand deposits." All the gimmicks mentioned below are merely each individual banks' method of "cheating" on the monopsonistic cartel.

later sixties and the start of the seventies. After all, if a rate of return of 9½ percent is available on safe, Aaa-rated bonds, who would leave much money in a local savings account at 5 percent?

The regulation of savings account interest rates has had serious consequences in another sector of the economy, the housing market. Since funds were flowing out of savings and loan associations, the source of available mortgage money dried up, for this is where such companies do their investing. The dearth of funds, aided by other factors, led to a sharp drop in new housing starts by the latter part of the sixties. In 1965, 1.4 million new units had been started, but only 1.1 million starts were made in 1966. Not until 1968 was the 1.4 million mark reached again, and at the time of this writing, the figure is still the same. By a circuitous but evident route, the regulation of savings accounts thus led to a "housing shortage" and to consequent higher housing prices.

Restrictions on economic variables aways have consequences by which some gain and some lose. Economic analysis can help identify both the effects of the restrictions and the groups affected. Restrictions on interest rates lead to curtailment of the supply of loans, with lower-income groups being most adversely affected.

THE IMPINGEMENT OF LOANSHARKING ON THE BANKING INDUSTRY*

RICHARD B. MILLER

When the National City Bank of New York announced its entry into the personal loan field in 1928, the move was acclaimed by the press with such headlines as:

> Loan Sharks Doom Sounded by Big Bankers
> Nation's Biggest Bank Fights Loan Sharks
> Usury Dealt Heavy Blow by Bank's Action

Since that step into an area untouched by the large commercial

---

* Reprinted from *The Bankers Magazine,* Winter 1966, pp. 84-91. Used with permission.

banks of the day, personal loan departments have grown to be a major part of modern banking. Yet the loanshark thrives. In fact, his influence has been spreading. Studies show that in some areas of the country, loansharks have even infiltrated banking institutions.

The World of the Loanshark

To most law-abiding citizens, the loanshark is a crude gangster who usually operates along the waterfront. And this description does apply to some loansharks. But it is only a partial description at best. Many criminal moneylenders are well-groomed, distinguished-looking men who ply their trade at almost every level of our society. One law enforcement official puts loansharking in "easily the billion-dollar-a-year class."

While membership or affiliation in a criminal syndicate is not a prerequisite for loansharking, it is almost a necessity if substantial sums of money are to be moved into the money-lending business.

Organization of the loanshark racket is usually composed of three main levels. On top are the underworld leaders, the heads of the Cosa Nostra (Mafia) families, who are the original sources of the money. It is to these chieftains that all the others owe their allegiance. The bosses distribute the funds to their chief lieutenants—the second level. These men are normally charged a fee of about 1 percent a week for the money. Incidentally, there is absolute responsibility for the use of the money at all levels, including distribution of funds and a profitable return on the capital. Each man is an independent contractor who can offer no excuses for failing to perform his part of the "contract."

The lieutenants are actually middlemen. They, in turn, distribute funds to the third level in the organization—the men who deal with the borrowers. Third-level operators are usually charged from .5 to 2 percent a week for their use of the money. And the borrower is charged at the rate of not less than 5 percent a week.

Collection Problems

Credentials or collateral, of course, have no place in the loanshark's operations. Yet payment is almost never a problem. As one of the most prominent loansharks in New York City described a meeting with a borrower:

> . . . the loanshark quite frankly stated to him that he doesn't need any credentials, number one. The man who had sent the borrower, the prospective borrower, into him—he was enough. His word that you, the prospective borrower, are okay, is enough for me. And the borrower didn't require any collateral. The borrower couldn't understand this too well. He was simply told in no uncertain terms that, "*Your body is your collateral.*"

Overt violence is rarely necessary. The loanshark's reputation alone is generally enough to instill sufficient fear to ensure payment. Sometimes "enforcers"—strong-arm men—are employed to encourage slow-paying borrowers to meet their obligations. But if a borrower can convince the loanshark of his inability to pay, loans may be re-negotiated. In rare cases, the loanshark will agree to halting interest charges for a certain period of time.

The Profit Incentive

Loansharking has long been a most attractive proposition to underworld operators. Of all the factors that have led to its popularity, the most important is the fantastic profits loanshark operations can generate. The extent of the profit potential was illustrated by Ralph Salerno, Sergeant of Detectives of the Criminal Intelligence Bureau of the New York City Police Department.

> A big racket boss could have a Christmas Party in his home to which he invites ten trusted lieutenants . . . He can take one million dollars, which is not an inconceivable amount of cash, and distribute one hundred thousand dollars to each of the ten men. All he has to tell them is, "I want 1 percent per week—I don't care what you get for it, but I want 1 percent per week."
>
> He does not have to record their names. He doesn't have to record the amount. These are easy enough to remember. And if you stop to think that 365 days later, at next year's Christmas party, the only problem this gang leader has is where is he going to find five more men to hand out a half a million dollars that he earned in the last year on the same terms . . . (a profit of) $520,000 a year.

If you carry out this example further, through the three organization levels, the million dollar "investment" can return a total of $4,160,000 in interest and other charges—in just one year!

Loansharks Links with Banks

In recent years there have been disturbing reports of organized criminal activities in banking operations. Probably the most detailed account on record of the extent loansharks have infiltrated banks was brought to light in the investigation in 1965 of the loanshark racket in metropolitan New York by the New York State Commission of Investigation.

Immediate Credit

Banks located in the garment center of New York City naturally cater to clothing manufacturers and employees. Because of the seasonal aspects of the business, the rapid turnover of cash and merchandise, and the sudden demands of style changes, there is often the need of cash in a hurry. In addition to making the garment industry a fertile field for the usurer, special customs and services have been developed by banks in the area. One of these banking services is called "immediate credit."

In the following excerpt from the public hearing held by the Investigation Commission, a former salesman for a dress manufacturer explained "immediate credit":

Q. Describe immediate credit.
A. Well, if our check was in the bank that same day that you wanted to make a deposit, in order to have it paid and not sent back to you, the bank would charge one dollar for each item.
Q. The bank would permit drawings against uncollected funds?
A. No, just on your own checks.
Q. Who used immediate credit—people in financial trouble?
A. Yes.

In other words, depositors were allowed to draw against uncollected checks upon approval of a bank officer and payment of a special fee. The net effect of this is that the bank was making a one-day loan for an interest charge of one dollar. Of course, such a bank-instituted service actually encourages a practice banks have been fighting for years—check kiting.

A Bank Employee's Story: The Panic Hour

The close working relationship that some loansharks may achieve with staff members of a bank was demonstrated at the same public hearing. The following is part of the testimony of a former employee who handled immediate credit at a bank in New York's garment center. His busiest time came in the afternoon during a period known in the area as "the panic hour."

Q. What does "panic hour" mean?

A. Well, at 2:30, checks are returned to the Federal Reserve, made good or not made good. If not good, they are returned. From 1:30 to 2:30 is the panic hour—one hour to deadline time. Though this actually depends on the account, because some accounts are held to 3:00 P.M. (This is the time when those who could would try to deposit cash to cover checks drawn against insufficient funds.)

Q. Did you see loansharks doing business on bank premises?

A. Yes . . .

Q. Did you ever refer anyone to a loanshark?

A. Not really. Kaufman* would hang around and hear if anyone needed money. He was allowed to hang around—especially during the panic hour. After the initial contact, I would give Kaufman financial information about the individual. He was never questioned by the guard.

Q. Did you ever get any money from loansharks?

A. Yes. About half the money and liquor at Christmas came from them by way of depositors.

Q. You mean the individual who borrowed money from the loansharks?

A. Yes.

Q. Were you ever told by the bank not to accept money from people doing business with the bank.

A. No.

Q. Were officers doing the same thing?

A. Yes, they set the pattern, we followed.

---

* Milton Kaufman, identified by the SIC as a well-known loanshark in the garment district, took the Fifth Amendment against self-incrimination thirty times in refusing to testify at the hearing about his activities. When arrested a few years earlier on charges of conspiracy to commit extortion, he was described as one of the city's biggest loansharks.

In later testimony, it was brought out that the employee actively assisted loansharks in contacting borrowers right in the bank. This was accomplished by a signal system where the employee would indicate what customers, after being refused credit by the bank, would be good prospects for a usurious loan. In fact, one witness told that, after being refused immediate credit, he was introduced to Kaufman. The bank employee, before the meeting, told the customer that Kaufman loaned money on a "6-5"* basis.

Other testimony by the bank employee showed that he was able to add about $2,000 a year—free and clear—to his regular earnings, most of it coming directly or indirectly from loansharks.

Tricks of the Trade

A former executive of a sportswear firm, currently serving a sentence for grand larceny, was allowed to testify at the hearing. To pay gambling losses, he borrowed from loansharks; to pay the sharks, he stole from his company. In the following exchange, the inter-relationship between loanshark, borrower, and bank employee is clearly illustrated.

Q.　What was your connection with Kaufman? (The same man mentioned earlier).

A.　I started taking checks from the company—made out to the company. I gave them to Kaufman who would cash them with no endorsement. They totaled about $200,000.

Q.　Did Kaufman discount the checks?

A.　Yes, 10 percent off the top.

Q.　Did you bank any of the money?

A.　Sometimes, at the same bank as Kaufman's. He introduced me to tellers and officers.

Q.　Did Kaufman say it would be necessary to hand them (members of the bank's staff) cash gratuities?

A.　Yes. Well, he said you could always count on them for a favor and naturally you should take care of them.

Q.　Then you began to pay the teller on a weekly basis?

A.　Yes. $10 a week. He (the teller) would tell me what checks I had to cover that day. Then I started to pay $15 a week.

---

* Loansharks will often supply small amounts of money for short periods of time. The usual terms are for $5 loaned, $6 must be repaid within a week.

Q. Did you pay money to the bank officer?

A. Yes.

Q. Did you ever have a conversation with Mr. Kaufman about how this money would be paid over to the bank officer?

A. Well, he mentioned to me, I had a check to be cashed, just slide the money underneath the check and that was sufficient.

Q. Would there be anything wrong with the particular check to be cashed which would entail an additional hazard to the banker, and were you paying him for this reason?

A. In some cases . . . It could have been a check drawn on an out-of-town bank, and naturally, usually it takes a long time for a check to clear . . .

Q. Was this same officer handling Kaufman's personal account?

A. To the best of my knowledge, yes.

Q. Was Kaufman using his personal account to transmit monies from these corporate checks?

A. Yes.

Q. Were any business transactions arising out of check larcenies conducted on bank premises?

A. Yes. I would call and arrange to meet Kaufman at the bank, turn over the checks to him, and he would make out personal checks and have them OK'd for cash by the officer.

Enter the Check Casher

The relationship and intermingling of loansharks and banking can take many twists, bringing others into the web. One group of outsiders are check cashers, found in many big cities and near where large numbers of people are employed. How check cashers become involved with loansharks and banks is shown in this excerpt from the testimony of the bank employee we met earlier:

Q. Do you believe there is a direct connection between check cashers and loansharks?

A. Yes. A loanshark will take a series of checks from an account. Now, we all know that if you clear X-amount of dollars worth of checks through your account, the income tax people can come in and check on it. It will show. Therefore, to get around this, you have to clear your checks without endorsing them personally. The best way I know how to do that is to go through a check casher who knows you and will cash the check without an endorsement.

Q. Isn't it against the law for a check casher to cash a check made payable to a corporate payee?

A. Yes. The loanshark would get a check payable to cash, made out by an individual, and endorsed by the individual. The loanshark would then take the check to a check casher and cash it without endorsing it.

Q. Does it also work this way? Would an individual, perhaps someone who had a partner in a corporate entity, and who didn't want someone to know that he had received a corporate check—would he use the same mechanism to cash a check?

A. Yes. The corporate officer would go to the check casher with the check payable to the XYZ company. He would cash it for a nominal fee. And providing that the check casher had an "in" in the bank, that check would be accepted for deposit on the check casher's account for clearance.

Q. Instead, could the check casher actually convey the check to a loanshark for further distribution to the borrower, and then the check would never go through the check casher's account?

A. Very possible.

Q. Isn't a check made payable to a corporation, isn't that supposed to be deposited only in the account of the corporation?

A. That is right.

Q. It is never cashed, or it isn't permitted to be transferred?

A. Unless it is OK'd and initialed by a bank officer.

Q. If a bank officer does that, he is not following the law, is he?

A. Right.

It might be well to note at this point that the officers and employees involved in the activities discussed in the hearings and in other findings of the Investigations Commission were discharged. In some cases, where criminal statutes were involved, the offending bank personnel were also brought up on charges.

Loansharks and the Law: The New York State Approach

Probably nothing has contributed more to the spread of loansharking than the lack of effective usury laws in the United States. To combat loanshark activities, police and public prosecutors have generally had to look for other criminal violations: extortion, assault and additional crimes of violence. In many cases, though, as mentioned earlier, loansharks rarely have to resort to violence. And when they do, the victims often are afraid to either report the assault or press charges.

Until this past year, only Florida and Illinois had laws of any consequence to control usury. Now, due in large part to the shocking disclosures of the New York Commission of Investigation, the State of New York has enacted the strongest law yet against the practice of usury. The new sections of the State's Penal Law provide:

> . . . The charging of interest at a rate greater than 25 percent per annum on a loan to any individual, partnership, association, or corporation constitutes a crime of "criminal usury," a felony. (This figure of 25% was set because it did not seem to restrict the flow of lending capital in higher risk areas of the economy.)
>
> . . . Possession of loanshark records is a misdemeanor. This section was included because individual borrowers from loansharks are often afraid to make formal complaints. And investigations show that the criminal lenders usually do keep detailed records of their transactions.

It is too early to make a judgment of the effectiveness of the 1965 changes in the New York State Penal Law. But the provisions outlined above, along with other measures to strengthen enforcement follow the specific recommendations of law enforcement agencies. A spokesman for the New York State Banking Department put it this way, "While the new law will certainly not end loansharking, it makes the operation that much riskier."

The Breadth and Depth of Criminal Activities

Loansharking operations are not confined to our largest metropolitan centers, but are in evidence in almost every city of size in the country.

A special banking subcommittee of the House of Representatives, investigating loanshark rackets run by criminal syndicates, has already uncovered 103 such operations in twelve cities: Boston, Buffalo, Chicago, Cleveland, Detroit, Kansas City, Los Angeles, Milwaukee, Miami, New York, and Philadelphia. And the investigations are still far from complete.

Bank Funds as Capital

The prestige and potential of bank operations appeal to many criminals. This can lead to more serious problems than the corruption of a bank employee.

The New York State Investigation Commission uncovered an instance where bank capital was actually used to finance usurious lending operations. This large-scale racket was run by John "Gentleman Johnny" Massiello. Though Massiello refused to answer questions at the hearing, witnesses revealed that at least 1.5 million dollars of the funds of a single branch bank were put to work for the loanshark. Other evidence indicated the operation was even larger.

Here is how the racket worked: A businessman-borrower, unable to obtain credit, applied to Massiello for a $6,000 loan. The loanshark required the borrower to execute a promissory note payable to him for $8,000. This note was then taken to the bank where it was discounted—with the approval of a corrupt loan officer—at the bank rate of 6 percent.

In addition to the basic scheme, Massiello would borrow large sums, with the aid of the corrupt bank official, at the going rate. The operation was kept going by continually pyramiding the base of the amount of the bank loans. At one point, a peak of $770,000 was on loan to the Massiello group using a variety of names and dummy corporations. Up to now, the bank has been able to recover only half that amount.

Hoodlum-Run Banks

Perhaps more dangerous are the reports of gangsters moving in on the management of some banks. Courtney Evans, retired as a senior official of the Federal Bureau of Investigation, warned last year that organized crime is expanding its efforts to take over banks and other financial institutions.

A Federal grand jury has been investigating the take-over of some banks by wealthy members of the Cosa Nostra crime syndicate. Though officials have refused to name the banks involved, or where they are located, they are not limited to the big cities. For the most part, according to reliable sources, they are in the East and Middle West.

Often used to conceal the transfer of "hot money" from gambling, narcotics, and other rackets into legitimate trade channels, the banks run by mobsters which will ignore the normal guidelines to sound banking are ideal investments for the mobsters. Though much of the racket money is funneled back into criminal operations, there are often considerable sums, called "mattress money," lying around untouched in shoe boxes or other caches. Besides providing a handy clearing house for their funds, a bank can be an excellent front against possible government scrutiny of their financial dealings. In addition, a bank provides a valuable aura of respectability.

Responsible Action

New laws, such as the New York State amendments to its criminal code, can play a significant part in controlling loan-shark operations. Still, it is doubtful that legislation will be enacted with any particular speed.

In the meantime, the situation demands that the institutions and the people involved move in a positive way. What can a bank do? Though there is probably no foolproof way to keep loansharks away, there are several measures a bank can and should take:

• *Exercise Better Control Over Loans.* In one of the banks mentioned in the hearings conducted by the New York State Investigation Commission, loans by some officers, as long as they were within the limits of their authority, were never reviewed.

• *Maintain Closer Supervision of Branch Offices.* There are advantages to allowing a branch to operate like a small unit bank. But control measures must be stringent enough to insure that operations conform to bankwide policies and procedures.

• *Review Overdraft Activity.* While, as a matter of customer relations, no bank can prevent all overdrafts, the transactions should be checked, as abnormal activity may indicate loan-sharking.

• *Improve Selection Procedures.* Though the inclination to

larceny is hard to detect, there may be some indications—overly large financial obligations, unsavory associates, a spotty employment record—which could point up potential problems.

• *Guard Against Loitering.* There's a difference between a friendly bank and a hangout.

• *Prohibit Receipt of Gratuities.* Particularly at Christmas, clients often want to show their appreciation for services rendered by gifts of liquor, food, money, and other presents. Many business firms have instituted campaigns among their employees to stop this practice because it puts the receiver under obligation—whether utilized or not. Banks can do the same thing, difficult as it might be on both officers and employees.

There are additional measures a bank can take that involve extra planning, or a longer time to put into effect. Along with other training procedures, a course or session could be included on "how to spot loansharks." It might be well for a bank to review its pay policies, too. The bank employee referred to earlier in the article gave his reason for cooperating with the loanshark as low pay. His salary was, in fact, lower than the average salary paid by other banks for the same position.

The use of bank money, bank employees, and bank premises by loansharks present problems and potential problems that are frightening. Several of the steps suggested to control the problems can be taken almost immediately. For many banks, there may be little time to lose.

The Loanshark's Glossary

BOOK: Lending capital provided to loansharks by underworld financiers.

COVER: A front, apparently legitimate, used to mask criminal activity.

FIVE PERCENTER: See "Shylock." Someone who lends money at 5 percent a week.

MOUSTACHES: Underworld bosses.

SHYLOCK: Used in the underworld to refer to anyone in the money-lending business. The words "shy" and "shell" are also used in the same way.

SIT-DOWN: Fixing a final figure of indebtedness by arbitration.

STEERER: A person who refers borrowers to the money lender, usually not a member or employee of a criminal syndicate.

VIGORISH: Interest and other penalties or charges imposed on a usurious loan. Also called "vig."

STOPPING THE CLOCK: The cessation of the accumulation of weekly interest and penalties. This only happens when the borrower has convinced the loanshark he cannot continue to pay the weekly payment.

BIBLIOGRAPHY

Books

Ashley, W. J.: *An Introduction to English Economic History and Theory.* London, 2 vols. 1906-1909, 4th ed.

Belloc, Hilaire: *Usury.* London, Sheed, 1931.

Challenge of Crime in a Free Society. A Report by the President's Commission on Law Enforcement and Administration of Justice. Washington, D.C., Government Printing Office, 1967.

Conrad, Joseph W.: *An Introduction to the Theory of Interest.* Berkeley, U of Cal Pr, 1959.

Cook, Fred J.: *The Secret Rulers.* New York, Duell, 1966.

Davis, Malcolm W.: *The Loanshark Campaign.* New York, Russell Sage, 1914.

Dawnay, Guy Payan: *Some Thoughts on Usury.* London, Industrial Christain Fellowship, 1944.

Dempsey, Bernard William: *Interest and Usury.* American Council on Public Affairs, 1943.

Eubank, Earle Edward: *Loansharks and Loan Legislation in Illinois.* New York, Russell Sage, 1917.

Ham, Arthur H.: *The Campaign Against the Loanshark.* New York, Russell Sage, 1912.

Hodson, Clarence (Ed.): *The Fair Rate of Interest for Small Loans: Anti-Loanshark Laws by States.* New York, Legal Reform Bureau to Eliminate the Loanshark Evil, Inc., 1923.

Mark, Jeffrey: *Analysis of Usury, With Proposals for Abolition of Debt.* London, J. M. Dent, 1935.

Mark, Jeffrey: *The Modern Idolatry, An Analysis of Usury and the Pathology of Debt.* London, Chatto and Windus, 1934.

Mills, James: *The Prosecutor.* New York, Farrar, 1969.

Nelson, Benjamin N.: *The Ideal of Usury, From Tribal Brotherhood to Universal Otherhood.* Princeton, N.J., Princeton U Pr, 1949.

New York State Commission of Investigation: *An Investigation of the Loanshark Racket*. New York, April 1965.

Noonan, John Thomas: *The Scholastic Analysis of Usury*. Cambridge, Harvard U Pr, 1957.

North, Douglas C. and Miller, Roger LeRoy: The economics of usury laws. *The Economics of Public Issues*, 2nd ed. New York, Harper and Row, 1973, pp. 44-49.

Ryan, Franklin Winton: *Usury and Usury Laws*. New York, Houghton, 1924.

Sillar, Robert George: *Usury*. London, Exeter Hall, 1885.

U.S. House of Representatives: *Investigation into Crown Savings Bank Failure*. Washington, D.C., Government Printing Office, 1966.

U.S. Library of Congerss. Division of Bibliography: *Select List of References on Loansharking*. No. 296, Washington, D.C., 1919.

Zeiger, Henry A.: *Sam the Plumber*. New York, VAL (Signet), 1970.

Articles

Confessions of a Six-for-Five Juice Man. *Burroughs Clearing House*, 49:40-1, April 1965.

Kaplan, Lawrence J. and Matteis, Salvatore: The economics of loansharking. *The American Journal of Economics and Sociology*, 27:239-251, July 1968.

Miller, Richard B.: The impingement of loansharks on the banking industry. *Banker's Magazine*, 149:84-91, Winter 1966.

New York State Appeals Court Upholds Waterfront Commission Revocation of Docker's License for Balking at Queries in Loansharking Probe. *The New York Times*, 70, June 3, 1959.

New York State Statutes. Chapter 328, Laws of 1965.

Seidel, John M.: Lets compete with loansharks. *Harvard Business Review*, 69-77, May-June 1970.

The loanshark problem today. *Law and Contemporary Problems*, School of Law, Duke University, 19, 1: Winter 1954.

Two watchmen held for loansharking. *The New York Times* 54, November 14, 1958.

Usurers beware. *Business Week*, April 27, 1957.

Waterfront commission charges Pontecorvo with loansharking. *The New York Times*, 1, April 10, 1958.

Waterfront commission hearing on loansharking against dockers. *The New York Times*, 18, March 20, 1959.

THE ECONOMICS OF NARCOTICS

INTRODUCTION

An AFFLUENT AMERICA today has not one but several drug problems, and those engaged in the business of supplying these products are very successful entrepreneurs. Nicotine is a drug, produced legally, which is probably responsible for the premature deaths of about 250,000 smokers annually. About 550 billion doses of nicotine are smoked yearly.

No other drug is so commonly a factor in homicides and suicides as alcohol, also legally produced. Over half the highway deaths and over half the arrests made in the United States are alcohol-related. It is estimated that alcohol addicts number five million, a conservative estimate, and that as many as nine million are drinking their way to irreversible brain and liver damage.

It is estimated that marijuana, an illegal drug, is smoked at the rate of about five million cigarettes a day. The National Institute of Mental Health estimated that there were two to three million *social users* of marijuana.*

But, manufacturers and distributors in the profitable drug empire handle many other products in great demand, including narcotics, stimulants, depressants, and hallucinogens, known more popularly as heroin, cocaine, hashish, methedrine, mescaline, LSD (lysergic acid diethylamide), and many others. The production and sale of these illicit drugs are accompanied by crime, corruption, and violence. As the risks in handling these products become greater, so do the profits. Those willing to accept great risks for great profits can always be found.

_____
* As of June 1975, Alaska became the first state to decriminalize home use of marijuana.

The first two selections in this chapter relate to heroin. The American heroin empire has come to be what it is because $350 worth of raw material can be worth $500,000 at retail, as indicated in the first article, "There Are People Who Say, 'Well, Business is Business.'" The heroin industry dollar volume is estimated at about $3 billion a year in the U.S. alone. The second article on "The Economics of Heroin," a condensed thesis, explains in some detail the movement of the raw material through the various middlemen until it reaches the addict.

The third article analyzes "The Socio-Economic Effect of Drug and Victimless Crime Prosecution." The fourth selection, Table 7-V, indicates profit possibilities for a list of the common drugs available in the New York Metropolitan Area in 1973.

THERE ARE PEOPLE WHO SAY, "WELL, BUSINESS IS BUSINESS"*

They say so because this is an industry where $350 worth of raw material can be worth $500,000 at retail.

It's an industry that runs to nearly $3 billion a year in the U.S. alone. Worldwide? It's anybody's guess.

It's a real growth industry, expanding in the U.S. at 10 percent or more yearly. The U.S. and the Far East are still the largest markets, but they may not be for long; the European market is exploding. Yet, nowhere in the world does the industry spend a dime in advertising.

Profitable? Incredibly so. Ten kilos (roughly 22 pounds) of the raw material costs $350. Processed and packaged, it can bring in anywhere from $280,000 to $500,000, with profits of perhaps 15 percent to 1,000 percent for everyone along the line. Naturally, there are risks: Whoever heard of a high-profit industry without them?

Of course, all figures on the industry are estimates. Hard statistics are impossible to come by. For not only is the industry large, growing and profitable, it's also illegal.

---

* Reprinted from *Forbes* magazine, issue of April 1, 1970, pp. 19-22. Used with permission.

The industry is the manufacture and sale of heroin.

Heroin addiction is, of course, a plague. It started in the slums of the nation's larger cities, but now rages almost everywhere in the U.S. including upper-middle-class suburbia. It has crossed the Atlantic to Italy, to France, where it was once almost unknown, and even to England, which boasted for years that it had the problem under control. It had destroyed the lives of nobody knows how many hundreds of thousands. It is responsible for three deaths a day in New York City alone.

A plague, yes, but it's an industry, too. In fact, such a plague, would not exist if thousands of people were not profiting from it.

One thing few law-abiding citizens understand is that a criminal enterprise obeys the same economic laws as any other business, including the law of supply and demand. Like any legitimate industry the heroin industry has its bankers, its exporters and importers, its manufacturers, jobbers, retailers, salesmen. Like legitimate businessmen, morever, the merchants of heroin strive constantly to diversify, and with a good deal of success. Heroin has financed many another enterprise.

How They Figure It

Anyone going into a business must first analyze his market. In the U.S. the market for heroin consists of about 100,000 men, women and children in New York City and 100,000 more elsewhere. This is a conservative estimate. Some experts put the number of heroin addicts in the U.S. at 250,000, and some say there could be as many as 250,000 users in the New York metropolitan area alone.

The Justice Department's Bureau of Narcotics and Dangerous Drugs keeps a record of known narcotics addicts. On December 31, 1968, the most recent date for which figures are available, they numbered 64,011; of these, over 60,000 were heroin addicts. Obviously, the vast majority of heroin addicts in the U.S. escape detection.

A spokesman for the Bureau of Narcotics and Dangerous Drugs says it is therefore not unreasonable to multiply the number of known addicts by three or four to get the total number of addicts. This would mean that on December 31, 1968 there were somewhere between 180,000 to 240,000 heroin addicts in the nation.

Also, assume that the number of known addicts increased by more than 25,000 in 1969. That would put the total addict population at somewhere between 220,000 and 280,000. Therefore, 200,000 on heroin does not seem an unreasonable figure.

Let's accept the estimate of 100,000 addicts in New York City. Heroin is less expensive in New York than in many parts of the U.S. and for a simple reason: Most heroin enters the country by way of New York because New York is the biggest port of entry for both planes and ships. According to Deputy Chief Inspector John P. McCahey, head of the New York City Police Narcotics Bureau, the average junkie in New York spends $35 a day for heroin. Some addicts spend as much as $100 a day, but teenagers just acquiring the habit may be able to get along on as little as $7 to $15.

Let's accept the estimate of $35 a day on the average. This means that every day in New York City addicts spend $3.5 million for heroin. That's $1.3 billion a year.

As heroin moves south and west, it naturally becomes more expensive. McCahey estimates that, in the country as a whole outside New York, the average junkie has to spend $40 a day. That's $4 million a day, or close to $1.5 billion a year.

It Starts in Turkey

The heroin industry, like every other, starts with raw material, in this case a flower called *papaver somniferum,* the "poppy of sleep." It can be grown in many parts of the world, but most of the poppies used in making heroin for the U.S. are grown in Turkey. The main reason is that, by international agreement, growing the "flower of sleep" is legal in Turkey. It yields a brown gum, opium, the base of codeine and morphine, which the medical world needs.

Under the international agreement, the Turkish government is supposed to buy up all the opium produced in the country. It pays about $120 for each ten kilos. However, the men who traffic in heroin pay as much as $350; and Turkish farmers are very poor.

Despite the Turkish government's efforts to prevent it, some 7 percent of the Turkish crop is diverted to opium brokers for the heroin industry. The brokers sell the opium for $400, a markup of nearly 15 percent, to dealers in Istanbul or Aleppo, Syria, or Beirut, Lebanon, getting it there by such bizarre means as having camels swallow rubber bags stuffed with opium. A camel has three stomachs, and, for that reason, takes a long time to digest anything.

Next the raw opium is converted chemically, by a relatively simple operation, into morphine base, a brown powder. This reduces the ten kilos to one, but makes that one kilo worth between $700 and $800. The converter sells the morphine base to a heroin laboratory, probably in France, adding $50 to $100 for the cost of shipping. Apparently by tacit agreement among the men in the heroin industry, the laboratories are run by Corsicans. There are heroin laboratories in Lebanon, the Far East and Mexico, but U.S. importers prefer the heroin made in France.

Converting morphine into heroin is a complicated process, requiring chemical skill, some equipment and several days' time. Three to seven people run each laboratory, usually on a profit-sharing basis. There are profits a plenty to share. The kilo of morphine base that cost, say $850, including transportation, is worth anywhere from $3,500 to $15,000 when converted into heroin. (The price fluctuates.)

Now the U.S. importer enters the picture. He must have a bankroll, not only to pay for the heroin but also because the cost of transporting heroin from Europe to New York is about $1,000 a kilo. That is supposed to cover the bribes and the risks.

Sharing the Risks

One practice is for the importer to pay 50 percent in cash before shipment. Then, if the heroin is seized, he and the exporter will lose equally. Suppose the importer buys 100 kilos at $5,000 a kilo, plus $1,000 a kilo for transportation. To put up half that amount would take $300,000 cash.

Very few people have that much ready cash, which is why

the heroin industry needs people to do for it what bankers do for legitimate business. Where do narcotics bankers get the money? From gambling, loansharking, extortion, and previous heroin imports. Where else?

Getting the heroin into the U.S. takes a great deal of ingenuity. The smugglers use circuitous routes, traveling by land, sea and air. They are constantly thinking up new ways to hide the heroin. Last December Customs and New York City police discovered heroin hidden in the bottoms of two five litre wine bottles under a glass partition with wine on top of the partition. The bottoms were hidden by raffia wrapping. This particular shipment came from Santiago, Chile.

Once the heroin is safely in the U.S., the money really starts rolling in. Says William Durkin, New York City regional director of The Bureau of Narcotics and Dangerous Drugs and a veteran of twenty years in narcotics work: "The heroin comes in 85 percent to 95 percent pure. The importer sells it, still pure, to one, two, three, or five number two men in ten- to twenty-kilo lots for anywhere from $12,000 to $22,000 a kilo, depending on the market. The latest quotation is $12,500. The number two men then resell it, still pure, in one- and two-kilo lots to maybe ten or fifteen number three men, just now at a price of around $22,000.

"The number three men have several choices: They can sell the stuff to number four men in half- or quarter-kilo lots for $28,000 to $29,000. Or they can short-weight, selling, say a ninth of a kilo as an eighth. Or else, they can dilute the heroin; pretend it's pure and charge the full price for it."

The number four men are the cutters. Their factories usually are one room in a slum apartment, where they employ eight or ten people to dilute the heroin. The preferred dilutant is quinine, but they also use Mennite® laxative or milk sugar though they have also been known to use roach powder. The resulting mixture is roughly 14 percent to 15 percent heroin. It could be more; it could be less. One ounce is worth $600 to $700 on today's market.

The mixture is packed in glassine bags, selling for $5 each. How much heroin in the bag depends on the going price of pure heroin—the higher the price of the pure stuff, the less heroin. At present, the bags contain roughly 100 milligrams each, about one-three hundredth of an ounce.

Customer as Salesman

People who sell the $5 bags on the street are called "pushers." Most are themselves addicts, who sell the stuff in order to make the money to buy it. To those in narcotics, this is the beautiful part about the industry. Almost every customer is in effect a salesman. They don't need Madison Avenue. Addicts feel comfortable only among addicts, and therefore push to get their friends on dope.

Given the variations in the quantity and quality of heroin a $5 bag contains, estimates of how much a kilo of pure heroin is worth when cut, packaged and sold at retail vary all the way from $225,000 to $500,000. In a time of panic, real or contrived, the worth will increase sharply. This from $350 worth of poppy juice.

Who runs the industry? Until a few years ago, this was an easy question: The Mob, the Mafia, La Cosa Nostra, the organized gangsters of Sicilian extraction in the U.S. Now the picture is cloudy.

An international consortium of Spanish-speaking criminals (Spaniards, Cubans, Puerto Ricans and South Americans) clearly has entered the business of smuggling heroin into the U.S. and distributing it. And some experts believe there are now small entrepreneurs in the business. Has La Cosa Nostra quit the heroin industry? On this, the experts disagree. Some argue that it has. The risks became too great, they say, after the conviction of La Cosa Nostra boss Vito Genovese in 1959 for narcotics conspiracy violation.

Says New York City's Deputy Chief Inspector McCahey, "La Cosa Nostra is probably not any longer in the mainstream of drugs. For one thing, those arrested and investigated now are in the Spanish group, not La Cosa Nostra. No Italians have been arrested in New York City in the past three or four years. For another, the Spanish-speaking group active in heroin aren't being retaliated against by La Cosa Nostra."

A more convincing argument comes from federal officials, particularly in the Bureau of Narcotics and Dangerous Drugs and the Bureau of Customs, which spends about 75 percent of its energies fighting the narcotics traffic. Sure, they say, The Mob no longer operates on the lowest (and riskiest) levels of the heroin industry, but it continues to run the industry from up high.

Two men who argue this view are Albert W. Seeley and Edward T. Coyne, senior Customs special agents. When interviewed, they kept interrupting and amplifying each other, so they can be quoted as one: "Narcotics is now organized worldwide mainly by three language groups—Italian, French and Spanish. Previously, there were only the Italians, in Italy and the U.S. They dealt with the French Corsicans. They permitted the Spanish-speaking group to get into the business only within the U.S. and only after the import stage and only well down the profit ladder between wholesaler and retailer. Beginning in 1963 —although we didn't get this information until 1968—the Mafia gave permission to the French Corsicans to deal directly with the Spanish, provided the Corsicans gave it a portion of the profit they made from their Spanish sales. Now the Spanish have these international contacts, play importer and, within the U.S. handle their own business from the top level all the way down to the retailer.

"Meanwhile, the Mafia takes its cut, yes, but makes still more from its own participation. It continues to import, and in large quantities like 50 kilos and up, and then handles its own distribution, at least at the top level and maybe down to the middle, too." Seeley and Coyne believe The Mob directly controls more than half the heroin supply in the U.S.; directly and indirectly, about 85 percent. Only it stays away from the actual "retail" level. It is the banker and the wholesaler.

Criminal U.N.

What makes narcotics agents believe this? Like all detectives, they uncover a clue and make a judgment. In July 1968, Customs seized a cache of heroin on a TWA plane that had just arrived at Dulles International Airport from Frankfurt, Germany. Investigation disclosed that it had been shipped by a kind of criminal United Nations, consisting of French-speaking, Italian-speaking and Spanish-speaking hoods. This gang had been smuggling 100 kilos of heroin into New York every month, for enough profit to deposit $1 million every month in Swiss banks.

The heroin was being smuggled in black and brown cotton socks, linked like sausages. Seely and Coyne say the heroin in the brown socks was for Italian customers; in the black socks, for Spanish speaking customers. The route to New York was by way of Washington, Denver and San Francisco. The delivery man to the Italians in New York was one Jean-Marc Montoya, a French national, who is now languishing in prison.

Coyne and Seeley say the Mafia mobsters were charged $7,500 a kilo; the Spanish-speaking, $11,000. "Whom do you charge a lower price for something?" Coyne asks. "Your biggest and best customer, of course." Coyne adds, "As long as there is a Mafia organization, they'll never get out of narcotics. *It's just too profitable.*"

In that final sentence, Coyne spelled out the whole problem of heroin addiction: For those who use heroin, the stuff is death. For those who merchandise this death, it's money. As the risks become greater, so do the profits. And there always are those willing to accept great risks for great profits.

Think about that next time you wonder why the governments haven't been more effective in stamping out the heroin plague.

THE ECONOMICS OF HEROIN*

Roy A. Feigenbaum

The Upper Levels of Heroin Distribution

It is the opinion of most narcotics law enforcement officials that the upper levels of the heroin distribution system operating

---

* This article is an excerpt from *A Comparison of Accumulated Total Revenues Between Organized Crime and Non-Organized Crime Elements in the Heroin Distribution System in New York City,* a thesis presented in partial fulfillment of the requirements for the degree of Masters of Arts in Criminal Justice, John Jay College of Criminal Justice of the City University of New York, February 1973. Used with permission.

in New York City are occupied by Cosa Nostra members. This does not imply that only "Mafiosi" occupy the two top levels. But in terms of this study's focus on the "Italian-Black system" it is presumed that the Cosa Nostra is *exclusively* responsible for the distribution system resulting from *its* participation in the narcotics trade.

The "Importer" Level

Generally each Cosa Nostra family which is involved in narcotics traffic appoints one man—usually a "captain"—to administer the family's interests in that area of crime. For the purpose of analysis this man must be considered the importer, though he is often not the major benefactor of the transactions he arranges. The importer is a supervisor, a "narcotics liason" between Cosa Nostra families, a "fund raiser," attempting to finance as large a shipment of heroin as possible. Usually the importer collects the sum for the purchase from members of his own "family." (These people are the wholesalers in the "Italian-Black system.") While most Cosa Nostra families which are involved in heroin at all will participate regularly, some families will buy infrequently. The importer will accommodate these other families as well.

The importer usually sends a representative, perhaps one of his "soldiers," to arrange the heroin transaction with an overseas contact. This contact may be located in Marseilles. Matters such as price, quality, and method of transportation must be agreed upon. Before the shortage of 1972, shipments of twenty to fifty kilograms of heroin were not uncommon, and ". . . it could go as high as 100 kilos [kilograms]." The price of "pure" heroin for importation has ranged from $6,500 per kilogram to as high as $10,000 per kilogram. Several factors may affect this price. Pressure from local authorities (in Marseilles, for example) may cause the overseas connection to raise *his* price in order to compensate for the increased risk. Or, the overseas connection's *costs* may have increased. The heroin manufacturing laboratory which had supplied this overseas connection with his stock may have been closed down by the police, thus causing him to seek his supply elsewhere. In "troubled times" the price of an illegal commodity generally rises, and all participants are affected. Since the price per kilogram of "pure" heroin has averaged about $8,000 this figure will be used in the analysis.

Assuming that a shipment of fifty kilograms was imported, the importer must have available a sum of $400,000. As mentioned above, he raises this amount by collecting from other Cosa Nostra members. The importer, however, does not merely act as an agent. He usually approaches his backers with an offer to sell each ten kilograms at what would be a "wholesale" price, e.g. $17,000 per kilogram. These backers will each pay in advance for their supply. The importer may deal in a "free on board" fashion—he may contact his backers initially to notify them of an impending deal and then collect the sums after the arrangements have been made overseas and the heroin shipped.

The importer arranges delivery of the parcels to his respective backers. He does not dilute the narcotic, nor does he repackage the shipment. In fact, since the importer usually has a representative handle the physical aspects of the deal, the importer probably never sees the shipment at all. For perhaps one or two month's work the importer can earn a profit of $450,000.

Summary of financial data on the "importer" level. The importer:

1. buys 50 kilograms of 90 percent pure heroin
2. pays $8,000 per kilogram
3. pays total of $400,000
4. does not process
5. sells 50 kilograms of 90 percent pure heroin
6. receives $17,000 per kilogram
7. receives total of $850,000
8. earns total profit of $450,000

The "Wholesaler" Level

The wholesaler is the importer's first customer. The wholesaler, a Cosa Nostra figure like the importer, will generally buy from five to twenty kilograms of heroin, depending upon the availability of the merchandise at the time. He behaves in a manner similar to that of the importer, in that he involves himself in heroin traffic as infrequently as possible. (It benefits all parties involved to handle a few large transactions rather than many small ones.) The wholesaler will thus try to sell his supply as soon as possible.

Whereas some Cosa Nostra families maintain a policy of control over the "wholesaler" level, usually the wholesaler is a free agent. And as long as he does not reveal his source (the importer), no one in "family" " . . . could care less about the wholesaler's clientele."

The wholesaler usually sells his supply without diluting it. He may, however, split the merchandise into half- or quarter-kilograms. But there is no hard and fast rule on this matter since the profit at this level is large and it may not be worth the risk to spend time repackaging the illegal commodity.

Thus the wholesaler differs little from the importer in terms of his pattern of operation. He does not dilute the narcotic, nor does he usually rebag the supply. His main interest is in realizing a large profit quickly and with as little risk as possible.

Nonetheless, the wholesaler must make an initial expenditure of $170,000, assuming that he has bought ten kilograms of heroin from the importer. At this point the wholesaler must decide whether to "stay within bounds" or to sell to a "non-affiliated" customer. That is, he may sell to a major supplier who is well-known and who may very well be a "soldier" in the Cosa Nostra, or he may sell to a Black, to whom the wholesaler could sell at higher prices. Since the proposition has been made that the wholesaler usually will neither cut nor split his stock in order to lessen the risk of arrest, it would follow that he would sacrifice the opportunity to earn a greater profit, thus selling to the more reliable Italian major supplier. Not having diluted the heroin, the wholesaler sells 90 percent pure heroin to his customers at $25,000 per kilogram. He may sell from two to five kilograms to each major supplier.

Summary of financial data on the "wholesaler" level. The wholesaler:

1. buys 10 kilograms of 90 percent pure heroin
2. pays $17,000 per kilogram
3. pays total of $170,000
4. does not process

5. sells 10 kilograms of 90 percent pure heroin
6. receives $25,000 per kilogram
7. receives total of $250,000
8. earns total profit of $80,000

The "Major Supplier" Level

The major supplier is the link between the Cosa Nostra and the "nonorganized" elements in the heroin distribution system. He buys his supply almost exclusively from the Cosa Nostra, and always sells to distributors, none of whom are "organized crime affiliated."

In its relation to the wholesaler, the nature of the "major supplier" level is generally valuable to him, but may also be seen as an obstacle. On one hand the "major supplier" level provides a buffer between Cosa Nostra and "the outside world;" however, the wholesaler must pay for this security since dealing directly with a distributor would result in greater profit for the wholesaler. Thus, for his own protection the wholesaler "stays within bounds" as he may very well have been "ordered" to do so by the other Mafiosi in the "wholesaler" level, or even by the importer.

The major supplier—in the "Italian-Black System" will usually be a "soldier" or an affiliate, in either case an Italian— will buy from two to five kilograms of yet unadulterated heroin. He pays about $25,000 per kilogram. Since it has been assumed that originally fifty kilograms were introduced into the system, it would not be unlikely for the major supplier to buy five kilograms from his wholesaler.

It is at this level that the adulteration process begins. The major supplier, having to operate outside the secure environment of the Cosa Nostra, will attempt to make his involvement in narcotics well worth his while. He "cuts twice"—dilutes the heroin in a 2:1 ratio, thus decreasing the quality of the narcotic from 90 percent purity to 30 percent purity. Quinine and either mannite or mannitol are used as dilutants. The entire cost of these adulterants is about $1,500. As a result, he now has a total of 30 percent pure heroin. The fifteen kilograms are then repackaged into quarter- or eighth-kilograms for sale. More often the major supplier will deal in quarter-kilograms, selling each for $9,000.

Usually selling about two kilograms of heroin net (eight quarter-kilograms) to each of his customers, the major supplier sells his entire stock of sixty quarter-kilograms for a total of $540,000. He therefore earns a profit well over $400 000, having paid $125,000 for his supply originally.

Summary of financial data on the "major supplier" level. The major supplier:

1. buys 5 kilograms of 90 percent pure heroin
2. pays $25,000 per kilogram
3. pays total of $125,000
4. dilutes in a 2:1 ratio
5. spends $1,500 on processing
6. sells 60 quarter-kilograms of 30 percent pure heroin
7. receives $9,000 per quarter-kilogram
8. receives total of $540,000
9. earns total profit of $413,500

The Lower Levels of Heroin Distribution

The lower echelons of the heroin distribution system are characterized by "exceptions to the rule" more than by any one uniform pattern. One "rule" which *can* be stated is that the lower levels of heroin distribution in New York City are composed of persons who are not members of the Cosa Nostra. Conversely, it can also be said that any member of the Cosa Nostra who is involved in heroin traffic will never appear in the lower echelons—the "distributor," "dealer," and "pusher" levels. Invariably, a member of the Cosa Nostra who is involved in heroin distribution is also involved in other illegitimate operations. Thus having too much to lose from a narcotics arrest which could result in twenty years of imprisonment, he avoids lower echelon activities. This problem does not confront those persons who are in the lower levels of heroin distribution since they are either predominantly or (as is the more common case) ". . . exclusively involved in narcotics."

The "Distributor" Level

In the "Italian-Black system" the "distributor" level is generally characterized by "mills" or factories"—locations in which the heroin is processed and prepared for consumption by addicts. Often a substantial operation, the factory is controlled by the distributor.

It is at this level that the risk of arrest and seizure is greatest. More time is spent with the narcotic physically than in any other level—a factory may operate over an entire weekend in order for its entire stock to be processed. The distributor, however, is usually never on the premises. He entrusts the supervision of the operation to several "lieutenants." These people are usually blood relatives, and there may be from four to eight lieutenants running a factory operation. The workers in the factory are usually women—five to six is the usual number—and each will receive a set wage of about $200 for a weekend's work. These women, who do the weighing, mixing, and "bagging" are reliable workers who possess an expertise in their technique. This is an important feature of any "mill" operation since a nonuniform mixture in a bag of heroin—perhaps an unusually high quality—can result in an addict's death from overdose.

The factory's outlet may be handled by "bundlemen," "ouncemen," or other specialists. It is at this point in the system that financial analysis can become difficult. If a distributor decides that the heroin be processed and packaged for addict consumption, the merchandise would then be handled by bundlemen, who would buy parcels of twenty-five bags of heroin, each bag worth $5 upon sale to an addict. Were the distributor to want only a quick (though sizeable) profit, not being interested in an operation which would provide a regular income, he would dilute his stock in a 2:1 ratio, selling ounce weights of 10 percent pure heroin. (These 10% pure ounces would be bought by persons who would then sell to a small "factory-type" operation. Thus it can be seen that the ounceman can be viewed as a dealer, *having purchased* heroin *from a distributor,* or he can be viewed as a distributor, *having sold to* an "entrepreneur" *factory operation.*) Nonetheless, these are only a few possibilities; there are many others. But in the "Italian-Black system" a mill operation which packages bundles is common and so this study will consider such a case as representative of the "distributor" level since the other options open to distributors are more typical of the "Cuban-Black" or Spanish systems in New York City.

The distributor purchases about two kilograms of heroin (usually in the form of quarter-kilogram packages) at a total cost of $72,000. Assuming that he operates a bundle-producing operation, his supply will be processed by five women—a total salary expense of $1,000—and then sold to dealers who, in this case, are bundlemen.

One additional point must be made concerning the lieutenants. A lieutenant may or may not be a bundleman. That is, he may choose to act solely in behalf of the distributor, or he may decide to involve himself in the actual dealing. For the purposes of this study it will be assumed that the lieutenant is as reluctant to risk imprisonment as is the distributor, and so, unwilling to jeopardize his position, will receive only a salary from the distributor. The lieutenant, therefore, will be viewed as a "co-distributor." His income will not be reflected in the financial analysis, as his share will derive from the distributor's final profit.

The expenses for processing are minimal, including only wages, cost of dilutants and packaging materials, and rental of the location. Since a 5:1 cut must be made in order to dilute the heroin from 30 percent purity to 5 percent—the most common quality for consumption—a total of ten kilograms of adulterant must be added. Of this weight, 10 percent is usually quinine and the remaining 90 percent is milk sugar. The cost of quinine (at $30 per ounce) is $1,050; the milk sugar costs about $100. A liberal estimate of $200 will be used as the monthly rent for the factory location.

The dilution of 5 percent yields a total weight of twelve kilograms. The weight of each dosage of heroin is one grain. Thus approximately 185,000 one-grain bags of heroin will be produced from this supply. Lately, as a result of recent legislation illegalizing the use of glassine envelopes for non-legitimate purposes, tin foil packets are being used instead. Despite this, the cost of packaging materials has remained the same—about $200 for 200,000 packets.

Since the heroin is sold in parcels of twenty-five bags, about 7,400 of these "bundles" are produced from the 185,000 bags. These bundles are sold to dealers at a price of $75 each.

Summary of financial data on the "distributor" level. The distributor:

1. buys 8 quarter-kilograms of 30 percent pure heroin
2. spends $72,000 on heroin
3. cuts 5:1 via factory operation
4. accumulates 12 kilograms of 5 percent pure heroin
5. spends $2,500 on processing
6. sells 7,400 bundles of 5 percent pure heroin at $75 per bundle
7. receives total of $555,000 from sales
8. earns total profit of $480,000

The "Dealer" Level

After the heroin has been processed it is sold to dealers in the form of bundles. Each bundle consists of twenty-five $5 bags of 5 percent pure heroin. A bundle costs the dealer $75, and it is not uncommon for the dealer to purchase ten bundles at a time. If a dealer were to purchase ten bundles, he would then have a total of 250 bags.

It is generally true that persons occupying the "dealer" level are themselves heroin users; however, a dealer, if he is a user, will always have enough to "stay straight"—in other words, to keep from getting sick. A dealer will consume from his own supply; that is, of the 250 bags he has purchased, he will sell 220, thus retaining 30 bags for his own habit. He sells these 220 bags of heroin as twenty-four "half-bundles"—parcels of *ten* $5 bags. Thus he is able to maintain his habit and still earn a profit from his participation in the distribution system. Selling his half-bundles at $40 each, the dealer earns about $130 in profit for each lot of ten bundles he has purchased. He has no processing expenses and concentrates mainly on selling his half-bundles and on keeping out of jail.

Summary of financial data on the "dealer" level. The dealer:

1. buys 10 bundles of 5 percent pure heroin
2. pays $75 per bundle

3. pays total of $750
4. does not process
5. consumes 12 percent of his total supply
6. sells 22 half-bundles of 5 percent pure heroin
7. receives $40 per half-bundle
8. receives total of $880
9. earns total profit of $130

The "Pusher" Level

The final level in the heroin distribution system is the "pusher" level. The pusher is always an addict. As will be shown, the only profit he earns is the heroin he needs for the maintenance of his own habit.

The pusher is the "street level" seller. He is vulnerable to arrest by the police and to robbery by other addicts. He will buy a half-bundle from the dealer, consume 20 percent of that amount, and sell the remaining supply in order to break even. He will usually follow this pattern three times a day. In addition, it should be noted that the pusher is vulnerable not only because he can be robbed and arrested but also because, as an addict, he will undergo considerable physical and psychological distress should he be deprived of heroin as a result of a decreased availability of the narcotic.

Summary of financial data on the "pusher" level. The pusher:

1. buys 1 half-bundle of 5 percent pure heroin
2. pays $40 per half-bundle
3. pays total of $40
4. does not process
5. consumes 2 of the 10 bags purchased
6. sells 8 bags of 5 percent pure heroin
7. receives $5 per bag
8. receives total of $40
9. earns no monetary profit

ANALYSIS

Four tables have been constructed for the purpose of this analysis. Table 7-I represents the buying and processing patterns of each of the six levels of distribution. Table 7-II represents the selling patterns and shows the profits earned by these levels.

Table 7-III shows the accumulation of the commodity, while Table 7-IV estimates the number of persons involved in the distribution system.

Table 7-I tabulates the facts and figures presented in Chapters 2 and 3 of this study. The ramifications of the data presented in those chapters and formulated in the table will be analyzed in this section.

Each level is represented by only one of its members; for example, were the major supplier to have sixty quarter-kilograms available for sale, the distributor would be shown as buying only eight of these quarter-kilograms. Considering that the original amount of heroin, fifty kilograms, is introduced into the system once every month, it is generally the case that the distributor will purchase eight quarter-kilograms but once. (In addition, there are "less substantial" distributors who may purchase only one or two quarter-kilograms at infrequent intervals.) The chart, then, illustrates single transactions, as the dealer, who is shown purchasing only ten bundles, will actually make this purchase twice a week, each week.

Within the "Amount Bought" column, the assumption is made that the wholesaler has purchased ten kilograms from the importer. This is based upon the probability that the importer was originally "backed" by *five* wholesalers, each of whom advanced equal payments to the importer. In turn, it is assumed that each wholesaler will sell five kilograms each to two major suppliers.

While neither the importer nor the wholesaler processes his stock, the major supplier and distributor do. Thus it must be remembered that the quantity of narcotic increases as a result of a dilution process, so that the major supplier will sell a *total weight* of fifteen kilograms, though he had bought only five. In addition, whereas the distributor buys only two kilograms of heroin (by weight) he sells a total quantity of heroin weighing twelve kilograms.

Table 7-II presents data on the sales and profit aspects of the system. The levels of distribution will be compared with regard to the final column: "Profit Per Original Amount Kilograms." This column, in effect, presents the combined profits earned by all persons in a particular level of distribution.

TABLE 7-I

COST FIGURES OF THE HEROIN DISTRIBUTION SYSTEM

Level of Distribution	Amount Bought	Percent Purity	Price Per Unit	Total Cost	Cut	Adulterants Added	Amount Adulterant Used	Total Cost of Adulterant	Packaging Expenses	Total Cost of Processing
Importer	50 Kilos	90	$ 8,000	$400,000			...........NO PROCESS........			
Wholesaler	10 Kilos	90	$17,000	$170,000			...........NO PROCESS........			
Major supplier	5 Kilos	90	$25,000	$125,000	2:1	Quinine Mannite	1 Kilo 9 Kilos 10 Kilos	$1,050 $ 315 $1,365	negligible	$1,365
Distributor	8 Quarter-Kilos	30	$ 9,000	$ 72,000	5:1	Quinine Milk sugar	1 Kilo 9 Kilos 10 Kilos	$1,050 $ 80 $1,130	$ 185 bags $ 200 rent $1,000 wage $1,385	$2,515
Dealer	10 Bundles	5	$ 75	$ 750			...........NO PROCESS........			
Pusher	1 Half-Bundle	5	$ 40	$ 40			...........NO PROCESS........			

TABLE 7-II

SALES AND PROFIT FIGURES OF THE HEROIN DISTRIBUTION SYSTEM

Level of Distribution	Amount Sold	Percent Purity	Price Per Unit	Price Per Kilo	Total Sales Receipts	Total Sales Profit	Profit Per Unit	Profit Per Kilo	Profit Per Total Amount Kilos for Sale at Level
Importer	50 Kilos	90	$17,000	$17,000	$850,000	$450,000	$9,000	$ 9,000	$ 450,000
Wholesaler	10 Kilos	90	$25,000	$25,000	$250,000	$ 80,000	$8,000	$ 8,000	$ 400,000
Major Supplier	60 Quarter-Kilos	30	$ 9,000	$36,000	$540,000	$413,635	$6,895	$27,580	$ 4,137,000
Distributor	7,390 Bundles	5	$ 75	$46,200	$554,250	$479,735	$ 65	$40,035	$36,031,500
Dealer	22 Half-Bundles	5	$ 40	$61,600	$ 880	$ 130	$ 6	$ 9,239	$ 7,982,500
Pusher	8 Bags	5	$ 5	$76,989	$ 40	0	0	0	0

The "Profit Per Kilogram" column will be used as the first step in the analysis. This column accurately represents the patterns of operation at each level since the *profit* at each level reflects not only the buying and selling prices but the processing costs as well.

The profit on one kilogram at the "wholesaler" level is 11 percent less than it is at the "importer" level. This is a result of three factors: first, the wholesaler does not process; second, he has had to do little more than "front" capital—make an advance payment—to the importer—third, the importer's higher profit can be understood in light of his having to spend much time and effort collecting money from his backers as well as arranging overseas transactions.

The greatest positive increase in the profit value of a kilogram occurs between the "wholesaler" and "major supplier" levels: +243 percent. This is explained by the fact that the major supplier triples his quantity by adding ten kilograms of dilutant to his original five kilograms of 90 percent pure heroin. Although the profit rate increases during the transaction between the major supplier and distributor, it falls sharply afterwards. The rate of change of profit per kilogram between the "distributor" and "dealer" levels is 76 percent; this is the percentage of decreased value from $40,035 to $9,239. One factor of this drop is an important characteristic of the "dealer" level, i.c. most dealers are themselves addicts and thus will consume a portion of their own supply.

The "Profit Per Original Amount Kilograms" column indicates the various profits earned by persons in all levels of heroin distribution. Whereas the column is divided into six sections, one for each of the six levels of distribution, a comparison will be made between the sum of the first three levels and that of the last three levels.

It has been shown in Chapter 2 that the common demoninator of the three "upper levels"—the "importer," "wholesaler," and "major supplier"—is affiliation with the Cosa Nostra. In fact, it is this alliance which has resulted in an entire system of distribution known as the "Italian-Black system." An analysis, therefore, will be made comparing the total revenue from heroin distribution accumulated by the "organized crime" element with that accumulated by the "nonorganized crime" element within the system—distributors, dealers, and pushers.

The total profit earned by the importer is $450,000. The five wholesalers to whom the importer has sold his stock earn a combined profit of $400,000. (At this point there are six members of "organized crime" involved in the system.) Each wholesaler sells his supply to two different major suppliers, each of whom earn $413,700 in profit. The total profit at the "major supplier" level, then, is $4,137,000. Thus the total combined profit for the first three levels—the profit earned by the "organized crime" element—is $4,987,000.

The distributor, whose factory operation provides him with a 644 percent profit rate, earns a profit of $479,735. All of the persons who operate within the "distributor" level accumulate a total profit of $36,031,500. (After the factory process there are nine hundred kilograms of 5 percent pure heroin available for sale to dealers.) The dealer's profit is lessened to an extent by the fact that he will consume a part of his own supply. Despite this, a sizeable profit totaling $7,982,500 is earned by all persons in the "dealer" level. At this point the desire for profit ceases to be a major factor as it is the physiological dependence on heroin which motivates the pusher to be involved in his transactions. The pusher will make just enough money from sales in order to buy another supply, a part of which he himself will consume. The "pusher" level accumulates no profit at all.

As compared with a figure of *$4,987,000* earned by the *"organized crime"* element, the *lower level* suppliers, who are not Cosa Nostra members, earn a total accumulated profit of *$44,014,000*. Thus the *lower levels* of heroin distribution accumulate *$39,027,000 or 780 percent more* than do the upper levels of distribution.

As shown in Table 7-III, approximately fourteen million bags of heroin are available to the addict population in New York City as a result of a fifty-kilogram purchase at the "importer" level. Assuming this fifty-kilogram purchase is made on a monthly basis, there are about 462,000 bags available for daily consumption. Thus, if it is accepted that the average addict uses five

TABLE 7-III

TOTAL ACCUMULATED PRODUCT

Level of Distribution	Accumulation Per Unit	Bulk Accumulation Per Kilo
Importer	50 Kilos	50
Wholesaler	50 Kilos	50
Major Supplier	600 Quarter-Bundles	150
Distributor	554,250 Bundles	900
Dealer	(Accumulated) 1,385,625 Half-Bundles / (For Sale) 1,330,200 Half-Bundles	900 Accumulated / 864 For Sale
Pusher	13,856,250 Bags (Accumulated) / 10,641,600 Bags (For Sale)	900 Accumulated / 691 For Sale

TABLE 7-IV

ESTIMATE OF THE NUMBER OF SUPPLIERS IN THE "ITALIAN-BLACK SYSTEM"

Level of Distribution	Usual Purchase	Frequency of Purchase	Estimated Number of Persons at Level[*]	Comment
Importer	50 Kilos	One purchase per month	1	may be a "caporegima" in any of New York's five Cosa Nostra families
Wholesaler	10 Kilos	One purchase per month	5	may be a "soldier" in any of New York's five Cosa Nostra families
Major supplier	5 Kilos	One purchase per month	10	usually affiliated but not a member of Cosa Nostra; may be Black
Distributor	8 Quarter-Kilos	One purchase per month	75	usually Black
Dealer	10 Bundles	Nine purchases per month	6,158	almost always Black; usually an addict
Pusher	1 Half-Bundle	Ninety purchases per month	14,778	usually Black; always an addict

Estimated Total of Persons in "Italian-Black System": 21,027

[*] For the purpose of analysis *one* importer is shown to occupy the "importer" level. Whereas there are several individuals who are importers in the *entire* system, they may not operate concurrently. Thus the table depicts the system as based upon a single transaction at the "importer" level. Similarly, the "estimated total of persons" by no means denotes a specific number of people. Actually, this figure represents the number of positions which can be occupied for the purpose of making a transaction within the system.

bags per day, then there are approximately 92,000 addicts (including pushers) who receive their heroin from suppliers operating in the "Italian-Black system." This figure can be derived from an alternate approach by utilizing Table 7-IV. As noted in Chapter 3, the pusher will make three "half-bundle" purchases a day. He therefore buys a total of thirty bags each day. Since the pusher is also a consumer (and it is assumed that an addict will use five bags per day), for every pusher in the system there are six addicts, one of whom is the pusher himself. Thus if there are about 15,000 pushers, as indicated in Table 7-IV, then again there are about 90,000 addicts (including pushers) who receive heroin from the "Italian-Black system."

THE SOCIO-ECONOMIC EFFECT OF DRUG AND VICTIMLESS CRIME PROSECUTION*

DENNIS KESSLER

As our urban centers battle for more Safe Street funds, they are by and large reaffirming the fact that most city streets do not provide a sense of security that was once a basic right of every American. Urbanites are especially feeling the encroachment of crime on their social and economic lives. As various schemes to rid the cities of crime are devised by urban policy planners we have yet to see an abatement of the problem.

If we view the problem as a condition symptomatic of contemporary urban mores we are overlooking some basic socio-legal principles. Crime is merely a legal category. As such, it describes a type of behavior that is contrary to the rules of a given society. What is criminal in one jurisdiction need not be criminal in another. We have sufficient evidence of this through our knowledge and understanding of various societies and cultures which treat the concept of "crime" as a cultural prescription which responds to societal demands. In essence then, we

---

* Summary of lecture. Brooklyn College, The City University of New York, 1973.

can accept the fact that crime has no inherent quality nor does it have an aspect of universality. The definitions of what conduct will be considered criminal are dependant upon the values a society embraces. Conceptually, law is a form of public policy which is engineered to regulate the behavior of its population. The behavior exhibited by any member of a society is labeled criminal by the formulation and application of criminal definitions. Crime is not, therefore, a quality inherent in a particular act.

An examination of our penal code reveals crimes were originally divided into two types of acts: those which are *mala in se*, or wrong in themselves, and those which are *mala prohibita*, or wrong merely because they are prohibited and punished by statute. The *mala in se* acts encompass the so-called common law offenses (felonious crimes, i.e. rape, murder, arson etc.). The *mala prohibita* acts, on the other hand, include acts which society currently deems illegal merely because they are forbidden—they are not otherwise wrong. The *mala prohibita* acts concern themselves with crimes such as gambling, drug use, pornography, prostitution and private sexual acts between consenting adults. The result of society engaging in the selective enforcement of these *mala prohibita* statutes has been adverse. It is adverse because of the palpable problem it presents in regulating morality and because legalized gambling as one example, is encouraged via the media as a legitimate form of profitmaking in both the religious and secular institutions. To gamble off-track in one of the Off-Track Betting parlors (now in operation in New York City) or in the sanctuary of the church under the rubric of fund raising is legally sanctioned. On the other hand, placing a wager on a basketball game becomes a violation of the law in most jurisdictions of the country. While police manpower is diverted to the enforcement of these statutes, more serious crimes are perpetrated and remain undetected.

Consider the inefficacy of the enforcement of victimless crimes. Our society is beginning to recognize the difficulties associated with the enforcement of such laws. The inherent

unenforceability of morals laws also presents a serious danger
to the constitutional rights of the so-called victims. The fact
that there is no complainant presents a law enforcement problem
as well. Because of the widespread reluctance on the part of
the participants involved in such crimes to testify, the police
must often use questionable methods to obtain evidence. These
questionable methods frequently border on entrapment, a clear
infringement of the suspects constitutional guarantees.

Equally futile is the enforcement of our drug laws, both
economically and socially. Heroin in the United States is rapidly
reaching epidemic proportions. An estimate of the number of
heroin addicts is in the neighborhood of four to five hundred
thousand. It is estimated that 50 to 75 percent of all crimes are
a result of drug addiction. Heroin addicts will spend about
fifteen million dollars satiating their habits. They will secure
a large portion of the necessary funds from crime. Throughout
the nation, addicts are responsible for a considerable number
of crimes against persons and property. The value of property
stolen by addicts was estimated at 2.8 billion dollars in a recent
study. The cost of combatting drug-related crime is 0.5 billion
dollars. The value of potential production lost due to drug
addiction is 1.1 billion dollars. Treatment costs are about 0.2
billion and education, prevention and research are 0.1 billion.
In all a cost of 4.7 billion dollars annually.[1]

The solution to this socially perplexing problem should be
of paramount concern to the medical as well as the legal profession. By repealing the current drug laws and thereby taking
the profit incentive out of the drug business and providing a free
fix for heroin users will do much to alleviate the already acute
crime problem. Although the British are currently in the process
of shifting from heroin to methadone, substituting one form of
addiction for another is questionable. Police efforts which concentrate on the arrest of both users and distributors is futile.
The solution rests in providing drug abusers with a free supply
regulated by local government control. By diminishing the
demand for the contraband, suppliers will be forced to seek

---

[1] "The High Cost of the Drug Problem," *U.S. News and World Report*
(September 11, 1972), p. 76.

TABLE 7-V

WHOLESALE AND RETAIL COSTS OF COMMON DRUGS IN THE NEW YORK METROPOLITAN AREA, 1973

		Wholesale	*Retail*
Heroin:			
Deck or bag	1 grain		*$5 to $10†
Ounce	437.5 grains	$700.00	*4,300.00†
One pound		*$15,000.00	$115,000.00†
One kilo	2.2 pounds	*$32,000.00	$250,000.00†
Cocaine:			
Deck			*$7.00
Spoon	⅛ oz.	$30.00	*$50.00
Ounce		$700.00	*$4,500.00
One pound		*$10,000.00	$125,000.00
One kilo		*$22,000.00	$275,000.00
Marihuana:			
Cigarette	5 grains		*$1.00
Nickel bag			*$5.00
Ounce	80 "sticks"	$30.00	*$80.00
One pound	1200 "sticks"	$200.00	*$1,200.00
One kilo	2500 "sticks"	*$400.00	$2,500.00
Hashish:			
One gram			*$10.00
Ounce		*$110.00	Assorted costs by
One pound		*$1,200.00	size of pieces
Liquid Hashish:			
Fluid ounce		*$550.00	
Methedrine:			
Deck			*$5.00
Spoon		$25.00	*$40.00
Ounce		$300.00	*$1,100.00
Mescaline:			
Caps or Tabs			*$5.00
Ounce		$300.00	*$500.00
One pound		*$4,000.00	$8,000.00
LSD & Other Hallucinogenics:			
Any type single dose			*$3.00
Other Narcotic Drugs:			
Morphine, Methadone, Dolophine, Demerol, Dilaudid, Codeine	Tabs, Caps or per 1 cc		*$5.00
Other Controlled Dangerous Substance or Legend Drug:			
Seconal, Tuinal, Amphetamine, Doriden, Darvon, and Dexedrine	Tabs, caps or per 1 cc		*$0.50

---

* Asterisk indicates suggested recovered property value.

† Retail values for heroin assume that the heroin content of any total amount is five (5) percent.

NOTE: Use wholesale value for drugs in bulk (pound, kilo), and retail value for drugs in individual packages.

Source: Narcotics police.

alternative avenues of income. The overall result of the decriminalization of the current drug law can be seen in the prospects of a society with a low urban crime rate, less death from drug overdose, and the obvious saving in tax dollars. Who would be opposed to such an altruistic notion? The current situation is only exacerbated by the law. If the *status quo* is maintained, we will see little accomplished to rid the cities of street crime while at the same time continuing to impair the physical and mental health of both the drug abusers and the citizenry of the urban population.

It has been indicated that crime is merely a classification of behavior. The crime index reflects how often people deviate from the accepted patterns. Far too many acts are considered criminal which ostensibly creates a higher crime rate. The way to reduce crime is to simply eradicate many of the acts now considered criminal. Current police programs geared toward eliminating prostitution, gambling, drug use etc., only produce more arrests, higher crime rates and no real reduction in the amount of "deviant" activity taking place. If we have agreed that there is no inherent deviance or criminality—through what justification does the state seek to prosecute for the above *mala prohibita* crimes? How does the state set the parameters of morality? Does eliminating a law mean such conduct is being condoned? The repealing of a law does not necessarily mean an increase in that conduct either. Certainly our society can continue to exist with the legalization and regulation of many of the current *mala prohibita* statutes, because without government regulation, we find that it flourishes in the shady atmosphere of organized crime operations which not so altruistically caters to the demands of the consumer public by providing goods and services not otherwise available.

If we are to make the euphemism "safe street" a reality then let us see a reduction in the crime rate via the elimination of the statutes that impinge on personal rights. Let sex acts which are now criminal become a private affair, whatever the partners choose to do. Let us take the profit out of the heroin business by providing free clinics for heroin. Let all victimless crimes become the concern of the alleged reticent victims. By realizing that legal institutions cannot possibly control the entire spectrum of human conduct we are recognizing that in a free society people should be able to select life styles compatible with their social and cultural beliefs. The real solution to the crime rate now rests with the elected officials who have the options open to them. *Status quo* or change?

BIBLIOGRAPHY

Books

Anslinger, Harry J.: *The Protectors. Our Battle Against the Crime Gangs.* New York, Farrar, 1964.

Anslinger, Harry J. and Oursler, Will: *The Murderers.* New York, Farrar, 1961.

Anslinger, Harry J. and Tompkins, William F.: *The Traffic in Narcotics.* New York, Funk and Wagnalls, 1953.

Ashley, Richard: *Heroin.* New York, St. Martin's Press, 1974.

Belli, Melvin: *Blood Money.* New York, Grosset, 1956.

Brecher, Edward M. and the editors of *Consumer Reports*: *Licit and Illicit Drugs.* Boston, Little, 1974.

Buse, Renee: *The Deadly Silence.* New York, Doubleday, 1965.

Chein, Isidor: *The Road to H: Narcotics. . . .* New York, Basic Books, 1964.

Cook, Fred J.: *The Secret Rulers.* New York, Duell, 1966.

Cressey, Donald R.: *Theft of the Nation.* New York, Harper and Row, 1969.

Demaris, Ovid: *Lucky Luciano.* Derby, Connecticut, Monarch, 1960.

DeRopp, Robert S.: *Drugs and the Mind.* New York, St. Martin's, 1957.

Feder, Sid and Joesten, Joachim: *The Luciano Story.* New York, McKay, 1054.

Frasca, Dom: *King of Crime.* New York, Crown, 1959.

Goulart, Ron: *Line Up Tough Guys.* Los Angeles, Sherbourne, 1966.

Green, Timothy: *The Smugglers.* New York, Walker, 1969.

Katcher, Leo: *The Big Bankroll.* New York, Harper and Brothers, 1953.

Kunnes, Richard, M.D.: *The American Heroin Empire.* New York, Dodd, 1974.

Maurer, David W. and Vogel, Victor H.: *Narcotics and Narcotic Addiction.* Springfield, Thomas, 1954.

McCoy, Alfred W.: *The Politics of Heroin in Southeast Asia.* New York, Harper and Row, 1972.

Moore, Robin: *The French Connection.* Boston, Little, 1969.

Moscow, Alvin: *Merchants of Heroin: An In-Depth Portrayal of Business in the Underworld.* New York, Dial, 1968.

Murtagh, John M. and Harris, Sara: *Who Live in Shadow.* New York, McGraw-Hill, 1960.

New York State Joint Legislative Committee on Crime, Its Causes, Control and Effect on Society. *Report on the Drug Abuse Problem at the State University of New York at Stony Brook.* Legislative Document No. 21, 1968.

Nyswander, Marie: *The Drug Addict as a Patient.* New York, Grune, 1956.

Partridge, Eric: *A Dictionary of the Underworld.* New York, Macmillan, 1961.

Prager, Ted, and Moberley, Leeds: *Hoodlums, New York.* New York, Retail Distributors, 1959.

Rice, Robert: *The Business of Crime.* New York, Farrar, 1956, Part 2. Narcotics.

Rosevear, John: *Pot: A Handbook of Marijuana.* New Hyde Park, New York, University Books, 1967.

Schur, Edwin: *Narcotic Addiction in Britain and America.* Bloomington, Ind., Ind U Pr, 1962, pp. 70-83, 205-206.

The Kefauver Committee Report on Organized Crime. New York, Didier, 1951.

U.S. President's Commission on Law Enforcement and Administration of Justice: *Task Force Report: Organized Crime.* Washington, D.C., Government Printing Office, 1967.

Varna, Anthony: *World Underworld.* London, Museum Press Limited, 1957, Chap. 9.

Weston, Paul B. (Ed.): *Narcotics, U.S.A.* New York, Greenberg, 1956.

Zinberg, Norman E. and Robertson, John A.: *Drugs and the Public.* New York, Simon and Schuster, 1974.

Articles

Ansley, Norman: International efforts to control narcotics. *Journal of Criminal Law, 50*: July-August 1959.

Blomquist, Edward: Operations narcotics. *Medical Times, 85*: March 1957.

Counter-measures on sales and smuggling. *The New York Times, 24,* January 24, 1958.

Federal government presses drive against trafficking by Mafia. *The New York Times, 30,* January 16, 1959.

Federal officials concerned over evidence that organized crime is trafficking in barbiturates and amphetamines. *New York Times, 13,* February 1, 1965.

Federal statutes governing traffic in marijuana. *University of Miami Law Review, 24*: Fall 1969.

Feigenbaum, Roy A.: A Comparison of Accumulated Total Revenues Between Organized Crime and Nonorganized Crime Elements in the

Heroin Distribution System in New York City. (unpublished Master's thesis) New York, John Jay College of Criminal Justice, The City University of New York, February 1973.

14-man 'Top Echelon' of largest narcotics ring in New York City seized in raids in four boros. *The New York Times*, 33, February 4, 1965.

Heilbroner, Robert L.: The microeconomics of the drug problem. *The Economic Problem*, 2:3, March 1970.

How hazardous are drugs from abroad. *U.S. News & World Report*, 53: December 17, 1962.

Howard, T.: Dope in his business. *Saturday Evening Post, 229*: April 27, 1957.

Irwin, T.: Crackdown on bootleg drugs: Campaign to end traffic in counterfeit drugs. *Today's Health, 45*: January 1967.

Judge Murtagh urges providing narcotics free to halt underworld trade. *The New York Times*, 13, February 24, 1958.

Kessler, Dennis: The Socio-Economic Effect of Drug and Victimless Crime Prosecution. (summary of lecture) Brooklyn, New York, Brooklyn College, The City University of New York, 1973.

Lindesmith, Alfred R.: Federal Law and Drug Addiction. *Social Problems*, 7: Summer 1959.

Mafia operations in smuggling naroctics from Montreal to New York City discussed. *The New York Times*, 1, May 9, 1967.

Marijuana: It's Big Business Now; House Select Committee on Crime Report. *U.S. News & World Report, 68*: April 20, 1970.

Moore, Mark H.: Economics of Heroin Distribution. Teaching and research paper No. 4. Cambridge, Mass., John F. Kennedy School of Government, Harvard University, 1971.

Moscow, A.: Merchants of heroin. *Readers Digest, 93*: September 1968.

Nisbet, Charles T., and Firouz, Vakil: Some social and economic characteristics of U.C.L.A. marijuana users. *Social Science Quarterly*, 179-189, June 1971.

Older underworld chiefs decide to get out of narcotics trafficking because of risk. *The New York Times*, 1, February 28, 1960.

$100 million crackdown. *Newsweek, 50*: September 16, 1957.

Operation impossible. Drive against drugs from Mexico. *Time, 94*: October 17, 1969.

Police smash multi-million-dollar drug ring; J. Russo identified as leader. *The New York Times*, 48, January 13, 1960.

Preble, Edward and Caesy, John J., Jr.: Taking care of business. *The International Journal of the Addictions, IV*:1-24, March 1969.

Rottenberg, Simon: The Clandestine Distribution of Heroin, Its Discovery and Suppression. *Journal of Political Economy*, 78-90, January-February 1968.

Schulz, W.: Smugglers of Misery. *Reader's Digest, 96*: April 1970.

Smith, Robert M.: New drug agency to fight pushers on lower levels. *The New York Times*, 1, January 19, 1972.

Survey on Reports that Mafia is Allowing Cuban and South American Racketeers to Takeover Large Part of Heroin Smuggling into U.S. *The New York Times*, 1, September 2, 1967.

There are people who say, "Well, business is business." *Forbes*, 19-22, April 1, 1970.

To drug or not to drug. *National Review*, June 4, 1968.

United States Congress. House. Select Committee on Crime: *Crime in America—Heroin Importation, Distribution, Packaging and Paraphenalia.* Hearings before the Select Committee on Crime. House of Representatives, 91st Congress, 2nd session, 1970.

U.S. government agents smash syndicate that smuggled $20 million worth of narcotics yearly into U.S. from France. *The New York Times*, 1, September 5, 1958.

U.S. and Mexico discuss illicit traffic in narcotic drugs. *Department of State Bulletin, 55*: December 26, 1966.

Vito Genovese, seized for conspiracy to import and sell narcotics. *The New York Times*, 1, July 8, 1958.

Walker, D. E.: Boom in smuggling. *Nation, 193*: July 15, 1961.

CHAPTER 8

CORRUPTION AND CRIME IN
LABOR UNIONS

INTRODUCTION

O VER 50,000 REGISTERED labor organizations represent this nation's twenty million unionized workers. Since their early beginnings these union groups have achieved significant benefits not only for their members but for millions of other nonunion workers. At the same time, however, labor racketeers and other criminal elements have infiltrated labor unions to exploit these organizations as well as their pension and welfare funds for personal enrichment.

In 1957 in response to public pressure the U.S. Senate appointed a Select Committee on Improper Activities in the Labor Management Field to be directed by Sen. John L. McClellan (D. Arkansas). The McClellan Committee concentrated on labor racketeering. After the first year of work, the Committee reported that it had found "Union funds in excess of $10 million were either stolen, embezzled, or misused by union officials over a period of fifteen years." The labor rackets investigation obtained evidence of gangster infiltration into seven unions with total membership of two million and domination of some fifty companies in the juke box, vending machine and garbage collection industries. Sen. McClellan's committee also found that organizational picketing was used as a weapon of extortion against management and that companies employed labor spies and consultants to defeat legitimate union activity.

The investigation probed the hidden ties between crooked

union officials and executives willing to pay for *sweetheart contracts.* The employer's advantages in such a collective bargaining agreement are that legitimate unions then have difficulty in organizing the shop; he pays less in wages and other benefits; and operates with few restrictions. The union racketeer benefits from the "payoff" he receives from the grateful employer, or the dues he collects from employees, or both. Sweetheart contracts were denounced by the AFL-CIO in its *Code of Ethical Practices.*

As a result of these disclosures, Congress in 1959 passed the Landrum-Griffin Act which was supposed to provide federally administered safeguards against racketeers' shocking exploitation of the unions. It provided that convicted felons would be barred from holding union office within five years after serving a prison term. It outlawed certain types of picketing, provided for secret ballot elections and limited the number of terms of office. It required financial reports of unions including balance sheets and a report on all financial transactions of all officials.

The first reading in this chapter details four fundamental operations employed by labor racketeers when Cosa Nostra members become labor brokers. The second reading, "Racketeering and Labor: An Economic Analysis," shows how organized criminals operate within trade unions. The third selection, by the editors, reviews the current situation.

DEMAND, SUPPLY, AND PROFIT*

DONALD R. CRESSEY

Because American business and industry has been extensively unionized, industrialists and businessmen seek black-market labor. Cosa Nostra meets this demand, and frequently cheats the businessmen who make it. Fraud, extortion, and bribery are the basic crimes involved when Cosa Nostra members work as labor brokers. But these same crimes, plus income-tax evasion, are

---

* Taken from "Demand, supply and profit." *Theft of the Nation* by Donald R. Cressey. Copyright 1969 by Donald R. Cressey. By permission of Harper and Row, Publishers, Inc., pp. 95-99.

the foundations of all the organizations' activities. In order to differentiate Cosa Nostra's activities in the labor field from its activities elsewhere, law-enforcement personnel some years ago began using the term "labor racketeering" to refer to the former. Unfortunately, this term directs our attention away from the fact that all Cosa Nostra operations are, basically, racketeering. It is quite appropriate to speak of Cosa Nostra involvement in "usury racketeering," "business racketeering," and even, in the case of monopolizing illegal bet-taking businesses, "racketeering racketeering." All involve extortion of the kind used by Lord Clive, founder of the British Empire in India, who in his youth formed a gang of fellow delinquents to collect tribute from shop-owners who did not wish to have their windows broken. All take organization.

Four fundamental operations are involved when Cosa Nostra members become labor brokers. Three of the operations, in their many variations, are provided as a service to greedy, crooked, or shady businessmen who have created the demand for a cheap supply of labor. In the fourth kind of operation, the Cosa Nostra member steals from his own union.

First, real unionization of some businesses is prevented by pretending, for a fee, that the shops are unionized. Nine men riding in two convertible-topped automobiles parked by the door of a sandwich shop. Two Cosa Nostra men walked into the shop. One handed the proprietor a business card and said, "You got to sign up with this union, right now." The proprietor, who had only four employees, replied, "I can't give you the answer right now." The second Cosa Nostra member was a bit persuasive: "Listen, you better sign, otherwise we know where you live." The man signed, but his employees never were really unionized. The employer paid their "initiation fee" and he regularly paid their "dues," all of which were simply pay-offs to the two men. He was never asked for a list of his employees, and the employees had no idea that they were union members. Since he paid his employees wages lower than the rates set by legitimate unions, the apparent extortion turned out to be a pretty jolly affair for all except the workers.

For a larger business, $5000 a year is a cheap price for a

nonunion "unionized" shop. One trucking firm is so well known to be controlled by Cosa Nostra that it is called a "mob's barn." The company is "unionized," but the workers do not get union wages. There is no "union trouble" in this company.

Second, in a variation of the first operation, employees are made members of fictitious "paper locals" which have been established in part to help greedy employers reduce labor costs. In the "sweetheart-contract" operation, a Cosa Nostra member for a fee writes a labor contract that cheats the workers out of wages and benefits they could legitimately obtain at the bargaining table. For example, most union contracts specify the names of the holidays to which the employees are entitled—New Year's, Christmas, Easter, Fourth of July, Rosh Hashonah, Passover, Washington's Birthday, Thanksgiving Day. But "sweetheart contracts" might restrict employees to only one or two holidays a year. In one such contract negotiated by the stupid Cosa Nostra president of a paper local, the only holiday granted to a work force made up exclusively of Catholic Puerto Ricans was Passover. A man who could neither read nor write was vice president of one fictitious Cosa Nostra local.

A company that manufactures chairs suddenly stopped manufacturing the cushions for the chairs. It began to purchase them, instead, from a newly formed company which was owned by a Cosa Nostra member. Shortly thereafter, a new union local was formed, and the son of the cushion company's owner became president of it. The union then "organized" both the chair company and the cushion company. About a dozen friends and relatives of the cushion company owner were put on the payroll of the chair company.

In a beautiful double cross, two Cosa Nostra members acting as business agents for a real union local agreed to let a shopkeeper pay them fees for a highly favorable contract. But later they went back for more. They told the shopkeeper that they had never reported the fraudulent contract to the local, then handed him a new contract with a different local, and demanded another pay-off. The shopkeeper paid, but he reported the matter to the district attorney, who convicted the two men of extortion, despite the fact that the shopkeeper's hands were by no means clean. But the district attorney never was able to find the second local, which simply disappeared. Its address was the same as that of a Cosa Nostra leader's office, but no union records could be found.

Fictitious locals are business properties. A low-level Cosa Nostra member engaged in gambling, usury, and narcotics financing simply purchased, for $30,000, a small town union local from a Cosa Nostra boss. Later he sold a part interest in the local to a friend.

Third, employers are threatened with labor strife or mayhem if they do not pay under-the-table fees to the Cosa Nostra members heading union locals, "paper" or otherwise. This, of course, is the outright extortion called "labor racketeering." It need not be, however. One man paid a union to picket his competitor, believing that the competitor wouldn't be able to pay them off because he had already done so. He was wrong. The competitor paid the officers of the local a high fee, and they picketed the originator of the plot.

It is not at all unusual for a Cosa Nostra union official to engage in a mild form of extortion by demanding that his relatives be put on the company payroll. In another thinly veiled form of extortion, some Cosa Nostra union "leaders" demand that the employing company hire them as "labor consultants." One company avoids paying some of its income taxes by overpaying one of its suppliers and then secretly taking the overpayment back. It uses the same scheme to bribe the president of a union local. Thus, it overpays a Cosa Nostra member for merchandise supplied by him. This man, in turn, passes the overpayment on to a second Cosa Nostra member, who is president of the local.

Cosa Nostra members have effectively used the National Labor Relations Board as part of their pressure for extortion. One man stated his "paper local's" terms to a shopkeeper, who refused them. The crook threatened to report him to the NLRB for unwillingness to negotiate, which is an unfair labor practice. As a variant, a Cosa Nostra union leader struck a company so that his brother, owner of a competing company, would get more business.

While some Cosa Nostra men get rich by threatening strikes

or slowdowns if businessmen do not pay under-the-table fees, others make a nice living by offering their services in the settling of "labor disputes" of this kind. In April, 1968, *The New York Times* reported that a grand jury had indicted the vice president of Spartan Industries—of which the billion-dollar E. J. Korvette chain of discount stores is a wholly owned subsidiary—for perjuring himself in testimony about such an arrangement. The indictment said the vice president had made a move for labor peace by seeking the aid of three hoodlums, two of them reputed Cosa Nostra leaders. In return for the help of the three "labor consultants," companies formed by them were to be given contracts to provide Korvette's with basic services such as window washing and garbage collection. The vice president was to share in the profits of the companies. Specifically, the indictment charged that the vice president had committed perjury when he told a grand jury he had never asked a reputed lieutenant in a New York Cosa Nostra "family" to help him persuade an unidentified labor union official to "lay off" in his demands. The case has not yet come up for trial.

Fourth, funds are stolen or otherwise obtained illegally from union funds or from union pension and welfare systems. This varies from the simple fraud of putting one's wife on the payroll to over-paying a consultant for services rendered. Funds are commonly embezzled by sending large checks to lawyers for nonexistent services. One local borrowed money from its own welfare fund, then used the money to buy Cadillacs for each of its Cosa Nostra officials. Two union locals jointly "purchased" a Cosa Nostra member's summer home for $150,000 but never used it. One union official bought a great deal of jewelry at one store with embezzled union funds. He was reported to the police by an irate union member who happened to notice the purchase and said, "Something crooked must be going on as no one pays full retail prices for jewelry, especially union officers who have many contacts."

The industries which seem to be most susceptible to shakedowns and to connivance between employers and union officials are those employing unskilled or only semiskilled labor. Significantly, it is the unions serving such industries that are most likely to be controlled by Cosa Nostra members. Many of the New York companies engaged in housewrecking are nonunion, and even the companies having union contracts hire nonunion personnel on occasion. There is a saving of some $2.50 per hour per man, and this difference permits the dishonest company to underbid the honest companies even when the dishonest company must pay an illegal fee to a corrupt union official. Cosa Nostra members seek control of the officers of union locals so they can get a share of the payoffs. "Control" may be secured legitimately, by helping an officer win a union election. More frequently it is achieved illegitimately, by outright extortion from an honest or dishonest official.

RACKETEERING AND LABOR: AN ECONOMIC ANALYSIS[*]

PAUL A. WEINSTEIN

Sub-rosa activities have largely been ignored in economic literature. Nowhere is this more noticeable than in the field of labor.[1] Instead of relegating this behavior to the limbo of a curiosum, we promote it in this article to a topic of economic interest for two reasons. First, it affects the allocation of resources. Second, it requires a stream of economic decisions for its economic well-being.

We shall examine the following problems: What substantive variations are there in labor racketeering? How do they emerge and what factors attract racketeers to some markets but not to others? What is the range of decision making open to the union racketeer? To what extent are racketeering activities comple-

---

[*] Reprinted from the *Industrial and Labor Relations Review*, Vol. 19, No. 3, April 1966, by Cornell University. All rights reserved. Used with permission.
[1] For accounts of union racketeering, see Harold Seidman, *Labor Czars*, Liveright, 1938; Daniel Bell, *The End of Ideology* (Glencoe, Ill., The Free Press, 1950), pp. 159-190; Philip Taft, "The Responses of the Bakers, Longshore and Teamsters to Public Exposure," *Quarterly Journal of Economics*, August 1960, pp. 393-412; Daniel Bell, "The Racket Ridden Longshoremen: A Functional Analysis of Crime," in W. Galenson and S. M. Lipset, eds., *Labor and Trade Unionism: An Interdisciplinary Reader* (New York, Wiley, 1960), pp. 245-264.

ments to or substitutes for one another? How do these practices affect resource allocation? Before constructing the model necessary to attack these problems, it will be necessary to clarify what activities are included in labor racketeering.

There are numerous types of racketeering associated with the trade union movement. Categorizing the causes of union corruption and the *modus operandi* of each form is a necessary starting place for analyzing this activity.

White-collar crime is one type of problem which can readily be dismissed. It involves a union official using union funds for personal gain without affecting the size of the treasury being raided. This is embezzlement and offers nothing unique simply because it takes place in the context of a union organization. The relative rarity of embezzlement of union funds may be attributable to the rather meager size of the funds available until recently for expropriation. In the early days of unions, however, it was not unknown for an official to appropriate the union treasury for private use.[2]

A second type of racketeering occurs when a labor leader uses his position for personal aggrandizement. Instances of union officials receiving graft—for example, by having it dropped into an umbrella—are part of the folklore of trade unionism.

The significant theoretical point about racketeering is that the individual who controls the flow of economic activity is in a strategic position to extract existing and potential quasi-rents. The potential for exploitation is always present. The sufficient conditions are a desire to exploit the situation, an arbitrary distribution system, and an inadequate legal system to penalize wrongdoers.

Entry of Racketeers into Trade Unions

Of the two areas of activity mentioned above which are open to the professional racketeer, the second is the most interesting. The decision maker may be either an inside union man who has defected or an outsider who enters the union area for the specific

---

[2] Robert F. Hoxie, *Trade Unionism in the United States* (New York, D. Appleton, 1923), pp. 11-33.

purpose of exploitation. Our interest here is in the latter type of criminal union leader.

The development of unions run by men associated with organized crime is largely a phenomenon of the thirties, although entry of criminals into the labor-management arena occurred during the twenties, when trade unions in the garment and fur industries, stymied by both legal and economic obstacles, turned to Lepke and Gurrah of Murder, Inc. for help.* The depression, however, marked the flowering organized criminal activity in trade unions.

A number of factors conspired to encourage the participation of organized crime in trade unions at this time. Unquestionably, one of the most significant factors was the repeal of prohibition. The cutting off of the organized criminal element from one of its largest sources of revenue encouraged a search for new income. Trade unions were an obvious target.

The racketeer's normal decision-making frame of reference especially encouraged the entry of organized crime into the labor-management field. A racket may be likened to a department store of illegal activity dependent in part on scale economies. One of the most productive "lines" of this multi-product firm is gambling. Certain aspects of the economics of this endeavor are significant for unions. A cluster of potential consumers of gambling activity reduces the variable costs of the line, as it facilitates taking bets and making payoffs. A portion of the market may be strongly influenced by the accessibility and cost of the service. For example, the market may contain a fringe of gamblers who will only buy (unfair) gambles at a zero cost.† Costless wagering, that is, where the placing of bets and collections involves no direct outlay of money or time, may be arrived at in numerous ways. It appears that the lowest cost per wager from the seller's position, however, is obtained at the work

---

* In fact this was done in retaliation against management toughs.

† Bets on numbers are made for very small amounts, frequently as little as 10 cents. To invest an extra dime in the wager increases the bias on what is, at best, an unfair gamble. (Telephonic interview, December 24, 1962, with members of New York City Police Department.)

place.† Inside the plant there is a need to control critical positions, principally those which involve tasks that legitimately require the touring of the work place and personal contact with the employees. The foreman, shop steward, and union agent are in such positions, and the last two have been the target of the gambling industry. While control of the latter official requires political control of the union local, which may be important for other reasons, the former does not. The election of the right kind of shop steward, however, might be simplified if the local were controlled. Thus, even if gambling were the sole activity of criminals, they would profit from union control.

Elements of Extortion

Better over-all, yet still imperfect, police control points to another way in which trade unions can be used as a vehicle for traditional racket activity. Extortion through the "protection racket" is an appropriate device when police enforcement is relatively ineffective. Improvements in law enforcement with the repeal of the Volstead Act required a substitute for threatened violence, and potential labor strife proved feasible.

Union domination of the work force facilitates branching, i.e. contact with large firms and the potential of much higher payoffs for protection. Thus, the absolute amount of protection bribes may be increased. Under the traditional protection game, using violence and its threat, it was not always possible to establish contact with large, profitable firms. With a trade union as the vehicle, there is both reason to contact large firms and economic leverage to apply against them.

Size of firm, rather than profit rate, is significant. It is less costly to extort the same absolute amount from one large establishment than from a group of smaller firms. This explains the racketeers' interest in firms which have high absolute profits rather than high profit rates. Positive quasi-rents are only a necessary condition for extortion.

---

† The largest number of individuals who take bets work on commission, while a smaller number of people transport the slips to banks. This latter group is salaried.

As mentioned above, a racket's need for scale economies may encourage a spread of the product line, both by integration and branching.* The costs of a racket are basically fixed and designed to meet capacity problems. These are the legal fees, bribes, etc., which are essential to the racket's very existence. Once an official is bribed, however, he is locked in for an assortment of activities. Branching out may involve some additional costs, but probably nothing like the fee paid at entry. The hired labor of the racketeer follows a similar pattern. Considerable muscle is needed for entry into an activity and for potential defensive activity. Branching spreads this overhead.

Horizontal integration into adjacent sub-rosa industries and product branching also may impede entry of potential rivals. Efforts to keep out rivals and the need to have a "front" to justify income receipts to the tax collector have caused integration of rackets into legitimate businesses. Restaurants, entertainment, and sports have been principal "beneficiaries" of this need to explain sources of income for tax purposes.

A necessary condition for the development of racketeering in the labor movement was the development of favorable public policy towards organized labor. The Norris-LaGuardia Act gave a legal umbrella to the racketeer in control of a union, along with added flexibility to the legitimate trade unionists, because it inhibited the enforcement of criminal law when the racket union's actions could be interpreted as "legitimate" pursuit of a "legitimate" end. The perversion of ends was thus accomplished in the penumbra of the law.

An Analytical Model

In order to appraise racket unions, it is necessary to develop a model of their organization. A partial explanation of previous failure to develop a theoretical structure for analyzing racket unions is found in a void in the analytics of trade union behavior

---

* Integration would be a move into an activity which has not been developed. Thus, for a narcotics distributor to enter gambling would involve integration, in this case horizontal. Branching, on the other hand, involves an extension of an activity into new areas. An example would be the extension of protection from dry cleaning to restaurants.

functions. Normally, a trade union is defined in such a way that the leadership and membership have parallel goals. A racket union, however, has been described as "an enterprise manipulated for the exclusive profit of the organizer."[3] This unduly restricts the field of labor racketeering. It is more appropriate to include those organizations which produce benefits for their members, but where the benefits are a necessary by-product of the racketeer's long-run profit goal.

A number of alternative approaches have been suggested. John T. Dunlop advises that racket unions may be analyzed with "the ordinary model of the business firm." He asserts that there is "a kind of demand relationship [which] would show expected gross receipts from dues and racketeering at various prices."[4] While this model is a step forward in the analysis, it is not quite correct. Arthur Ross, on the other hand, explicitly negates at consideration of the problem by assuming that the activities of the institutional leaders are on behalf of the union and not for their own political or economic gain. He recognizes, however, that there may be abnormal cases where "in the absence of identification, personal ambitions will come first."[5]

Unquestionably, the most interesting analysis to date is by Gary S. Becker.[6] Becker introduces the racketeering problem within the context of an upward-sloping supply curve of labor where, at the wage established by the unions, the union leadership expropriates the producer's surplus. This is the distance measured by the perpendicular between the voluntary offer price at *each* point on the supply curve to the union-firm, and the price established by the union in the labor market. While this analysis is correct and in part is at the root of this article, the following analysis goes further and focuses on a number of relations.

---

[3] John T. Dunlop, *Wage Determination Under Trade Unions* (New York, August M. Kelley, 1950), p. 32.

[4] *Ibid.*

[5] Arthur Ross, *Trade Union Wage Policy* (Berkeley, Calif, University of California Press, 1956), p. 27.

[6] Gary S. Becker, "Union Restriction on Entry," in Phillip B. Bradley, ed., *The Public Stake in Union Power* (Charlottesville, University of Virginia Press, 1959), pp. 209-224.

That it is impossible to use an ordinary model of the firm to analyze the racket union becomes obvious when one tries to analyze the problem with Dunlop's "kind of demand relationship." While there is an aggregate surplus which may be expropriated by the racketeer, it consists of rents originating in the product market and in the factor market. While the total is important and serves as a limit for the gains, the distribution between the two markets has economic meaning. The lower the wage rate, the greater is the likelihood that the expropriation may have to come from the worker in the industry rather than directly from the firms. Alternatively, monopoly control of the labor market and perfectly elastic supply functions of other inputs may place the surplus exclusively in the workers' hands.

Prior to domination of an industry by the racketeer, the quasi-rents may be divided along a number of lines: all may be taken by entrepreneurs who are able to use normal monopoly and monopsony power; or the rents may be seized by the laborers through organizing the labor market along monopoly lines; or a bargained distribution may result from bilateral monopoly. The racketeer may be able to cut something extra out of this pie by resorting to extralegal methods. Generally, the use of these methods may not depend upon union control, but the union power position may well lower the cost of the marginal surplus. For example, the state of the labor market may prohibit perfect monopsonistic discrimination, but the entry of the racketeer may open this up as a marginal source of surplus.

The following model is applicable to what shall be called here the economic racketeer, one who depends primarily upon the use of strife and the threat of loss of profits in order to achieve his goals. It is assumed that the union leaders are entrepreneurs running the trade union for their own benefit. It is useful to think of the union as a firm acting as an organizational link between the factor and product markets. The problems are how much of the racketeers' resources should be used in each market and what procedures or decision-rules should be employed in the markets?

Economic Pressure on Employers

A racketeering union would almost always choose to concentrate its efforts on the employers in an industry. Only when the product market prohibits direct operations against the employers does the employee become subject to direct pressure. The firm is the efficient side of racketeering activity.

The economic leverage used against firms by racket union leaders is the threat of labor trouble. Posed in another and more meaningful way, the union sells a factor of production, which when not purchased forces the net return of entrepreneurship to fall to zero. Protection is a perfectly complementary input.

One potential union policy was envisioned by Henry C. Simons, who perceived unions pressing firms with high fixed investments to the point where they would receive no profits at all and hence be driven from the market. This procedure involves the squeezing out of the quasi-rents of the individual entrepreneurs. It is clearly a short-run policy and represents only one alternative open to the union.

If an industry is in perfect competitive equilibrium, with each firm having a roughly identical cost structure, the union is forced to impose a uniform charge on all members of the industry. This addition to fixed cost will find some firms closing in the long run, with the new equilibrium price for the industry above the old and output decreased. Assuming that firms are not alike, but range along a continuum from low- to high-cost producers, then a variable-charge policy would be followed. The larger the number of firms in the industry, the more difficult and costly is control. Similarly, in an industry operating under pure competition, ease of entry serves as a continuing threat to the existing firms as well as to the racketeering union. In such an industry the union is faced with a high potential cost of collection and of maintaining control. The racketeer is under continuous threat from the arrival of new firms entering with hopes of being able to avoid the payment of tribute.

A classic case of racketeers attempting the organization of competitive industries occurred in the late twenties. Both the garment industry and the fur industry were the targets of organized rackets. Since both were almost ideal types of competitive organization with apparently free entry, organization of the industries by racketeers might have seemed unreasonable, unless the object were to exploit the workers, which could have been a sufficient explanation. The geographic clustering of both industries in confined sections of New York City, however, made entry controllable by the racketeers. In turn, control of entry and the clustering of firms minimized operating costs and made branching profitable.

In the case where there is less than perfect competition, the analysis is more clear cut. The potential gains to the racketeer are the profits of the firms, which may be limited by potential entrants but nonetheless are positive and expropriatable. The union can extract all abnormal profits without affecting the output or price of the product. In this case, the racketeer only redirects the flow of quasi-rents, and as economists we are left with no clear case against the union. The organization of the industry, however, should force a Cournot monopoly adjustment that would reduce output and increase price, which is objectionable.

Establishing Entry Barriers

Now it is apparent that a properly run racket has a very real interest in the structure of the industry within which it is operating. It may also be seen that there is a substantial reason for cooperation between racketeer and firms in the industry. The limiting aspect to higher prices and profits at all times for firms is potential entry into the industry. If entry barriers are raised above normal heights, it then becomes possible to raise the price and consequently the rent of management. A long-run profit-maximizing union might well develop a rule of behavior which would take a residual share of the pure profits, either with or without some minimum guaranty.

The union in this case might offer an inducement to the firms, a *quid pro quo* for extracting some rent. The payoff for the existing members of the industry comes in the maintenance of the current industry structure despite increases in prices and profits. The union may, in this situation, refuse to sign an agreement with a new firm or let it be known that any new firm will be faced with great labor difficulties. A further inducement may be in the form of lower labor costs, either through a sweetheart contract or failure to pursue the grievances of the workers.

In either case, there must be some significant latitude in wages. (Failure to receive high wages may be due to high demand elasticities and a union employment preference, however, and may not be the work of a racket organization.) There also must be strong market imperfections, or the firms with sweetheart contracts will be unable to satisfy their manpower needs. The sweetheart contract is a broad type of exploitation against all the workers and is unlikely to be uncovered. It allows the racket union to collect its funds without having to resort to more unsavory and inefficient exploitative techniques discussed below.

Union control must involve the creation of labor problems in adjacent industries to retard product substitution. The union must maintain the relative advantage of the firm despite an increase in absolute costs. Under these circumstances, a group of firms may be able to do better with a racketeering union as their "agent" than if they had an incorruptible union.*

In terms of resource utilization, the impact of this type of racketeering is as follows. A union sharing in the profits of management would have an incentive to reduce labor costs. While the rate of pay can not readily be altered, although the sweetheart contract is not impossible, the efficiency of labor could be increased. One should expect to see high labor productivity, accompanied by relatively low pilferage and insurance losses and general slack time. Discipline should be the rule and efficiency the goal.

We may sum up our conclusions as follows: A racket union can attack the management of an industry for the profits it receives; the union will be better off the less competitive the industry structure and may become the industry's agent to raise entry barriers and reduce unit labor costs.

---

* The gains of industry organization go to the owners of the firms and the union leaders. A nonracketeering union without any employment preference might welcome an offer by management of high wage rates, etc., if the union effectively stopped the entry of new firms and policed the industry.

Economic Pressure on Employees

Only when certain market conditions are not fulfilled have there been attempts to extract rents directly from the employees of an industry. These cases are rare, but result in such bizarre activity that they have received attention far in excess of their economic significance or importance in labor racketeering. They amount to last-resort activities and are truly deviant behavior in what is already a deviant enterprise.

In order for this type of racketeering to exist, certain market characteristics must be present. *First*, the firms in the industry must not be open to organization, and/or some employers must be out of reach, say, the government. This eliminates expropriation from the firms or increases the firms' surpluses, for example, through the sweetheart contract. *Second*, the labor markets must be disorganized and characterized by immobility, excess supply, etc. *Third*, a will to use the situation for personal gain must exist. At this point it is uncertain whether economics will be able to clarify why human motives differ, but there are cases where the potential for racket activity against the membership was possible, but not used. With these guidelines, we can examine the racketeers' direct activities against the worker.

Assume that the union faces a group of workers who are potential union members, whose motives are pecuniary, and who have a continuous range of occupational choice (including no occupation) at every moment. Essentially, their sole interest is in maximizing their expected take-home pay over some time period.

These workers at any moment have different opportunities with respect to employment and income. At the lower extreme are workers on the border of being unemployable. In one sense, the best alternative that they have facing them is that of relief payments. In the same economic category for our purposes are moonlighters, attracted by high hourly rates. A floater group may be of importance in the racketeer's sales plan. At the other extreme would be people who have potential employment at rates of pay comparable to the controlled occupation.

Under these circumstances, each man employed through the agency of the union would receive a quasi-rent or producer's surplus by being employed in the unionized trade rather than an alternative occupation. The quasi-rent would be largest for the worker with the lowest possible alternative income, zero for the man who can get just as good a position in another industry, and negative if the alternatives are better than those offered by the union. The quasi-rent in a given occupation will vary directly with the contracted-for wage in the industry and inversely with the societal minimum. The distance of the industry wage above the social minimum wage may be determined by the needs of the industry for a large supply of workers, by the government through its role as employer, or by the national union.* It is likely that the rent function is not smooth, but a step function, the discontinuities representing classes of workers. This does not vitiate the analysis but, instead, provides a rationale for a core membership that is not exploited. The core's function is to support the leadership of the union against political insurgents.

Work Permits

Assume that the union is a firm selling work permits, which are a necessary condition for employment in the industry. These permits have to be purchased on a continuing basis; failure to keep up the payments immediately involves loss of the job and the long-term discounted stream of quasi-rents. The union faces a downward-sloping curve for the permits. As the price of the permit is reduced, more workers are willing to purchase the permits—given some income guarantee. The exact shape of the curve is determined by the expected quasi-rents in this occupation for the relevant group. For any wage rate contracted by the union with the industry or firm, there exist both maximum and minimum prices. The maximum would be paid by the least efficient worker earning the highest quasi-rent, while at the other extreme workers would become attached only if the price per permit were zero or negative.

The racketeering union's operation has a cost as well as a demand function. The union must make its collections and

---

* Racketeering may be on a local basis in industries where contract terms are set by the national union.

protect its members from workers outside the organization. In addition to the normal overhead, one would expect a very high component in the form of legal fees and bribes. We shall assume in the analysis, which follows a rising marginal cost function for this racketeering activity. While total unit costs may be declining, it would be unreasonable to assume declining marginal costs, since these would be mostly labor charges. For ease of exposition, the marginal cost function is assumed to be linear.

The organizations must establish a tariff for the work permits or determine the number of permits to sell in order that the treasury will be maximized.† It is important to notice that the union has a number of alternatives which it can follow, depending on whether it chooses to act as a perfectly discriminating monopolist or as an ordinary monopolist. These alternatives are indicated in Figure 8-1. The union acting as a monopoly would solve its problems by equating marginal revenue and marginal cost. Doing so, it would sell OA permits at price OC. Its profits would be BEJ. This profit is the treasury out of which the leadership can expropriate funds.

Selling permits at a single price OC is a long-run policy, designed to keep the membership satisfied, for the membership will still be receiving some quasi-rent, represented by the area ECG. Thus, one finds numerous unions with a history of racketeering, but with the membership refusing to oust the leadership.

Alternatively, the union may decide to discriminate in the sale of permits, charging each worker the value of his quasi-rent. The first worker would pay the extreme price OE, while the lowest price for a permit would be OH. In this case, the union determines the output by equating its marginal cost with its average revenue, for the average revenue curve is the incremental revenue schedule for the discriminating monopolist.*

---

† In white-collar crime the treasury was assumed given and outside the decision-making ambit of the embezzlers.

* If the union decided to act as a perfectly discriminating monopolist, its cost schedules might be affected by this policy. Generally, we would surmise that to act in this fashion would result in a shift upwards in the cost schedules due to the difficulty of extracting the added quasi-rent. Where discrimination exists, we would always expect that the added revenue exceed the addition to costs, or the racketeering organization would have to be considered irrational.

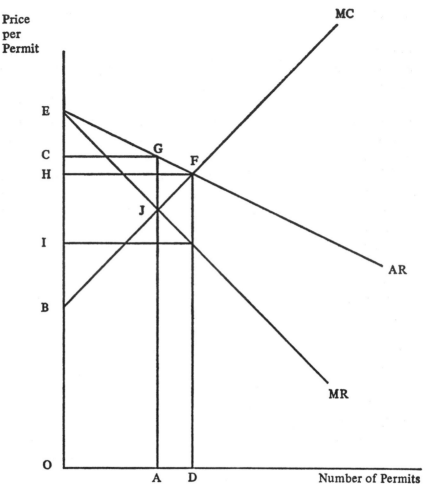

Figure 8-1. Union alternatives in determining number and price of permits.

Kickbacks

To openly follow this policy might not be wise in terms of community relations, inviting punitive legal action. The same end could be achieved in a more discreet fashion. The union would charge a flat fee for the permit, but the number to be sold would again be determined by the intersection of marginal cost and average revenue curve. The price for the fee would be OH, but OHFD would not be the total receipts of the union racketeer. The permit would be a necessary but not a sufficient requirement for obtaining work in the trade. The union would institute kickbacks. The full kickback would be equal to the difference between the cost of the permit and the quasi-rent. This alternative has an advantage, in addition to its secrecy, which should not be overlooked. The added payments would not appear in the union's accounts and, therefore, as income which could be examined for tax purposes.

When the discriminating monopolist applies himself fully, his profit increases by FEJ over what it would have been if he acted as an ordinary monopolist. When the kickback is used, the union reports as dues only the OHFD, while EHF (the shakedown) would not be counted as part of the union's and, therefore, the racketeer's income. The analysis clearly explains the conditions uncovered in the waterfront investigations. The union dues are low, while the apparent rate of pay is high. This results in many workers joining the union. The firm is not able to hire all the workers who have fulfilled the necessary condition for employment. The union allocates employment through the shapeup system,† requiring members to be available on a continuous basis, so that at any shapeup there is a surplus of workers which should help facilitate the payment of the kickback.

The union may employ a regular gang of workers who would not pay any tribute to the union, with a fringe of outsiders selected as candidates for irregular jobs which are dependent upon a bribe. This is shown in Figure 8-2, where the demand for the permits is a step function. Each horizontal section of the curve represents a group of workers, the A-B group having inferior opportunities to the C-D group. The marginal cost curve is rising and intersects the average revenue schedule at G. This indicates that a price of GJ would be set with OJ permits demanded. The loyalist group IJ would be the regularly employed crew members who are not exploited. The groups AB

---

† Alternatives to the shapeup are loansharking or forced charity. The loanshark forces borrowing, with employment contingent on being in debt.

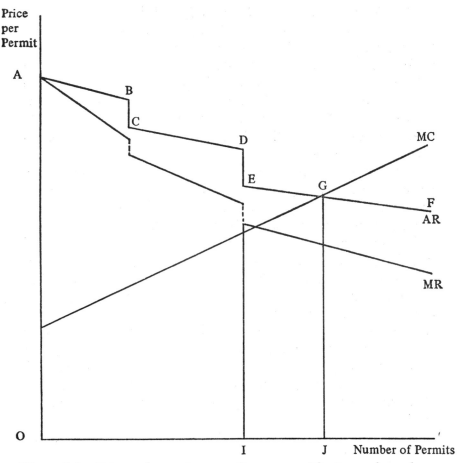

Figure 8-2. Prices of permits according to qualifications of employee groups.

and CD are the irregulars who are subjected to price discrimination, possibly within each group as well as compared to other groups. The larger the desired loyal power base, the more steps above the EF level will pay only the GJ formal dues.

Numerous implications may be drawn from the analysis of price discrimination. The system encourages higher membership by lower formal dues and fees than a racket union acting as an ordinary monopolist. Another characteristic suggested by the model is that preference in hiring for irregular jobs would go to the least able worker, hence causing lower labor productivity. One may infer that the fringe of unemployed workers would be made up of those who were likely to be the most able workers and hence had the lowest potential rent in this trade. A complement to this is that productivity would be lowest under discrimination against the employees and would decrease directly with the degree of discriminate pricing. This raises an interesting question about supply. What would be the effect of stringent discrimination upon supply?

As we approach complete expropriation, there would possibly occur a falling off of the supply of labor to the industry. The absence of total expropriation may be due to two causes. First, the union may leave some quasi-rent if for no other reason than that the collection costs are too high. Second, the residual is to maintain a constituency. Apparent complete discrimination may still not cause a collapse of the supply function to the firm. There may be some slack in the model that might be theoretically observable. One characteristic of disequilibrium i.e., total discrimination, might be a falling away of discipline and consequently a decrease in productivity and high loss from breakage. In effect, this is a deliberate attempt to lower the disutility of labor. Second, and related to the above, is the presence or extent of pilferage. Thievery by the work force may become the source of the laborers' surplus.* Pilferage is interpreted not as a conscious policy on the part of the racketeers, but as a necessary by-product of their pricing policy.

A further implication of the model is that this type of a hard-driving racket union would not choose to have a substantial entry fee. First, this would retard entry and reduce the unemployed fringe, making it more difficult to discriminate. Second is the problem of the size of the fee. With discriminatory pricing, one can adjust the permit price quickly to changes in rent, while the initiation fee would require an estimation of discounted stream of rent. High initiation fees are therefore a sign of monopoly organization, for the benefit of existing membership

---

* This material would have to be checked on a pier-by-pier or multipier group in longshoring. Such a search was not feasible for the author and may very well be impossible, given record retention practices.

and a device to retard entry rather than an indication of racketeering.

Areas Favorable to Racketeering Activity

Finally, there is the problem of specialization in labor racketeering. It should be quite clear that the expropriation can never be as high from workers as from employers. The shapeup system has not been widespread, most likely because it is inefficient. It thrives where access to the industry is difficult, as in the case of government docks. The major potential for racketeers lies in the industry and in keeping workers contented enough so that the union leadership is not voted out of office, with sweetheart contracts used whenever the market permits.

Given the goals of the racketeer, we must attempt to specify the conditions attracting organization. For example, highly perishable commodities are generally considered to be significant in drawing racketeers into an industry. Superficially this idea has appeal, but careful analysis leads to a different conclusion. Industries with highly perishable products are not an important part of labor racketeering, nor do all such industries have a history of racketeering. In fact, perishability may only be a proxy for profits, which are the significant variable. If perishability were the true variable, one would expect firms to leave the industry as a consequence of their losses and a permanently low level of activity to result.

The racketeer is concerned with his profit position. His advantage is in selling his wares to a cluster of firms or an industry where the absolute payment is high relative to absolute cost of collection. His costs are related to maintaining barriers to entry in the industry. If the structural conditions for market control and entry are inappropriate, there is a natural barrier to organization by racketeers (or unions).

Examine instances where there is no history of pressure upon firms by racketeers. The picture that one draws is of firms with little economic myopia. For example, stone, clay and glass, metal products, chemical and allied products do not have a history of racketeering, while contract construction, shipping, and entertainment are involved in racket organization. What conditions make for control of one activity and not another? Essentially, they are the factors which encourage or impede strong unionization.

Multiplant firms may be controllable by racketeers, but the cost of control, one suspects is excessive. The fact that some industries are oligopolistic in nature and may exhibit high returns shows only part of the relevant picture. If the firms have geographically dispersed production and marketing units, the cost of applying economic pressure may outweigh the gains, since it may involve taking over a number of union locals spread throughout the country. The absolute cost to the racketeer may be high enough to reduce the rate of return to an uneconomic level.

High clustering of firms reduces the cost of control and implies relatively low costs of controlling entry. If the firms in the industry are few in number and already making large absolute profits, so much the better for the racketeer. The larger the number of firms or the more difficult the control of entry, the less likely is racket organization because of the expense.

An implication of this thesis is that the emergence of national crime organizations is a response to changes in industrial organization and is not due to exogenous factors.

Union racketeering, and more broadly criminal activity, is a reasonable area for economic study. The model provided will hopefully cause increased economic research on this problem. The sociology of crime, while important, leaves too many areas unexplored. These are problems which are amenable to the paraphernalia of economics.

THE CONTINUING PROBLEM OF LABOR RACKETEERING

LAWRENCE J. KAPLAN AND DENNIS KESSLER

Evidence continues to mount that labor racketeers are still exploiting unions. The situation today is as bad as it was in 1959 when Congress approved the Landrum-Griffin Act.

In March 1974 four fur union officials were convicted for

having accepted payoffs. Criminal justice officials hailed the convictions as a significant gain in the long and generally futile effort to crack labor racketeering in the garment industry. The union leaders are officials of the Furriers Joint Council which represents most of the workers in the industry. According to the Federal District Court, the four union officials conspired to receive $35,000 in payoffs from unionized fur shops for ignoring illegal subcontracting to nonunion shops.

In the same month James R. Hoffa, the former president of the International Brotherhood of Teamsters, filed a lawsuit against former President Nixon and former Attorney General William B. Saxbe, charging that they had illegally prevented him from holding union office. Mr. Hoffa was released from a Federal prison in Lewisburg, Pa., on December 22, 1971, after Mr. Nixon granted executive clemency. Mr. Hoffa had been in prison since March 7, 1967 after receiving a thirteen-year sentence for mail fraud and jury tampering. The order releasing Mr. Hoffa stipulated that he "not engage in direct or indirect management of any labor organization prior to March 6, 1980." Among the allegations is the charge that the Government barred union activity by Mr. Hoffa in return for favors from the current teamster president, Frank E. Fitzsimmons. The stipulation in President Nixon's grant of clemency prohibiting union activity by Mr. Hoffa for ten years was designed to protect Mr. Fitzsimmons from being forced out of office by Mr. Hoffa, the suit alleges. In return, the suit contends, Mr. Fitzsimmons contributed political aid, campaign donations, and other services for Mr. Nixon and certain of his assistants.

In a third news item, a former teamsters' union pension fund consultant, was enjoying a golfing vacation in Southern California and has yet to be arrested, even though he had been charged a month earlier in a Federal indictment in a $1.4 million pension fund fraud. According to Justice Department sources, the unusual delayed arrest was a special consideration extended by a top aide of the United States Attorney in Chicago, where the indictment was returned. This individual was the only one of seven defendants who had not been arrested. Federal law enforcement officials noted that the vacationing ex-teamster aide had a history of association with Mafia figures and, after he was indicted, he was seen by law enforcement agents playing golf with a Chicago-based mobster. Only three months ago, this consultant had been released from Federal prison where he served nine months of a one-year sentence for his part in a $55,000 kickback from a $1.5 million pension fund loan.

These three case studies appeared within a two-week period in March 1974. The evidence seems to support the view that labor racketeering, corruption, and tyranny continues unabated. It is time for a new Federal inquiry.

The constitution of the American Federation of Labor-Congress of Industrial Organizations provides for the powers required to keep itself free of corruption. It declares that it "must remain free from any and all corruption influences" and authorizes a watchdog committee to keep the AFL-CIO "free from any taint of corruption." In recent years this committee has been inactive, and according to labor insiders there has developed a climate of tolerance and even immunity for union exploiters. In view of this resurgent union criminality it is time once again to review the adequacy of labor laws as well as their enforcement. Congress should establish again a select committee to investigate racketeering and to develop necessary legislation for combatting it.

BIBLIOGRAPHY

Books

Cressey, Donald R.: Demand, supply, and profit. *Theft of the Nation.* New York, Harper and Row, 1969, pp. 95-99.

Demaris, Ovid: *Lucky Luciano.* Derby, Connecticut, Monarch, 1960.

Dineen, Joseph F.: *Underworld U.S.A.* New York, Farrar, 1956.

Hostetter, Gordon L. and Beesley, Thomas Quinn: *It's A Racket!* Chicago, Les Quinn Books, 1929.

Johnson, Malcolm A.: *Crime on the Labor Front.* New York, McGraw-Hill, 1950.

Keating, William J. and Carter, Richard: *The Man Who Rocked the Boat.* New York, Harper and Brothers, 1956.

Kennedy, Robert F.: *The Enemy Within.* New York, Harper, 1960.

Leiserson, William H.: *American Trade Union Democracy.* New York, Columbia U Pr, 1959.

Lipset, Seymour M.; Trow, Martin A. and Coleman, James S.: *Union Democracy*. Glencoe, Free Press, 1956.

Martin, Raymond V.: *Revolt in the Mafia*. New York, Duell, 1963.

McClellan, John L.: *Crime Without Punishment*. New York, Duell, 1962.

Raymond, Allen: *Waterfront Priest*. New York, Henry Holt, 1955.

Smith, Alson J.: *Syndicate City*. Chicago, Regnery, 1954.

Taft, Philip: *Corruption and Racketeering in the Labor Movement*. Ithaca, New York State School of Industrial and Labor Relations, 1958.

Taft, Philip: *Organized Labor in American History*. New York, Harper and Row, 1964.

Thompson, Craig and Raymond, Allen: *Gang Rule in New York*. New York, Dial, 1940.

Tyler, Gus: *Organized Crime in America*. New York, Harper, 1963.

United States Senate, Committee on Improper Activities in the Labor-Management Field, *1st Interim Report*, 85th Congress, 2nd Session, 1958.

United States Senate. Select Committee on Improper Activtiies in the Labor-Management Field. *Final Report*. Senate Report No. 1139, 86th Congress, 1960.

United States Senate, Committee on Government Operations, *Labor Racketeering Activities of Jack McCarthy and National Consultants Associated, Ltd.*, 90th Congress, 1st Session, Report No. 192, 1967.

Zeiger, Henry A.: *Sam the Plumber*. New York, NAL (Signet). 1970.

Articles

AFL convention expels ILA in first such action for corruption. *The New York Times*, September 23, 1959, p. 1.

Anti-Trust Gets New Role as Key Weapon in Drive on Rackets. *Business World*, March 14, 1959.

Attorney General Kennedy Reports Justice Department Gains in Dealing With Corrupt Labor Leaders and Employers. *The New York Times*, 18, January 25, 1962.

Attorney General Lefkowitz reports many Puerto Ricans and Negroes exploited by racketeering unions and employers. *The New York Times*, 25, August 9, 1961.

Bell, J. F.: Corruption and union racketeering. *Current History*, June 1959.

Case against Hoffa. *New Republic, 137*: September 2, 1957.

Containerized cargo in port of New York. *The New York Times*, 90, March 9, 1969.

Contract. *Time, 69*: March 11, 1959.

Featherbedding and the federal anti-racketeering act. *University of Chicago Law Review, 26*: Autumn 1958.

Elkins, J. B.: Story of a union and underworld ties. *U.S. News and World Report, 42*: March 8, 1957.

Graham, Fred P.: U.S. aide charges labor-crime link. *The New York Times,* 1, March 30, 1967.

Grutzner, Charles: 2 restaurateurs tell of union payoffs. *The New York Times,* 20, March 6, 1969.

Guys and doll. *Newsweek,* 5, June 24, 1968.

Here's what labor probe means. *Nation's Business, 45:* April 1957.

How unions can avoid rackets. *U.S. News and World Report, 42:* April 5, 1957.

Johnson, Earl J.: Organized crime: Challenge to the American legal system. *Journal of Criminal Law, Criminology and Police Science,* December 1962.

Justice Department representative charges ILA and Teamster are linked with each other and with Cosa Nostra crime syndicate. *The New York Times,* 1, March 30, 1967.

Kennedy, John F.: Labor racketeers and political pressure. *Look, 23:* May 12, 1959.

Kennedy, John F.: Union racketeering; the responsibility of the bar. *American Bar Association Journal, 44:* May 1958.

Kihss, Peter: Lumbard on State Drive to Control Crime. *The New York Times,* 1, 82, May 7, 1967.

Labor-management reporting and disclosure act of 1959: A Symposium. *Georgetown Law Journal, 48:* Winter 1959.

Labor racketeers. *Business Week,* August 17, 1957.

Labor racketeering. *Fortune, 52:,* July 1955.

Labor vs. racketeers. *U.S. News and World Report, 41:* September 7, 1956.

Labor, violence and corruption. *Business Week,* August 31, 1957.

Loan Rackets. *The New York Times,* 28, May 17, 1968.

Longshoremen bargain for new contract. *The New York Times,* 73, December 21, 1968.

McClellan committee hearing on Teamsters. *The New York Times,* 11, June 26, 1959.

McClellan committee labels Hoffa boss of *hoodlum empire. The New York Times,* March 26, 1958, p. 1.

McClellan, J. L.: Can the labor racketeer be stopped? *U.S. News and World Report, 45:* October 10, 1958.

Mollenhoff, C.: How labor bosses get rich. *Look, 18:* March 9, 1954.

Mitchell, John P.: Labor racketeering. *Vital Speeches, 23:* March 15, 1957.

N.Y. SLRB warns against 'racketeering' unions that prey on poorly educated workers from minority groups. *The New York Times,* 83, May 3, 1964.

None so blind: Labor racketeering. *Reader's Digest, 69:* August 1956.

One year struggle against gangsterism. *Political Affairs,* 772, October 1961.

Phony unions. *America, 100:* July 4, 1959.

Racketeers in labor. *Commonwealth, 64:* May 18, 1956.

Rackets. *The New York Times*, May 24, 1949.

Riesel says gangsters and communists use same methods to gain control of labor movement. *The New York Times*, 28. December 17, 1956.

Senate spotlight on labor rackets. *Business World*, January 26, 1957.

St. Louis blues; Labor rackets in the construction industry. *Fortune, 50*: July 1954.

SLRB chairman asks federal, state and local prosecutors to help curb gangster use of labor law as shield for corrupt unions. *The New York Times*, 1, June 2, 1959.

Sweetheart contracts in Chicago restaurants. *The New York Times*, 1, July 9, 1958.

Union agent use of violence in forced hiring violates federal anti-racketeering act. *Harvard Law Review, 66*: March 1953.

Unions vs. racketeers. *U.S. News and World Report, 42*: February 1, 1957.

U.S. Assistant Attorney General Vinson says several labor leaders in New York area will be indicted for corruption in Justice Department drive against infiltration of organized crime into labor unions. *The New York Times*, 30, June 28, 1967.

Velie, L.: Our secret labor bosses. *Readers Digest, 74*: March 1959.

Waterfront commission begins sweeping probe of criminal influence on docks. *The New York Times*, 74, November 2, 1961.

Waterfront commission subpoenas top ILA leaders in probe of return of underworld elements to piers. *The New York Times*, 58, September 2, 1959.

Waterfront commission opens drive to rid port of criminals and racketeers; Aims at ex-convicts who hold secret posts in ILA. *The New York Times*, 1, September 5, 1958.

Weinstein, Paul A.: Racketeering and labor: An economic analysis. *Industrial and Labor Relations Review, 19*:3, 402-413, April 1966.

When Mafia gangsters muscle into unions. *U.S. News and World Report, 45*: July 11, 1958.

Why the new move to investigate racketeering in labor unions? *U.S. News and World Report, 40*: June 15, 1956.

Worst invasion of New York metropolitan area unions by gangsters since 1933. *The New York Times*, 1, April 24, 1952.

CHAPTER 9

INFILTRATION INTO LEGITIMATE BUSINESS

INTRODUCTION

O NE OF THE MOST disturbing problems in the area of organized crime is the fact that criminals and racketeers are investing the profits of their illicit activities into legitimate enterprises. A gangster in a legitimate business does not become an honest entrepreneur. The methods used to achieve success in racketeering and gambling enterprises continue to be used in a legitimate business. The gangster-businessman will use unscrupulous and discriminatory business practices, extortion, bombing and other forms of violence to eliminate competitors and to compel customers to buy products sold by the mobsters. A racketeer with contempt for law will not hesitate to engage in illegal practices. This gives him a considerable advantage over more timid competitors and is used frequently to push the competition out of business.

It has been estimated that the investment of organized criminals amounts to about $30 billion. It is also estimated that this sum is invested in 15,000 to 50,000 domestic business firms, providing the Syndicate with ownership or "decision-making influence." If we assume that this involvement is confined to the 5,000 "family" members, the holdings would approximate three to ten firms per crime associate. The average net worth of companies owned by organized crime associates probably ranges between $1 million to $2 million.

What impact does this have on our economy? Professor

Simon Kuznets of the National Bureau of Economic Research estimated the total value of industrial and business assets for the United States economy at approximately $3,000 billion dollars, or $3 trillion dollars, as of 1969. If organized crime controls as much as $30 billion, their share is 1 percent. This is an impressive proportion, and a cause for concern because a sum of $30 billion proves the success of illicit enterprise, and serves as an incentive to continue illegal operations. In addition, these holdings represent a reservoir of economic power which enables organized crime to further strengthen its position in both legal and illegal activities.

The first selection lists about fifty areas of business enterprise infiltrated by organized crime, as identified by the Kefauver Committee in 1951. The lead article, "How Criminals Solve Their Investment Problem," provides some of the specific details on criminal money in real estate, banks, securities, the garment industry, and a host of other enterprises. The next article written by an expert on organized crime in the United States examines infiltration from the viewpoint of business executives. He shows how businessmen are victimized by organized crime, what kinds of ruses and machinations are used by the underworld, and how the typical businessman's attempts to extricate himself get him into deeper trouble still. Then he analyzes how an executive can detect inroads into his company by organized crime and what counteraction he should take.

How Criminals Solve Their Investment Problems*

By latest official estimates, organized crime in America is now producing "an annual income of billions."

And the crime bosses, faced with the problem of what to do with their illegal wealth, are moving ever deeper into a variety of legitimate businesses.

The problem is emerging as one of urgent concern to federal, state and local authorities all across the United States.

In recent months, it has been discovered that mobsters with long criminal records are infiltrating multimillion-dollar business

---

* Reprinted from *U.S. News & World Report*, March 30, 1964.

AREAS OF BUSINESS ENTERPRISE INFILTRATED BY ORGANIZED
CRIME, THE KEFAUVER COMMITTEE LIST*

Advertising
Amusement industry
Appliances
Automobile industry
Baking
Ball rooms, bowling alleys, etc.
Banking
Basketball
Boxing
Cigarette distribution
Coal
Communications facilities
Construction
Drug stores and drug companies
Electrical equipment
Florists
Food (meat, sea food, dairy products, groceries, cheese, olive oil, fruit)
Football
Garment industry
Gas stations and garages
Hotels
Import-export business
Insurance

Juke box and coin-machine distribution
Laundry and dry cleaning
Liquor industry
Loan and bonding business
Manufacturing (gambling equipment, broilers, etc.)
Nevada gambling houses
News services
Newspapers
Oil industry
Paper products
Racing and race tracks
Radio stations
Ranching
Real estate
Restaurants (taverns, bars, night clubs)
Scrap business
Shipping
Steel
Surplus sales
Tailoring (haberdashery)
Television
Theaters
Transportation

* Reprinted from United States Government document, United States Senate, Special Senate Committee to Investigate Organized Crime in Interstate Commerce (the Kefauver Committee), *Final Report*, 82nd Congress, 1st Session, Report No. 725 (1951), p. 152. Used with permission.

enterprises. These include banks and Wall Street brokerage houses, big real estate syndicates, sizable corporations serving the public in many ways.

One clear fact emerges: The underworld's invasion of legitimate enterprises has become big business. Racketeers—many of them associated with the underworld secret society known as the Mafia—now have so much illegally acquired money that they're hard pressed to find ways to put it to work profitably.

Consequently, much of the criminal world's excess capital is flowing into legitimate fields.

From officials and authoritative sources in Washington and other cities, "U.S. News & World Report" obtained a picture of how organized crime is gaining control of more and more U.S. businesses:

Real Estate

In New York City alone, U.S. District Attorney Robert M. Morgenthau estimates, underworld investments in real estate run into "hundreds of millions."

Mafia members are major stockholders in a group operating two famous skyscraper office buildings, according to Mr. Morgenthau, "This is a third-of-a-billion-dollar operation," he said.

One of the alleged participants is a particularly notorious criminal—head of a Mafia "family" blamed for numerous murders. He was one of the hoodlums arrested at a convention of racketeers at Apalachin, N.Y., in November 1957.

Activities of this real estate group are being probed by the U.S. Senate's Permanent Subcommittee on Investigations, headed by Senator John L. McClellan.

Gangsters also are said to be large holders of shares in one of the best-known skyscrapers in Manhattan.

In New York, at least one well-known hotel is owned outright by criminals, U.S. officials said. Gangsters also own hotels and motels in Miami and Miami Beach, Las Vegas, Detroit, Chicago and other cities. Law-enforcement officers in other large cities throughout the country can name important properties owned by known criminals.

In Tucson, Ariz., two mobsters named before the McClellan Committee as Mafia leaders acquired blocks of downtown business property and acres of other real estate, officials said. Vigorous police action finally drove them out of Tucson.

Another identified leader of the Chicago Mafia has large real estate holdings—including hotels—in Chicago, Las Vegas and other cities.

Banks

Enforcement officials believe racketeers and gamblers have gained a foothold in many large banks through stock purchases. They attempt to use their position as stockholders to obtain special favors—and often succeed.

In Detroit, one medium-seized bank, now under investigation, is owned outright by "the mob," a Washington official said.

"It is known as the 'hoodlums' bank,'" the official stated. "We have reason to believe that it makes unsecured loans to Mafia leaders. It lets them open big accounts through fictitious names or dummies—no questions asked. It has a tie-up with large business interests controlled by the Mafia."

In Miami, an almost identical situation is said to exist in a bank, also under official scrutiny. And in New York City alleged gangster control of at least two banks is being investigated.

"We have evidence of one bank officer making highly questionable loans to Eastern racketeers," a Justice Department official said.

As far back as 1950, the Senate Investigating Committe headed by the late Senator Estes Kefauver learned that a New Jersey gambling ring had bought a large block of stock in a New York bank. Thereafter, it used this bank as its clearing house for checks obtained in payment of gambling losses. These checks ran into millions of dollars.

A Chicago police official told the Committee: "In the past few years, they [criminals] are becoming very active in the finance industry, particularly in small-loan companies, in banks."

Securities

Official files are bulging with instances—including convictions —of penetration of brokerage offices by gang-connected racketeers. Some involve firms with previously spotless reputations. Others are "boiler room" operations, set up to unload worthless stocks through high-pressure sales tactics.

"All in all," a Washington official said, "frauds in which the underworld and the financial world are linked have bilked the public of many millions."

Sometimes the 'stocks" peddled by racketeers through brokerage offices are worthless certificates in nonexistent companies.

One Brooklyn mobster, sentenced to jail for frauds in connection with Wall Street operations, also has interests in real estate and other "legitimate" businesses. Among other things, investigators say, he manufactures eyeglasses that are sold through a labor union's medical fund.

Recently, federal investigators have begun looking closely at every case involving a major financial scandal. They have found links to the Mafia or to Las Vegas gambling interests in many multi-million-dollar frauds.

Garment Industry

The dress-manufacturing business, centered in New York, long has been known to be over-run with racketeers. Many have become millionaires.

Investigators attribute these successful operations to the fact that many of these racketeers run nonunion shops. This keeps their costs well below those of nonracketeer competitors.

The racketeers keep the unions out of their shops, investigators say, by hiring Mafia killers and strong-arm men as "labor consultants."

U.S. Attorney Morgenthau, with the aid of the Federal Bureau of Investigation, presented evidence recently to a federal grand jury on New York Mafia activities. One of his main cases involves an alleged Mafia boss who owns interests in a string of dress factories in New York and Scranton, Pa., and is said to be a multimillionaire.

Other Businesses

As the chart on this page shows, mobsters are in many legitimate businesses. So far as is known, they have not taken over large industries such as heavy manufacturing. But, from time to time, the underworld manages to penetrate the fringes of heavy industry.

A number of years ago, the Kefauver Committee discovered, mobsters from Cleveland, Ohio, put up part of the money to finance a merger of two steel companies. This underworld association since is said to have been dissolved.

A leading auto manufacturer, "U.S. News & World Report" was told, has been able to cut its former ties with a car hauling company in which a New Jersey gangster was a major owner.

One alleged leader of the Detroit Mafia at one time had a close connection with a stove works in Detroit. He also had a lucrative contract for the factory's scrap metal. He now is in the auto wash and filling station business.

Sudden emergence of sons or sons-in-law of Detroit Mafia racketeers as contractors for scrap metal handling at big Detroit plants is commonplace.

In Detroit alone, Mafia members have infiltrated legitimate businesses worth at least $50 million, George Edwards, then police commissioner of that city, told the McClellan Committee. He named ninety-eight businesses which can be traced to the Mafia. Many of the Mafia leaders live in Grosse Pointe, a residential district favored by Detroit's top industrialists.

A figure named by police as one of the five "dons" who comprise the Mafia's ruling council in Detroit has many legitimate business connections. These include a wholesale produce company with gross annual sales in the millions, a large baking company, a coach line, and a large beer distributorship.

Commissioner Edwards also named a race track operating near Detroit, and testified: "We think there is a major influence on [the race track] from the top echelon of the Mafia, and that some of the proceeds of this million-dollar-a-year operation undoubtedly are available for Mafia purposes."

The fields of entertainment and sports—big business in the U.S.—also are heavily infiltrated by the underworld, a Justice Department aide said.

Hoodlums—Who Are They?

Who are these hoodlums who have invaded U.S. business? How do they operate?

The Mafia and other criminal gangs exist in every sizable city in America. New York, Chicago, Philadelphia, Detroit, Cleveland, St. Louis, Boston, New Orleans, Pittsburgh, Buffalo, Kansas City, Miami and Miami Beach, Tampa, Providence and Las Vegas are known to investigators as the centers.

Many of the richest gangsters of today made their millions in the old prohibition days. Then repeal and income tax prosecutions ended that era.

Now the big money in crime, officials say, is made in gambling, narcotics and "loansharking"—the lending of money at exorbitant interest rates. These illegal activities provide the billions which the underworld is funneling into legitimate businesses.

When a businessman falls behind on his payments to a loan shark, the gangster often simply takes over the business.

The New Image

In the new world of gangster-businessmen operations, the gangster has taken on a new image. As a rule, the top level gangster no longer is a crude, flashily dressed, fast-living character. More often, he wears Ivy League suits. He lives quietly, often in the best residential communities, and sends his children to select colleges. Sometimes he hires public-relations firms to add luster to his image.

"We have fifty important Mafia leaders living in Nassau County on Long Island," District Attorney William Cahn told "U.S. News & World Report." "They live circumspectly, in houses costing upward of $75,000. They take part in civic projects and are liberal with their charitable contributions.

"They all claim they are respectable businessmen. Until we began exposing them, many citizens did not know that they were narcotics pushers, gamblers, labor racketeers, blackmailers and panderers, with hired killers to do their dirty work."

Officials say that criminals often have "devious reasons" for entering legitimate businesses. Often they want the business as a respectable "front" for their illegal activities.

"Criminals are smarter now about income tax matters," an investigator said. "They try to show enough 'legitimate' income and keep out of trouble."

War on Crime

Director J. Edgar Hoover of the FBI views underworld's vast invasion of the legitimate business world as a menace. He says it enables criminals to gain a "respectable front" for their illicit activities.

Within the Department of Justice, former Attorney General Robert F. Kennedy has strengthened the organized crime and racketeering section of the criminal division. An intelligence unit has been set up. It draws on the resources of more than twenty-five federal enforcement agencies. These include the FBI, the Securities and Exchange Commission, and the Treasury Department, including the Internal Revenue Service, Secret Service, Narcotics Bureau and Customs.

Selected police departments throughout the country also cooperate. In return, they receive information from the Government.

"We keep track of 1,100 racketeers," says William G. Hundley, chief of the rackets section.

Thus, a constant battle is being pressed forward by the nation's law-enforcement agencies. Its aim: to bring under control what the U.S. Attorney General calls "the increasing encroachment of the big businessmen of the rackets into legitimate business."

HOW TO LOCK OUT THE MAFIA*

CHARLES GRUTZNER

The success of organized crime is no longer news to business leaders. It has been well publicized in *The New York Times, The Wall Street Journal, Life,* and many other periodicals. Nevertheless, well-intentioned businessmen continue to play into the hands of underworld organizations. Judging from reports, they are victimized almost as easily now as they ever were. Unwittingly, many often seem to act like passive allies of criminal organizations; and when they are duped into that role and finally wake up to the fact, they don't seem to know what to do to extricate themselves. Other businessmen are really victims of their own greed; they become involved with organized crime in the hope of gaining an advantage or turning a profit.

These statements are not limited to the proprietors of grocery stores, laundries, appliance outlets, and other small businesses.

They apply to the top executives of prosperous, respectable, well-established corporations of all sizes and in many industries. This is one of the facts which I, along with other reporters and many law enforcement officials, find most alarming. What I shall try to do in this article, therefore, is to help business leaders to understand the nature of the problem, and to show them that there are countersteps they can take which are relatively simple, direct, and effective—without jeopardizing their own safety or that of their families.

To begin, let us examine the nature of organized crime and how it infiltrates legitimate business, focusing on the facts and aspects that are important for effective counteraction purposes.

Role of "Silent Majority"

Despite the efforts of law enforcement agencies and such business organizations as the U.S. Chamber of Commerce, the National Industrial Conference Board, and others, the flood of underworld money, muscle, and managerial activity seems to be spreading faster than it can be drained off. A large part of the explanation is businessmen's reluctance, for one reason or another, to turn over to official investigators and prosecutors their specific suspicions and evidence of infiltrative attempts. The reticence of this "silent majority" has made matters far easier for the underworld—and far more difficult for legitimate business.

Goldfinger Lends a Hand

Perhaps the best way to illustrate the role played all too often by uncommunicative businessmen is to take an actual example from recent experience:

• The Progressive Drug Company in New York, a respectable family enterprise that prospered into a $10 million-a-year wholesale business, was sold after the founder's death to the Pawnee Drug Company. Strange things began to happen. As the State Investigation Commission found out later, Twentieth Century Industries, a giant conglomerate whose top officers had dealings with identified members of the Mafia, had created Pawnee for the sole purpose of acquiring Progressive. Under the new ownership, Progressive was milked dry for the benefit of underworld figures and other subsidiaries of Twentieth Century Industries. It went into bankruptcy with losses to creditors.

The weird sequence of events in the rape of the Progressive Drug Company began with a switch in the company's labor contract, which had been with a reputable AFL-CIO union, to a local of the unaffiliated Teamsters Union. The ploy, listed in the Chamber of Commerce's *Deskbook on Organized Crime*° as a telltale indicator of possible hanky-panky, went apparently unnoticed by Benjamin Goldfinger, who had been a vice president of Progressive and whom the new owners kept in the same post after the sale.

Goldfinger was directed by one of his new bosses to put one Dominick (Nicky) Bando on the payroll at $150 as a guard at the company's warehouse in the Bronx, and to hand to Bando an additional $100 in cash each week "to insure labor peace." Testifying as a subpoenaed witness before the State Investigation Commission after the bankruptcy, Goldfinger swore he had been ignorant that Bando was an ex-convict and an associate of Mafiosi. Bando's record showed prison terms for dealing in narcotics and for the acid blinding of Victor Riesel, the journalist who had exposed the labor racketeering of John (Johnny Dio) Dioguardi.

It developed that Goldfinger had also made cash payments in amounts of $100 to $200 at a time to a man he said he knew only as "Abe," who was neither an employee nor a creditor of Progressive but who was connected with another subsidiary of Twentieth Century Industries. There were other payments that Goldfinger knew were, to use the kindest word, "irregular"—$13,405 to an affiliate company for "merchandise" never delivered, and $2,000 to the comptroller of another affiliate firm for nonexistent "services rendered."

Goldfinger, a slightly built man who had receding gray hair and who wore glasses, was unable to hide from himself the obvious illegality of these and other transactions. Although he kept silent until the State Investigation Commission people called

---

° Available from the U.S. Chamber of Commerce, 1615 H Street, N.W., Washington, D.C. 20006 ($2 per copy, reduced rates for quantity orders).

him in (too late to save the company and its creditors), he was keeping a private journal in which he listed the cash payments against a possible day of reckoning. The Commission induced him to testify at open hearings in 1969 after giving him immunity from prosecution. Other witnesses, from ex-convict Bando to Martin Goldman, Vice President of Twentieth Century (which controls or has interests in mining, drug, soft drink, and plastics companies) invoked the Fifth Amendment against self-incrimination in refusing to answer questions at the hearings.

Results of Reticence

The Progressive Drug case was one of more than a dozen in different industries laid bare by the Commission in seven days of public hearings in New York City. Each case made clear one or another of the ways in which organized crime gains an interest or complete domination of a hitherto legitimate business and either operates it in unlawful or unethical ways to increase its profits and destroy competitors, or else bankrupts the captive company by siphoning off its assets. The perpetrators were found to be at work in the areas of banking, insurance, restaurants, bagel baking, butcher knife grinding, trucking, kosher meat, supermarkets, and plastics.

In not a single case did the legitimate entrepreneur who was the target of the illegal maneuver step forward to inform federal or local law enforcement agencies of the obvious evidence. Such early information, along with a willingness to testify, *could* have thrown the invasion strategy off balance, saved many businesses from ruin, averted puffed-up costs for legitimate competitors and inflated prices for consumers, and transferred some of the underworld agents from executive offices to prison cells.

Of course, *some* of the invaders have gone to prison, along with the businessmen and public officials they corrupted. There have been convictions for fraud, labor racketeering, income tax evasion, extortion, larceny, perjury, conspiracy, and other specific crimes connected with business take overs. But these convictions represent only a fraction of the cases known to enforcement officials. An even larger number of flagrant cases of underworld infiltration gather dust in prosecutors' files often until statutes of limitation wash them out, while investigators search desperately for witnesses whose testimony is essential for a court case.

The public, including businessmen, frequently wonders why disclosures by Congressional committees and state investigation commissions of clearly illegal activities fail so many times to result in criminal prosecution. The answer is simple. It is one thing to produce the testimony of investigators and subpoenaed books, records, and bank accounts at public hearings, with the public drawing its conclusions from the repetitive invoking of the Fifth Amendment by the principals. But it is an altogether different thing to get people involved in or innocently affected by the criminal acts to mount the witness stand in a courtroom and give the kind of testimony required for conviction.

Some of the information about the infiltration of legitimate business has resulted from routine surveillance of known members of the criminal organization, some from tedious checking of corporate records, some from wiretaps and electronic bugs, some from underworld informers. But *almost none* has been supplied voluntarily to official agencies by legitimate businessmen who became unwilling or willing associates of criminals.

Masks of the Mafiosi

How do the leaders of "America's number one growth industry," as it has been called, get inside legitimate businesses? In answering this question, which has an obvious bearing on the strategy of counteraction by legitimate companies, it would be well to keep in mind the two principal motives of the underworld's "top management":

  1. It wants to put the profits of its illegal enterprises to work earning more money. The huge take from gambling and loan-sharking, for instance, cries for reinvestment in other ventures. This need is so pressing that every major Mafia borgata has its own "money mover"—a member or associate whose function it is to find the weak or willing spots in the business community where the ill-gotten gains can be used as seeds for further profits.

The idea of unemployed capital is as repugnant to the bosses of organized crime as it is to any banker or captain of legitimate industry. And the infusion of tainted capital into the nation's business and industrial fabric requires an underworld organization and highly skilled "money movers." The difficulty of such reinvestment without a coordinated organization is illustrated in the sad plight of "Newsboy" Moriarity, a highly successful, bigtime numbers-game operator in Jersey City who remained independent of the criminal syndicate. Without a "money mover" to handle his surplus from gambling, Moriarity couldn't put his profits to work as fast as they rolled in. The police eventually found $2,500,000 in cash stashed away in the trunk of a car he kept in his garage. The government got most of it for income taxes and penalties.

The No. 1 "money mover" for organized crime is Meyer Lansky (Maier Suchowljansky), a hoodlum who got his start breaking heads in the wars between garment sweatshop bosses and union organizers, and graduated to rum-running, where he became an associate of the Mafia bosses of organized crime and showed a genius in handling their financial investments here and abroad. Lansky's public boast is "We're bigger than U.S. Steel."

2. Many underworld leaders want to seed legitimate businesses with the profits from criminal rackets in order to provide a visible source of earned income. The principal channels of wealth remain underground. Income from reputable corporations provides a basis for income tax filings, however false in terms of total income, as well as a veneer of respectability.

The Hood Samaritans

Like guerrilla campaigners in other fields, the agents of organized crime infiltrate their target areas along devious trailways where possible. In the guise of labor relations consultants, they entice businessmen who are willing to pay a price for substandard labor contracts into making deals with labor racketeers. Or they offer to supply merchandise at prices so far below market quotations that only a merchant blinded by avarice doesn't spot it as stolen goods or sequestered stock from a fraudulent bankruptcy.

Once a businessman has compromised himself with the underworld, he is vulnerable to further advances. These may take the form of a suggestion that the labor consultant, the phony union leader, or the cut-rate supplier has a friend with some idle funds he would like to invest in the business. Or the seducer may suggest making a loan to expand the business or to handle an influx of new business which he can guarantee. To illustrate:

• A supplier promised a meat purveyor that he could get for him, practically overnight, the business of the city's major restaurants and hotels. "There was strong hint that the restaurants and hotels would change purveyors because they did what 'a powerful guy' told them to do," said a federal prosecutor who eventually sent the businessman and his Mafia associates to prison for bankruptcy fraud. "The businessman wasn't so dumb as not to realize that the promise involved coercion of the hotels and restaurants. No, he wasn't dumb that way. He was just greedy dumb."

The loanshark approach is used to entrap hard-pressed businessmen who would not otherwise have any dealings with racketeers. This is widely employed in industries like garment manufacturing where competition among small entrepreneurs produces a rags-to-riches business climate. Because of the high business mortality, garment makers often find it difficult to get bank credit for the capital they need each season to try their luck with a new fashion line. They borrow from usurers, confident that their line will become a popular success and that they will be able to repay the loan with exorbitant interest and still come out ahead. But if the season isn't a smashing success and the businessman is unable to meet his obligation to the loan shark, the racketeers settle for a partnership—and then they are on their way.

Contrary to a popular impression, the foregoing approach is not limited to high-risk industries. The loansharks and their underworld bosses like nothing better than to hook onto a substantial, long-established business whose owners may be hard up for ready cash to ride out a temporary emergency. The New York State Investigation Commission learned that certain bank employees were tipping off Mafia money men whenever a business customer had exhausted his line of credit and was unable to get further conventional financing.

Sometimes, as indicated earlier, business executives take a more active role in becoming associated with the Mafia. Once again, though, an apparently simple liaison may lead to an unintended result for the company:

• A large Detroit corporation was willing to do business with the local Mafia to get a mortgage loan from a Teamster union pension fund. As a consequence it found itself in the middle of a dispute between two criminal groups. The strange involvement came to light with the indictment of thirteen men, ten of them identified by the government as Mafiosi, on charges of conspiring to pay kickbacks to a pension fund officer. The defendants are awaiting trial in federal court.

The Mid-City Development Company of Detroit, according to the government, needed a large loan to buy an industrial building complex in Warren, Michigan in 1964. Management sought help from Dominick Corrado of Grosse Point Park, a top Mafia figure in the Detroit area. Samuel Marroso, a public relations man in Warren, who is also under indictment now, was drawn into the orbit of the scheme and became instrumental in getting a mortgage loan of $1,050,000 from the Teamsters Central States Southeast and Southwest Areas Funds.

Later, according to the government, Mid-City Development sought Mafia help to obtain an additional loan, that one for $200,000. But there was some bickering with the Detroit Mafia over terms. The company allegedly tried then to make a deal for mortgage money through James Plumeri, a captain in the New York Mafia family of the late Thomas Luchese. This led to a dispute between the Detroit and New York Mafia groups.

The Mafia's nine-man national commission, known as the Supreme Court of the Underworld, ruled that the dispute should be settled on neutral ground by a neutral referee. Frank Amato, seventy-five-year-old alleged Mafia boss of southwest Pennsylvania, sat in judgment at a hearing in a Pittsburgh suburb, according to federal investigators, and made this decision: Detroit having priority on the local deal, would handle the enitre matter;

after the loan was received by Mid-City Development, the New York Mafia would get a cut of the take. The indictment alleges that an illegal kickback of $5,000 was paid to David Wenger, a certified public accountant and auditor of the Teamster pension fund, to influence his decision on the mortgage application. The $200,000 loan never materialized from the pension fund despite the alleged conspiracy and kickback payment, according to the government.

Corporate Cahoots

Organized crime uses some of its illegal profits to set up its own companies, usually under false fronts or proxies. What appears to be a legitimate mortgage and loan company is sometimes a blind for loansharking and unorthodox transfers of real estate. Or a trucking company and a union local, both established by the same criminal group, may work in cahoots in the pilferage of millions of dollars of cargo at piers and airports. For instance, large scale infiltration along the waterfront and at Kennedy International Airport has been uncovered by the New York-New Jersey Waterfront Commission and by the New York Investigation Commission.

Further, Mafia-controlled companies having branches in Latin America and interests in Europe serve as conduits for the outflow of profits from illicit operations in the United States. Some of the funds go to the smugglers of raw opium from the Near East; some to the refiners of heroin in France and Italy; others to coded accounts in Swiss banks whence some of the money comes back, through U.S. banks, in the form of untraceable investments in major American corporations or equally untraceable "loans" to the very underworld bosses who started the funds on their roundabout journeys. In the latter instance, a gangster, sending his illicit profits deviously into a Swiss bank account, "borrows" his own money from his unidentifiable Swiss account and gets it back as "clean" money to be used in becoming a shareholder in any legitimate U.S. business in which he wants a stake.

A highly profitable form of infiltration is that practiced by some "money movers":

• An agent of a criminal organization ingratiates himself with a branch manger of a large bank or a top executive of a medium-sized bank by placing the accounts of the borgata's businesses in the selected bank. Through strategic deposits and social cultivation of the bank executive, the "money mover" manages to be made a director in the bank (such instances have been verified by law enforcement investigators). He eventually attains an eminence where he can approve, or get a higher bank official to approve, the lending of large amounts, sometimes unsecured, at perhaps 8 percent. The borrower, a fellow conspirator, is a loanshark who puts the money out on the street at interest of anywhere from 120 percent to 500 percent.

I could describe other methods, but the foregoing should make the point that underworld leaders today usually present a businesslike appearance and do their business by negotiation. Gone, for the most part, are the days of frontal attacks on business when gangsters walked into nightclubs and saloons and declared themselves partners, with their shares to be handed over each week—refusal to be followed by beatings, bombings, vandalism, and other acts of terror and destruction. *Some* vestiges of terror tactics have survived, e.g. in garbage collection and waste removal, but they no longer are characteristic.

Ingredients of Infiltration

Now let us look at several cases that highlight typical tactics of criminal infiltrators, the all too characteristic pattern of response of target businessmen, and likely results of such a response for the victims and their companies.

A Pinch of Extortion

A classic in the annals of infiltration began in August 1967 when Maurice Minuto, the president of the Nylo-Thane Plastics Corp. at Farmingdale, New York, was looking for capital to expand his operations, which were built around a formula for speeding the vulcanizing of rubber. Alan Morrell (not identified further in the subsequent testimony) telephoned Minuto to say he had an investor who wanted to meet with him alone that evening in his office. Instead of an investor, there arrived five or six thugs, two of whom put knives to Minuto's sides while a third put a gun to his head. (In this respect, at least, the criminals' approach lacked contemporary finesse.) The leader, identified later from a rogue's gallery photo as Julius (Julie) Klein, a notorious Long Island racketeer and ex-convict, announced, "We're going to kill you unless you give us $25,000."

Minuto was held overnight in a motel, where he wrote a check for $25,000. He was released next day after one of the kidnappers had cashed the check, according to testimony he gave to the State Investigation Commission nearly two years later. (The Commission happened to learn about Minuto's involvement with members of organized crime during the course of another investigation.) Minuto said he did not report the kidnapping and extortion to the police because of Klein's threat to kill his wife and children. But, he did go to see "Gentleman Johnny" Masiello, a major loanshark who had been publicly identified by the FBI as a "soldier" in the Genovese borgata of the Mafia. Minuto's move was a common type of mistake by businessmen victims; hoping to save himself by backstage maneuvering, he succeeded only in making matters worse.

An Offer of Cozy Credit

The circumstances of the visit to Masiello, as related by Minuto to the Commission, remain somewhat clouded. Minuto said he had previously borrowed money from Masiello but swore he had not known that the dapper "Gentleman Johnny" who wore striking ensembles of electric blue and a huge diamond pinky ring, was a loanshark or a Mafioso. Minuto said his reason for calling on Masiello was to enlist help in preventing further forays against him by Klein and his desperadoes. He said also he went to borrow $25,000 from Masiello in order to reimburse his company, Nylo-Thane Plastics, for the check he had written against its account.

Masiello agreed to arrange a loan. He sent Minuto to the Royal National Bank, whose president and board chairman, William Goldfine, was a friend of the Mafioso's, with instructions to Minuoto to take out a loan of $50,000 and "lend" half of it to Masiello. Minuto said he did just that, hoping that his "loan" to Masiello would "get the Long Island hoodlums off my back." Masiello got *most* of the $50,000, instead of half the amount.

Neither Klein nor his gang ever bothered Minuto thereafter. But the manufacturer, already out $50,000, was far from free of the toils of organized crime. Masiello repeatedly induced him to take out new loans from Royal National, to pledge Nylo-Thane shares for the loans, and to sign over other shares of Nylo-Thane to the Mafioso and his associates. In testimony about one transfer of 25,000 shares to the president of the Masiello-controled Setmar Holding Company, Minuto explained, "I felt an obligation to Setmar. I just handed this [stock] over to Mr. McKeever and said: 'Thank you for everything you've done for me in the past.' Later Mr. Masiello called me and said, 'Thank you for the shares.'"

Nylo-Thane, which had been offered at $4 a share when it first went public, began in 1967 a meteoric rise to $88 a share. After trading in it had twice been suspended by the SEC, the stock had leveled off at about $22 by March 1969, when the State Investigation Commission hearings were held. By November it had plummeted to 2¾.

As for Minuto himself, the Commission's hearings revealed that he had become obligated for $515,000 in bank loans, of which he had received only $13,500 for himself. A total of $292,500 had gone to Masiello and his associates, and $179,000 had been eaten up by interest, bank discount, premiums on a policy issued by an Oklahoma insurance company, premiums on a fidelity bond of a Florida surety company for collateral for some of the bank loans, other fees, and $45,000 given by Minuto to two Las Vegas hotels to liquidate the gambling debt of a known racketeer. In addition, $1.3 million of Minuto's Nylo-Thane stock was either held by the bank as collateral on unpaid loans or had been given to Masiello and his associates.

The Commission's chart showing all this was captioned: "The High Cost of Protection."

A Dash of Respectability

Not content with his mulcting of the Long Island business-man, Masiello managed also in 1967 to get $466,000 from the

United States Government in the form of Small Business Administration loans. In this, as in his dealings with Minuto, the Mafioso had help from the banker Goldfine. The Royal National Bank put up 25 percent of the amount of the loans to meet the federal requirement for Small Business Administration outlays. As Paul Kelly, Associate Counsel to the State Investigation Commission, later declared, this chain of events in effect "put the federal government in the position of financing Masiello's loanshark activities." Masiello, a jaunty witness, invoked the protection of the Fifth Amendment in refusing to answer any of the twenty-one questions put to him at the Commission's hearing, including whether he had used the federal loans for loansharking.

Goldfine made an interesting witness. Although admitting to a first-name friendship of many years with Masiello, he swore that he never knew Masiello was a loanshark or a Mafioso—matters that had been reported prominently in newspapers over the years. And although Goldfine had sponsored Masiello for the federal loan, he said under questioning that Masiello and his companies constantly were overdrawn by more than $100,000 at the Royal National Bank. At that time, Setmar Holding Company (one of Masiello's organizations) owed the bank $106,000; and A.N.R. Leasing Corp., a truck company headed by Masiello's son, John, Jr., owed the bank $135,000.

Goldfine acknowledged that at a dinner marking his seventieth birthday, he had been pledged 5,000 shares of Nylo-Thane by Masiello. He said that the stock was turned over to the Hebrew Home for the Aged in Riverdale, beneficiary of the birthday dinner.

A red-faced Small Business Administration called in the loans to A.N.R. Leasing. The area administrator, pleading ignorance of Masiello's background, explained that the agency customarily relied on information supplied by the sponsoring bank about the prospective recipient. A.N.R. Leasing Corp. also had $2 million in contracts for truck rentals to the Post Office Department. Masiello is awaiting trial in federal court on charges of bribery of postal employees in connection with those contracts.

An Industrious Insider

Less dramatic perhaps, but equally deadly to the target company, was the plot engineered by members of two Mafia borgatas against Murray Packing Company, supplier of meat, poultry, and eggs to wholesalers and markets. The action began when the legitimate owners, a father and son and their partner, found themselves short of working capital. Joseph Pagano, a salesman for the company, arranged for a loan from the Jo-Ran Trading Corporation.

How Pagano, a convicted narcotics trafficker and a member of the Genovese borgata, had got the job as salesman is not clear (from testimony at the trial later on). It developed, though, that Jo-Ran Trading Corporation was a loanshark operation owned by Peter Castellana, a member of the Carlo Gambino borgata, and by Carmine Lombardozzi, "money mover" for Gambino. The versatile Castellana was also the president of Pride Wholesale Meat and Poultry Corporation, a Brooklyn organization which was soon to become part of the action.

Jo-Ran Trading lent Murray Packing Company $8,500 at interest of 1 percent a week. As the debt increased, the legitimate owners could not resist Castellana's demand that Joseph Pagano be moved up and made an executive with check-writing authority to "protect the investment."

A systematic looting of the company got under way, simultaneously with a tenfold increase in its purchases from processing plants. As shipments of meat and poultry rolled into the Murray Packing plant in the Bronx, much of it was "sold" at less-than-cost prices to Pride Wholesale Meat and Poultry Corporation. In this way Pride Wholesale and the retail markets controlled by the Mafia were able to undercut legitimate competitors.

This was all done within the thirty day period before Murray Packing's payments to the processors became due. The siphoning off of the funds was accomplished with underworld finesse. Checks from Pride Wholesale to Murray Packing covering the enormous sales to Castellana's company, would be taken by a messenger (who was another Gambino Mafioso) to the bank along with Murray Packing checks made out to cash by Joseph

Pagano in the same amounts as the Pride Wholesale checks to Murray.

A phone call from Pagano to an official of the bank then insured that the exact amount of cash would be awaiting the messenger, who had only to go to the designated teller, hand him the checks, and pick up a bundle of money. In a short time $745,000 was stolen. During the bankruptcy proceedings that followed, the conspirators sequestered another $112,000 of Murray Packing's assets. The losers, besides the original owners, were the processors and other creditors.

Castellana, Pagano, the Mafia messenger, and the three original owners were convicted of bankruptcy fraud. In a plea for leniency for the latter, their lawyer described them as victims of "a situation with which they could not cope" and told the court they had not profited from the looting of the company. Judge Dudley B. Bonsal, directing his remarks to the trio, said, "It taxes my credulity that you couldn't see that the creditors were being defrauded."

Or Perhaps a Consultant

After the Chrysler Building was sold in 1960, there was a strike of service and maintenance men. The new owners, Sol Goldman and Alex DiLorenzo, hired S.G.S. Associates, a self-described "labor relations" firm, to help them. Subsequently, the strikers complained that "goons" with guns in holsters arrived at the building in Cadillacs and took over elevator operations. The strike was settled with the help of the Mayor's office, and the complaint about the "goons" went into limbo.

Five years later, when FBI agents were questioning clients of S.G.S. Associates in connection with another investigation, *The New York Times* revealed that the "G" in the firm's name was Carlo (Don Carlo) Gambino, boss of a Mafia borgata whose members operated in a wide range of legal and illicit enterprises. Gambino's partners of record in S.G.S. Associates were Henry H. Saltzstein, a convicted burglar and bookmaker, and George Schiller. The newspaper disclosed that S.G.S. Associates had been employed to handle labor relations for major industrial and business companies, among them Howard Clothes, Bond Clothes, William J. Levitt, most of whose massive building operations used nonunion labor, the Concord Hotel at Kiamesha Lake, New York, and Flower and Fifth Avenue Hospital in New York City.

These and other contracts with business companies had brought the Mafia-connected "labor consultants' an estimated $500,000 a year.

With Gambino's connection now made public, however, S.G.S. Associates lost clients as a maple loses leaves in a November gale. Spokesmen for most of the legitimate business companies involved professed ignorance of Gambino's partnership. Some revealing anecdotes of the infiltration process were given, of which the following is an example:

• Dr. Ralph E. Snyder, President of Flower and Fifth Avenue Hospital, said S.G.S. Associates had first been called in during a strike of hospital employees in 1962. He told the story in these words, "We didn't know what to do. One of our doctors said he had a patient who was a labor relations expert and might help us. It was Mr. Saltzstein. With the settlement of the strike, hospital management and the union agreed on Saltzstein as impartial arbitrator of the contract. Since learning about Gambino I think we ought to eliminate Mr. Saltzstein as impartial arbitrator when the contract expires at the end of this year."

Counteraction Against Crime

Why have members of the business community so often failed to respond to evidence of inroads into their companies by organized crime? Is the failure due to naïveté or inability to read the telltale signals? If so, why have the widely circulated warnings made by law enforcement agencies and other experts somehow failed to get across to businessmen? Or is the failure due to fear of physical or economic reprisal—or perhaps to the strain of larceny which is said to lurk in most humans? If so, do many businessmen *really* believe they can profit from a limited involvement with organized crime without eventually becoming its victims?

Whatever the explanation, it is not likely to hold up under analysis. And it is not an excuse for a businessman to say there is an absence of good alternatives. When signs of criminal inroads are observed, there *are* steps a businessman can take to cope with the problem without inviting reprisals against himself, his family, or his company.

Warnings to Watch For

To begin with, there is no good reason for failure of any businessman to recognize the first overture or stratagem of organized crime. The Chamber of Commerce's *Deskbook on Organized Crime.*[1] spells out how to recognize the different approaches and tells how businessmen, acting individually or through trade associations, can effectively counter such attempts. Similar information and advice is being given by the National Council on Crime and Delinquency, which has in the last two years sponsored, in city after city, meetings and conference at which business executives and corporate security officers have discussed specific problems with experts such as Will Wilson, Assistant Attorney General in charge of the Department of Justice criminal division, state and county prosecutors, police officials, and investigators.

Among the situations listed in the Chamber's *Deskbook* and described at the conferences as indicators of possible infiltration attempts, I believe the following should be singled out for attention:

• A change of ownership, not publicly announced, of a customer company.

• A marked increase in a customer's orders unrelated to a seasonal increase in business. This could be a tip-off to a fraudulent bankruptcy scheme.

• A new account with a name very similar to that of an established company, perhaps even with an address in the same building as the offices of the better known company.

• A sudden outbreak of bookmaking or numbers-game activity in an industrial plant. This may mean that organized crime has established a beachhead for other operations.

---

[1] *Ibid.*

• Picketing by nonemployees, followed by a visit from a "labor relations consultant" offering to "take care of things" for a fee.

• Any offer to arrange a labor contract with conditions less favorable to the employees than those prevalent in the industry. Such "sweetheart" contracts are often used by labor racketeers as leverage to open the way to criminal infiltration.

• Offers of loans from persons or companies of unchecked background. Such an offer, coming when a legitimate business is known to be in a credit squeeze, is frequently the opening gambit of a loan shark who seeks to put the businessman in his debt as a prelude to a partnership demand.

• Merchandise offered at less than wholesale prices, which is likely to be stolen goods.

• A series of incidents causing damage to a company's property or equipment, followed by solicitation to join a "trade association" of unfamiliar background.

• Discovery that paychecks of several employees are endorsed over to the same person. This could mean that a loanshark or bookmaker is at work and could be particularly dangerous if any employees in sensitive positions become deeply indebted.

Procedure for Reporting

Suppose an executive notices warning signals like the foregoing. Or worse, suppose he does not see them in time and becomes embroiled as did Goldfinger, Minuto, and the others in the examples described earlier. What is his next step?

He can get in touch immediately with the police and tell them what has been going on. The trouble with this step is that other agencies may be in a better position to help. Also, it may lead to reprisals—or, at least, the businessman may *think* it will cause reprisals. Nevertheless, this step should not be discounted; it has turned out to be safe and effective many times.

As an alternative, the executive can consult immediately with his lawyer or with the executive director of his trade association. From them he can gain information as to which law enforcement agency or regulatory body should be contacted for most effective results. Also, perhaps they can act for him and report the situation to the proper authorities. However, this procedure, too, may seem unsatisfactory to the businessman, especially if the warning signals are quite inconclusive. And if he ends up as witness in court, the prospect of reprisals becomes a problem again.

There is a third course of action which, in my opinion, avoids the difficulties just mentioned and could be especially effective. This approach has been suggested by Alfred J. Scotti, rackets bureau chief for New York District Attorney Frank S. Hogan. Its virtues are that it preserves the businessman's anonymity at the same time that it relieves him of the burden of trying to evaluate whether the suspicious situation he knows about is an isolated phenomenon or part of a larger picture. Scotti proposes that local commerce and industry groups set up committees to which businessmen could make confidential reports. Then, when a committee has reports from half a dozen or more sources in the same industry—as would be likely if infiltration were attempted— the complaints could be brought by it to the proper law enforcement agency without putting the spotlight on just one cooperative witness.

Establishment of such a committee is practicable because it can be done within the framework of the association or organization that exists in almost every industrial community. It is timely because increasing publicity about organized crime has made so many Americans uneasy. If the idea were supported by business leaders, it could be implemented quickly with existing personnel, at least in the beginning.

The need for such a step is *now*. All over the nation, judging from available reports, prosecutors are failing to get businessmen's cooperation. For two cases in point which I believe to be typical, let me refer to the experiences of Scotti and Robert M. Morgenthau, former U.S. Attorney for the Southern District of New York, where there are more business headquarters than in any other part of the nation. (Morgenthau resigned in January to become Deputy Mayor of New York City.) Both those prosecutors have sent bosses of organized crime and their associates to prison for bribery of public officials to get contracts, and for coercion, fraud, extortion, hijacking, perjury, and illegal business practices. Businessmen have testified for the prosecution in some cases, *but only after being subpoenaed to corroborate evidence the lawmen had dug up on their own.*

Where businessmen were found to have been in cahoots with the criminals, they testified in some cases after being named as co-conspirators. But *none* of the businessmen, whether innocent victims or bilked partners, came forward voluntarily at a time when the acts of infiltration could have been aborted. If industry committees such as those proposed were created, some real progress might be made in correcting this abysmal record.

Tighter Security

One vulnerable area in which many companies have been lax is that of internal security. Because of the extent of underworld infiltration and the multiplicity of ways the syndicate has of recruiting employees having no criminal background, management should tighten employment safeguards and, so far as is possible without spying on employees, be more alert to signs of personal problems that might put an employee under obligations to the underworld. Examples of such signs are a person's involvement in an outbreak of gambling in the office or plant, garnishments against his salary, indications he has fallen behind in payments to a loanshark, and deviations from normal standards of conduct.

The infiltration of a company may occur at the ownership level, among top or middle executives, or among supervisors, clerks, mechanics, and other types of workers. The recently publicized stock thefts on Wall Street, accounting in 1969 for the loss of $45 million in negotiable securities, indicate how the bosses of organized crime may strike through employees:

• During the surge of stock buying and selling in 1969, when the paperwork of brokerage houses, including actual transfers of stocks, was months behind the telephoned transactions in many cases, securities houses were beefing up their backroom staffs as best they could. A tight labor market for qualified clerical help led to many hirings without the checking of references and without personal history investigations.

As a result, underworld groups could steal millions of dollars in securities from offices without their disappearance being noticed until months later, when it was difficult or impossible to trace them. An anonymous informer, who told the New York State Legislative Committee on Crime how $1 million in stock certificates was stolen from one nationally known brokerage firm, said that organized crime had gone into Wall Street in a big way "because there is big money and we are getting more educated people (into criminal ranks) who know how to steal with an IBM machine."

• Sometimes the underworld has deliberately planted one of its own in a sensitive business spot. In one such instance, a young messenger who reported he had been held up and relieved of a fortune in negotiable securities, was found to be a nephew of a man highly situated in the Mafia. The messenger appeared several times before the grand jury investigating the possibility that the "holdup" had been faked. While the investigation was under way, the messenger's corpse was found, covered with stab wounds.

These instances illustrate the potential price of loose internal security in any urban business area, not just Wall Street. There is no reason that they could not be repeated on LaSalle Street, Market Street, or other centers of commerce.

New Legal Approaches

A stronger business counteroffensive against organized crime would take on added significance because of the actions of law enforcement agencies. At both the national and local levels, official agencies are stepping up their efforts against the infiltration of legitimate business and are readying some new tools for the job. As a result, executives who report evidence of possible infiltration can be surer than ever that it will be evaluated carefully; there are both more ways of using such evidence and more personnel interested in following it up.

One promising development is the effort to use antitrust procedures in civil actions against crime-tainted businesses in cases where criminal prosecution would be ineffective. This approach was first suggested in March 1969 by Attorney General John N. Mitchell, then only eleven weeks in office. In an address to the American Bar Association's antitrust section, Mitchell said:

If we can convict a Mafia lieutenant and place him in jail, another may take his place. Perhaps we should investigate the deterrent of financial loss. . . . If we can levy fines on their real estate corporations, if we can seek treble damages against their trucking firms and banks, if we can seize the liquor in their warehouses, I think we can strike a critical blow at the organized crime conspiracy.[2]

Despite doubts about the workability of such a novel approach —for example, Ralph Salerno's opinion that organized crime's "perfect conglomerate . . . need not fear the Antitrust Division"— the first such cases are being prepared by the Antitrust Division for a special federal grand jury sworn in on November 8, 1969, in New York. The special grand jury, impaneled for eighteen months, will work with the Antitrust Division and a special federal-state-city task force on investigation of links between organized crime and business, with especial interest in monopoly trends.

Another innovation is the use of special task forces, started about two years ago as federal combinations of agents of the Internal Revenue Service, Securities and Exchange Commission, Bureau of Narcotics, Department of Labor, and other agencies. These task forces are sent into areas of heavy organized crime activity to cooperate with the resident U.S. attorneys. They are now operating in a dozen or so cities, and some of their work— in New Jersey, for instance—has been widely publicized. The first of the special strike forces was sent from Washington to Buffalo, New York, where the resident effort against organized crime and its business allies had been less energetic and successful than the Department of Justice felt it could be. The result, in indictments and pressure on the underworld, was quite successful, and there is every indication that similar task forces in other cities will be effective.

In addition, the Internal Revenue Service, which struck its first telling blows against organized crime a generation ago by sending Al Capone, Johnny Torrio, and other Mafia overlords to prison for tax cheating when other agencies were unable to convict them, is again directing a large part of its manpower to

---

[2] Reported in *The New York Times*, March 28, 1969.

exploring the profits, legal and illegal, of crime syndicate members. IRS Commissioner Randolph W. Thrower has revealed that a recent sampling of 113 major underworld characters showed ninety-eight of them having controlling interest in 159 different legitimate businesses. It is less difficult, generally, to put a syndicate member behind bars for income tax evasion than it is to prove specific acts of violence, bribery, or narcotics traffic. Often it is sufficient, in gaining an income tax conviction, to show a jury that the defendant's scale of living is beyond his declared income.

Another development is the growing realization by state governments that they, too, can crimp the profits of racketeers and in some instances drive them out of a particular business field altogether without having to convince twelve jurors that, beyond any reasonable doubt, an abhorrent crime has been perpetrated. A few states have new laws which in effect could put an apparently legitimate enterprise out of business if it can be shown that a substantial interest is controlled by persons connected with organized crime. In Florida such a law has been invoked by the State Attorney General in civil suits to revoke the charters or the Florida operating permits of a number of hotels, motels, and other businesses allegedly infiltrated by the mob. The outcome of the Florida suits is being awaited by other states which recently adopted similar laws or whose legislators have such proposals under consideration.

Conclusion

There can no longer be any doubt in the minds of perceptive business executives that there has been a massive infiltration of the national economy by members of organized crime. Law enforcement agents and investigators who are best able to observe this phenomenon agree that there is not a commercial, industrial, or professional field in which an honest dollar can be made which has not already been infiltrated or marked for an entry attempt by underworld organizations.

Some of the industries already infiltrated have been mentioned in this article. What about those marked for future infiltration? Investigators who try to anticipate where the underworld will attempt to establish its next beachheads are surveying at least three major business areas which they believe are tempting to the syndicate's "money movers":

• The shipping companies are almost the only waterfront business not already infested by organized crime. Because of competition from air freight and air passenger travel, ocean shipping is not attracting all the new capital it requires, here or abroad. Of particular interest to the underworld would be the possibility of using the ships, especially those under foreign registry, as conduits for the international movement of "hot" cash and goods, including narcotics. With members of organized crime already in sensitive dockside positions, the coupling of this advantage with an inside track on the ocean lanes would make a winning parlay indeed.

• Some law enforcement agents believe that the criminal syndicate already has placed "sleepers" at the executive level in one or more of the airlines. An "in" at the operational and policy level of the air transportation industry would have advantages similar to, and perhaps greater than, those resulting from infiltration of ocean shipping. Ground operations at international airports are at present permeated by the syndicate or by men under its control, from cargo handling, trucking, and maintenance to some of the ancillary services.

• The public sale in 1969 of more than $900 million in oil and gas leases in Alaska appears to have brought the underworld to that state, along with many new legitimate business enterprises. Both Douglas Bailey, U.S. Attorney for Alaska, and Mel Personett, State Commissioner of Public Safety, report evidence that organized crime has begun to move in on the economic upsurge in Alaska. Personett says most criminal activity is in the area of legitimate business. The bosses of organized crime apparently feel that if they are going to extend their operations as far as Alaska, it will be for more substantial gains than those of gambling or loansharking.

It will be interesting to say what role, if any, businessmen will play in resisting the Mafia's attempts to organize these new areas. Management *could* play a significant role in countering infiltration—just as it could do so in all other industries.

To be sure, the task of actually rooting out the despoilers is one for professionals, not executives in ordinary business. And it must be left up to federal and local prosecutors, the heads of regulatory agencies, police officials, and other experts to decide, after consultation, how to handle a particular situation—whether under conspiracy and extortion statutes, under the labor or antimonopoly laws, as income tax cases, or by initiating other criminal or civil proceedings. But to achieve their purpose they need information from the businessmen who first see signs of infiltration attempts, and they need witnesses who are willing, if required, to take the stand in court or at other hearings.

Each individual manager must decide for himself, as must the directors of his corporation, whether his fear of possible business or personal recrimination outweighs his courage. He must decide whether the lure of immediate competitive advantage from dealing with suspect individuals or companies means more to him than his responsibilities as a citizen and the preservation of sound business practices.

BIBLIOGRAPHY

Books

Brennan, Bill: *The Frank Costello Story*. Derby, Connecticut, Monarch, 1962.

Cook, Fred J.: *The Secret Rulers*. New York, Duell, 1966.

Demaris, Ovid: *Lucky Luciano*. Derby, Connecticut, Monarch, 1960.

Frasca, Dom: *King of Crime*. New York, Crown, 1959.

Gartner, Michael (Ed.): *Crime and Business*. Princeton, N.J., Dow Jones, 1971.

Katcher, Leo: *The Big Bankroll*. New York, Harper and Brothers, 1958.

The Kefauver Committee Report on Organized Crime. New York, Didier, 1951.

Maas, Peter: *The Valachi Papers*. New York, Putnam, 1968.

Martin, Raymond V.: *Revolt in the Mafia*. New York, Duell, 1963.

McClellan, John L.: *Crime Without Punishment*. New York, Duell, 1962.

Messick, Hank: *The Silent Syndicate*. New York, Macmillan, 1967.

Murtagh, John M. and Harris, Sara: *Who Live in Shadow*. New York, McGraw-Hill, 1959, pp. 63-73.

Prager, Ted and Moberley, Leeds: *Hoodlums, New York.* New York, Retail Distributors Inc., 1959.

Reid, Edward: *The Grim Reapers.* Chicago, Regnery, 1969.

Starr, John: *The Purveyor.* New York, Holt, 1961.

Thompson, Craig and Raymond, Allen: *Gang Rule in New York.* New York, Dial, 1940.

U.S. President's Commission on Law Enforcement and Administration of Justice. *Task Force Report: Organized Crime.* Washington, D.C., Government Printing Office, 1967.

U.S. Senate. Special Senate Committee to investigate organized crime in interstate commerce (the Kefauver Committee). *Final Report,* 82nd Congress, 1st Session, Report No. 725 (1951).

Zeiger, Henry A.: *Sam the Plumber.* New York, NAL (Signet), 1970.

Articles

AFL-CIO president Meany scores probe of juke box industry; says labor involvement is negligible. *The New York Times,* 18, March 3, 1959.

Brooks, L. J.: Rhode Island routs the auto rackets. *American Mercury, 87:* September 1958.

Businessmen: Partners in crime busting. *Nations Business, 55:* January 1967.

Cole, Robert J.: How crime is infiltrating Wall Street. *The New York Times* (Sec. 3, Business and Finance), 1, November 30, 1969.

Cort, J. C.: Crime and big business. *Commonweal, 54:* April 27, 1951.

Detroit juke box operator testifies; operators paid $6,000 to Teamsters President Hoffa to bar competitors from getting Teamsters charter. *The New York Times,* 25, April 8, 1959.

Doty, Robert C.: Sicilian Mafia moving from crime into business and politics. *The New York Times,* April 21, 1967.

Echoes of Capone; senators hear restaurants' troubles. *U.S. News and World Report, 45:* July 18, 1958.

Federal investigators report members of Mafia families who direct most large-scale gambling and loansharking operations in Westchester, seek to gain control of most legitimate business in county. *The New York Times,* 26, June 22, 1967.

Fight against crime is costly to business. *The New York Times,* 1, May 1, 1969.

Gangland grip on business. *Business Week,* May 12, 1951.

Gangland infiltration of coin-operated machines business. *The New York Times,* 30, December 1, 1958.

Government agencies have begun coordinated nation-wide attack on Mafia infiltration of legitimate business. *The New York Times,* 1, February 22, 1967.

Grutzner, Charles: How to lock out the Mafia. *Harvard Business Review,* 45-58, March-April 1970.

Grutzner, Charles: Gambino called in state inquiry. *The New York Times,* 18, May 7, 1968.

Grutzner, Charles: New state study on crime begins. *The New York Times,* 43, March 15, 1968.

Grutzner, Charles: State hearing told of Mafia tie to 20th Century Industry, Inc. *The New York Times,* 48, March 7, 1969.

Grutzner, Charles: 98 of 113 underworld figures found tied to legal businesses. *The New York Times,* 1, October 14, 1969.

Highwayman: Accident-rigging racket. *Newsweek, 58:* August 21, 1961.

Hoover, J. Edgar: How you can help smash it. *Parade,* September 15, 1963.

Hoover, J. Edgar: The deficit of crime. *Monitor,* 1-3, January-February 1968.

How criminals solve their investment problem. *U.S. News and World Report, 56:*74-76, March 30, 1964.

Industrial laundry taken over by Teamsters in Chicago. *The New York Times,* 1, August 2, 1958.

Kennedy, Robert F.: Gangster invasion of business grows. *Nation's Business,* 47: May 1959.

Lacey urges Jersey to make refuse industry 'public trust.' *The New York Times,* 22, January 16, 1970.

Lefkowitz, Louis: Infiltration of the securities industry. *Annals,* May 1963.

McClellan committee to probe role of Mafia in unions and business. *The New York Times,* 1, June 29, 1958.

Methvin, E. H.: Mafia war on the A&P. *Reader's Digest,* 97: July 1970.

The mob. *Life,* September 1, 8, and 25, 1967.

New ways gangsters muscle into business. *Nation's Business,* August 1965.

Rackets probers eye employer. *Business Week,* April 13, 1957.

S. Braden reports anti-crime commission finds evidence of organized crime in food, garment, trucking, and building industries. *The New York Times,* 1, February 16, 1953.

Schanberg, Sydney H.: Rockefeller wants pier agency to police major airports here. *The New York Times,* 1, February 9, 1968.

Schendel, G.: How mobsters grabbed a city transit line. *Colliers, 128:* September 29, 1951.

Special report by task force on organized crime warns that growing penetration of legitimate business by Cosa Nostra threatens increased corruption of local government officials. *The New York Times,* 1, May 15, 1967.

There are people who say, "Well, business is business." *Forbes, 105:* April 1, 1970.

Thugs in business. *Business Week,* May 19, 1951.

Trouble in the garbage industry. *U.S. News & World Report, 43:* November 22, 1957.

Underworld moves in on business. *U.S. News & World Report, 66*: May 5, 1969.

Underworld reportedly expands control over nightclubs, bars and motels in New York area. *The New York Times,* 81, October 16, 1966.

United States attorney says *the mob* is *taking over* in New Jersey. *The New York Times,* 1, November 30, 1969.

Velie, L.: Rackets in the juke box. *Reader's Digest, 67*: November 1955.

Vinson, F. M.: New ways gangsters muscle into business. *Nations Business, 53*: August 1965.

ECONOMIC IMPLICATIONS OF
PORNOGRAPHY AND PROSTITUTION

INTRODUCTION

T HE PORNOGRAPHY INDUSTRY in the United States is small when compared with other national economic enterprises. Yet, estimates of gross sales range between $1.5 to $2.5 billion a year. The pornography business is one of the illegal economic activities in which organized criminals are intimately involved.

In October 1967 Congress created the Commission on Obscenity and Pornography to investigate traffic in these areas. Its membership consisted of eighteen commissioners from the fields of law, religion, business, sociology, psychiatry and teaching with William B. Lockhart, dean of the University of Minnesota law school, as chairman. On September 30, 1970 the Commission sent its report to the President. Even before it became public, the report kicked up a storm. A majority of the Commission's members said that all curbs on *smut* should be ended. The dissenting Commissioners charged that the panel was biased.

The first selection in this chapter, "How Big is the *Smut* Industry?" abstracts material from the report of the Commission on Obscenity and Pornography. For each of the major areas of activity in pornography, it estimates dollar volume of gross sales.

The second article, *"Hard-Core* Grows Fashionable—And Very Profitable,"* is an analysis of the film *Deep Throat*. With an investment of $25,000, the film grossed over $3.2 million in more than seventy theaters across the country. Federal and local law enforcement officials assert that the pornography industry ". . . is falling increasingly under the domination of the Mafia."

Prior to World War I, the major profits of organized criminals were obtained from prostitution. For a variety of reasons commercialized prostitution became less profitable, and convictions of organized crime figures in prostitution cases during the thirties and forties made executives in the criminal syndicate fearful of association with this enterprise.

In "The Porno War," Pete Hamill suggests that "if prostitution were legalized, the massage parlors would become the basis of the system. Instead of having cops posing as johns at our expense, the parlors would be brought into the tax system, the women would be licensed and forced to have medical check-ups against venereal disease, and a big hunk of hypocrisy would go out of our lives."

The fourth selection, "The Economics of Prostitution," analyzes the business aspects of the occupation, including employment and earnings.

HOW BIG IS THE "SMUT" INDUSTRY*

The Commission on Obscenity and Pornography says the "smut" industry is not nearly so big as many people think.

In its report released September 30, the Commission said it "can state with complete confidence that an estimate of $2.5 billion sales grossly exaggerates the size of the 'smut' industry in the United States under any reasonable definition of the term."

The report also stated, "The size of this industry is small when compared with the overall industry in books, magazines and motion pictures, and the business in explicit sexual materials is insignificant in comparison with other national economic enterprises."

Motion Pictures

Sex-oriented films for limited audiences, including so-called "art" films and "skin flicks," will take in $156 million at the box

---

Reprinted from *U.S. News & World Report*, issue of October 12, 1970.

office this year—14 percent of the $1.1 billion of receipts estimated for all movie theaters.

Movies released for general audiences "have become more sexually explicit" in recent years, the Commission noted, and the trend is accelerating. Films rated "R"—barred to persons under seventeen unless accompanied by an adult—or "X"—no one under seventeen admitted—now account for nearly one third of the market, with box-office receipts of $335 millions expected in 1970.

Mass-Market Magazines

Retail sales of sex-oriented periodicals, such as "confession" magazines for women, "barber-shop" or "men's sophisticates," total less than $200 million a year.

Mass-Market Books

"Tens of millions of paperback books with some degree of sexual orientation are sold each year" to general readers.

"Adults-Only" Bookstores

"The Commission estimates that 25 to 30 million 'adults only' paperback books were sold in 1969, for a total retail value of $45 to $55 million; 'adults only' magazine sales were approximately $25 to $35 million, for fourteen to eighteen million copies."

Mail-Order Erotica

Mailers, centered in New York City and Los Angeles, send out forty-five to forty-eight million letters a year offering sexually oriented material.

Retail sales "probably did not exceed $12 to $14 million" in 1969.

"Under-the-Counter" Pornography

The total market in "stag films," photo sets and picture magazines sold "under the counter" is estimated to be between five and ten million a year. But traffic of this sort—largely picture magazines—"appears to be growing," with an increase in imports from Scandinavia.

What sort of person buys pornographic materials?

The Commission said the most frequent purchaser is a college-educated, married male in his thirties or forties who is above average in socioeconomic status.

"People who are more socially and politically active are more exposed to erotic materials. People who attend religious services more often are less likely to be exposed to erotica." The Commission adds: "Actually, most people who see erotic materials do not buy them. They get them free, from friends."

"HARD-CORE" GROWS FASHIONABLE— AND VERY PROFITABLE*

RALPH BLUMENTHAL

With a budget of $25,000, a handful of $75-to-$100-a-day actors and actresses and a vivacious, gifted sexual performer he signed to a year's contract, Gerard Damiano, a veteran pornographic film producer, spent six days early this year shooting a 35 mm. color film in Miami.

Since then the following has happened:

• The film, "Deep Throat," with its star, Linda Lovelace, has grossed over $3.2 million in more than 70 theaters across the country, including some $700,000 in New York alone since its June 12 opening, making it the greatest porno hit ever.

• It has gone on trial here and elsewhere in significant obscenity test cases that hinged not on whether explicit sex is depicted—for surely it is—but whether the film is socially redeeming and in conformity with current standards of display. It has also become a symbolic target in Mayor Lindsay's attempt to rid the Times Square' area of commercialized sex. At this writing, Criminal Court Judge Joel J. Tyler is mulling over the more than 1,000 pages of expert testimony given in a colorful, ten-day non-jury trial before deciding if "Deep Throat" is obscene.

• It has drawn an average of 5,000 people weekly to the New Mature World Theater on West 49th Street here, including celebrities, diplomats, critics, businessmen, women alone and dating couples, few of whom, it might be presumed, would previously have gone to see a film of sexual intercourse, fellatio and cunnilingus.

• It has become a premier topic of cocktail party and dinner table conversation in Manhattan drawing rooms, Long Island beach cottages and ski-country A-frames.

• It has, in short, engendered a kind of porno chic.

Now "Deep Throat" is the story of a young woman (Linda Lovelace) who is disappointed to find herself surprisingly indifferent to sex—until an examination by her doctor solves the mystery: Because of an eccentricity of her anatomy, she finds oral sex more gratifying than conventional intercourse.

The sixty-two minute film, according to the recent charges, depicts fifteen sex acts, including seven of fellatio and four of cunnilingus. Characteristically for a hard-core or—as those in the trade themselves call it—porno film, the sex acts are clearly, clinically, shown, in contrast to the deep-breathing simulations of soft-core sex movies.

Such explicitness is hardly unusual in itself anymore—one need only walk down 42nd Street these days for an unmistakable vista of sexploitation gone berserk. But "Deep Throat"—or "Throat" as the more decorous newspaper ads would have it—is by general agreement a better product than its porno predecessors, for as well as raw sex, it offers viewers a sense of humor and story line. To some film critics, that is still measuring progress in millimeters, but the film does seem to be an undeniable improvement over the genre's ordinary offering, which all too often betrays the film maker's contempt for his audience: The sound is warped, the color thin and faded and grainy. And the story, well, there is really no story, just coupling—exhaustive, boring, mechanical, relentless minute-after-minute of poker-faced fornication in "loops," so-named for the splicing of the film into ten minute repeating cycles.

"Deep Throat," on the other hand, attempts some comedy —and is rewarded by guffaws virtually unprecedented in porno movie houses. (The jokes, unfortunately, may not be repeated here.) The sound track, too, is sprightly and haunting, so much so that when Herman Tarnow, an attorney serving with the

Police Department, returned home one day after viewing the film preliminary to a bust, he caught himself absent-mindedly humming the theme song.

"Compared with what came before," says David Vandor, a young, black-bearded Hungarian who keeps track of porno for the Mayor's Office of Midtown Planning and Development, " 'Deep Throat' is an excellent film. It is better than most situation comedies or grade-C comedies."

This quality, coming along in a time of "permissiveness," is apparently enough to persuade a lot of people that there is no harm or shame in indulging their curiosity—and perhaps even their frankly prurient interest—by going to see "Deep Throat." Recent "Deep Throat" audiences are said to have included people like Johnny Carson, Mike Nichols, Sandy Dennis, Ben Gazzara and Jack Nicholson. Some French United Nations diplomats went and insisted on paying with traveler's checks. Some off-duty policemen went and became the objects of search in the theater by fellow officers. Members of *The New York Times* news staff went *en masse* during a recent lunch hour, to be followed a few days later by a group from the Book Review. Members of the in-crowd from Elaine's announced one night that they were going for the second time.

Truman Capote, who went after dinner one night "with a bunch of people I thought were fun," says he went because "Mike Nichols told me I just had to see it."

Was he scandalized? "Not the least little bit," he says. "I thought the girl was charming." Did he think it was for every-one? "Oh," he says, "I know a lot of people who don't want to see that sort of thing and so they don't. They probably couldn't stand it. You see it at your own peril."

One recent evening the audience included two well-dressed, apparently well-to-do middle-aged women laden with Christmas packages. They left after 20 minutes. "I was bored," one could be heard to comment. "It was boring," the other concurred, quickly. Then she giggled, "Peggy would have died." "We left too early," the first decided.

Herbert Kassner, attorney for the New Mature World Theater, who argued the recent obscenity case, maintains that "it's a fad.

You know how these things catch on in New York."

"Once it broke in the society columns, it was O.K. to go," says Allison Verrill, the astute and respected thirty-year-old reporter and film critic of *Variety*. The film has been cited by columnists and critics and newsmen ranging from Bob Salmaggi of WINS to Andrew Sarris of *The Village Voice* to the syndicated Suzy Knickerbocker to Al Goldstein of *Screw* magazine who became an immediate booster and gave "Deep Throat" the top mark of 100 on his original rating scale.

Not only are a lot of people interested in seeing for themselves: They will gladly pay the hefty $5 admission, a fact that makes hard-core pornography an enticing investment opportunity.

Terry Levine of Aquarius Film Releasing, Inc., the company that distributed "Deep Throat" and other leading porno films in the East, says that "sex theaters do better than nonsex." He estimates that a film generally has to gross at the box office five times its production cost for the producers to begin making a profit. But others in the industry put the multiple at only three. By last estimate, of course, "Deep Throat" had grossed twenty-eight times its production cost in its New York run alone.

The $5 price may itself be an important part of the porno-house image. Early in the run of "Deep Throat," Bob Sumner, the twenty-six-year-old operator of the New Mature World Theater, lowered the admission to $3 and then watched his gate drop because porno fans concluded that hard-core could not be seen at such a bargain rate.

Perhaps the firmest indication that pornography can be profitable is the assertion of federal and local officials that the industry is falling increasingly under the domination of the Mafia and has become the mob's fastest growing racket in a decade in the metropolitan area. Law-enforcement officers confirmed recently that they are looking into a number of porno films—including "Deep Throat"—as a part of their ongoing investigations of organized crime in the industry.

No one yet accuses the producers of "Deep Throat" of any wrongdoing, but the firm's financial history did take an intriguing turn that remains unexplained. It all began when Gerard Damiano, a droll, stocky film maker with a white-flecked goatee, rounded up his cast early last year in Miami. Damiano, who goes under the professional pseudonym of Jerry Gerard, started shooting with a bankroll of $25,000 put up by two partners, Lou Perry and Phil Parisi. The cast included an engaging porno-film stalwart who goes by the name of Harry Reems and is in particular demand in the industry for his ability to perform virtually tirelessly and on command. Then there was Damiano's particular find, a 21-year-old party girl from Bryan, Tex., with Medusa locks and virtuosic talent for fellatio. Damiano gave her the name of *Linda Lovelace*. With the concurrence of her manager-companion, she was signed to a year's contract at a figure put by Damiano's backers at between $100 and $200 a week. The manager got expenses but no salary.

The film took six days to shoot and another three months to edit and complete. There are different versions of what happened next.

According to Lou Perry, Damiano, the third partner in Film Productions, Inc., asked to sell his share when the film faced legal problems and had not yet begun to make money. "He was compensated what he asked for—$25,000." Perry said. "He was even asked to stay. This was his decision."

One of Damiano's acquaintances has a different story, however. According to him, Perry and Parisi, once the film began to draw well at the box office, informed Damiano that the three-way split was over and they would give him $25,000 for his one-third share of the future profits.

That sounds like a bad deal, I told Damiano as we sat one night with associates in a restaurant on Eighth Avenue.

"I can't talk about it," Damiano said.

Why?, I wanted to know.

"Look," he said, "you want me to get both my legs broken?"

When I pressed the question, Damiano just rolled his eyes and said nothing. The chatter around the table had also suddenly stopped.

In any case, some weeks ago, before trial publicity increased the take, Perry would acknowledge that "Deep Throat" had earned the—two—partners well over $500,000 as their share of the gate and, "we figure we might end up with a million." Not bad for a $25,000 investment.

As intriguing as its financial history, however, is "Deep Throat's" legal history, a saga that serves as a good introduction to the complexities of the obscenity laws.

Last summer, during the Mayor's campaign to clean up the midtown area, Criminal Court Judge Ernst Rosenberger reviewed "Deep Throat" and, finding it obscene, ordered it seized under a New York Court of Appeals ruling establishing such a procedure as proper. The next day, made aware of a contradictory ruling by the U.S. Federal Court of Appeals that requires an adversary hearing, permitting the exhibitor to defend the film before it can be seized, Judge Rosenberger returned the film. The U.S. Supreme Court will now have to rule on which procedure is proper; meanwhile the run of "Deep Throat" continues.

The operator of the New Mature World Theater, Mature Enterprises, Inc., had meantime been charged with two counts of promoting obscenity, misdemeanors each carrying a $5,000 fine, and the trial began last Dec. 18. The trial was entertaining in itself. It started in a Fifth Avenue screening room where Judge Tyler and court officers viewed the film. Then testimony began, with the defense presenting Arthur Knight, film critic for *Saturday Review* and professor of film at the University of Southern California. He contended that "Deep Throat" had redeeming social value because it helped people to expand their sexual horizons and particularly emphasized that a woman's sexual gratification was as important as a man's.

Unlike the cruder sexploitation films, Professor Knight testified, "Deep Throat" was not devoted to "deep breathing sex."

"Didn't you hear the female in the opening scene breathing deeply?" Judge Tyler wanted to know—until the professor explained that he was speaking metaphorically. When the professor used the term "missionary position" to refer to the conventional position for intercourse, Judge Tyler did not understand and the professor had to explain it to him. "It's worthwhile for me, if nothing else happens, to have gotten this education," the judge commented.

Another witness for the defense, John W. Money, professor of medical psychology at Johns Hopkins University, testified that "Deep Throat," by showing explicit acts of fellatio, cunnilingus and intercourse, convinced viewers there was nothing shameful about sex and therefore produced saner, healthier attitudes about it. "It puts an eggbeater in people's brains" was the way he expressed it.

Disputing this approach and testifying for the prosecution, Dr. Max Levin, a seventy-one-year-old semiretired psychiatrist, said the film was harmful in that it distorted "the true nature of female sexuality." People with sexual hang-ups, Dr. Levin testified, might become confused and experience "sexual fantasies of an unhealthy nature." Dr. Levin, formerly clinical professor of neurology at New York Medical College, ended his cross-examination in a cloud of confusion over whether he was talking about "Deep Throat" or film shorts on the same bill. He entered the theater in the middle of the show, he explained, and couldn't tell where one film ended and the others began.

If all of this made for good newspaper copy—and excellent free advertising for the movie—it also seemed to be leading to a judicial precedent.

For it is unusual that the question of "Deep Throat's" obscenity is being debated in a New York City courtroom at all, some legal observers point out. According to the State Penal Law a performance or material is obscene if all of the following three conditions are met: "(a) considered as a whole, its predominant appeal is to prurient, shameful or morbid interest in nudity, sex, excretion, sadism or masochism, and (b) it goes substantially beyond customary limits of candor in describing or representing such matters, and (c) it is utterly without redeeming social value."

Needless to say, many of these words—"predominant," "substantially," "utterly," "social value"—have proven hellishly difficult to apply to a given film or book, and city prosecutors have preferred to permit exhibitors of pornography to plead guilty to a charge not having to do with obscenity—disorderly conduct, for example—rather than risk a trial that could result in a ruling that a film of hard-core pornography is not obscene. In this case they have chosen to charge the corporation, rather than individuals, with promoting obscenity, to allow trial by judge instead of the jury proceeding mandated for charges against individuals. The city apparently fears a sophisticated jury would never rule a film obscene. In fact, a Binghamton, N.Y. jury recently found "Deep Throat" not obscene.

Such legal harassment has not done much, however, to limit the pornographic film business in midtown. Pleading guilty to disorderly conduct doesn't prevent an exhibitor from continuing to show his film, and in any event, his case may not come up until long after the film in question has completed its run and the exhibitor has made his money from it. Having pleaded guilty, the exhibitor has to pay a fine, but he can consider that an acceptable expense, easily absorbed by his profitable operation. In the meantime, Time Square films fare has grown raunchier.

Conviction on an obscenity charge, however, may result in heavier fines, or even a jail term. So, according to legal observers like Leon Friedman, a lawyer on the staff of the Association of the Bar of the City of New York, if Judge Tyler rules that "Deep Throat" is obscene, and if his ruling holds up on appeal, it could in time have a substantial inhibiting effect on midtown exhibitors. In effect, it would establish a legal limit to obscenity at some relatively soft-core point between your average X-rated Hollywood film and "Deep Throat," and the dirty movie business would no doubt respect the limit, at least for a time.

More intriguing, however, would be a ruling by Judge Tyler that "Deep Throat" is not obscene, given the nature of the recent trial. Expert witnesses called to establish that the film has redeeming social value not only cited its artistic qualities, they went on to argue that in these times of general concern about problems of sexuality, the explicit display of sexual intercourse, fallatio and cunnilingus is socially valuable in itself.

For the court to accept this principle would seem to eliminate the possibility of any obscenity finding for any film, however explicit, that depicts and illuminates virtually any aspect of human sexuality.

As the trial proceeded it began to create a rather serious question about its own relevance and that of the Mayor's effort to make war on sexploitation in midtown, for the newspaper publicity resulting from the trial more than doubled the weekly gate receipts of "Deep Throat." The Mayor and the legitimate threater owners and other businessmen might like to wipe out the pornography industry, but it nevertheless seems to be meeting a substantial public demand.

William G. Bardel, head of the Mayor's Office of Midtown Planning and Development, who is coordinating the city's drive on Times Square sexploitation, believes, or at least hopes, that the current interest in "Deep Throat" is only superficial. "The repetition of oral sex . . . I don't think it will create the mass demand for this sort of thing," he says, with evident distaste.

And, in fact, if porno chic has thus arrived, some patrons still seem to have satisfied their curiosity with their first and last hard-core film.

One group of three couples in their late twenties I interviewed one night as they emerged from "Deep Throat" acknowledged having been completely turned off by the film.

"I think is was gross," said one of the group, named William. "Too graphic. I never watch what I do. I was disappointed. It had such a contrary effect."

"It was like watching cattle," said another member of the party, Lynn.

And if critics can applaud the fact that a movie like "Deep Throat" is slightly better in quality than more traditional porno movies, it remains true that pornography is at best a limited form of art. Andrew Sarris, for example, complains that for all its comic moments, good color, bouncy music and vivid action, "Deep Throat" still features disengaged sex organs, the human beings attached to them having been lost somewhere on the way to the orgasm.

Also, porno films characteristically are overwhelmingly male chauvinist, catering to male sexual fantasies and apprehensions. The women are submissive, and the men are but inexhaustible. (Except for gay porno films—a flourishing subcategory—male homosexual contact seems to be taboo in hard-core and soft-core films. Lesbian scenes, on the other hand, are common, but for the titillation of men, not women.)

On the other hand, porno producers and operators believe in a promising future, and are backing their belief with hefty investments. One producer and director who goes by the name of Danny Stone recently made a film called "High Rise," scheduled to open here in coming months, with the unusually high budget for porno of $75,000. And he dreams of producing a quarter-million-dollar hard-core film that, he says, will be "the 'Ben Hur' of porno."

Perry and Parisi are going on to shoot "Deep Throat II" in New York. Its completion was recently announced in a large ad in *Variety*. "We're going to make lightning strike twice," it said. "If you like 'Throat,' you'll love 'Throat II.' "

The ad portrayed Damiano as the director. However, in another intriguing twist, it turns out that the sequel has not been finished at all—although Parisi insists shooting has begun. Moreover, Damiano has nothing to do with it; it is being made by another porno film maker, Joe Sarno. Asked about the peculiarly misleading ad, Parisi explained, "You know how the motion-picture business is. Sometimes ads tend to be misleading. But there's a reason for it." The reason, apparently, is that others had their eye on producing a sequel, and Perry and Parisi wanted to establish their claim on "Deep Throat II" with the name that made "Deep Throat" such a success.

The sequel, according to Perry, is budgeted at $70,000. It also stars Linda Lovelace—"in a kind of 'Perils of Pauline' plot," says Perry. For a week's shooting, she gets $1,000 a day plus expenses for her and her manager, plus a percentage of the future box office receipts.

Meanwhile, Perry says, negotiations are under way with a publisher for a "Deep Throat" film book and, he adds, "We're considering releasing the album."

THE PORNO WAR*

PETE HAMILL

Politicians can usually think of more ways to waste money than ordinary mortals can, and the current "war" on pornography,

* Reprinted from the *New York Post*. Copyright November 29, 1972, New York Post Corporation. Used with permission.

peep shows and massage parlors is a good example. This is a city which can't raise enough money to rebuild Brownsville, clean the streets, fill the potholes or catch the crooks and it has its cops and other employes running around chasing skin. It's bizarre.

The Time Square area does have a seedy, crawly look to it these days, but the sex clean-up isn't going to change things very much. The prostitutes will be on the streets as long as heroin addiction eats away at the city's heart, and as long as there are johns willing to pay for the services of the women. A crackdown does not stop prostitution; it only moves the prostitutes to another part of town.

If the people running the crackdown were serious, they wouldn't waste the time of the cops and the others who chase around the town. They would be pressing for full legalization of everything.

If prostitution were legalized, the massage parlors would become the basis of the system. Instead of having cops posing as johns at our expense, the parlors would be brought into the tax system, the women would be licensed and forced to have medical check-ups against venereal disease, and a big hunk of hypocrisy would go out of our lives.

The brothels would exist in the open; a generation would grow up knowing about their existence, and choice would be left to the individual.

This does not mean that people would be forced to use the places, any more than legalizing abortion meant that women had to have abortions. It simply means that what exists, and what will always exist, is recognized, and made available to those who care to use it.

In cases of prostitution, pornography, and peep shows there is no true crime; the law is making a moral judgment and asking cops to enforce that moral judgment.

A certain element of the population objects to the existence of prostitution, but that does not mean that prostitution will go away. All it means is that somebody objects.

But the basic tactic of those who truly object is to refuse. They do not have to use brothels, buy pornographic books or magazines, or line up at the peep shows. But some people want, perhaps even need, those things, and in a free society, they should have that right.

Legalization would also mean regulation. There could be specific zoning codes to control the more blatant sort of advertising. And there could be some regulation of prices.

Most civilized nations have red light districts, and those countries which have abolished them (like France and Italy) have found to their chagrin that the system goes haywire, that venereal disease spreads, and that the pimps and racketeers continue to provide the services, but with a vicious undertone.

New York now has legalized gambling on horse-racing, and the public morals did not suffer; the horseplayers simply moved from the illegal bookmaker to the legal bookmaker.

Within a few years, all sports gambling will almost certainly be legalized with the only objections coming from the mob guys, and after that we will no doubt have full casino gambling, along the lines of Las Vegas.

If that happens, it will be absurd to have a continuing crackdown on the sex shows, massage parlors and pornographic book stores. You don't have to like pornography: I personally find most pornography boring, poorly written and frequently violent. But I don't drink rum or smoke cigars either.

If a person wants such things, they should be available. And a city can then get on to attacking the true obscenity: street crime, violence, poverty, drug addiction, rotten housing.

To continue to ask grown men and women to go chasing around after skin is a waste of time.

THE ECONOMICS OF PROSTITUTION

LAWRENCE J. KAPLAN AND DENNIS KESSLER

Prostitution in the United States is big business. In 1936 Lucky Luciano was described as New York's "vice czar" for running the biggest prostitution racket the city had ever seen. Today, we find the role of organized crime in prostitution is much less pervasive than it had been in previous years. Prostitution in most of our urban centers today is primarily a free lance operation. Reliable estimates as to the number of women involved in the world's oldest profession are hard to determine. On the national scene, the range spans from a conservative 100,000 to a possible one half million. "No village, town, city or metropolis is entirely free of covert prostitution. And, according to the American Social Health Association, which has been investigating hired love for fifty years, 'conspicuous prostitution' exists in 27 percent of all U.S. communities."[1]

The Role of Pimps and Madams

The control of the lucrative prostitution industry has shifted from organized management to the small operator. Many prostitutes are operating as street walkers or call girls under the watchful eye of their panderer, more familiarly known as the "pimp," or known on the distaff side as the "madam."

The pimp plays an important role in the life of the prostitute. His promise of protection and glamour as well as providing money for the clothes and fashionable living quarters makes his role indispensable. In addition, it is the pimps who pay the fines and put up the bail for the girls that get them back on the streets.[2] The motivation behind the pimps' efforts are certainly not altruistic. Garishly dressed pimps are easily recognizable in the New York area and are capable of pocketing from $750 to more than $1,000 per week through control of as few as three or perhaps four prostitutes.[3] The prostitute frequently relies on the pimp to provide her with emotional and psychological support. It is for these reasons that the overwhelming majority of street prostitutes rely on the services and support of the pimp. In turn, the pimps enjoy a certain social status among the deviant subcultures and are in fact, the real money makers in the prostitution relationship.

In most of the cities throughout the country, prostitution

---

[1] "A Consumers Guide to Prostitution," *Moneysworth*, June 23, 1973, p. 1.

[2] Murry Schumach, "Police Unit Aims at Curbing Pimps," *The New York Times*, July 12, 1971, p. 19.

[3] Edward C. Burks, "Lenient Laws Lure Prostitutes Here," *The New York Times*, January 27, 1969, p. 1.

apparently flourishes while public officials wage a rhetorical war against it. As the moral debate ensues, prostitution is spreading to the rich uptapped rural markets with alacrity. The mobile brothel house is playing an important role in facilitating this exodus. "Prostitutes have found lucrative new markets by taking their services to smaller towns with regional airstrips, to commercial suburbs and to convention centers and clumps of motels and bars outside core cities where salesmen and other transients pass time away from home and are too timid, fearful or lazy to go downtown."[4]

In these rural areas, it is the madam who usually assumes the role of manager for the girls. Her main function, something like that of the pimp, is to run the establishment as a profitable business enterprise which means maximizing profits and producing the least amount of consternation among the girls, their customers and the law.

Massage Parlors

The urban counterpart to the brothel is now euphemistically termed the massage parlor. Massage parlors generally provide a number of services including illicit sex. Many advertise their services in local newspapers or even in the yellow pages as most operate behind thin but legal fronts. Many offer legitimate if cursory services such as steam baths or back rubs. The concept of the massage parlor has gained such popularity that they have begun to proliferate in Los Angeles and New York.[5] One of the reasons why law enforcement officials have met with so little success in deterring massage parlors from opening is the way the law is constructed in favor of the parlor operator. As a result, it is often difficult to make a legal arrest in a massage parlor. Customers will frequently enter these establishments in a lawful fashion and go to a private room with a masseuse. The masseuse is cognizant of the law which forbids her from soliciting any sexual relations. The sexual overture must be

---

[4] James P. Sterba, "Prostitution is Flourishing in Rich Exurban Markets," *The New York Times,* June 9, 1974, p. 55.

[5] *Ibid.*

made by the customer and, if that customer is a police officer, he has violated the law of entrapment.

Despite the police interference and frequent harassment parlor operators must live with, it is apparently well worth the trouble. Fantastic profits with minimal overhead are realized by parlor operators. "A massage parlor with two masseuses can gross $50,000 a year in Minneapolis. Masseuses in Des Moines legally earn $250 to $300 a week."[6] In New York City where the volume is apparently much greater, the profits surpass the smaller operations. Gross revenues have been estimated by the New York City Police Department vice members at $2000 to $3000 daily in some of the more profitable sex shops.

Earnings

Economics is probably one of the prime factors which lures women into the trade. Annual earnings are dependent upon numerous variables including: age, location of operation, pimp or madam percentage, and, of course, supply and demand. In some communities, a prostitute applying her efforts full-time may gross $9,000 per annum, but she usually keeps less than one half, the balance going to the various parasites of the trade.[7] A breakdown of where the brothel dollar goes is provided by sociologists Charles Winick and Paul M. Kinsie in their recent work, *The Lively Commerce*. "Fifty cents to the Madam, twenty cents to the pimp, eight cents for room and board, two cents for the doctor (for periodic venereal examinations) and twenty cents for the girl."[8] The vast disparities in the estimates of the earning potential can best be illustrated by citing David Reuben's account of the upper-class prostitute.

> Based on an eleven month work schedule, the average upper-level hooker should gross about $78,000 if she services her full quota of customers. Expenses, calculated conservatively, run to about $48,000. Her take home pay figures about to $30,000, before subtracting the contingency fund. With abortions and arrests her

---

[6] *Ibid.*

[7] *Moneysworth, loc. cit.*

[8] *Ibid.*

net income runs about $20,000. For about 3200 assorted acts of sexual intercourse she reaps about $7 a trick for herself.[9]

Earnings are also dependent upon the location of operation. In New York City it is reported that girls who openly solicit ask between $15 to $25. Most are unafraid of the law and are frequently permitted to operate in certain sectors of the city. Other girls who are under the strict domination of the pimp are forbidden to come home until they have earned a certain amount of money. One hundred and fifty to $200 is not an uncommon demand.[10]

Additional income is usually obtained by many of the girls working with the hotels they frequent. Some of the smaller hotels, in order to augment business, will give the girls a kick-back of $2 to $3 on a room that costs the customer $5 to $8 for no more than half an hour's occupancy.[11] Considering all of the above variables, the average urban prostitute grosses between $100 to $200 daily, less expenses.

Prospects of Legalization

St. Thomas Aquinas said in the thirteenth century that prostitution was a permanent evil and should be kept in a restricted place to protect those in other places. Apparently, Thomas Aquinas was correct in his evaluation of the permanence of prostitution since we have yet to see an abatement of this activity. Prostitution exists in probably every urban center in America despite the existence of laws which prohibit it. City-wide crackdowns on prostitution are announced with monotonous regularity. The net result of these administrative actions, however, is usually another ineffective program to curb the activity.

In view of this situation, many of our cities would make a wise choice to consider the possibilities of legalizing prostitution. Most cities have by now recognized the fact that legislative

---

[9] David Reuben, *Everything You Always Wanted to Know About Sex* (New York, David McKay, 1969), p. 257.

[10] Burks, *loc. cit.*

[11] Thomas F. Brady, "Prostitutes, Most of Them Young, Now Work the Day Shift Along Eighth Avenue," *The New York Times*, May 29, 1970, p. 55.

bodies cannot eliminate prostitution by laws. In the United States today prostitution is legal only in the state of Nevada on a local option basis. While it has been in existence in Storey County, Nevada, for many years, prostitution there is now legalized and licensed. The license fee is $1,000, and revenues from this source furnish a sizable portion of the county budget. The county has a population of about 700.[12]

In addition to Nevada, prostitution is now legalized in England, Scandinavia, West Germany and other countries. In these places prostitution is taxed under the general business law, and is also regulated by health officials. In West Germany, prostitutes gross $250 million annually.[13]

A realistic appraisal of the overall situation indicates that prostitution will flourish despite laws which prohibit it. Legislators would do well to consider legalization which would bring supervision, health examinations, and, at the same time, reduce crime associated with prostitution while increasing government revenues. Those individuals who elect not to indulge in prostitution would be free to abstain by their own choice. While legalization is not a panacea, it does offer economic and social compensations which make it worthy of serious consideration.

BIBLIOGRAPHY

The Economics of Prostitution

Brady, Thomas F.: Prostitutes, most of them young, now work the day shift along Eighth Avenue. *The New York Times,* 30, May 29, 1970.

Burks, Edward C.: Lenient laws lure prostitutes here. *The New York Times,* 1, January 27, 1969.

Demaris, Ovid: *Lucky Luciano.* Derby, Connecticut, Monarch, 1960.

Egen, Frederick W.: *Plainclothesman: A Handbook of Vice and Gambling Investigation.* New York, Greenberg, 1952.

Feder, Sid and Joesten, Joachim: *The Luciano Story.* New York, McKay, 1954.

---

[12] Steven Roberts, "Expansion of Legal Prostitution Weighed by Counties in Nevada," *The New York Times,* February 14, 1971, p. 40.

[13] "German Brothels Face Competition," *The New York Times,* November 19, 1967, p. 29.

Messick, Hank: *Syndicate in the Sun.* New York, Macmillan, 1968.

Messick, Hank: *Syndicate Wife.* New York, Macmillan, 1968.

Mullady, Frank and Kofoed, William H.: *Meet the Mob.* New York, Belmont Books, 1961.

Reuben, David: *Everything You Always Wanted to Know About Sex.* New York, McKay, 1969.

Shenehon, Eleanor: Prevention and repression of prostitution in North America. *International Review of Criminal Policy, 13*: October 1958.

Thompson, Craig and Raymond, Allen: *Gang Rule in New York.* New York, Dial, 1940.

Thornton, Robert Y.: Organized crime in the field of prostitution. *Journal of Criminal Law, 46*: March-April 1956.

Varna, Anthony: *World Underworld.* London, Museum Press Limited, Chap. 6, 1957.

Winick, Charles and Kinsie, Paul M.: *The Lively Commerce: Prostitution in the United States.* Chicago, Quadrangle, 1971.

The Economics of Pornography

Blumenthal, Ralph: Hard-core grows fashionable—and very profitable. *The New York Times Magazine,* January 21, 1973, pp. 28-34.

Clark, Alfred E.: Crime cashing in on pornography. *The New York Times,* 54, September 28, 1969.

Hamill, Pete: The porno war. *New York Post,* November 29, 1972.

Dirkson, Senator Everett M.: A new plan to fight pornography. *Reader's Digest,* November 1969, pp. 113-116.

How big is the smut industry? *U.S. News and World Report,* October 12, 1970, p. 62.

Kristol, Irving: Pornography, obscenity and the case for censorship. *The New York Times Magazine,* 1, March 28, 1971.

Lubasch, Arnold H.: Hearing assails the smut 'flood.' *The New York Times,* 44, February 19, 1970.

Report of the Commission on Obscenity and Pornography. New York, Bantam, 1970.

Roberts, Steven V.: Pornography in U.S.: A big business. *The New York Times,* 1, February 22, 1970.

Schumach, Murray: Sex exploitation spreading here. *The New York Times,* 1, July 11, 1971.

See, Carolyn: *Blue Money.* New York, McKay, 1974.

The Economics of Other Criminal Activities:

Hijacking, Stock Fraud

Air-cargo losses triple in 2 years. *The New York Times,* 33, February 14, 1970.

Belair, Felix, Jr.: Secret Service warns of spurt in counterfeiting and forgery during election years. *The New York Times,* January 4, 1969.

Bootlegging is back: now it's cigarettes. *U.S. News and World Report,* November 6, 1967.

Bull market in thievery: Stealing of securities. *Forbes, 102:* December 15, 1968.

Charlton, Linda: Fireworks bootleggers thriving. *The New York Times,* 1, July 4, 1971.

Cigarette racket is costly to state. *The New York Times,* September 10, 1967.

City studies bids of indicted firms. *The New York Times,* August 22, 1968.

Coburn, R. F.: New York seeks tighter airport security. *Aviation Week and Space Technology, 88:* January 1, 1968.

Cohane, T. and Melchiorre, G. (Eds.): How I fell for the basketball bribers. *Look, 17:* January 13, 1953.

Cole, Robert J.: 361 arrest records uncovered by Wall Street fingerprinting. *The New York Times,* 1, February 5, 1970.

Conn, H.: G.I. housing: Bribes and bribers. *New Republic, 127:* September 15, 1952.

Grutzner, Charles: Use of stolen credit cards investigated. *The New York Times,* 35, November 21, 1969.

McGuire, E.: *The Forgers.* Bernardsville, New Jersey, Padric. 1969.

Phalon, Richard: Hooded 'informer' reveals stock theft. *The New York Times,* 1, December 12, 1969.

Pick, F.: Billion dollar black market. *Nation's Business, 41:* October 1953.

Ranzal, Edward: 5th suspect seized in securities plot. *The New York Times,* 27, July 30, 1969.

Rice, Robert: Annals of crime: S. Sollazzo and bribing of basketball players. *New Yorker, 31:* March 5, 1955.

Rice, Robert: Part 1. Arson; Part 3. Counterfeiting; Part 4. Smuggling. *The Business of Crime.* New York, Farrar, 1956.

Senate approves bill making it a federal offense to use interstate commerce facilities to influence outcome of sports events by bribery. *The New York Times,* 18, September 13, 1962.

Senator Keating sponsors bill making it federal crime to fix sports events. *The New York Times,* 6, January 26, 1962.

Severo, Richard: Extortion is laid to a mafia figure. *The New York Times,* January 4, 1969.

Shanahan, Eileen: Stock-theft ring hinted by Haack. *The New York Times,* 55, February 27, 1969.

Sondern, F., Jr.: World's happiest smugglers: Smuggling of American cigarettes. *Reader's Digest, 63:* July 1953.

Stern, Michael: A&P fires here laid to the Mafia. *New York Times,* 1, July 13, 1969.

Stump, A.: Shame of college sports. *Coronet, 39:* January 1956.

Sutherland, Edwin H.: *White Collar Crime.* New York, Holt, 1961.

21 arrested in steal to order car-theft ring. *The New York Times,* 28, January 29, 1970.

U.S. agency fears loans aided Mafia concerns. *The New York Times,* 18, January 6, 1970.

U.S. House of Representatives Committee on Govt. Operations (90:1) *Hearings: The Federal Effort Against Organized Crime.* Part 2, 1967, pp. 137-138, 153-154. (Infiltration of ethical drug industry).

Whitney, Craig: Jury here indicts 16 in stock fraud. *The New York Times,* 1, November 20, 1970.

FINANCIAL OPERATIONS OF ORGANIZED CRIME

INTRODUCTION

T HE BANKING BUSINESS is a mysterious activity to most people except those involved in the banking profession and those who make a determined effort to understand its operations. Basically, a bank performs a set of functions which are essential to a nation's economy. In providing its services, a bank does not discriminate between the honest businessman, the prudent saver, or the criminal who uses the bank as a refuge for his illegitimate gain.

Swiss banks are particularly attractive, especially to those with larcenous intentions, because by Swiss penal law its banks are committed to secrecy as to names of account holders, volume of activity, or personal information. Any Swiss bank employee who breaks the code of professional secrecy is subject to both fine and/or imprisonment. It is no wonder then that for the past hundred years, Switzerland has been "a cool place for hot money."

While secrecy has been a dominant trait of Swiss banking for a century, a new twist was added in the 1930's, namely, the "numbered-account." Actually, *all* Swiss accounts have a number, in the same way that every American account has a number. But, in Switzerland, for those who want it, the banks omit the customer's name on all records and statements. The identities of numbered account holders are locked in a special safe, with very limited access. All transactions for the account are handled by *number only*.

This is the ideal arrangement for the criminal who wants to transform illegal rackets money into legitimate money for investment in a business. The process is referred to as *laundering*, and involves depositing "dirty" money in a secret numbered bank account and then bringing it back "clean" to the United States in the form of a phony loan. Not only does the criminal *launder* the money in the snows of the Swiss Alps, but the arrangement also enables him to hide the original illegal income from the Internal Revenue Service and to acquire a deduction when he prepares his tax return, namely, the interest on the make believe loan. There is no way to find out the original source of the money because it can be traced back only to the Swiss banks, which will not divulge the names of depositors.

A few underworld leaders have perfected these money-laundering operations. They have developed a worldwide network of couriers, middlemen, bankers, and front men who collect the profits from illegal enterprises, send them halfway around the world, and then bring the money back laundered clean to be invested in legitimate business.

A treaty between the U.S.A. and Swiss Confederation on Mutual Assistance in Criminal Matters was signed at Bern on May 25, 1973. If ratified by the Swiss Federal Assembly and the U.S. Senate, it would enable law enforcement authorities in the U.S. for the first time to obtain *secret* bank information where organized crime is involved.

The first reading in this chapter provides a summary of the kinds and limits of Swiss banking service, including gold, silver, currency trading, time deposits, trust arrangements, securities, precious stones, and special accounts. The second reading indicates the techniques for using secret numbered accounts as well as the procedure for taking over banks which can then be converted to serve the special needs of criminals. The third reading, based upon information obtained at congressional hearings, details some of the intrigue used by organized criminals in their financial operations.

SWISS BANKING SERVICES—
EVERYTHING FOR ANYBODY*

LESLIE WALLER

We have seen how the Swiss banking system developed, and why. We have noted its special appeal for both law-abiding and law-breaking people who have unreported cash. We have referred, in passing, to the fact that Swiss banks provide virtually every sort of financial service.

To understand the unique value of the system—and perhaps to set the record straight for anyone planning to stop off in Switzerland on his next trip abroad—this summary of the kinds and limits of Swiss banking service should prove useful.

Gold

By presidential proclamation it is illegal for any United States citizen to own gold "either directly or indirectly." In theory this means that we can buy neither gold bullion, nor gold coins minted after 1933, nor any stock or bond whose value is based even in part on gold, nor an investment trust or mutual fund that holds in its portfolio this kind of gold-backed security or other investments.†

So much for theory.

To learn about the practical side of the gold question, however, take a stroll some pleasant morning along Zurich's Bahnhofstrasse and Paradeplatz, with its expensive shops for furs and watches and its dull-faced, graystone bank buildings.

On the upper floors of these Victorian edifices you will often see bright spots of color, usually geraniums in window-ledge planters. But on the ground floor of these banks, carefully displayed behind plate glass, you will find the flash of only one color—gold.

---

* From *The Swiss Bank Connection* by Leslie Waller. Copyright 1972 by Leslie Waller. Reprinted by arrangement with The New American Library, Inc., New York, New York.

† Editor's Note: As of January 1, 1975, ownership of gold became legal for American citizens.

Strolling past these windows is like an open-air lesson in geography and history. Displayed on discreet, black velours plaques are gold coins from every corner of the world, ranging from rare Cape Verde escudos to the scarce afghani of Afghanistan.

Faces from the past haughtily turn their profiles to us: French napoleons, various monarchs of France on the 20-franc "louis d'or," English sovereigns, Dutch tientje, Swiss vreneli, and even the good old U.S. $10 gold piece featuring neither king nor president, but an eagle instead.

Inside the bank gold is for sale in various sizes of bars and all modern coinages. The back-and-forth convertibility is flawless: One can exchange currency for gold or turn in gold for currency. The Swiss accommodate both transactions.

Moreover, even more highly sophisticated forms of gold are for sale behind these dark gray façades. Gold futures, for example, are contracts by which you agree to buy or sell bullion at a fixed price and time, a good investment or a bad one, depending on what is happening to the future price of gold. Gold shares carry less risk. They are simply shares in South African gold mining companies. They are traded at the Zurich stock exchange, and any of these banks will execute such sales.

Behind these gray walls few bankers ask your nationality. They are not concerned for one simple reason: It is not against Swiss law to buy and sell gold in any of its forms. As long as you do not violate a Swiss law, your banker has no further interest in the transaction, which, of course, is covered by Swiss banking secrecy.

Is gold buying and selling one of the Swiss banking system services popular with U.S. citizens? It seems hard to believe that Americans do not regularly buy gold, for so many generations a prime hedge against devaluation and inflation.

It seems even harder to believe that when U.S. citizens open discretionary investment accounts in Swiss banks (see later), the portfolio does not include gold shares and perhaps even some direct trading in gold.

Silver

Not as secure as gold, silver is nevertheless attractive to some investors, particularly nervous Americans for whom it is not a forbidden metal. There exists, of course, in this new age of government supervision of private finance, the distinct possibility that at some future time a president of the United States may very well forbid investment in silver as was done with gold.

The minimum quantity of silver you can buy in Switzerland is 5,000 ounces, for which you pay a storage fee of about $50. Silver is also available in all the paper forms in which gold can be bought, including futures. As a metal, however, it is a much bulkier investment than gold.

Currency Trading

This service of the Swiss banks is not for the average investor. It takes two forms. The first, called "arbitrage," is really only for major institutional investors with millions of dollars to move about as they see fit. Treasurers of large international corporations shift company cash reserves from one currency to another, taking advantage of minute fluctuations in rates of exchange that may earn, for example, a few pennies on a dollar. Multiplied by millions, of course, and always assuming the guesswork preceding the move was accurate, arbitrage is a low-yield but extremely low-risk investment that Swiss bankers manage with consummate skill.

The second form of currency trading is similar to other kinds of futures. The investor contracts to buy or sell a currency for a fixed price at a certain time. He gambles on either a rise or a fall and sets his transaction accordingly, all handled for him by his Swiss banker. The attraction of this form of investment, at least as the Swiss offer it, is that the investor doesn't need to cover the full cost of the transaction. He can trade "on margin," usually a small percentage of the real contract. In effect, the bank lends him the money and charges interest.

Time Deposits

In Switzerland these are not quite the savings type of account your own U.S. bank will open for you. It resembles the two-year savings certificates available in the U.S. Instead of the unlimited deposit and withdrawal privileges of the typical American savings account, the typical Swiss time deposit is for a fixed amount and period of time at a guaranteed interest. The shorter the period of time, the lower the interest rate. Time-deposit accounts can be opened for as few as three months. There is a quarterly penalty of 2 percent on such deposits by foreigners.

The interest earned by these deposits is taxed by the Swiss at a flat 30 percent, half of which you can have refunded to you *if* you report the interest as income on your IRS return for that year. There are, indeed, many reasons why people would rather not announce to the IRS that they have a Swiss account, in which case they surrender 15 percent of their interest for that deception.

Trust Arrangements

It is not clear if it was a Swiss banker who first uttered the maxim: "What the hand of man can do, the hand of man can undo." But the fact remains that through a trust agreement, the Swiss will help you evade not only the 15 percent owed the IRS but the other 15 percent owed the Swiss as well.

This trust agreement is a legal fiction, a contract between you and the bank that certifies that you have not actually deposited your money in Switzerland. The bank is acting as your agent.

In fact, the bank simply places your deposit in a third country, where it earns a decent rate of interest. The deposit is made in the Swiss bank's name; yours never enters the transaction.

Naturally, under those circumstances, the 30 percent Swiss tax on interest is not levied. In exchange for a management fee, the Swiss have made it possible for you to cheat them of their tax.

International Securities

These take many forms, from stocks and bonds to various kinds of debentures and even commercial paper, a form of lending. Through your Swiss bank you can trade on virtually any stock exchange in the world, including the Big Board in New York. And you can do it anonymously, behind the façade of the bank's name.

Or you can become involved in the high-yield, high-risk commercial paper market. Here your money is lent to a company, often to an individual businessman, occasionally to a government or municipality, at a fixed term and interest rate.

Some Swiss banks sell certificates of deposit, which resemble time deposits. Others sell a variety of what in the U.S. are called mutual funds, but of an almost bewildering variety. For example, you can buy shares in funds whose portfolios are exclusively in Japanese securities, all-European stocks, utilities only, Swiss securities only, and many other mixtures of investment.

Precious Stones

Another form of investment that is not for the dilettante, this one is easily managed through a Swiss bank, which can handle purchase and sale, appraisal, and, of course, storage in a safe deposit box.

Special Accounts

In addition to the time-deposit accounts mentioned previously, Swiss banks offer many other kinds of accounts.

The "deposit account" yields a low rate of interest and can be had either in dollars or Swiss francs, although the Swiss banks at this writing will not accept direct dollar investments, preferring instead that you convert your money to a harder currency before bringing it to them. This situation changes back and forth.

The "investment account" works this way. You send along your check for $5,000, the minimum most Swiss banks will accept in this type of account, although some refuse anything under $10,000. You empower the bank to invest your money in one of two ways. Either you agree to tell the bank what you want them to buy for you, or you sign what amounts to a power of attorney giving them the right to invest your money at their discretion.

Many investors prefer the discretionary form of investment account because they believe it reduces their liability—or culpability—in the eyes of U.S. fiscal authorities should some of this money happen to be invested in the forbidden metal. You are not, of course, immune from prosecution or from the 2 percent per quarter penalty on deposits from foreigners.

The only advantage of the discretionary account is that, like all Swiss accounts, it is secret. As long as you break no Swiss laws, the T-Men will be butting their heads against a blank wall. In the eyes of some investors this gets to be quite an advantage.

There are other, minor kinds of accounts of small interest to the average investor. But perhaps the one that has captured the imagination of most Americans is the "numbered account."

It is usually assumed that the mob uses only these anonymous numbered accounts for laundering cash. Along with the Syndicate, however, popular imagination pictures numbered accounts as being the secret depositories for the looted treasuries of South American dictators, Arab sheikdoms, American cardiologists, and other proprietors of large amounts of cash.

By and large, the additional charge the Swiss bank makes for an anonymous account is wasted money. The Swiss banking secrecy protects *all* types of accounts and, in fact, all types of banking transactions.

Having a numbered account simply means that fewer people in your particular bank know the real identity of the account holder. Perhaps only the officer who opened the account and one or two other people ever know. In short, the numbered account doesn't guarantee anonymity at all. It simply reduces to a minimum the number of knowing bank people whose secrecy is, in any case, already guaranteed under Swiss law.

Nevertheless, the passion of some depositors for utter secrecy is so great that Swiss banks have often gone to ludicrous lengths to satisfy the craving. In addition to numbers, these anonymous accounts can be opened under mysterious code names. Secret passwords are also possible.

Correspondence from the bank will be sent in plain envelopes with no return address. If not delivered, they will be returned to Switzerland where the postal officials know by the postage meter number on the envelope to which bank the envelope must be returned.

Banks will even mail correspondence from a country other

than Switzerland, to avoid the arrival at a depositor's office or home of an envelope with a Swiss postmark. In some cases, if the customer is paranoid enough to insist on and pay for it, all transactions will be handled by couriers, face to face. In other cases, only transactions within the bank will be allowed, as the customer directs.

Naturally, this obsession with supersecrecy leads to a variety of problems, some of them laughable. Evita Peron, beloved wife of the former Argentine dictator, is said to have opened several numbered accounts in which some $15 million was quietly laid to rest. The interment proved final because, so the story goes, Little Eva forgot to tell Juan what the account numbers were before she died at a prematurely early age. He has yet to get his hands on the money. It sits there to this day.

Something of the same order happened a few years back to U.S. authorities who went to Switzerland to locate some $7 million belonging to the Texas operator Billie Sol Estes. He had apparently evaded paying U.S. taxes on the $7 million, a crime in the U.S. but not in Switzerland. As far as is known, the Swiss flatly refused to locate the money or even to admit that there was such an account.

The whole question of Swiss banking secrecy is a matter of some confusion to non-Swiss, leading many to ask for numbered accounts when they really don't need them, others to trust so implicitly in Swiss secrecy that they overlook taking normal precautions, and still others to curse the Swiss as criminals and associates of criminals.

While there was a time when banking secrecy was enforced in many other European countries, as well as in Switzerland, it was a tradition more than a restriction, and shortly after World War I the governments of most countries began to violate their native traditions of secrecy so thoroughly that only Switzerland was left.

By 1934, with the rise of Fascist and Nazi dictatorships to the south and north of Switzerland, people were beginning to flee from neighboring lands for asylum in neutral Switzerland. It was at this moment in history that the Swiss parliament decided to codify banking secrecy and make it part of the penal code. Article 47 of the law puts the matter this way:

> Whoever intentionally in his capacity as an officer or employee of a bank . . . violates his duty to observe silence of professional secrecy; or whoever induces or attempts to induce a person to commit such an offense, shall be fined not more than 20,000 francs, or shall be imprisoned for not longer than six months, or both.

This federal law supplements cantonal codes that had already defined Swiss banking secrecy. But the Swiss took still a further step. Banking information had always been considered a "trade secret." Under Article 273 of the Criminal Code, trade secrets were separately protected in the words:

> Whosoever explores trade secrets in order to make them accessible to foreign governments or foreign enterprises or foreign organizations or their agents, and whosoever makes such trade secrets accessible will be punished by imprisonment.

With Articles 47 and 273 in effect, the Swiss have felt, with good reason, that their banking secrecy was secure. There have been occasions, though, when the secrecy was violated either accidentally or by the corruption of a bank employee. Two cases come to mind:

> In one the traveling representative of a Swiss bank carried with him as an aid-memoire a little black book with the names of account holders he normally visited on his travels. The story goes that on one occasion, by means known only to them, the police of Franco's Spain got their hands on such a list and immediately collared the Spaniards whose names indicated that they had Swiss accounts. Sorely pressed by the Franco regime—which many of them supported fervently—the depositors sued the Swiss for damages and jointly recovered nearly $6 million. It is said that any Swiss courier who is unable these days to memorize the names of his customers is well advised to ask for a different sort of job at the bank.
> In another case it was learned that an employee of a Swiss bank made photostatic copies of a list of names matched with their account numbers. He turned this over to some unsavory characters who used the list for several years to blackmail the people whose names were on it. The terror ended, so the tale goes, when one victim gathered up enough courage to report the blackmailers to the police.

Where it can be proved that Swiss law has been violated, or when a Swiss court can be convinced to issue a court order, secrecy can be revoked.

In a classic case from the mid-1950's, loot stolen from a Canadian bank was suspected of having been hidden away in Swiss accounts. Canadian police forwarded serial numbers of the stolen currency to Switzerland and the Swiss police circularized all banks. Eventually some of the bills were located, and a depositor's name was supplied by a Swiss bank. This led, finally, to the apprehension of the criminals. In this case, bank robbery and the smuggling in of stolen currency were crimes in both Canada and Switzerland, and the serial numbers were proof of the crime.

It seems clear enough that the whole question of Swiss banking secrecy has been misunderstood and misinterpreted by people in all walks of life, from criminals to the highest officials in governments throughout the world. Since this secrecy is one of the most important reasons for Swiss banking popularity and success, the nature of it can stand further examination.

TURNING CASH INTO CREDIT*

MICHAEL DORMAN

Much of the money invested in legitimate business by the Mob is first funneled through secret numbered bank accounts in such countries as Switzerland, the Bahamas, Panama, Liechtenstein, Luxembourg, and West Germany. This process is known as "laundering"—that is, making illegal rackets money appear legitimate. Usually, it is accomplished by depositing the money in a secret bank account abroad, then bringing it back to the United States in the form of a make-believe loan. The racketeer pretends he is borrowing the money from a foreign investor, but actually is just juggling his own funds. Besides "laundering" the money, the technique provides the mobster several other benefits. It allows him to hide the original illegal income from the Internal Revenue Service. And, when he prepares his tax return, he deducts the interest on the make-believe loan.

Will Wilson, Assistant Attorney General in charge of the Justice Department's Criminal Division, says the "laundering" process helps the Mob solve the problem of how to use the large supplies of cash it accumulates. "Anyone who has a large quantity of cash would have some difficulty in using it because most large transactions are credit transactions," Wilson points out. "People don't go into a stock brokerage house and buy a hundred thousand dollars' worth of stock and pay in cash generally. And, if they do, it raises questions right off as to where they got it and why they are paying in cash, rather than a check. So it is not easy to do business in the American system in large denominations using cash, and therefore the racketeers' problem is to take cash that they get from the numbers racket or other illegal business and turn it into usable credit. They do that through the process of taking the cash by courier to some foreign bank and then bringing it back in the form of credit."

Robert Morgenthau, former United States Attorney for the Southern District of New York, says his investigators uncovered numerous examples of use of secret foreign accounts by organized crime. "We found many transactions by American hoodlums through banks and brokerage firms in the Bahamas," he says. In addition, it was found that millions of dollars worth of securities stolen from Wall Street brokerage firms wound up in the hands of Mob figures. The racketeers then sold the stolen securities "through foreign banks both in Nassau and in Switzerland," Morgenthau says.

Secret accounts, he points out, are also instrumental in the Mob's international narcotics smuggling operations. "Our investigations into the importation and sale of heroin revealed that accounts in foreign banks are frequently depositories for the proceeds of heroin transactions. Because those accounts are secret, attempts to uncover persons directing the international dope traffic frequently end up in complete frustration. Generally, money received for the sale of heroin in the United States is either carried to Europe by courier or hand-carried to a local money exchange or bank, where it is forwarded to an account in a Swiss bank. This account is often in the name of a paper (dummy) corporation with an office in Switzerland. From that account, the money is transferred to an account in a European country under the direct control of the initial supplier of the heroin."

Morgenthau recalls one case in which just such a technique was used by a narcotics ring that ultimately smuggled into the United States heroin worth $60 million on the retail market:

> The facts in this case revealed that, as part of the payments for smuggling heroin during a three-week period, $950,000 was sent to a Swiss bank account of a Panamanian corporation with offices in Geneva, which was known as the Me Too Corporation. Couriers delivered $800,000 in cash to two money exchange houses in New York City. From there, the money was forwarded to the Secret Swiss account of the Me Too Corporation. While the appearance of unknown persons with large sums of money might have been questioned by the money exchanges, an official of the Swiss bank had previously advised them about the expected delivery of funds. Because of their substantial business connection with the bank, the exchanges accepted these transactions as a professional courtesy. The other $150,000 in currency was deposited in the account of a South American brokerage firm with the First National City Bank in New York City. On the instructions of an authorized signatory of the account, a check for $150,000 was drawn on the First National City Bank and mailed to the Swiss bank for the account of the Me Too Corporation. Although there was no evidence that the money exchanges or the New York bank or the Swiss bank had any knowledge of the underlying narcotics transactions, the vital part they played in the heroin traffic is unmistakable.

In some cases, Morgenthau says, racketeers are not even content merely to make use of foreign banks' secret accounts; they actually take control of the banks. "A startling development of recent years has been a significant change in the identity and ownership of foreign banks," he points out. "Today, numerous banks in Switzerland and the Bahamas are owned and controlled not only by Americans, but in some cases by American hoodlums closely linked to loansharking, gambling rackets, and other illegal businesses. Such a bank does not need a large working capital to be a useful element of an illegal business. Its function is not to provide funds for the business so much as to provide an unreachable depository for illegal profits."

Congressman Wright Patman, chairman of the House Banking

and Currency Committee, has spearheaded a drive to tighten U.S. laws in order to make it more difficult for mobsters and others to conceal their dealings through the use of foreign accounts. Chiefly at Patman's instigation, Congress has recently approved legislation requiring American banks to keep more detailed microfilm records of their transactions, particularly those involving foreign commerce, and requiring all American citizens and corporations to disclose whether they hold secret foreign accounts. Meanwhile, American officials have persuaded the Swiss government to relax its strict banking secrecy laws slightly in order to help track down concealment of Mob money. Despite these steps there are still broad loopholes that allow racketeers ample opportunity for illegal manipulation of money through foreign accounts. As Patman puts it, "Secret foreign bank accounts are the underpinning of organized crime in this country. They are a haven for unreported income. They can be used to buy gold in violation of American law. They can be used to buy stock in our market or in the acquisition of substantial interests in American corporations by unidentified persons under sinister circumstances."

While making use of secret accounts in foreign banks, the Mob has simultaneously moved to gain covert control over domestic banks throughout the United States. In some cases, through front men with clean records, racketeers buy their way into actual ownership of the banks. In other cases, the mobsters achieve control over key bank officials through such tactics as threats and payoffs.

There is virtually no limit to the number of ways in which the Mob can benefit from a bank takeover. Once gangsters get their hooks into a bank, a Federal official says, the bank begins doing "an inordinate amount of business with racket-controlled guys that a legitimate bank wouldn't touch." Suddenly, he says, all the accounts of an area's known racketeers are switched to a single "hoodlums' bank." The bank then makes large loans to mobsters, their relatives and friends—with no questions asked, no collateral, no credit checks. A penciled okay from a top racketeer is all it takes for a loan to be approved.

The bank furnishes excellent credit references on the gangsters' accounts. Often, it allows them to open huge accounts under false names in order to stymie investigators. Bank officials may falsify their records to camouflage Mob transactions. In addition, bank cashiers may deliberately fail to make the required reports to the Treasury Department on abnormally large deposits of currency. Such reports on major cash deposits are used as a "flag" to the Internal Revenue Service—indicating possible sources of illegal income.

THE UTILIZATION OF THE NUMBERED SWISS ACCOUNT BY ORGANIZED CRIME*

MATTHEW W. RAFFA

This article will document various types of crime that are perpetrated with the aid of Swiss banks. It will analyze the process by which the skim from gambling, loansharking, and narcotics finds its way into numbered Swiss bank accounts.

There are three main ways through which illegal monies reach Switzerland. The first method, which is used extensively, is that of courier. Almost daily, couriers transport illegally acquired monies from any one of America's numerous airports. The number of such couriers is astonishingly large since each man makes only two or three trips per year. To make more than this would alert Customs or Immigration officials, and they would question these semiannual vacations. Under the provisions of H.R. 15073, section 231 of the year 1970, no person is allowed to leave the United States with more than five thousand dollars in cash. However, each time a courier leaves America, he carries at least a quarter of a million dollars in cash. The courier usually receives a flat rate for his service, usually 2 to 5 percent. The main goal of the courier is to insure that the money reaches the designated Swiss bank.

---

* This article is an excerpt from "The Utilization of the Numbered Swiss Account by Organized Crime," a thesis presented in partial fulfillment of the requirements for the degree of Master of Arts in Criminal Justice, John Jay College of Criminal Justice of the City University of New York, September 1974. It is printed with the author's permission.

A courier is usually a man who is remotely connected with organized crime. He must not have an arrest record in the United States, and his reasons for international travel must not arouse suspicion. Having done business with the Crime Syndicate before, he knows what happens to a courier who tries to abscond with the money. Besides, his business and his family usually remain behind as collateral against loss or theft of his cargo.

The use of couriers became so rampant that it prompted the aforementioned law to be passed limiting the amount of money that can leave the United States at any one time. However, these laws are seldom enforced. Searches at airports are confined primarily to determining whether weapons or explosives are being smuggled aboard the aircraft. There is no criminal penalty for failure to fill out a Customs form declaring the amount of money being transported. Any such information supplied by a traveler is generally given voluntarily. Searches do not provide adequate means for tracing mob couriers because couriers generally have no criminal records. They thus prove a perfect tool for organized crime. Through them, the Crime Syndicate freely transfers millions of dollars daily into their numbered accounts and avoids scrutiny by law enforcement agencies.[1]

In his book *Lansky*, Hank Messick offers an example of the courier type operation as it is presently utilized by organized crime. Large amounts of cash are carried out of the United States by couriers and deposited in the International Credit Bank of Switzerland. Once these monies are safely deposited in numbered accounts, they are returned in the form of loans to persons and corporations controlled by the National Crime Syndicate.[2]

In addition to the extensive use of couriers, organized crime has the option of sending their monies to Switzerland via Swiss

---

[1] Leslie Waller, *The Swiss Bank Connection* (New York, New American Library, 1972), pp. 11-19. The author explains in detail the use of couriers by organized crime.

[2] For more details on the large-scale use of couriers, see Hank Messick, *Lansky* (New York, Berkley Publishing Corporation, 1971), p. 199.

banks that have branches in the United States. Many Swiss banks have opened foreign branches in the larger American cities, having discovered that in order to facilitate such large scale deposits, they must operate on an international basis.†

Anyone may readily open a Swiss account in a Swiss bank in downtown Wall Street, New York. He is free to conduct all business transactions anywhere in the world via his Swiss bank.

American banks are the third conduit for illegal monies that reach Switzerland. Fearful of cutting off business opportunities for themselves, American banks will accommodate any client who wishes to transfer money into a numbered account. American banks also protect Swiss bank secrecy by not divulging information concerning their depositors' Swiss transactions. For example, in 1969 the First National City Bank refused to submit records of a $200,000 deposit certificate transferred from the Geneva branch to the New York account of an organized crime figure. Even after they were informed that the certificate was to be used as evidence in a large stock fraud case that was being prosecuted at the time, they still refused to divulge any information.[3]

All three methods of funneling monies into Swiss banks are presently being utilized by organized crime. Any efforts to curb these illegal transfers would have to take these three methods into account.

In attempting to define the term "numbered account" in his book, *What The Prudent Investor Should Know About Switzerland and Other Foreign Money Havens,* Harry Schultz presents some of the basic concepts of this type of account. He declares that, "Apart from the fact that Swiss banks never knowingly accept 'illegal' money, the whole concept of the numbered account is vastly overrated and misunderstood."[4]

Like all bank accounts, the numbered account has a number

---

† Swiss banking facilities can now be secured through any major banking institution in the United States.

[3] Leslie Waller documents this case in his chapter describing the career of U.S. Attorney Robert Morgenthau, pp. 90-108.

[4] Harry Schultz, *What The Prudent Investor Should Know About Switzerland and Other Foreign Money Havens* (New Rochelle, N.Y., Arlington House, 1970), p. 110.

precisely the same way that any account would be numbered. (Actually, every bank account in Switzerland is afforded the term "secret account.") Because of the expressed needs of individuals to conceal large amounts of cash, the Swiss bankers officially omit from all records the names of the holders of deposit slips, checks, and deposit certificates. This information is available only to a few senior officers of the bank. It is kept in a locked safe, and any breach of confidence is a federal offense in Switzerland. When the customer has correspondence with the bank, he signs his account number instead of his name. If the customer deems it necessary, he may refer to his account by a coded word such as "account Juno." Any further correspondence from the bank will be mailed directly or indirectly to the designated person. It will contain official bank statements signed by the bank official. It will be mailed in a plain envelope and no letterheads or return address will appear.

Should the letter be lost, it can be returned to the bank by the post office which will know the sender of the letter by a special postage stamp number. If correspondence arrives at the bank, the bank official will refuse to accept it unless it specifically mentions the account number or the account name. The banks will go as far as to accept only certain dates and a special mailing address when receiving foreign correspondence. In addition, the banks will, upon request, act with the power of attorney over any account. They will underwrite any number of stocks and advise on investment in Euro-dollars. There is no limit to the number of services that the numbered account can confer upon its holder. Upon agreement, the banks will assume any responsibility that will earn money and pass inspection on paper. Aside from looking after the fiduciary interests of their clients, the Swiss banks have little or no regard for so-called conventional banking practices despite Schultz's contentions.[5]

In connection with the numbered Swiss accounts, certain crimes are being committed. Violations of the Securities and Exchange Commission involving margin requirements, illegal

[5] For a detailed discussion of the services that Swiss banks provide, see Schultz, p. 103-114.

trading in gold, maintenance of dummy corporations, evasion of taxes, concealment of large amount of ill-gained income, stock manipulation, and profiteering by U.S. Army personnel from service club corruption are but a few of the large number of crimes that are committed and legally protected under the Swiss secrecy code.

This type of operation was developed, and is still being conducted, by members of the Crime Syndicate of the United States. A prime example of the procedure may be found in the machinations of Meyer Lansky. Lansky began his criminal career in 1929 when the worldwide depression left many businessmen bankrupt. He turned to bootlegging whiskey and since then has risen to the highest position that the Crime Syndicate offers—"Chairman of the Board." During his reign, the Mob built a modern, sophisticated organization that relied on a large cash flow, political connections, and influence on every level of government. His operation is worldwide, and the men that he controls range from the very lowly to highly placed corporate executives and very wealthy individuals.

Lansky has for many years avoided indictment and prosecution because of the highly placed people with whom he is connected and his uncanny ability to conceal his personal fortune, which is estimated at about 300 million dollars. He controls the Miami National Bank through one of his associates. The former U.S. Attorney for the Southern District of New York, Robert M. Morgenthau, uncovered enough evidence to convict men close to Lansky. He found that the Exchange and Investment Bank of the International Credit Bank of Switzerland are mob-controlled banks. He also found that the Exchange and Investment Bank handles most of Lansky's personal fortune. His operation is financed and supported through a series of loans and investment programs that are handled by his associate, John Pullman. The Miami National Bank sends millions of dollars into the Exchange and Investment Bank of Switzerland. These monies are transferred through a series of banks that are worldwide in their scope of operation. The monies return to the U.S. in the form of loans to meet mortgage payments on real estate transactions. Furthermore, the interest on these loans is deducted from tax returns.[6]

Lansky has become so powerful that he is virtually untouchable by Federal Law Enforcement authorities. He controls every situation involving top Mafia chieftains and every important step taken by the National Crime Syndicate. Perhaps more than any other person, Lansky has shaped and guided the Syndicate and made it an integral part of our political and economic systems in the U.S.[7]

The success of Lansky in building his empire may be attributed to the zealous work of John Pullman who resides in Switzerland. Mr. Pullman is a seventy-year-old former bootlegger and rumrunner who recently renounced his U.S. citizenship. According to federal law enforcement authorities, he is the mastermind for the flow of millions of dollars in and out of Swiss banks. He is alleged to have handled the skim from the gambling operations of Las Vegas, prostitution, loansharking, and narcotics for America's crime families. His principal function is to arrange for these illegal profits to be returned to their American depositors as "clean money." These cleansed profits are usually in the form of loans from the depositors' own Swiss bank, and they are then invested in legitimate businesses and in the purchase of real estate. This type of operation illustrates graphically the freedom and secrecy with which Pullman is able to function. His operations in Switzerland violate none of the Swiss federal or cantonal laws. The U.S. harbors no formal charges against him although it is rumored that the government maintains close surveillance on him whenever he visits Canada or Europe. He manages to elude U.S. enforcement agencies by staying out of the U.S. By 1964, he was a permanent resident of Lausanne, Switzerland, where he is reported to have set up

---

[6] For detailed information on the transfer of illegal monies see the U.S. Congress, Senate Committee On Banking and Currency, *Foreign Bank Secrecy*, Hearings before a subcommittee of the Senate Committee on Banking and Currency on S. 3678 and H.R. 15073, 91st Cong., 1st sess., 1970, pp. 58-61. This will hereafter be referred to as *Senate Hearings*.

[7] Lansky's influence on the American lifestyle is described by Messick, p. 268.

an intricate network of connections among bankers, lawyers, and couriers for the skim for America's crime families. Having branched out, he is now handling the proceeds of various illegal activities, and his profession is listed as "financial adviser." The Intelligence Division of the I.R.S. and the Treasury Task Force on Banking Secrecy would like to question Pullman about his working knowledge of the system of Swiss banking. It is widely believed that he controls the monies not only of Meyer Lansky but also of Mafia chieftain Vito Genovese, who is estimated to have $30 million hidden away in Switzerland.[8]

The process by which illegal monies enter Switzerland and then return to the U.S. was described by Whitney North Seymour, former U.S. Attorney for the Southern District of New York. In his testimony before the U.S. Senate, he stated:

> A racket-controlled domestic corporation borrows $200,000 from a foreign bank. The loan is collateralized by the same $200,000 which never leaves the Swiss bank. We refer to this as a plug loan. The corporation then loans the $200,000 of the illegally obtained funds to one of its officials, describing the foreign bank as the source of this money. Everyone benefits—the corporation deducts the interest on its foreign loan from its tax returns; the racketeer official deducts the interest he pays the corporation; more significant, he justifies the possession of the $200,000 and defeats efforts to prove a net worth tax case. The foreign bank receives interest on the money which it retains. The domestic money, illegally obtained, surfaces as clean money to be used in further illegal activities or to penetrate legitimate business.[9]

In attempting to define the large scale maneuvering that is involved in Swiss banking, it may help illuminate the reasons why only criminals, and the powerful and the rich can participate. Some of the crimes that are made possible by numbered Swiss accounts are listed and described below.

---

[8] Messick, p. 268. For more details on John Pullman see Charles Grutzner, "Ex-bootlegger Manages Money in Swiss Banks for U.S. Mobs," *The New York Times,* March 2, 1969, p. 1.

[9] *Senate Hearings,* pp. 57-58.

Violations of the Securities and Exchange Commission Involving Margin Requirements

At the time of the Senate and House of Representatives hearings, American buyers of stock were required to pay 80 percent of the purchase price in cash when acquiring stock. However, in Switzerland the law concerning the purchase of stock on margin has always been far more liberal. The general rule at that time was 20 percent down in any Swiss transactions. Violating this law, many Americans purchased millions of dollars of stock on the open market via their Swiss bank. They concealed the ownership of the stock by using their numbered account as the purchasing agent. They also violated Securities and Exchange Commission rulings by putting down 20 percent instead of the 80 percent required by U.S. regulations. In one case that was described by Mr. Seymour, a group of Americans purchased large amounts of stock, thus generating an escalation in stock prices to $16 a share. They sold out at the high price, and in the process depressed the stock prices to $1 a share. While these operators reaped millions of dollars of profits, numerous investors were financially hurt because of the violation of margin requirements.[10]

Illegal Trading in Gold

According to U.S. law it is strictly illegal for an American to own, purchase, or deal in gold bullion.* However, Swiss banks deal heavily in gold bullion and gold backed bonds. In one case, an American purchased $50 million worth of gold in the period of one week during 1968. In the course of this time, he resold the gold and realized a profit of over $9 million. Morgenthau, then the U.S. Attorney for the Southern District of New York, had the case under investigation. Due to lack of corroborative evidence and no real means of investigating the crime, the investigation was never concluded, and no further action was taken.[11]

---

[10] For specific case studies, see *Senate Hearings*, p. 62.

* As of January 1, 1975, ownership of gold became legal for American citizens.

[11] *Senate Hearings*, p. 267.

Dummy Corporations

This type of scheme is especially useful to those whose businesses involve transactions abroad. Investigations by Morgenthau found numerous examples of the so-called dummy corporation. Most of the companies were concealing large amounts of money and were not reporting the income to the I.R.S. For instance, a company was formed in Liechtenstein where the laws preserve the secrecy of stockholdings. An American business that deals abroad escaped taxation, by opening a numbered account; and in making purchases, bought twice as much as it reported and, using double invoices, reported the smaller amount for tax purposes and deposited the added gains to its numbered Swiss account. By understating the actual amount paid, these companies defrauded the I.R.S. on taxes, yet their dealings were legally protected under Swiss law.

Many Liechtenstein dummy corporations are headed by a dishonest lawyer who serves as the president and the sole employee of each business enterprise. From his office, this executive conducts the same type of operation for numerous dummy corporations and funnels millions of dollars in phony sales into Swiss accounts.[12]

Evading Payment of Taxes

The evasion of taxes is one of the major functions of the numbered account when it is utilized by a member of organized crime. There is a constant need to funnel money into Swiss accounts for the sole purpose of evading taxes. Any portion of legally or illegally obtained funds are immune from taxation once they have reached Switzerland. Any attempt to determine the actual amount of money in a Swiss account proves useless, and this is a major reason why tax evaders have utilized the numbered account.[13]

Concealment of Large Amounts of Ill-Gained Income

This is perhaps the major function of a numbered account.

---

[12] *Senate Hearings*, p. 66.

[13] For a complete analysis of tax evasion and its relationship to the numbered account see Harry Browne, *How to Profit from a Monetary Crisis*. (New York, Macmillan, 1974), passim.

Organized crime has been quick to discover that their ill-gained monies from gambling, loansharking, narcotics, and hi-jacking are totally untraceable once they are in a numbered account. This concealment of illegally obtained funds serves a dual role. Once the money is in the Swiss account, it is returned to its original depositor in the form of a loan from the Swiss bank. Not only is the ill-gained money concealed, but the same funds turn up later as legitimate monies that can be accounted for. This procedure eradicates any efforts to prove income tax evasion. The original "dirty money" has been laundered by the Swiss bank, and then is free to return to America to infiltrate legitimate business.[14]

Stock Manipulation

A numbered Swiss account provides an excellent means by which the manipulation of stock can be executed. Former U.S. Attorney Robert Morgenthau had many forms of this crime under investigation. In one instance, an "insider" violated Securities & Exchange Commission Rules and took advantage of a corporate position to sell unregistered stock. He realized a profit of more than one-half million dollars in a quick turnover because of that vehicle. Morgenthau also investigated numerous cases where stock manipulation was a prelude to a corporate takeover attempt by organized crime. Morgenthau illustrates this procedure with specific cases.[15]

Illegal Profits from the Sale of Narcotics

Due to the fact that the sale and distribution of narcotics has assumed worldwide proportions, the use of Swiss banks to conceal the monies involved has surfaced in the last few years. One case in particular that was under investigation by the U.S. Attorney for the Southern District of New York charges that a numbered account was the vehicle used for conveying the proceeds of heroin trraffic from the seller of heroin to the Swiss

---

[14] See *Senate Hearings* in which former U.S. Attorney Whitney North Seymour describes the concealment of ill-gained income and its impact on legitimate business, p. 58.

[15] *Senate Hearings*, pp. 260-268.

bank. In this one case alone, $950,000 was sent to Switzerland to be handled and concealed by the numbered account.[16]

Profiteering by U.S. Army Personnel

An American Army Sergeant Major was involved in service club corruption during the Vietnam War. He succeeded in funneling $362,000 into a numbered account under the coded name of "Account Fish Head." It is believed that the banks have been used extensively to conceal illegal profits by former and present members of the Armed Forces.[17] In another instance, the U.S. Attorney referred to the case of two partners in a supply company for military post exchanges. They had, over a period of three years, succeeded in sending over three million dollars into Swiss banks under the title of Continental Trade Establishment of Vadux, Liechtenstein. Later this company proved to be a dummy corporation operated by two Swiss lawyers from Liechtenstein. The U.S. Attorney stated:

> Secret accounts are also used for the bribery of public officials. Seven indictments returned in February 1970, in the Southern District charge former employees of the military post exchanges with conspiring to subvert the honesty of the exchanges by accepting bribes. The indictments charge that the sales agency which paid the bribe handled part of the money through numbered Swiss accounts.[18]

Profiteering by Government Contractors

In another case the U.S. openly charged the Union Bank of Switzerland, the largest bank in Switzerland, of "aiding and abetting" two men who succeeded in stealing an estimated $4.6 million from the U.S. Treasury. These two men were involved in a scheme that defrauded the U.S. Navy out of money on contracts on missile launchers. Not only did the banks help the men to conceal their illegal monies, but they went so far

---

[16] For detailed information on this particular case, see *Senate Hearings,* p. 266.

[17] For detailed information on this particular case, see the *Senate Hearings,* p. 267. Also Charles Grutzner documents the case in an article in *The New York Times,* March 2, 1969, p. 1.

[18] See *Senate Hearings,* p. 60, for complete documentation of this case.

as to act as middlemen by helping them smuggle another $500,000 worth of munitions to Europe, Latin America, and the Mideast. In this particular case, the Union Bank of Switzerland provided fictitious letterheads and forged documents in an attempt to mislead the Justice Department and the I.R.S.[19]

However, after an exhaustive investigation, it was found that corruption was becoming the rule rather than the exception. In this one case, there were twenty-five senior businessmen and a number of vice presidents in the U.S. alone implicated for their participation. The U.S. Attorney commented on this as follows:

> Corporate financial transactions probably provide the greatest area of misuse of secret banking facilities. A secret foreign bank account provides an ideal vehicle for a corporate insider to buy and sell securities of a corporation in which he holds a fiduciary position. We have evidence of the use of Swiss accounts in the allocation of new "hot" issues of stock. We are currently investigating several instances where corporate insiders and underwriters arranged for the sale of hot issues to Swiss banks which actually were acting as nominees for the very people who arranged the sales. These fraudulent transactions involve direct violations of the Federal Reserve Board's margin requirements.[20]

The U.S. Attorney cited the investigation that was pending at that time against Weiss Credit Bank of Switzerland and Shearson Hammill & Co., a New York brokerage firm. These two firms were linked to a scheme whereby the American brokerage firm purchased millions of dollars of stock by using the name of the Swiss corporation. The American firm violated the Securities and Exchange Commission and Federal Reserve Board rulings because they purchased stock using the 20 percent Swiss cash down payment instead of the 80 percent required by U.S. regulations at that time. This agreement was contrived not only to circumvent the margin requirement in the U.S., but also to cloak the identity of those involved.

---

[19] Charles Grutzner documents these cases in his article "Ex-bootlegger Manages Money in Swiss Banks for U.S. Mobs," *The New York Times*, March 2, 1969, p. 1. For further documentation of this case see Waller, p. 173.

[20] *Senate Hearings*, p. 60.

In view of these case studies, can there by any conceivable means of government control to eliminate such illegal transactions?

Representative Wright Patman stated that the use of the Swiss banks has become a national scandal. He has been urging legislation that would curb the use of Swiss bank accounts and make it illegal for an American citizen or an American corporation to have a secret account unless all transactions were reported to the U.S. Treasury.[21]

The widespread use of the secrecy provided by Swiss accounts by Americans who wish illegal gain has been an ever present evil and the subject of comprehensive studies not only by law enforcement agencies, but also by reporters of the *The New York Times*, the *Wall Street Journal*, and *The New York Post*.[22] Most knowledgeable persons involved agree that until the Swiss cooperate, if ever, any efforts at control will be in vain.

Here we touch upon a critical question that appears to be the crux of the entire problem. At the present stage, Swiss legal authorities need not cooperate in apprehending violators of American tax frauds or bond trading ventures simply because they are not part of the Swiss penal code. Security trading laws do not exist in Switzerland, and as far as the Swiss are concerned, there has been no crime committed. This is the prime reason why stock manipulation and illegal bond trading ran rampant in 1969-1970. Unlike their American counterparts, the Swiss at that time could purchase common stock by borrowing 80 percent of the cost, whereas the down payment rate in America at that time was about 80 percent. In addition to this loophole, American laws that relate to mail fraud are also nonexistent in Switzerland. A Swiss banker who helps an

---

[21] Rep. Wright Patman suggested that laws be passed which would curb the flow of money to Swiss bank via couriers. He points to current loopholes which enable organized crime to utilize the numbered Swiss account in the *Senate Hearings*, passim.

[22] See Neil Sheehan, "Crooked Deals in Swiss Accounts Aided by Inaction of Banks," *The New York Times*, December 1, 1969, p. 42; William Woodward, "Swiss Bank Accounts & Those Secret Numbers," *New York Post*, February 15, 1969, p. 24; "The Feds Push Prosecution for Tax Evasion as a Weapon Against Organized Crime," *Wall Street Journal*, June 17, 1970, p. 1.

American to break the law has not broken a law in his own country.*

In addition to these factors it has become increasingly apparent that America's organized crime families have succeeded not only in utilizing the Swiss device, but in gaining partial or full control of several banks. For example, the Exchange and Investment Bank and the International Credit Bank are reputed to be controlled by the Crime Syndicate. The Weiss Credit Bank and the Union Credit Bank of Switzerland are both connected with organized crime. Although they are not directly controlled by the Syndicate, they do have close ties and are more than willing to engage in deals that will yield large profits.

This dramatic change from customer to ownership will eventually prove to be the most detrimental aspect of the banking system to law enforcement authorities. Instead of having to deal with the Swiss bankers, law enforcement authorities will now be confronted by American crime families who run every aspect of the illegal business.

A bank organized and operated by a crime family functions only to serve the illegal activities of organized crime. It provides a safe conduit for monies and then conceals these illegal funds in a maze of untraceable transactions. Moreover, these funds can also be transferred to more reputable Swiss banks in an effort to erase all means of tracing these funds.[23]

Organized crime by using their own banks for their own purposes are able to obtain loans from a Swis bank if that is required. This loan to an American business venture is then totally cloaked under the Swiss secrecy code. In an attempt to establish the magnitude of an operation such as a mob-controlled bank, and in order to reiterate the need for legislation, Morgenthau, a former U.S. Attorney, declared:

> Taking these different types of operations together—the genuine foreign bank, the foreign branch of an American bank, and the foreign bank controlled by Americans and American hoodlums—I

---

* These contentions are supported by printed material listed in footnotes 5, 10, 20 and 21.

[23] For background information on the tracing of illegal monies see Hank Messick, pp. 269-275.

would conservatively estimate that their secret accounts hold hundreds of millions of dollars which have been used in or are fruits of violating American law.[24]

The full extent of this problem requires examination of two very important procedures in banking. The primary effort at control would require institutions to keep clear and precise microfilm copies of all checks, certificates, and money orders. It is virtually impossible for the I.R.S. and Treasury enforcement agencies to track large amounts of cash flow without the aid of the banks involved. The banks take the position that any extra amount of office work such as microfilming or record keeping would add great cost and not be worth the effort expended. Such contentions by the banks tend to lose their credibility since we know, for example, that every bank within the United States and abroad maintains these records as a matter of course, especially in this highly technical age of computers and with the growing size and complexity of the business transactions on Wall Street. Moreover, in order to present a tax evasion case, a stock fraud case, an insider trading case, or a bribery case, the prosecution must detail in the minutest fashion the various monies expended in the operation. Thus, any move by the banks to minimize their record-keeping processes would encourage this special form of criminality through the Swiss banks.

This leads one to suspect the motives of the banks, and forces law enforcement agencies to ask a second question, which is actually the crux of the problem. If an American-owned branch of a Swiss bank refuses to allow inspection of checks and money orders, on the grounds that Swiss banking secrecy extends to the shores of America, is it within its rights?

This blatant denial by banking officials to open their records for inspection was particularly aggravating to men like former U.S. Attorneys Morgenthau and Seymour. Morgenthau refers to a number of cases that were under investigation by his office and were hindered because of lack of cooperation by bank officials. In the course of these investigations, it was found in the vast majority of cases that the checks, certificates and money

---

[24] *Senate Hearings*, p. 262.

orders had been cleared through various American-based banks. Had bankers cooperated to a greater extent, and had the records been kept in a more suitable manner, the investigations would have proven a less formidable task. The fact is that virtually every Swiss bank maintains accounts in the larger American banks. In the majority of cases where fraud, theft, or organized crime are suspected, the actual transactions thus took place right here in the United States. Had accurate records been made available to the investigators, a greater number of such cases could have been prosecuted successfully. By the same token when an American bank opens a branch abroad, it refuses to make records available. As Morgenthau has noted,

> I find it shocking that an American bank, by opening a branch abroad, can lend its facilities to citizens who are defrauding the common revenue and violating our laws and then successfully deny its obligation to make account records available to the Justice Department, by claiming that the laws of a foreign country could be violated.[25]

Due to the fact that both the U.S. and Switzerland operate according to principles of free enterprise, one can readily see how this special form of banking secrecy fits virtually every need that an American could contrive. Criminals want a safe haven for their money, and the Swiss simply act out their roles as bankers. This in essence defines the clear-cut system of Swiss banking as we know it today. However, perhaps the most important reason why American banks defy the law and openly refuse to permit inspection of their records is that they do not wish to cut off business opportunities for themselves. Their political and economic bargaining power is so powerful that they succeed in circumventing numerous rules and manage to avoid accountability. Only recently has the public come to understand the relationship that exists between some banks and organized crime. The manipulation of large sums of money that in turn will produce a large return is often the sole criterion of a bank's transactions. One author summed up this point succinctly when he stated, "Perhaps under the skin, all bankers are Swiss."[26]

---

[25] *Senate Hearings*, p. 261. Waller, p. 96.
[26] Waller, p. 158.

BIBLIOGRAPHY

Browne, Harry: *How to Benefit from a Monetary Crisis.* New York, Macmillan, 1974.

Cole, Robert J.: Swiss may aid U.S. on bank accounts. *The New York Times,* 67, April 8, 1970.

Congress told U.S. tax cheats use Swiss banks for evasion. *The New York Times,* December 10, 1968.

Crime and secret bank accounts. *U.S. News and World Report,* 65: December 23, 1968.

Dorman, Michael: Turning cash into credit. *Payoff: The Role of Organized Crime in American Politics.* New York, McKay, 1972, pp. 277-282.

Errors and omissions. *The New York Times,* 38, February 26, 1970.

The feds push prosecutions for tax evasion as a weapon against organized crime. *The Wall Street Journal,* 1, June 17, 1970.

Fowler. Glenn: Foreign fund to aid building in midtown of two skyscrapers. *The New York Times,* 1, June 9, 1970.

Giniger, Henry, Liechtenstein: A tiny corner of Europe that is doing big things. *The New York Times,* 5, April 16, 1971.

Grutzner, Charles: Ex-bootlegger manages money in Swiss banks for U.S. mobs. *The New York Times,* 1, March 2, 1969.

McInnes, N. M.: No small change: Swiss bankers play down secrecy, promote expansion. *Barrons,* May 1, 1972.

Messick, Hank: *Lansky.* New York, Putnam, 1971.

Morgenthau, Robert M.: *Statement* Before House Banking and Currency Committee, December 9, 1968.

Portmann, H.: A view from Zurich. *The Banker,* April 1971.

Pick, Franz: *The Numbered Swiss Account.* New York, Pick, 1972.

Porter, Sylvia: Swiss bank accounts. *New York Post,* 40, April 30, 1970.

Ranzal, Edward: Tax fraud is laid to Lombardozzi. *The New York Times,* 50, February 21, 1969.

Reid, Ed: *The Grim Reapers: The Anatomy of Organized Crime in America.* Chicago, Regnery, 1969.

Schultz, Harry: *What the Prudent Investor Should Know About Switzerland and Other Foreign Money Havens.* New Rochelle, N.Y., Arlington House, 1970.

Sheehan, Neil: Crooked deals in Swiss accounts aided by inaction of banks. *The New York Times,* 42, December 1, 1969.

Sheehan, Neil: House votes curb on fraud in using Swiss accounts. *The New York Times,* 1, May 26, 1970.

Sheehan, Neil: More Americans cheating with Swiss bank accounts. *The New York Times,* 1, November 30, 1969.

Sheehan, Neil: Panel votes curb on Swiss accounts. *The New York Times*, 1, March 18, 1970.

Sheehan, Neil: Thousands linked to Swiss deposits. *The New York Times*, 22, December 5, 1969.

The shenanigans of the Swiss banks. *Newsweek*, December 23, 1968.

Smuggling: The Swiss connection. *Newsweek*, 71-72, April 8, 1974.

Swiss Restrictions: Old lady Gnomes. *The Economist*, July 15, 1972.

Switzerland agrees to aid in tracing gangsters' funds. *The New York Times*, 24, July 8, 1969.

Tunley, Roul: Zurich's Bahnhofstrasse is the world's richest street. *The New York Times*, 3, Section 12, International Travel, February 12, 1974.

Two Swiss banks seek to ease pressure in U.S. against secret accounts. *The New York Times*, 11, March 6, 1970.

Vicker, Ray: *Those Swiss Money Men*. New York, Scribners, 1973.

Waller, Leslie: *The Swiss Bank Connection*. New York, NAL, 1972.

Walsh, Denny: Rebozo bank and gambling in Bahamas attract election spending investigators. *The New York Times*, 1, January 21, 1974.

Woodward, William: Swiss bank accounts: The secret numbers. *New York Post*, 24, February 15, 1969.

CHAPTER 12

CONCLUSIONS

INTRODUCTION

On July 23, 1965, former President Johnson established a nineteen-member Commission on Law Enforcement and Administration of Justice, because of the urgency of the Nation's crime problem and the lack of knowledge about coping with it. In February 1967, the Commission issued a 308-page report on its eighteen-month study of crime which proposed more than 200 recommendations to reduce crime. They varied from controversial demands for birth control programs and a guaranteed minimum family income to noncommittal positions on the death penalty and wiretapping.

The Commission in the course of its work established nine Task Forces to study and analyze particular areas of interest. One was an Organized Crime Task Force which released a 126-page report. Appendix D of the report, prepared by Harvard economist, Thomas C. Schelling, entitled "Economic Analysis of Organized Crime," is reprinted in this chapter.

Professor Schelling states that "racketeering and the provision of illegal goods (like gambling) have been conspicuously neglected by economists." He proposes "a more professional, *strategic* analysis of the criminal underworld . . . that would draw heavily on modern economics and business administration."

He further states that "such an analysis, in contrast to *tactical* intelligence aimed at the apprehension of individual criminals, could help in identifying the incentives and the limitations that apply to organized crime, in evaluating the different kinds of costs and losses due to crime, in restructuring laws and programs to minimize the costs, wastes, and injustices that crime entails, and in restructuring the business environment in which organized crime occurs with a view to reducing crime or, at least, its worst consequences."

Organized crime is part of the fabric of American life. Over half a century ago Americans understood and accepted the fact that gangsters and racketeers controlled the business of bootlegging. And, political leaders reflected popular thinking of the Prohibition Era and made no effort to enforce the Eighteenth Amendment to the Constitution. Eventually, it was repealed as unenforceable.

Today, the same attitude prevails, and the American people cooperates with criminals by buying their illegal services and products, such as gambling, usurious loans, and smuggled cigarettes. The problem is aptly stated by Salerno and Tompkins, "Organized crime will not disappear by itself and armies of policemen will not solve the problem. To correct the conditions in which organized crime thrives, we as citizens will have to stop cooperating with criminals. This may mean uncomfortable changes in our behavior. We will have to stop buying smuggled, tax-free cigarettes. We will have to seek legal outlets for our gambling instincts and refuse to bet with the bookmakers and lottery operators of organized crime. Businessmen will have to give up the services of 'labor consultants' who earn their food by victimizing workers."*

ECONOMIC ANALYSIS AND ORGANIZED CRIME†

Thomas C. Schelling

At the level of national policy, if not of local practice, the dominant approach to organized crime is through indictment and conviction, not through regulation, accommodation, or the re-

---

* Ralph Salerno and John S. Tompkins, *The Crime Confederation* (New York, Doubleday and Company, 1969), p. 393.

† Reprinted from United States Government document. President's Commission on Law Enforcement and Administration of Justice, *Task Force Report: Organized Crime*, 1967, Appendix D, pp. 114-126.

structuring of markets and business conditions. This is in striking contrast to the enforcement of antitrust or food and drug laws, or the regulation of industries affecting the public interest. For some decades, antitrust problems have received the sustained professional attention of economists concerned with the structure of markets, the organization of business enterprise, and the incentives toward collusion or price cutting. Racketeering and the provision of illegal goods (like gambling) have been conspicuously neglected by economists. There exists, for example, no analysis of the liquor industry under prohibition that begins to compare with the best available studies of the aluminum or steel industries, air transport, milk distribution, or public utility pricing.

Evidence of the lack of professional attention to the economy of the underworld is the absence of reliable data even on the magnitudes involved, of techniques for estimating them—even of a conceptual scheme for distinguishing profits, income, turnover, transfers, waste, destruction, and the distribution of gains and losses due to crime. Yet a good many economic and business principles that operate in the "upperworld" must, with suitable modification for change in environment, operate in the underworld as well, just as a good many economic principles that operate in an advanced competitive economy operate as well in a Socialist or a primitive economy. They operate differently, though, and one has to look carefully to see them.

In addition to sheer curiosity there are good policy reasons for encouraging a more professional, "strategic" analysis of the criminal underworld, an analysis that would draw heavily on modern economics and business administration. Such an analysis, in contrast to "tactical" intelligence aimed at the apprehension of individual criminals, could help in identifying the incentives and the limitations that apply to organized crime, in evaluating the different kinds of costs and losses due to crime, in restructuring laws and programs to minimize the costs, wastes, and injustices that crime entails, and in restructuring the business environment in which organized crime occurs with a view to reducing crime or, at least, its worst consequences.

A number of questions need to be pursued. Many are professionally challenging and ought to appeal to economists and others whose talents and energies could be enlisted in the unending campaign waged by the authorities concerned with law enforcement. As an example, what market characteristics determine whether a criminal activity becomes "organized?" Gambling, by all accounts, invites organization—extortionate monopoly organization based on intimidation of small operators and competitors—while abortion, by all accounts, does not. In the upperworld, automobile manufacture is characterized by large firms while machine tool production is not; banking is subject to concentration while the practice of law is not; collusive price fixing occurs in the electrical machinery industry but not in the distribution of fruits and vegetables; retail price maintenance can be legally enforced in the branded liquor industry but not in the market for new cars. The reasons may not be entirely understood, but they are amenable to study. The same should not be impossible for illegal gambling, extortion, abortion, and contraband cigarettes.

Some Economics of Organized Crime

A useful distinction that we can borrow from the legitimate economy and apply to the economy of organized crime is the difference between an organized economy and an organized business. We should distinguish—within the organized underworld itself—between the organized economy within which criminal business operates and the highly organized criminal enterprise (firm), in particular the monopolistic enterprise.

Only some crime is organized in the second sense, in large-scale continuing firms with the internal organization of a large enterprise, and in particular with a conscious effort to control the market. Gambling syndicates and the better organized protection rackets qualify for this category.

Other criminal businesses, like "unorganized" robbery, would not meet the definition of "organized crime" in the restricted sense of a criminal firm. They nevertheless operate in, and participate in, a highly "organized" economic framework. That is, these "unorganized" but professional criminals are part of the underworld communication system, recruitment system, marketing system, and even diplomatic system (in relations with the world of law enforcement), and may consider themselves part of a highly organized criminal society.

Still other crimes, including those committed by amateur criminals but also apparently by abortionists, embezzlers, and ordinary dishonest businessmen, are outside the organized economy of the underworld. They may, however, have intermittent contact with it or make occasional use of the services available in it. In some cases the police themselves constitute part of this underworld society (at least from the point of view of the long-operating prostitute or abortionist, or the regular purveyor of liquor to minors).

Our interest at this point will be in the firms and trade associations that qualify as "organized crime" in the more restricted sense. But the two cannot be entirely separated. The organization of the underworld itself is undoubtedly affected, perhaps in a dominant way, by the occurrence of large-scale monopolist organizations and cartels. Indeed, the role of "government" within the underworld, including diplomatic relations with the legitimate world, may have to be played by large organizations originating from market forces, not political forces. It may require a large firm or cartel to represent the underworld in its relations with the legitimate world, to impose discipline and procedures for the adjudication of disputes, and to provide a source of recognizable leadership.

In fact, some of the central questions (to be investigated) about the functioning of the highly organized criminal firms are the extent to which they condition the underworld itself. This includes the extent to which organized crime lives off the underworld rather than directly off the upperworld, the extent to which the underworld benefits or loses by this kind of market dominance and leadership, and the extent to which relations of the underworld with the legitimate world depend on the emergence of some large, economically viable organization with the incentive and capability to centralize diplomatic and financial relations.

A closely related question is the extent to which organized crime itself depends on at least one major market occurring in which the returns to tight and complex organization are large enough to support a dominant monopoly firm or cartel. Not all businesses lend themselves to centralized organization; some do, and these may provide the nucleus of well-financed entrepreneurship and the extension of organizational talent into other businesses that would not, alone, support or give rise to an organized monopoly or cartel.

A strategic question is whether a few "core" criminal markets provide the organizational stimulus for organized crime. If the answer turns out to be yes, then a critical question is whether this particular market, so essential for the "economic development" of the underworld and the emergence of organized crime, is one of the black markets dependent on "protection" against legitimate competition; or is, instead, an inherently criminal activity? This question is critical because black markets always provide, in principle, the option of restructuring the market, of increasing competition as well as reducing it, of compromising the original prohibition in the larger interest of weakening organized crime, in addition to selectively relaxing the law or its enforcement. If, alternatively, the core industry is one that rests principally on violence, on the intimidation of customers (extortion) or competitors (monopoly), then compromise and relaxation of the law are likely to be both ineffectual and unappealing. Restructuring the market to the disadvantage of such criminal business is accordingly a good deal harder.

A Typology of Underworld Business

One of the interesting questions in analyzing organized crime is why some underworld business becomes organized and some remains unorganized; another is what kinds of organization we should expect to occur. These questions indicate that a workable classification of organizations has to be broader than simply "organized crime." A tentative breakdown is suggested as follows:

Black Markets

A large part of organized crime involves selling commodities and services contrary to law. In the underworld, this can include dope, prostitution, gambling, liquor under prohibition, abortion, contraceptives in some states, pornography, and contraband or stolen goods. Most of these tend to be consumer goods.

In what is not usually considered the underworld, black-market goods and services include gold, rationed commodities and coupons in wartime, loans and rentals above controlled prices, theater tickets in New York, and a good many commodities that, though not illegal *per se*, are handled outside legitimate markets or are diverted from subsidized uses.

In some cases, i.e. gambling the commodity is to be excluded from all consumers; in others, i.e. cigarettes some consumers are legitimate and some, i.e. minors not. In some cases what is illegal is the failure to pay a tax or duty. In some cases, it is the price of the transaction that makes it illegal. In some it is public hazard—carrying explosives through tunnels, producing phosphorus matches in disregard of safety regulations. In some cases, i.e. child labor, illegal immigrant labor it is buying the commodity, not selling it, that is proscribed.

Some black markets tend to be "organized" and some not. In some black markets both parties to the transaction know that the deal is illegal; in others only one party to the transaction is aware of illegality. The innocent party to the transaction may have no way of knowing whether the goods were illegally obtained or are going into illegal channels.

Racketeering

Racketeering includes two kinds of business, both based on intimidation. One is extortion; the other, criminal monopoly.

"Criminal monopoly" means the use of criminal means to destroy competition. Whether one destroys a competitor, or merely threatens to make him go out of business, by deterring new competition, by the threat of violence or by other unfair practices, the object is to get protection from competition when the law will not provide it (by franchise, tariff protection). Such protection cannot be achieved through legal techniques (such as price wars, control of patents, or preclusive contracts).

We can distinguish altogether three kinds of "monopoly": Those achieved through legal means, including greater efficiency than one's competitors, or the inability of the market to support more than one firm; those achieved through means that are illegal only because of antitrust and other laws intended to make monopoly difficult; and monopolies achieved through means that are criminal by any standards, means that would be criminal whether or not they were aimed at monopolizing a business.

It is evident from the history of business abuses in the nineteenth and twentieth centuries that "unfair competition" of a drastic sort, including violence, has not been confined to the underworld. So it is useful to distinguish between firms that, in excess of zeal and deficiency of scruples, engage when necessary in ruthless and illegal competition, and between the more strictly "racketeering" firms whose profitable monopoly rests entirely on the firm's propensity for criminal violence. It is the latter that I include under "criminal monopoly"; the object of law enforcement in the other case is not to destroy the firm but to curtail its illegal practices so that it will live within the law. If the whole basis of business success is the use of strong-arm methods that keep competition destroyed or scared away, it is a pure "racket."

"Extortion" means living off somebody else's business by the threat of criminal violence or by criminal competition. The protection racket lives off its victims, letting them operate and pay tribute. If one establishes a chain of restaurants and destroys competitors or scares them out of business, he is a monopolist. If one merely threatens to destroy people's restaurant business, taking part of their profits as the price for leaving them alone, he is an extortionist; he likes to see them prosper so that his share will be greater.

For several reasons it is difficult to distinguish between "extortion" that, like a parasite, wants a healthy host, and "criminal monopoly" that is dedicated to the elimination of competitors. First, one means of extortion is to threaten to cut off the supply of a monopolized commodity—labor on a construction site, trucking, or some illegal commodity provided through the black market. In other words, one can use a monopoly at one stage in the production process for extortionate leverage on the next.

Second, extortion itself can be used to secure a monopoly privilege. Instead of taking tribute in cash, a victim signs a contract for the high-priced delivery of beer or linen supplies. The result looks like monopoly but arose out of extortion. (To a competing laundry service this is "unfair" competition; criminal firm *A* destroys competitor *B* by intimidating customer *C*, gaining an exclusive right to his customers.)

Evidently extortion can be organized or not; there are bullies and petty blackmailers, whose business is localized and opportunistic. But in important cases extortion itself has to be monopolized. Vulnerable victims may have to be protected from other extortionists. A monopolistic laundry service, deriving from a threat to harm the business that does not subscribe, may have to destroy or intimidate not only competing legitimate laundry services but also other racketeers who would muscle in on the same victim. Thus, while organized criminal monopoly may not depend on extortion, organized extortion needs a large element of monopoly.

Black-Market Monopoly

Just as monopoly and extortion may go together in racketeering, monopoly and black markets go together. Indeed, any successful black marketeer enjoys a "protected" market in the same way that a domestic industry is protected by a tariff, or butter by a law against margarine. The black marketeer gets automatic protection, through the law itself, from all competitors unwilling to pursue a criminal career. The law gives a kind of franchise to those who are willing to break the law. But there is a difference between a "protected industry" and a "monopolized industry;" abortion quacks are protected by the laws against abortion, and charge prices accordingly, but apparently are seldom monopolized, while gambling and prostitution are often organized monopolies, locally if not regionally, within a market from which the bulk of their competitors are excluded by the law and the police. Thus abortion is a black-market commodity but not a black-market monopoly; a labor racket is a local monopoly but not a black-market one; the narcotics traffic has both elements: the monopolization of an illegal commodity.

Cartel

An interesting case is the "conspiracy in restraint of trade" that does not lead to single-firm monopoly but to collusive price fixing, and is maintained by criminal action. If the garment trade eliminates cut-throat competition by an agreement on prices and wages, hiring thugs to enforce the agreement, it is different from the monopoly racket discussed above. If the government would make such agreements enforceable (as it does with various retail-price-maintenance laws in some states) the businesses might be happy and in no need of criminally enforcing discipline on themselves. Similarly a labor organization can engage in criminal means to discipline its members, even to the benefit of its members, who may be better off working as a block rather than as competing individuals; if the law permits enforceable closed-shop agreements or dues collection, the criminal means becomes unnecessary.

Cheating

"Cheating" means all the things that a business can do to cheat customers, suppliers, tax authorities, and so forth. Tax evasion, adulteration of goods, some kinds of bankruptcy, are always available in greater or lesser degree to any business firm; all it takes is a dishonest or unscrupulous employee or proprietor and some cheating can occur. (The main distinction between cheating and straightforward stealing is that the victim—tax collector, customer, supplier—either does not realize that he has been cheated or has no recourse at law.) The only relation between this kind of dishonest business practice and the underworld, or organized crime, is that criminals have special needs and uses for businesses in which they can cheat. They may want a "front" in which to disguise other earnings; they may want to make money in legitimate business and, being criminally inclined, have a propensity to go into business where it is advantageous to cheat. If they already have connections by which to corrupt law enforcement, they will have a comparative advantage toward the kind of cheating that depends on bribery and intimidation.

Organized Criminal Services

A characteristic of all the businesses listed above is that they involve relations between the underworld and the upperworld. The ultimate victim or customer is not a career criminal, possibly not a criminal at all except insofar as the transaction in question is illegal. But just as businesses in the upperworld need legal services, financial advice and tax advice, credit, enforcement of contract, places to conduct their business, communication facilities, even advertising, so in the underworld there has to be a variety of business services that are "domestic" to the underworld itself. These can be organized or unorganized. They are in the underworld, but not because they do to the underworld what the underworld does to the legitimate world. And, of course, they can operate in both worlds; the tax lawyer who advises a gambling casino can help them break the law and still have other customers in legitimate businesses.

Corruption of Police and Politics

Legitimate businesses have been known, through bribery and intimidation, to corrupt legislatures and public officials. Criminal organizations can do likewise and are somewhat like lobbies in that respect. The gambling rackets have as great a stake in antigambling laws as the dairy farmers in margarine laws or textile manufacturers in tariffs. But organized criminals have more need and more opportunity for corrupting officials whose job is law enforcement, especially the police. They need protection from the police; they can use police support in excluding competitors; they can even seek recruits among the police. What is special about the police is that they operate in both the upperworld and the underworld and do so in a more official capacity than the lawyers who have customers in both worlds.

The Incentives to Organization

Any firm prefers more business to less, a large share of a market to a small share. But the inducements to expansion and the advantages of large-scale over small are especially present in some markets rather than others.

The simplest explanation for a large-scale firm, in the underworld or anywhere else, is high costs of overhead or other elements of technology that make small-scale operation impractical. The need to utilize full equipment or specialized personnel often explains at least the lower limit to the size of the firm.

Second is the prospect of monopolistic price increases, If most of the business can be cornered by a single firm, it does not merely multiply its profits in proportion to its expansion but can, if it keeps new competition from entering the market, raise the price at which it sells illegal services. Like any business, it does this at some sacrifice in size of the market; but if the demand for the goods is inelastic, the change in profit margin will be disproportionate to the reduction in output. Decentralized individual firms would have just as much to gain by pushing up the price at which they sell, but without discipline it will not work. Each firm will attempt to undercut its competitors, and profit margins will be shaved back to where they were. Thus where entry can be denied to newcomers, centralized price setting will yield monopoly rewards to whoever can organize the market. With discipline, a cartel can do it; in the absence of such discipline a merger may do it; but intimidation, too, can lead to the elimination of competition and the conquest of a monopoly position by a single firm.

Third, the larger the firm, and especially the larger its share in the whole market, the more "external" costs will become formal and attributable to the firm itself. "External costs" are those that fall on competitors, customers, by-standers, and others with whom the firm deals.

Collection of all the business within a single firm causes the costs that individual firms inflict on each other to show up as costs (or losses) to the larger centralized firm now doing the business. This is an advantage to it. It is an advantage because the costs were originally there but neglected; now there is incentive not to neglect them.

Spoiling the market in various ways is often an external cost. So is violence. While racketeers have a collective interest in curtailing violence in order to avoid trouble with the public and the police, the individual racketeer has little or no incentive to reduce the violence connected with his own crime. There is an analogy here with, say, the whaling industry, which has a collective interest in not killing off all the whales. The individual whaler will pay little attention to what he is doing to the future of the industry when he maximizes his own take. But a large organization will profit by imposing discipline, by holding down the violence if the business is crime, by holding down the slaughter of females if the business is whaling.

There are also other "external economies" that can become internalized to the advantage of the centralized firm. Lobbying has this characteristic, as does cultivating relations with the police. No small bookie can afford to spend money influencing gambling legislation, but an organized trade association or monopoly among those who live off illegal gambling can collectively afford the influence legislation to protect their monopoly from legitimate competition. Similarly with labor discipline: the small firm cannot afford to teach a lesson to the industry's labor force, since most of the lesson is lost on other people's employees but a single large firm can expect the full benefit of its labor policy. Similarly with cultivating the market: if a boss cultivates the market for dope by hooking some customers, or cultivates a market for gambling in a territory where the demand is still latent, he cannot expect much of a return on his investment since opportunistic competitors will take advantage of the market he creates. Patent and copyright laws are based on the notion that the investment one makes in inventing something, or in writing a song, has to enjoy monopoly protection, or else the thing is not worth inventing or the song not worth writing. Anything that requires a long investment in cultivating a consumer interest, a labor market, and ancillary institutions or relations with the police can be undertaken only by a fairly large firm that has reason to expect enjoyment of most of the market and a return on its investment.

Finally, there is the attraction of not only monopolizing a particular market but also of achieving a dominant position in the underworld itself, and participating in its governing. To the extent that large criminal business firms provide governmental structure to the underworld, helping to maintain peace, setting rules, arbitrating disputes, and enforcing discipline, they are in a position to set up their own businesses and exclude competition. Constituting a kind of "corporate state," they can give themselves the franchise for various "state-sponsored monopolies." They can do this either by denying the benefits of the underworld government to their competitors or by using the equivalent of their "police power" to prevent competition. (They may even be able to use the actual police power if they can dominate diplomatic and financial relations with the agencies of law enforcement.) Where the line between business and government is indistinct, as it appears to be in the underworld, dominant business firms become regulators of their own industries, and developers of state monopolies.

Evaluating the Structure of Gains and Losses

In evaluating the consequences of organized crime an arithmetical accounting approach gives at best a crude bench mark as to magnitudes, and not even that for the distribution of gains and losses. The problem is like that of estimating the comparative incidence of profits taxes and excise taxes, the impact of a minimum wage law on wage differentials, or the social costs of reckless driving and hurricanes. Especially if we want to know who bears the most, or to compare the costs to society with the gains to the criminals, an analysis of market adjustments is required. Even the pricing practices of organized crime need to be studied.

Consider, for example, the illegal wire service syndicate in Miami that received attention from Senator Kefauver's committee. The only aspect of the situation that received much explicit attention was the estimated loss of State revenues due to the diversion of gambling from legal race tracks, which were taxable, to illegal bookmakers, whose turnover was not taxable. No accounting approach would yield this magnitude; it depended (as was pointed out in testimony) on what economists call the "elasticity of substitution" between the two services—on the fraction of potential race track business that patronized bookmakers. Some people bet at the track out of preference; some who patronize bookmakers would be diverted to the track if that were the only place they could gamble; and to some of the bookmaker's customers, the race track is either unavailable or unappealing. (There may even be some who bet at the location that offers the more attractive odds.)

Similar analysis is required to determine at whose expense the syndicate operated, or what the economic consequences of the syndicate's removal would have been. The provision of wire service was of small economic significance. It accounted, on a cost basis, for less than 5 percent of the net income of book-makers (of which the syndicate took approximately 50%). And cheaper wire service might have been available in the absence of the syndicate, whose function was not to provide wire service but to eliminate wire-service competitors.

The essential business of the syndicate was to practice extor-tion against bookmakers—to demand half their earnings against the threat of reprisals. The syndicate operated like a taxing authority, levying a substantially ungraduated tax on the earnings of bookmakers. (It also provided some reinsurance on large bets.) It apparently did not attempt to limit the number of bookmakers so long as they paid their "taxes."

How much of this tax was passed along to the customer (on the analogy of a gasoline or sales tax) and how much was borne by the bookie (on the analogy of an income or profits tax) is hard to determine without knowledge of the demand for betting. If the customer tends to bet a certain amount per month, the tax would be rather easily passed along to the customer in the form of less advantageous odds. If the customer tends to budget his losses, allowing himself to lose only a certain average amount per month (betting more when he wins and less when he loses), the total take of the bookmakers would tend to be a constant not much affected by the spread between buying and selling rates in the market for bets; and the tax would tend to be borne by bookmakers. Alternatively, if the customer tends to bet less when the odds are less favorable, as a consumer of some com-modity may buy less when the price rises, the bookie's net earnings will be limited by a declining market and a smaller volume of total business. The incidence of the tax will then be shared between bookmakers and customers, but some bookmakers will leave the business and some customers go unsatisfied to an extent not measured by the revenue yield.

If we assume that bookmakers' earnings are approximately proportionate to the volume of turnover (equal to the product of turnover times rate spread) and that their customers, though sensitive to the comparative odds of different bookmakers, are not sensitive to the profit margin and that they tend, consciously or implicitly, to budget their total bets and not their rate of loss, we can conclude that the tax is substantially passed along to the customer.

In that case the bookmaker, though nominally the victim of extortion, is victimized only into raising the price to his customers, somewhat like a filling station that must pay a tax on every gallon sold. The bookmaker is thus an intermediary between an extortionate syndicate and a customer who pays the tribute voluntarily on the price he is willing to pay for his bets.

The syndicate in Miami relied heavily on the police as their favorite instrument of intimidation. It could have been the other way around, the police using the syndicate as their agency to negotiate and collect from the bookmakers. If the syndicate had had no other way of intimidating bookmakers, and if the police had been organized and disciplined as a monopoly, it would have been the police, not the syndicate, that we should put at the top of our organizational pyramid. From the testimony, though, it is evident that the initiative and entrepreneurship came from the syndicate, which had the talent and organization for this kind of business, and that the police lacked the centralized authority for exploiting to their own benefit the power they had over the bookmakers. Leadership came from the syndicate; and, though collectively the police dispensed the power that intimidated the bookmakers, organizationally they were unable to exploit it on their own. Presumably—though there were few hints of this in the hearings—the syndicate could have mobilized other techniques for intimidating the bookmakers; the police were the chosen instrument only so long as the police share in the proceeds was competitive with alternative executors of the intimidating threats.

What the long-term effect was on police salaries would

depend on how widespread and nondiscriminatory the police participation was, especially by rank and seniority in service. Recruiting would be unaffected if police recruits were unaware of the possible illegal earnings that might accrue to them; senior members of the force who might otherwise have quit the service or lobbied harder for pay increases would presumably agitate less vigorously and less successfully for higher wages if their salaries were augmented by the racket. One cannot easily infer that part of the "tax" paid by the bookmaker's customer subsidized the police force to the benefit of nonbetting taxpayers; mainly it supported a more discriminatory and irregular earnings pattern among the police—besides contributing, unwillingly, to a demoralization of the police that would have made it a bad bargain for the taxpayer anyway.

This is just a sketch, based on the skimpy evidence available, of the rather complex structure of "organized gambling" in one city. (It is not, of course, the gambling that is organized; the organization is an extortionate monopoly that nominally provides a wire service but actually imposes a tribute on middlemen who pass most of the cost along to their voluntary customers.) Similar analysis would be required to identify the incidence of costs and losses (and gains of course) of protection rackets everywhere. Monopoly priced beer deliveries to bars or restaurants, if the price is uniformly high among competing bars and restaurants, will lead to a rise in the price the customers pay for beer. Vending machines installed in bars and restaurants under pain of damage or nuisance can raise the price of machine-sold commodities if the increase is uniform among competing establishments. But it may also tax away whatever profit the establishment formerly made from the sale of the item. The latter "tax" is probably passed along to the customer only to the extent that it reduces the attractiveness of the bar and restaurant business and causes some decline in the market.

These considerations are important because they help to explain the extent and nature of the victim's resistance. A bar that has to pay an extortionate price for its beer can seek relief in either of two ways. It can seek to avoid paying that extortionate or monopolized price; alternatively, it can insist that its supplier achieve similar concessions from all competing bars, to avoid a competitive disadvantage. An individual bar may suffer little if the wholesale price of beer goes up; it suffers if competitors' prices do not go up.

The logical extreme of this economic phenomenon is "self-imposed" extortion: if all the bars jointly organize, and sign exclusive contracts with their own firm for distribution of beer, charging themselves higher prices for their beer, they achieve a technique for disciplining themselves with respect to a collusive price increase. No individual bar has an incentive to cut the new high price of beer, and they enjoy their beer profits in the form of dividends from their own wholesale company. If, of course, they can police themselves with respect to an agreement on the price of beer, they have no need of the jointly owned wholesale company, the function of which is merely to enforce the agreed higher price of beer. There is evidence that in the garment trades, and some others, price discipline has been enforced by the direct threat of damage to the price cutter; and there is no economic anomaly in a potential price cutter's favoring such discipline.

Other aspects of the "costs" of crime, the incidence of these costs, and the incentive effects of these costs, need to be similarly analyzed. Insurance, for example, spreads the costs and makes them less uncertain. (It also raises them through the costs of insurance itself.) There can be no doubt that people, who would ordinarily stay home if they lacked liability and collision insurance, drive on slippery roads, just as there is no doubt that over-insured buildings have invited arson, that insured home-owners are a little less careful about locking their doors, insured travelers a little less careful with their cameras and suitcases, and theft-insured drivers a little less careful about locking their cars. The extreme is reached in a fake burglary or holdup which, unlike arson, does not sacrifice the value of the insured property. The incentive effects are appreciated by those laws, by police efforts to discourage the payment of ransom in kidnapping cases, and by occasional efforts of the police to keep insurance companies from buying back stolen jewelry and thus provide a market for stolen jewels.

Besides insurance, there are other important aspects of the costs and losses due to crime. One is "self-protection," in the form of locks, alarms, guards and watchmen, and other specialized commodities and expenses that are unmistakably a response to the threat of crime.. (Whether they actually reduce crime, or mainly divert it to other targets, could be an important question if there were a good way of answering it.) These items are unlikely to be overlooked and not difficult to tabulate although such things as modifications in the design of buildings would be hard to estimate and probably not worth estimating. But a wide range of other expenses taking the form of "protective adaptation" would be left out of that tabulation, and might indeed be worth estimating.

An obvious one is the use of taxis where, if the streets were safer, people would walk or, if the subways were safer, would use cheaper transport. Less obvious and harder to disentangle is the role of crime-avoidance in choosing a place of residence. Crime may be so mixed with other disagreeable environmental factors, and so many other neighborhood characteristics determine residential choice, that no simple technique will provide a good estimate, and even the best estimates will be unreliable. In view of the number of people whose choice of residence is determined by how safe for play streets are because of the volume of automobile traffic, it is evident that the degree of adaptation can be significant.

A special reason for examining some of these costs— as distinct from merely the costs entailed by the crimes that are executed— is to get a better idea of what it is worth to reduce crime and to whom it is worth it. (If the beneficiaries of crime reduction ought to pay for the cost of reducing crime, or can be induced to pay for it, it is worthwhile knowing who they are.) There is a tendency to think of the "costs" of crime as the costs inflicted on society by the crimes that occur. Evidently if private protection and law enforcement were so effective that no crime occurred, the costs of crime would be nil—but the costs of living in an environment of potential crime could be high. Evidently, too, if streets became so dangerous that nobody walked, street crime could disappear while the "cost" would be enormous.

There is no direct relation between the level of crime and the costs of crime; a given percentage reduction in crimes executed does not mean necessarily a similar reduction in the costs and losses due to crime.

Evaluating Costs and Losses

One consequence of the analyses suggested here should be a better appreciation of just what it is about crime that makes it deplorable. Crime is bad, as cancer is bad and war is bad; but even in the case of cancer one can distinguish among death, pain, anxiety, the cost of treatment, the loss of earnings, the cost of uncertainty about life expectancy, the effects on the victim and the effects on his family. Similarly with crime. It is offensive to society that the law be violated. But crime can involve a transfer of weath from the victim to the criminal, a net social loss due to the inefficient mode of transfer, the creation of fear and anxiety, violence from which nobody profits, the corruption of the police and other public officials, costs of law enforcement and private protection, high prices to customers, unfairness of competition, loss of revenue to the State, and even loss of earnings to the criminals themselves who in some cases may be ill-suited to their trade. There may be important trade-offs among these different costs and losses due to crime in the different ways that government can approach the problem of crime. There will be choices between reducing the incidence of crime and reducing the consequences of crime, and other choices that require a more explicit identification and evaluation of the magnitude and distribution of the gains and losses due to crime.

If there were but one way to wage war against crime, and the only question was how vigorously to do it, there would be no need to identify the different objectives (cost and consequences) in devising the campaign. But if this is a continual campaign to cope with some pretty definite evils, without any real expectation of total victory or unconditional surrender, resources have to be allocated and deployed in a way that maximizes the value of a compromise. The different consequences are divided among quite different parts of the population, so that the immediate victim of a gambling syndicate is itself a criminal class (illegal bookmakers) or the immediate victims of a high-priced criminal monopoly service are indifferent so long as their individual competitive positions are not harmed.

When we turn to the black-market commodities, it is harder to identify just what the evils are. In the first place, a law-abiding citizen is not obliged to consider the procurement and consumption of these illegal commodities as inherently sinful, as entailing negative value to society. We have constitutional procedures for legislating prohibitions. The outvoted minority is bound to abide by the law but not necessarily to agree with it. The minority can campaign to become a majority and legalize liquor after a decade of prohibition, legalize contraceptives in states where they have been prohibited, prohibit the importation of firearms, legalize marijuana, or make it a crime to sell plastic model cement to minors. Even those who vote to ban gambling or saloons or dope may do so not because they consider the consumption sinful but because some of the consequences are bad enough to make it preferable to prohibit all consumption if selective or discriminating prohibition is infeasible. If it is infeasible to prohibit the sale of alcohol to alcoholics, or gambling to minors, we have to forbid all of it in order to forbid the part that we want to eliminate.

The only reason for rehearsing these arguments is to remind ourselves that the evil of gambling, dope, prostitution, pornography, smoking among children, or the dynamiting of trout, is not necessarily proportionate to how much of it goes on. The evil may be much greater or much less than will be suggested by the gambling or the consumption of narcotics that actually occurs. One might conclude that the consumption of narcotics that actually occurs is precisely the consumption that one wanted to eliminate. One might equally conclude that the gambling laws eliminate the worst of the gambling, and what filters through the laws is fairly innocuous (or would be, if its being illegal per se were not harmful to society), and that the gambling laws thus serve the purpose of selective discrimination in their enforcement if not in their enactment.

The evils of abortion are particularly difficult to evaluate, especially because it is everybody's privilege to attach his own moral or theological values to the commodity. Are the disgust, anxiety, humiliation, and physical danger incurred by the abortionists' customers part of the net cost to society, or is it positively valued as punishment for the wicked? If a woman gets an abortion, do we prefer that she have to pay a high price or a low one, and do we count the black-market price that she pays as a cost to society, as a proper penalty inflicted on the woman, or merely as an economic waste? If a woman gets a safe, cheap abortion abroad, is this a legitimate bit of international trade, raising the national income like any gainful international trade, or is it even worse than her getting an expensive, more disagreeable, more dangerous abortion at home because she evaded the punishment and the sense of guilt?

These are not entirely academic questions. There are serious issues of public policy in identifying just what it is we dislike about criminal activity, and especially in deciding where and how to compromise. The case of prostitution is a familiar and clear-cut example. Granting the illegality of prostitution, and efforts to enforce the law against it, one may still discover that one particular evil of prostitution is a hazard to health—the spread of venereal disease, a spread that is not confined to the customers, but transmitted even to those who had no connection with this illicit commodity. There may be some incompatibility between a campaign to eradicate venereal disease and a campaign to eradicate prostitution. Specifically, one may legislate a public health service for prostitutes and their customers even at the expense of "diplomatic recognition" of the enemy. One may need to provide certain kinds of immunity both to prostitutes and to their customers, to an extent required by medical and public health services. One may not; just as one may not want the Commerce Department to keep income figures out of the hands of the taxing authorities, or courts to exempt witnesses from self-incrimination. The point is that a hard choice can arise, and ideology gives no answer. If two of the primary evils connected with a criminal activity are negatively correlated, one has to distinguish them, separately evaluate them, and make up his mind.

A similar case exists with abortion. At the very least one could propose clinical help to women seeking abortion for the very limited purpose of eliminating from the market those who are actually not pregnant, providing them to diagnosis that an abortionist might have neglected or preferred to withhold. Going a step further, one may want to provide reliable advice about postabortion symptoms to women who may otherwise become infected, or may hemorrhage, or otherwise suffer from ignorance. Still a step further, one might like to provide even an abortionist with a degree of immunity so that he could call for emergency treatment, for a woman in such need, without danger of self-incrimination. None of these suggestions yet compromises the principle of illegality; they merely apply to abortion some of the principles that would ordinarily be applied to hit-and-run driving or to an armed robber who inadvertently hurts his victim and prefers to call an ambulance.

One has to go a step further, though, on the analogy with contraception, and ask about the positive or negative value of scientific discovery, or research and development, in the field of abortion itself. Cheap, safe, and reliable contraceptives are now considered a stupendous boon to mankind. What is the worth of a cheap, safe, and reliable technique of abortion, one that involves no surgery, no harmful or addicting drugs, no infection, and preferably not even reliance on a professional abortionist? (Apparently the laws in some states make it illegal to perform an abortion but not to undergo one, except to the extent that undergoing abortion makes the patient an accomplice to the crime.) Or suppose some of the new techniques developed in Eastern Europe and elsewhere for performing safer and more convenient abortions became technically available to abortionists in this country, with the consequence that fewer patients suffer but also the consequence that more abortions are procured? How do we weigh these consequences against each other? Each of us may have his own answer, and a political or judicial decision is required if we want an official answer. But the question cannot be ignored.

The same questions would arise in the field of firearm technology. Do we hope that nonlethal weapons become available to criminals, so that they kill and damage fewer victims, or would we deplore it on grounds that any technological improvement available to criminal enterprise is against the public interest? Do we hope to see less damaging narcotics become available, perhaps cheaply available through production and marketing techniques that do not lend themselves to criminal monopoly, to compete with the criminally monopolized and more deleterious narcotics, or is this a "compromise" with crime itself?

Evidently judgments of this sort are made, even if only implicitly. Consider the reaction to gangland killings, of which the number in the Boston area alone, in recent years, is reported to be forty-four. People seem appalled that they can occur, because they are evidence of the existence of organized crime and of the impotence of the law to deal with it. People seem less concerned that they do occur, because they eliminate individuals who may be considered to be undeserving of the protection of the law anyhow. And the question whether these killings denote a deterioration of peace and discipline within the underworld or a tightening of discipline, whether the result will be more crime or less, more violence or less violence outside the underworld itself, more illegal gains taken from the innocent or more illegal gains taken from black market customers, or more illegal gains taken from criminals themselves, or less, is an important matter of "strategic" intelligence and evaluation. Like the Red Guard in China, it is a significant phenomenon that needs to be understood, and one that goes beyond the immediate beatings and killings and display of arrogance and disdain for the law.

Should Crime Be Organized or Disorganized?

It is usually implied, if not asserted, that organized crime is a menace and has to be fought. Evidently the crime itself is a menace; and if the crime would disappear with the weakening or elimination of the organization, the case for deploring organization, and combating it altogether, would be a strong one. If the alternative is "disorganized crime"—if the criminals and their opportunities will remain, with merely a lesser degree of organization than before—the answer is not so easy.

There is at least one strong argument for favoring the monopoly organization of some forms of crime. It is the argument about "internalizing" some of the costs that fall on the underworld itself but go unnoticed, or ignored, if criminal activity is decentralized. The individual hijacker might be tempted to kill a truck driver to destroy a potential witness, perhaps to the dismay of the underworld, which may suffer from the public outrage and the heightened activity of the police. A monopoly or a trade association could impose greater discipline. This is not a decisive argument, nor does it apply to all forms of organization nor necessarily to all criminal industries if it applies to a few; but it is an important point.

It may be that modern society "contracts out" some of its regulatory functions to the criminals themselves. Surely some of the interests of organized crime coincide with those of society itself—minimization of gangland feuds, minimization of all those violent byproudcts of crime, even a kind of negotiated avoidance of certain classes of crime. If society has no legal means of policing some kinds of crime, or lacks the political authority to compromise directly with the criminals, maybe what society does is to let the underworld itself provide some of the necessary discipline; that may require the existence of organizations strong enough to impose discipline. That is, organizations that can offer or withhold employment, punish recklessness, and at least passively try to stick to the business of criminal transfer of cash and property rather than destruction of wealth and harm to people.

Just as in war one may hope that the enemy government remains intact, thus assuring that there is an authority to negotiate with and to discipline the enemy troops themselves, maybe in the war on crime it is better that there be a "command and control" system intact on the other side.

If so, it should not be taken for granted that we want all crime to be less organized. It may even be that we should prefer that some kinds of crime be better organized than they are. If abortion, for example, will not be legalized and cannot be eliminated, there may be ways to minimize some of the extremely deleterious side effects of the rather dirty black market in abortion. One of the ways might be better organization; and though a policy of actually encouraging such organization would be too anomalous to be practical (and perhaps not wise if it were practical), a choice might arise between acquiescing in a degree of organization or preventing it.

A large organization could probably not afford to mutilate and even kill so many women. It could impose higher standards. It would have some interest in quality control and the protection of its "goodwill," of a kind that the petty abortionist is unlikely to have. As it is, the costs external to the enterprise—the costs that fall not on the abortionist but on his customer or on the reputation of other abortionists—are of little or no concern to him, and he has no incentive to minimize them. By all accounts, criminal abortion is conducted more incompetently and more irresponsibly than the illegal control of gambling.

Compromising with Organized Crime

It is customary to deplore the kinds of accommodation that the underworld reaches, sometimes, with the forces of law and order, with the police, with the prosecutors, with the courts. Undoubtedly there is corruption of public officials, including the police—bad not only because it frustrates justice and enforcement of the law but also because it lowers the standards of morality among the public officials themselves. On the other hand, officials concerned with law enforcement are in the front line of diplomacy between the legitimate world and the underworld. Aside from the approved negotiations by which criminals are induced to testify, to plead guilty, to surrender themselves, and to tip off the police, here is undoubtedly sometimes a degree of accommodation between the police and the criminals—tacit or explicit understandings analogous to what in the military field would be called the limitation of war, the control of armament, and the development of spheres of influence. A little coldblooded appeasement is not necessarily a bad thing; it was bad at Munich mainly because it failed, but it does not always fail.

The problem seems to be this. In other fields of criminal business, that is, of criminal activity by legitimate business firms, such as conspiracy in restraint of trade, tax evasion, illegal labor practices, or the marketing of dangerous drugs, regulatory agencies can be established to deal with the harmful practices. One does not have to declare war on the industry itself, only on the illegal practices; regulation and even negotiation are recognized techniques for coping with those practices. But when the business itself is criminal it is harder to have an acknowledged policy of regulation and negotiation. In the international field one can coldbloodedly accommodate with the enemy, or form expedient alliances, limit warfare and come to understandings about the kinds of external violence that will be resisted or punished and the kinds of activities that will be considered nonaggressive, or domestic, or within the other side's sphere of influence. Maybe the same approach is somewhat necessary in dealing with crime itself. And if we cannot acknowledge it at the legislative level, it may have to be accomplished in an unauthorized or unacknowledged way by the people whose business requires it of them. These people are those whose responsibility is to oppose crime—by enforcing the law, by apprehending criminals, or by any other techniques that minimize the costs, the losses, and violence due to criminal activity.

The Relation of Organized Crime to Enforcement

It is important to distinguish between the black-market monopolies dealing in forbidden goods, and the racketeering enterprises, like extortion and the criminal elimination of competition. It is the black-market monopolies that depend on the law itself. Without the law and some degree of enforcement, there is no presumption that the monopoly organization can survive competition—or, if it could survive competition once it is established, that it could have arisen in the first place as a monopoly in face of competition. Some rackets may also depend on the law itself, some labor rackets, some blackmail, even some threats to enforce the law with excessive vigor. But it is the black-market crimes—gambling, dope, smuggling, etc.—that are absolutely dependent on the law and on some degree of enforcement. That is, without a law that excludes legitimate competition, the basis for monopoly probably could not exist.

In fact, there must be an optimum degree of enforcement

from the point of view of the criminal monopoly. With virtually no enforcement, either because enforcement is not attempted or because enforcement is infeasible, the black market could not be profitable enough to invite criminal monopoly (or not any more than any other market, legitimate or criminal.) With wholly effective enforcement, and no collusion with the police, the business would be destroyed. Between these extremes there may be an attractive black market profitable enough to invite monopoly.

Organized crime could not, for example, possibly corner the market on cigarette sales to minors. Every twenty-one-year-old is a potential source of supply to every nineteen-year-old who is too young to buy his own cigarettes. No organization, legal or illegal, could keep a multitude of twenty-one-year-olds from buying cigarettes and passing them along to persons under twenty-one. No black-market price differential great enough to make organized sale to minors profitable could survive the competition. And no organization, legal or illegal, could so intimidate every adult so that he would not be a source of supply to the youngsters. Without any way to enforce the law, organized crime would get no more out of selling cigarettes to children than out of selling them soft drinks.

The same is probably true with respect to contraceptives in those states where their sale is nominally illegal. If the law is not enforced, there is no scarcity out of which to make profits. And if one is going to intimidate every drugstore that sells contraceptives in the hope of monopolizing the business he may as well monopolize toothpaste or comic books unless the law can be made to intimidate the druggists with respect to the one commodity that organized crime is trying to monopolize.

What about abortions? Why are they not organized? The answer is not easy, and there may be too many special characteristics of this market to permit a selection of the critical one. First, the consumer and the product have unusual characteristics; nobody is a regular consumer the way a person may regularly gamble, drink, or take dope. A woman may repeatedly need the services of an abortionist, but each occasion is once-and-for-all. Second, consumers are probably more secret about dealing with this black market, and secret especially among intimate friends and relations, than are the consumers of most banned commodities. Third, it is a dirty business and too many of the customers die; and while organized crime might drastically reduce fatalities, it may be afraid of getting involved with anything that kills and maims so many customers in a way that might be blamed on the criminal himself rather than just on the commodity that is sold. We probably don't know which reason or reasons are crucial here, but it would be interesting to know. (In particular it would be worth knowing whether organized abortion is less harmful than unorganized.)

Black Markets and Competition

An important difference between black-market crimes and most of the others, like racketeering and robbery, is that they are "crimes" only because we have chosen to legislate against the commodity or service they provide. We single out certain consumer goods and services as harmful or sinful; for reasons of history and tradition, as well as for other reasons, we forbid dope but not tobacco, forbid gambling in casinos but not on the stock market, forbid extramarital sex but not gluttony, forbid erotic stories but not mystery stories. We do this for reasons different from those beehind the laws against robbery, parking in front of fire hydrants, and tax evasion.

It is, in other words, a matter of policy that determines the black markets. Cigarettes and firearms are two borderline cases. We can, as a matter of policy, make the sales of guns and cigarettes illegal. We can also, as a matter of policy, make contraceptives and abortion illegal. Times change, policies change, and what was banned yesterday can become legitimate today; what was freely available yesterday can be banned tomorrow. Evidently there are changes in policy on birth control; there may be changes on abortion and homosexuality, and there may be legislation restricting the sale of firearms.

The pure black markets, in other words, in contrast to the rackets, tend to reflect some moral tastes, economic principles, paternalistic interests, and notions of personal freedom in a way that the rackets do not. A good example is contraception. We can change our policy on birth control in a way that we would not change our policy on armed robbery. And evidently we are changing our policy on birth control. The usury laws may to some extent be a holdover from medieval economics; and some of the laws on prostitution, abortion, and contraception were products of the Victorian era and reflect the political power of various church groups. One cannot even deduce from the existence of abortion laws that a majority of the voters, especially a majority of enlightened voters, opposes abortion; and the wise money would probably bet that the things that we shall be forbidding in fifty years will differ substantially from the things we forbid now.

One of the important questions is what happens when a forbidden industry is subjected to legitimate competition. We need more study of this matter. Legalized gambling is a good example. What has happened to Las Vegas is hardly reassuring. But the legalization of liquor in the early 1930's rather swamped the criminal liquor industry with competition. Criminals are alleged to have moved into church bingo, but they have never got much of a hold on the stock market. What happens when a forbidden industry is legitimized needs careful analysis; evidently criminals cannot always survive competition, evidently sometimes they can. A better understanding of market characteristics would be helpful. The question is important in the field of narcotics. We could easily put insulin and antibiotics into the hands of organized crime by forbidding their sale; we could do the same with a dentist's novocaine. (We could, that is, if we could sufficiently enforce the prohibition. If we cannot enforce it, the black market would be too competitive for any organized monopoly to arise.) If narcotics were not illegal, there could be no black market and no monopoly profits, and the interest in "pushing" it would probably be not much greater than the pharmaceutical interest in pills to reduce the symptoms of common colds. This argument cannot by itself settle the question of whether, and which narcotics or other evil commodities, ought to be banned, but it is an important consideration.

The greatest gambling enterprise in the United States has not been significantly touched by organized crime. That is the stock market. (There has been criminal activity in the stock market, but not on the part of what we usually call "organized crime.") Nor has organized crime succeeded in controlling the foreign currency black markets around the world. The reason is that the market works too well. Furthermore, Federal control over the stock market, designed mainly to keep it honest and informative, and aimed at maximizing the competitiveness of the market and the information for the consumer, makes tampering difficult. Ordinary gambling ought to be one of the hardest industries to monopolize, because almost anybody can compete, whether in taking bets or providing cards, dice, or racing information. Wire services could not stand the ordinary competition of radio and Western Union; bookmakers could hardly be intimidated if the police were not available to intimidate them. If ordinary brokerage firms were encouraged to take accounts of customers and buy and sell bets by telephone for their customers, it is hard to see how racketeers could get any kind of grip on it. And when any restaurant or bar or country club or fraternity house can provide tables and sell fresh decks of cards, it is hard to see how gambling can be monopolized any more than the soft drink business, the television business, or any other. Even the criminal-skilled-labor argument probably would not last once it became recognized that the critical skills were in living outside the law, and those skills became obsolete with legalization.

We can still think gambling is a sin and try to eliminate it; we should probably try not to use the argument that it would remain in the hands of criminals if we legalize it. Both reason and evidence seem to indicate the contrary.

Essentially the question is whether the goal of somewhat reducing the consumption of narcotics, gambling, prostitution, abortion, or anything else that is forced by law into the black market, is or is not outweighed by the costs to society of creating a criminal industry. In all probability, though not with certainty, consumption of the proscribed commodity or service is reduced. Evidently it is not anywhere near to being eliminated because the estimates of abortions run to about a million a year, the turnover from gambling is estimated in the tens of billions of dollars per year, and dope addiction seems to be a serious problem. The costs to society of creating these black markets are several.

First, it gives the criminal the same kind of protection that a tariff might give a domestic monopoly: It guarantees the absence of competition from people who are unwilling to be criminal, and guarantees an advantage to those whose skill is in evading the law.

Second, it provides a special incentive to corrupt the police, because the police not only may be susceptible to being bought off, but also can be used to eliminate competition.

Third, a large number of consumers who are probably not ordinary criminals—the conventioneers who visit houses of prostitution, the housewives who bet on horses, the women who seek abortions—are taught contempt, even enmity, for the law, by being obliged to purchase particular commodities and services for criminals in an illegal transaction.

Fourth, dope addition may so aggravate poverty for certain desperate people that they are induced to commit crimes or can be urged to commit crimes because the law arranges that the only (or main) source for what they desperately demand will be a criminal source.

Fifth, these big black markets may guarantee enough incentive and enough profit for organized crime so that the large-scale criminal organization comes into being and maintains itself. It may be—this is an important question for research—that without these important black markets crime would be substantially decentralized, lacking the kind of organization that makes it enterprising, safe, and able to corrupt public officials. In economic development terms, these black markets may provide the central core (or infrastructure) of underworld business, capable of branching out into other lines.

A good economic history of prohibition in the 1920's has never been attempted, so far as I know. By all accounts, though, prohibition was a mistake. Even those who do not like drinking and want to prohibit it have to reach the conclusion that prohibition was a mistake. It merely turned the liquor industry over to organized crime. In the end we gave up—probably not only because there was disagreement whether drinking was bad or, if it were, whether it was properly a political question—but also because the attempt was an evident failure and an exceedingly costly one in its social byproducts. It may have given underworld business in the United States what economic developers call the takeoff into self-sustained growth.

Institutional Practices

A variety of institutional practices in the underworld needs to be better understood. What, for example, is the effect of the tax laws on extortion? Why does an extortionist put cigarette machines in a restaurant or provide linen service? Do the tax laws make it difficult to disguise the payment of tribute in cash but easy to disguise it (and make it tax deductible) if the tribute takes the form of a concession or the purchase of high-priced services? Why does a gambling syndicate bother to provide "wire services" when evidently its primary economic function is to shake down bookies by the threat of hurting their businesses or themselves, possibly with the collusion of the police? The Kefauver hearings indicate that the wire service syndicate in Miami took a standard 50 percent from the bookies. The 50 percent figure is itself remarkable. Equally remarkable is the fact that the figure was uniform. Similarly remarkable is the fact that the syndicate went through the motions of providing a wire service when it perfectly well could have taken cash tribute instead. There is an analogy here with the car salesman who refuses to negotiate the price of a new car but is willing to negotiate quite freely the allowance on the used car that one turns in. The underworld seems to need institutions, conventions, traditions, and recognizable standard practices much like the upper world of business.

A better understanding of these practices might lead not only to a better evaluation of crime itself but also to a better understanding of the role of tax laws, social security laws, and various regulatory laws on the operation of criminal business.

Even the resistance to crime would be affected by measures designed to change the cost structure. Economists make an important distinction between a lump sum tax, a profits tax, and a specific or ad valorum tax on the commodity an enterprise sells. The manner in which a criminal monopolist or extortionist prices his service or demands his tribute should have a good deal to do with whether the cost is borne by the victim or passed along by the customer. The uniform "tax" levied by the racketeer on all his customers may merely be passed along in turn to their customers, with little loss to the immediate victims if the demand in their own market is inelastic. Similarly, legal arrangements that make it difficult to disguise illegal transactions and make it a punishable offense to pay tribute, might help to change the incentives.

In a few cases the deliberate stimulation of competing enterprises could be in the public interest. Loansharking could be somewhat combatted by the deliberate creation of new and specialized lending enterprises. And some of the worst side effects of crime itself might be mitigated by the developing of institutions to deal directly with the criminal underworld. Examples would be the provision of public health services to prostitutes, confidential medical advice to dope addicts, and clinics for the determination of pregnancy so that at least the women who are not pregnant need not participate in a traumatic illegal experience that is unnecessary.

BIBLIOGRAPHY

Anti-trust laws invoked for first time to curb rackets. *The New York Times,* 20, March 20, 1959.

Attorney General Brownell charges democratic administrations let gangsters prosper by failing to enforce Hobbs Anti-Racketeering Act. *The New York Times,* 40, April 23, 1955.

Attorney General Clark reports task force against organized crime which proved effective in 9-month test in Buffalo, will be used in other cities. *The New York Times,* 35, November 15, 1967.

Attorney General Kennedy offers program to combat organized crime and racketeering. *The New York Times,* 1, April 7, 1961.

Attorney General Kennedy urges legislature to combat organized crime. *The New York Times;* 1, March 20, 1961.

Attorney General Rogers offers program to combat organized crime. *The New York Times,* 25, May 25, 1959.

Bachelder, W. K.: Suppression of bookie gambling by a denial of telephone and telegraph facilities. *Journal of Criminal Law and Criminology, 40*: July-August 1949.

Bar association offers anti-crime plan. *America, 88*: March 14, 1953.

Bill making mandatory fingerprinting of those arrested for bookmaking. *The New York Times,* 1, April 19, 1960.

Blow at the rackets. *Newsweek, 45*: May 2, 1955.

Commissioner Murphy holds public alone can halt numbers racket. *The New York Times,* 17, June 26, 1964.

Coon, R.: What good did the Kefauver Crime Commission really do? *Cosmopolitan, 134*: April 1953.

Crime must be attacked at the local level: Summary of report of U.S. Senate's special committee to investigate organized crime in interstate commerce. *American City, 66*: October 1951.

Crowley, W. F.: New weapon against confidence games. *Journal of Criminal Law and Criminology, 50*: September-October 1959.

Denaturalization and deportation of racketeers. *The New York Times,* January 2, 1953.

Denison, G.: Legal weapon the Mafia fears most. *Reader's Digest, 96*: June 1970.

Effect of restriction of communication facilities on bookmaking racket. *California Law Review, 39*: March 1951.

Federal regulation of gambling. *Yale Law Journal, 60*: December 1951.

Feds vs. gangland, lynchland. *Life, 49*: June 1, 1959.

Finney, John W.: Senate approves measure to fight organized crime. *The New York Times,* 1, January 24, 1970.

Gangbusters: Richard Nixon's campaign against organized crime. *Newsweek, 73*: May 5, 1969.

Governor Kirk sets up private police force to fight organized crime. *The New York Times,* 56, January 8, 1967.

Governor Rockefeller urges more vigorous drive on organized crime. *The New York Times,* 1, March 13, 1959.

Grafton, S.: What has happened to law and order in the United States? *Look, 26*: July 3, 1962.

Graham, Fred P.: Wiretapping and bugging rise here under new federal law. *The New York Times,* 50, February 16, 1969.

Grutzner, Charles: How to lock out the Mafia. *Harvard Business Review, 48*: March 1970.

Grutzner, Charles: Mafia expert sees enforcement lag. *The New York Times,* 29, October 11, 1969.

Hoover, J. Edgar: FBI's war on organized crime. *U.S. News & World Report, 61*: August 8, 1966.

House of Representatives committee drafts bill to complete master file on all racketeers. *The New York Times,* 4, April 16, 1960.

Indirect control of organized crime through liquor license procedure. *Journal of Criminal Law, 49*: May-June 1958.

Justice Department asks $200,000 to continue for one year Attorney General's special group to prosecute organized crime. *The New York Times,* 50, February 15, 1959.

Kefauver cure for crime. *U.S. News & World Report, 30*: May 11, 1951.

Kefauver speaking. *Newsweek, 37*: April 2, 1951.

Kihss, Peter. Police expert urges tighter state conspiracy laws aimed at crime leaders. *The New York Times,* 37, June 17, 1970.

King, Rufus G.: The control of organized crime in America. *Stanford Law Review, 4*: December 1951.

Lawrence, David: Only the people as a whole can cure crime. *U.S. News & World Report,* 92, March 9, 1970.

Mattei, Kenneth D.: Use of taxation to control organized crime. *California Law Review, 39*: June 1951.

McClellan, J. L.: Crime war: Key senator lauches a broad attack on organized crime: excerpts from Senate statement on March 11, 1969. *U.S. News & World Report, 66*: March 24, 1969.

McClellan, J. L.: Weak link in our war on the Mafia. *Reader's Digest, 96*: March 1970.

McClellan, J. L.: Organized crime in the United States. *Vital Speeches, 35*: April 15, 1969.

McClellan, J. L. and Smith, B.: What we learned about labor gangsters. *Saturday Evening Post, 230*: May 3 and May 10, 1958.

Mitchell, J. M.: Fighting crime in America. *U.S. News & World Report, 67*: August 18, 1969.

More aid for cities in war against crime. *U.S. News & World Report, 68*: February 23, 1970.

Nixon, Richard M.: The control of crime. *The New York Times,* 64, (Message to Congress), October 12, 1969.

Peterson, V. W.: Fighting nationally organized crime: address. *Vital Speeches, 25*: December 15, 1958.

President creates a council on crime. *The New York Times,* 14, June 15, 1970.

Re-examination of the Fifth Amendment as applied to federal registration of gamblers. *U.C.L.A. Law Review, 14*: March 1967.

Robert Meyner pledges war on labor racketeers. *The New York Times,* 25, October 13, 1953.

Senator Keating offers bill to mobilize full power of federal government against organized crime. *The New York Times,* 2, February 16, 1959.

Rockefeller, Nelson A.: *Governor's Message,* at Opening of New York State Legislature (Crime Control), *The New York Times,* 30, January 8, 1970.

Senate approves six of eight bills urged by Attorney General Kennedy to curb organized crime. *The New York Times*, 17, July 29, 1961.

Senator Keating readies bill to mobilize federal government against *perilous* rise in organized crime. *The New York Times*, 14, January 24, 1961.

Smith, Dwight C., Jr.: Cooperative action in organized crime control. *The Journal of Criminal Law, Criminology and Police Science*, 59, 4: 1968.

State crime commission first report urges creation of permanent commission of investigation. *The New York Times*, 1, January 26, 1953.

Swanson, Warren L.: Legal methods for the suppression of organized crime. *Journal of Criminal Law*, 48: November-December 1957.

Thrower, R. W.: Significant developments in tax administration: organized crime. *Vital Speeches, 36*: November 15, 1969.

We can break the grip of the mob. *Life, 63*: September 8, 1967.

What the 'Feds' can do in the fight against organized crime. *New York Times*, News of the Week Section, 13, April 27, 1969.

INDEX

A

Abortion, 324
Accardo, Tony, 40
Accountants, 115
AFL-CIO, 246, 271
Amato, Frank, 290
American Bar Association, 9
American Telephone & Telegraph,
    40, 47
Annenberg, Moe, 40
Anomie, 18
A.N.R. Leasing Corporation, 295
Aqueduct Race track, 78
Arrests, 7
Assault, ix
Athens, 180
Australia
    gambling in, 122
    horse racing, 74
Auto theft, ix

B

Backstraps, 68
Bahamas
    banking, 344
Bail bondsmen, 115
Bailey, Douglas, 306
Baker, Bobby, 46
Baltimore
    gambling in, 43
Bando, Dominick, 285
Bardel, William G., 322
Baseball
    wagering, 88
Basketball
    wagering, 89
Beccaria-Bonesana, 17
Becker, Gary S., 17, 18, 256

Belgium
    usury, 181
Belmont Race Track, 76, 83
Bentham, Jeremy, 17, 180
Betting and Gaming Act, 167
Billiard parlors, 66
Biloxi, Mississippi
    gambling in, 44
Bingo games, 55
Black Hand, the, 25
Black-market monopoly, 374
Boiler room, 189
Boleda, 110, 124
Bonger, William, 17
Bonsal, Dudley B., 297
Bookies, 56
Bookmakers, x, xi, 79, 89, 90, 92, 93,
    95, 100
    France, 169
    Australia, 173
    Nevada, 174
Bookmaking, 143, 145, 146, 378,
    380-382
Breakage, 78, 79
Britain
    gambling in, 122
Brownsville, N.Y., 324
Brooklyn
    number, 112-113, 124-125
Buffalo, N.Y.
    gambling in, 44
Bureau of Narcotics and
    Dangerous Drugs, 8, 214
Burger, Warren, 13
Burglaries, 10
Burglary, ix, 6, 12, 14, 21

C

Cahn, William, 282
California, vii

Cape Verde, 336
Capone, Al, 40, 304
Capote, Truman, 316
Carr-Hill, 18
Carson, Johnny, 316
Casino gambling, 142
Casinos, 153
  revenue potential, 156
Cheese boxes, 69
Chemin de fer, 167
Chicago, 40
Chinatown, 113
Cohen, Mickey, 40
Combination bet, 93, 110
Concord Hotel, 298
Connecticut
  horse racing, 74
  lottery in, 137
Continental Press, 40
Cosa Nostra, 47, 199, 207, 218, 221-
  225, 246-251
Coughlin, John, 43
Coyne, Edward T., 219-220
Cressey, Donald R., 95
Crime
  Economics of, vii
Criminal usury, 190
Criminology, 15, 16, 20-23
Currency trading, 338

D

Damiano, Gerard, 314, 317-318
Deep Throat, 314-322
Dennis, Sandy, 316
Deterrence, 18
Dewey, Thomas E., 43
DiLorenzo, Alex, 297
District of Columbia
  gambling in, 44
Dog racing, 142
Dog tracks, 38
Dragna, Jack, 40
Durkin, William, 217
Drunkenness, 13-14
Dunlop, John T., 256

E

Economists, 16
Edwards, George, 281
Eisenhower, Dwight D., 49
Embezzlement, 252
England, 17-18, 63
  horse racing, 74
  sports pool cards, 161
  usury, 181
Estes, Billie Sol, 342
Euro-dollars, 351
Evans, Courtney, 207
Extortion, 254

F

Far East, 213
Fascell, Dante B., 27
Fascists, 342
Federal Bureau of Investigation, 26,
  189, 283
Federal campaign fund laws, 45
Federal Trade Commission, 27, 47
Fitzsimmons, Frank E., 270
Football
  wagering, 88, 92
Football pool cards, 96
Ford Motors, 35, 47, 117
Forlano, Nicholas, 49
France, xiii, 8
  gambling in, 122-123
  horse racing, 74
  prostitution, 325
Friedman, Leon, 321
Fund for City of New York, 126, 130

G

Gallagher, Congressman, 46
Gambino, Carlo, 296-297
Gambling, x, 10, 11, 13, 15 ,36, 37
  control of, 40
  in cities, 43, 44
  legal aspects, 148
  police corruption, 41, 42
  relation to numbers, 105

Gazzara, Ben, 316
General Electric, 35, 47
General Motors, 27, 35, 47
Genovese, Vito, 218, 354
Gerard, Jerry, 318
Germany
  sports pool cards, 161
Gold, 336
Gold futures, 337
Goldburg, Arthur, 81
Goldfine, William, 293, 295
Goldfinger, Benjamin, 285
Goldman, Martin, 286
Goldman, Sol, 297
Goldstein, Al, 317
Greece, 63, 180
Gross National Product, 4, 13
Guzik, "Greasy Thumb," 40

H

Harlem, New York, 117
Harrison tax law, 37
Hawaii, vii
Head to head betting, 151-152
  arguments against, 160
  revenue potential, 155
Henry II, 63
Heroin, xiii, xiv, 3-9, 18-19, 107
  addiction, 215, 238
  and crime, 238
  dealer level, 228
  distribution level, 226
  lower level distribution, 225
  major supplies, 224-225
  pusher level, 229
  wholesaling, 222-223
Hines, Jimmy, 43
Hoffa, James R., 270
Hogan, Frank S., 301
Holland
  usury, 181
Homicide, 14
Hoover, Herbert, 38
Hoover, J. Edgar, 49, 282
Horse room, 65
Horse tracks, 38

I

Illinois
  gambling in, 43
I.B.M., 35
I.R.S., 43, 118, 150, 187, 189, 304, 335,
  344, 354
International securities, 339
Iron Curtain, 174
Italy, xiii
  prostitution, 325
Italian lottery, 107

J

Jacobs, Eugene, 86
Japan
  horse racing, 74
Jersey City, N.J., 118
  gambling in, 50
  loansharking, 156
  numbers, 288
Jo-Ran Trading Corporation, 296
Johnson, President L. B., 44, 49, 366
Justice, Department of, 10, 27, 47

K

Kansas City, 40
Kassner, Herbert, 316
Kaufman, Milton, 202-204
Kefauver Commission, 35, 42, 44, 47,
  105, 276, 280
Kefauver, Estes, 279, 379
Kelly, Paul, 295
Kenna, Hinky Dink, 43
Kennedy, Robert F., 282
Kentucky, 39
Kentucky Derby, 76, 87
King, Rufus, 36, 49
Klein, Julius, 293-294
Knickerbocker, Suzy, 317
Knight, Arthur, 319
Krumpe, Jack, 84
Kuznets, Simon, 276

L

La Cosa Nostra, 24, 105
Labor racketeering, xiii, 268
Labor unions
  kickbacks, 264
Landrum-Griffin Act, 269
Lansky, Meyer, 24, 46, 47, 288,
  352-354
Las Vegas
  loansharking, 183
Laundering, 335
Law Enforcement Assistance
  Administration, 3, 11, 12
Lawyers, 115, 116
Lebanon, xiii
Legal gambling
  arguments against, 157, 158-159
  arguments for, 159-161
Legalized gambling, xi
  recommendations, 164-169
Levin, Max, 320
Levine, Terry, 317
Levitt, William J., 298
Liechtenstein
  banking, 344
Lindsay, John, 80, 121
Loanshark, xii
  glossary, 209-210
Loansharking, xi, 10, 49, 50
  collection, 199
  dispursement of money, 51
  garment industry, 189
  in American cities, 206
  interest rates, 179, 183-185
  legal recommendations, 191-203
Loansharks, 47
  and banking, 201
Lockhart, William B., 311
Lombardozzi, Carmine, 296
Long, Huey, 43
Lorrado, Dominick, 290
Los Angeles
  loansharking, 183
Lottery, 10
  London lottery, 108
Louisiana, 39
Luciano, Lucky, 325

Luxembourg
  banking, 344

M

Mafia, 24, 103, 105
Manhattan way
  numbers, 112
Mapp v. Ohio, 65
Marcello, Carlos, 40
Marijuana, 4
Maryland, vii, 39
  horse racing, 74
  lottery in, 137
Massachusetts, vii
Massage parlors, 327
  Los Angeles, 327
  New York City, 327
Massiello, 207
McCahey, John P., 215, 218
McClellan, John L., 245, 278
McGarth, Attorney General M., 42
Mennite, 217
Methadone, xiv, 238
Mid-City Development Company,
  290-291
Middle Ages, 180
Middle East, xiii
Minimum wage, 262
Minuto, Maurice, 292, 293-294, 300
Mitchell, John M., 304
Mobil Oil, 81
Money, John W., 320
Morgenthau, Robert M., 278, 280, 301,
  345-346, 357-363
Moriarity, "Newsboy," 50
Morphine, xiii
Morrell, Alan, 292
Murder, Inc., 253

N

Narcotics, x, xiii, xvi
  dealers, 47
  relation to numbers, 105

National City Bank of New York,
182, 198
National Commission on Marihuana
and Drug Abuse, 13
National Commission on Marihuana
and Prevention of Violence,
The, 14
National Council on Crime and
Delinquency, 120
National Labor Relations Board, 249
Nazis, 342
Nevada, xi, 41
casinos, 153, 154
numbers, 118
New Hampshire
legal lotteries, 120
lottery in, 137
New Jersey
casinos, 162, 163
legal lottery, 126-127
lottery in, 137
New Orleans, 40
gambling in, 56
New York, vii, 9
casinos, 153-154
gambling in, 56
horse racing, 75
loansharking, 183
lottery in, 137
wagering in, 100
New York City, 4, 19
bookmaking, 93
garment center, 201, 202
horse racing, 77, 79
jobs in numbers game, 117
labor unions, 259
numbers operation, 114
sports betting, 88
New York City Commission
of Investigation, 206
New York State, 10, 11, 13, 36
casinos, 156, 162
horse racing, 63
legal gambling, 158
loansharking, 205
lottery, 121
numbers, 118

race tracks, 121
usury laws, 182
New York State Banking Law, 190
New York State Commission of
Investigation, 178, 186, 188, 190
New York State Crime Commission,
186
New York State Investigation
Commission, 207, 289, 293
New York State Joint Legislative
Committee on Crime, 103
New York Racing Association, 74, 75,
78, 83, 84, 85, 86
New York Stock Exchange, 339
New Zealand
horse racing, 74
gambling in, 122
Nichols, Mike, 316
Nicholson, Jack, 316
Nicotine, 18, 19
Nixon, Pres. Richard M., 8, 270
Norris-La Guardia Act, 255
North America, 17
North German Federation
usury, 181
Numbers
banker, 115
how to compute, 124
legal operation, 126
legal payoffs, 130
legalization of, 144
legalized, aspects of, 148
payoffs, 130, 149
revenue potential, 155
selection of, 131
taxes on, 150
Numbers, legal
discussion of, 135

O

O'Dwyer, William, 78
Off Track Betting, 11, 55, 63, 73-76,
79-83, 85, 88, 93, 104, 121, 131,
137, 145, 163, 237
Australia, 172-173
Czechoslovakia, 174

France, 169
Great Britain, 166
Ireland, 174
Nevada, 174
New Zealand, 171-172
Poland, 174
Puerto Rico, 173-174
Sweden, 174
West Germany, 174
Opportunity cost, 18, 21
Organized crime, x, xi, xiii, xvi, 24,
    26, 35, 38
  activities, 54
  black market, 393
  criminal services, 376
  drug sales, 234
  dummy corporations, 356
  economics of, 369
  enforcement, 392
  in Boston, 187
  in Buffalo, 187
  in Chicago, 187
  in Cleveland, 187
  in Detroit, 187
  in Kansas City, 187
  in Las Vegas, 187
  in Miami, 187
  in New Orleans, 187
  in New York, 187
  in Philadelphia, 187
  in Pittsburgh, 187
  in Providence, 187
  in St. Louis, 187
  in Tampa, 187
  in U.S.A., 24
  infiltration into legitimate
      business, 187-189, 275
  investments in real estate, 278
  loansharking, 177
  numbers operation, 108
  racketeering, 372
  revenues, 106, 146
  stock dealing, 279
  stock manipulation, 357
  syndicates, 42
Organized Crime Control Act, 10

P

Pagano, Joseph, 296-297
Patman, Wright, 360
Panama
  banking, 344
Parisi, Phil, 318
Peron, Evita, 342
Perry, Lou, 318
Pittsburgh
  loansharking, 183
Plea bargaining, ix, 7
Plumeri, James, 290
Point spreads, 90-91
Policy, 37
Policy banks, 114
Political contributions, 56
Pool card betting, 152
Pool cards, 98, 100, 152
  revenue potential, 155
Pool selling, 144
Pornography
  books, 313
  magazines, 313
  mail order, 313
  pictures, 312
Preakness, 76
Precious stones, 340
President's Crime Commission, 105,
    106
Professional criminals, xii
Progressive Drug Company, 284
Prohibition, 25, 26, 37, 187, 386
Prostitution, x, 37
  earnings, 328
  England, 330
  legalization, 329
  morality, 324
  Nevada, 330
  pimps, 326
  Scandinavia, 330
  West Germany, 330
Pullman, John, 352-354
Pure Food and Drug Act, xv

Q

Quayle Survey, 88, 100

R

Ragen, James E., 40
Rangel, Charles, 120
Rape, 14
Recidivism, 21
Rehabilitation, 18, 22
Rockefeller, Nelson, 81, 142
Robbery, ix, 14
Rogers, William P., 48
Rome, 180
  usury, 194
Ross, Arthur, 256
Russell Sage Foundation, 182

S

Salerno, Ralph, 200, 304
Salmaggi, Bob, 317
Saltzman, Henry H., 297-298
Samuels, Howard, 80-82, 84-88, 121
Saratoga Springs, New York, 39
Saratoga Springs Racetrack, 83
Saxbe, William B., 270
Scarne, John, 48
Schiller, George, 297
Schultz, Dutch, 40, 109
Scotti, Alfred J., 301
Scranton, Pennsylvania
  gambling, 44
Seattle
  gambling in, 43
Secret Service, 189
Securities and Exchange Commission,
    189, 304, 351, 357
Seeley, Albert W., 219-220
Shearson Hammill and Co., 359
Silver, 338
Simons, Henry C., 258
Single action, 124
Slot machines, 37
Smith, Adam, 17
Snyder, Ralph E., 298
Social Science, 16
South Africa, 337
South Carolina

gambling in, 43
Special accounts, 340
Sports betting, 150-152
  legalization of, 144
St. Luke, 180
Standard Oil, 27
Stein, Charles, 49
Stone, Danny, 323
Street crime, 12, 14
Supreme Court, 69
Sweden
  gambling in, 122
Sweetheart Contract, 248
Swiss banks, 220, 291
  in relation to numbers, 106
Swiss Federal Assembly, 335
Switzerland
  banking, 344
Syria, xiii

T

Thrower, Randolph W., 305
Time deposits, 338-339
Times Square, 324
Torrio, Johnny, 304
Trade unions, 252
Turkey, xiii, 8, 9
Tweed, Boss, 43
Twentieth Century Industries, 285
Tyler, Joel J., 314
Tyler, Judge, 319

U

United States, xiii, 8, 9
  usury, 181
U.S. Steel, 27, 35, 47
United States taxes, 342
Usury, 177
  federal regulations, 197
  saving and loan associations, 197
  United States, 181

V

Valachi, Joseph, 48
Vanderbilt, Alfred G., 83-84
Vandor, David, 316
Verrill, Allison, 317
Violent crime, 6
Volstead Act, 26

W

Washington, D.C., 6, 10
Weiss Credit Bank, 359, 361

Wenger, David, 291
West Germany
  banking, 344
White collar crime, ix, xiv, xv, 5
White slave act, 37
Wickersham Commission, 38, 43
Wilkes-Barre, Pennsylvania
  gambling in, 44
Wilson, Will, 345
Wire room, 67
Wire services, 40
World War I, 25, 37
World War II, 26, 38